To an exemplary
high school staff.
Thanks for your
contribution.

Paul George
Spring 2000

The Exemplary High School

Paul S. George
University of Florida

C. Kenneth McEwin
Appalachian State University

John M. Jenkins
University of Florida

The Exemplary High School

Paul S. George
University of Florida

C. Kenneth McEwin
Appalachian State University

John M. Jenkins
University of Florida

Harcourt College Publishers

Fort Worth   Philadelphia   San Diego   New York   Orlando   Austin   San Antonio
Toronto   Montreal   London   Sydney   Tokyo

Publisher	Earl McPeek
Acquisitions Editor	Carol Wada
Developmental Editor	Emma Guttler
Project Editor	Claudia Gravier
Art Director	David Day
Production Manager	Andrea Archer

ISBN: 0-15-503199-6
Library of Congress Catalog Card Number: 99-63307

Address for Domestic Orders
Harcourt College Publishers, 6277 Sea Harbor Drive, Orlando, FL 32887-6777
800-782-4479

Address for International Orders
International Customer Service
Harcourt College Publishers, 6277 Sea Harbor Drive, Orlando, FL 32887-6777
407-345-3800
(fax) 407-345-4060
(e-mail) hbintl@harcourtcollege.com

Address for Editorial Correspondence
Harcourt College Publishers, 301 Commerce Street, Suite 3700, Fort Worth, TX 76102

Web Site Address
http://www.harcourtcollege.com

Harcourt Brace College Publishers will provide complimentary supplements or supplement packages to those adopters qualified under our adoption policy. Please contact your sales representative to learn how you qualify. If as an adopter or potential user you receive supplements you do not need, please return them to your sales representative or send them to: Attn: Returns Department, Troy Warehouse, 465 South Lincoln Drive, Troy, MO 63379.

Printed in the United States of America

9 0 1 2 3 4 5 6 7 8 039 9 8 7 6 5 4 3 2 1

Harcourt College Publishers

To our families, who taught us
what high schools must be:
Andrew George, Evan George, Lia George, Stace McEwin,
Amy Lyons, Jill Sands, John Jenkins, and Bob Jenkins

PREFACE

The Exemplary High School is designed for use by prospective high school teachers and other educators who are seeking a comprehensive understanding of the challenges, successes, and promise of high schools. It also provides experienced high school educators, enrolled in graduate classes or involved in professional development efforts, with valuable information regarding the high school knowledge base. A major feature of this book that makes it unique from more traditional texts is its focus on programs and practices at highly successful high schools from across the nation.

The Exemplary High School acknowledges, but does not dwell upon, the shortcomings of the American high school. Rather it follows the premise that significant and dramatic reform is needed if high schools are to reach their full potential and serve all students well. Each chapter addresses topics that are relevant to this reform and supplements that knowledge with materials from high schools that have been nationally recognized for their excellence.

Several features are included to assist instructors. Each chapter begins with recommendations from *Breaking Ranks: Changing an American Institution,* published by the National Association of Secondary School Principals. This provides instructors with the option of tying study of these chapters to these influential recommendations. However, the book is designed to stand alone and is not intended to be an extension of the recommendations made in this document. The scope of the book goes well beyond the content of the recommendations.

Each chapter begins with "What You Will Learn in This Chapter," which provides readers with a preview of some of the most important topics addressed. Figures, which frequently include reproductions of materials from high schools, are used throughout the book. End of chapter features include "Action Steps," which consist of suggested activities to enhance the learning of readers, and "Discussion Questions," which focus on key topics included in the chapters. A complete listing of high schools and their addresses is found in the appendix section.

The book team at Harcourt also deserves special recognition and thanks: Carol Wada, Acquisitions Editor; Emma Guttler, Editorial Assistant; Claudia Gravier, project Editor; Andrea Archer, Production Manager; and David Day, Art Director. The authors wish to acknowledge the contributions of educators from more than 130 high schools. These people took time from their busy schedules to share materials that described their schools and agreed to have the names and addresses of their schools listed in the appendix so that readers can contact them for additional information.

Paul S. George
C. Kenneth McEwin
John M. Jenkins

BRIEF CONTENTS

Introduction xix
Chapter One: The Evolving American High School 1
Chapter Two: The Emergent High School Curriculum.........................42
Chapter Three: New Directions for Instruction....................................67
Chapter Four: Technology in the Emergent High School......................113
Chapter Five; Responding to Affective Needs Through Advisement
    and Advocacy 131
Chapter Six: Alternative Scheduling for Teaching and Learning..........167
Chapter Seven: The Organization of Teachers and Learners 211
Chapter Eight: School/Family/Community Partnerships 263
Chapter Nine: The High School Teacher...296
Chapter Ten: Leading High Schools in the New Century 322
Roster of High Schools...349
Author Index..357
Index of High Schools 361
Subject Index 363

TABLE OF CONTENTS

Introduction   xix

Breaking Ranks: The Changing of an American Institution   xx
High Schools Featured in This Book   xxi
Organization of the Book   xxi
The New High School   xxii
References   xxv

Chapter One
The Evolving American High School   1

What You Will Learn in this Chapter   1
The American High School: Serving Multiple Masters   2
The Earliest American Secondary Education   2
The First High Schools   5
Reformation of the High School Curriculum: Three Goals Persist   8
The Contemporary American Comprehensive High School   21
A Nation at Risk and Its Aftermath   28
Summary   36
Connections to Other Chapters   38
Action Steps   39
Discussion Questions   39
References   39

Chapter Two
The Emergent High School Curriculum   42

What You Will Learn in this Chapter   42
High School Curriculum   43
A National Core Curriculum   45
Recasting Standards at the Local Level   48
Values as Basic Education   50
Interdisciplinary Curriculum   52
Writing Across the Curriculum   55
Learning to Use the Mind Well   56
The Application of Knowledge and Skills   57
Summary   62
Connections to Other Chapters   63
Action Steps   63

Discussion Questions   64
References   64

Chapter Three
New Directions for Instruction   67

What You Will Learn in This Chapter   67
Modifying Traditional Teacher-Directed Whole-Class Instruction   68
Modifying Traditional Instruction to Account
    for Growing Student Diversity   70
Recognizing the Limitations of Teacher-Directed Instruction   74
Differentiating Instruction   75
Alternative Instructional Strategies for the
    New High School Classroom   77
Summary   108
Connections to Other Chapters   109
Action Steps   110
Discussion Questions   110
References   111

Chapter Four
Technology in the Emergent High School 113

What You Will Learn in this Chapter   113
The Impact of Technology   114
Planning for Technology   115
Coordinating the use of Technology   117
Instructional Uses of Technology   117
Technology in Traditional Academic Programs   123
Administrative Uses of Technology   124
Creating Learning Environments: Technology and the Future   125
Summary   128
Connections to Other Chapters   129
Action Steps   129
Discussion Questions   129
References   130

Chapter Five
Responding to Affective Needs Through Advisement and Advocacy   131

What You Will Learn in this Chapter   131
Providing for the Affective Needs of Adolescents   132
High School Guidance and Counseling   132
Student Assistance and Peer Counseling Programs   134

Peer Mediation Programs   136
Teacher Advisory Programs   137
Advisory Programs as Integral Components of Guidance   138
The Nature of Advisory Programs   139
Goals and Objectives of Advisory Programs   140
Characteristics of Successful Programs   141
Scheduling the Advisory Program   143
Roles of the Advisor   144
The Advisory Curriculum   147
Evaluation of Advisory Programs   157
Concluding Statements   162
Summary   163
Connections to Other Chapters   163
Action Steps   164
Discussion Questions   164
References   165

Chapter Six
Alternative Scheduling for Teaching and Learning   167

What You Will Learn in this Chapter   167
Scheduling the High School   168
The Emerging High School Schedule   168
Copernican-Style Schedules   170
Alternating Day (A/B) Schedules   178
The 4 × 4 Semester Plan   187
Various Combination Schedules   198
Issues Associated With the Transition to a New Block Schedule   203
Research on the Block Schedule   207
The Future of the High School Schedule   208
Summary   208
Connections to Other Chapters   209
Action Steps   209
Discussion Questions   209
References   210

Chapter Seven
The Organization of Teachers and Learners   211

What You Will Learn in this Chapter   211
Interdisciplinary Organization in High Schools   212
Academic Teaming   213
Academic Teaming in Various Settings   228

School-Within-School Strategies 243
The House Concept   247
Heterogeneous Grouping   253
The Talent Development High School   257
Summary   258
Connections to Other Chapters   259
Action Steps   259
Discussion Questions   261
References   261

Chapter Eight
School/Family/Community Partnerships   263

What You Will Learn in this Chapter   263
Family, Community, and High School Partnerships   265
Changing Perspectives of Partnership Roles   266
Parent and Family Involvement in a Changing Society   266
Meaningful Partnership Roles for Family and Community   267
National Standards for Parent/Family Involvement Programs   268
Barriers to Successful Partnerships   268
Successful Strategies for Outreach Activities and Programs   269
Effective Communication with Families, Community,
        and Other Stakeholders   287
Building Strong Partnerships   290
Concluding Remarks   291
Summary   291
Connections to Other Chapters   292
Action Steps   292
Discussion Questions   293
References   293

Chapter Nine
The High School Teacher   296

What You Will Learn in this Chapter   296
The Changing Roles of Teachers in the New High School   297
The Effects of the Expanding Knowledge Base on Teacher Roles   299
Teaching the New Curriculum   300
The National Board for Professional Teaching Standards   301
Professional Development for the New High School   302
Standards for Staff Development at the High School   303
New Paradigms for Staff Development   304
Staff Development Practices in the New High School   306
Teacher Preparation for the New High School   309

Professional Development High Schools and Other
Collaborative Partnerships   310
High School Teachers Meeting the Challenges of
New High Schools   316
Summary   317
Connections to Other Chapters   318
Action Steps   318
Discussion Questions   319
References   319

Chapter Ten
Leading High Schools in the New Century   322

What You Will Learn in this Chapter   322
The Nature of Instructional Leadership   324
The Performance-Based Principalship   325
Reforming High Schools   327
A Prototype Design Statement   334
Action Research   338
Efforts to Reform Schools   339
Total Quality Management   342
Leadership and School Accountability   343
Summary   344
Action Steps   345
Discussion Questions   346
References   346
Roster of High Schools   349
Author Index   357
Index of High Schools   361
Subject Index   363

INTRODUCTION

Nationwide, 485,000 teenagers dropped out of school last year, according to the U. S. Department of Education. In cities like Chicago and New York, barely one of every two entering freshmen graduates in four years. And these numbers don't include the multitudes who crawl into class indifferent, tired and just plain angry. The Carnegie Council on Adolescent Development has estimated that one in four young people—or seven million—is "extremely vulnerable to multiple high-risk behaviors and school failure" (Kotlowitz, 1998, p. 32).

Most high schools are at best average. They serve some students well and others poorly. International comparisons of achievement show that the United States ranks near the bottom in several academic areas. The poor methodology of these comparisons helps us rationalize some of the differences, but it does not provide a full explanation. Critics of the high schools place blame on everything from rampant anti-intellectualism, to overemphasis on interscholastic sports, to poorly prepared teachers, to the failure of many homes to support the efforts of high school educators.

Walberg (1984) identified nine factors that contribute significantly to school productivity. Among the instructional factors that influence student learning were the amount of time students engage in learning and the quality of the instructional experience, including psychological and curricular aspects. The largest instructional effects were registered by mastery learning, acceleration programs and the quality of the home environment. Surprisingly, Walberg found that open systems of education produced results that pleased parents, students and educators while leading to results on standardized achievement tests similar to those of students in more conventional schools. Goals such as cooperation, critical thinking, self reliance, constructive attitudes, lifelong learning, and independence were more likely to be attained in schools committed to flexible approaches to education.

In 1983 the National Commission on Excellence and Education issued a stinging criticism of our nation's high schools in a report titled *A Nation at Risk*. The Commission blamed the public schools for the nation's fall from grace in commerce, industry, science, and technological innovation when compared with competitors throughout the world. The high school curriculum was viewed as a type of smorgasbord, giving students too many choices and lacking a central purpose. The report recommended more homework, a longer school day and year, the strengthening of graduation requirements, better textbooks, and achievement testing from one level of schooling to another (The National Commission on Excellence, 1983).

In February, 1990 Admiral James Watkins, Secretary of Energy in the Bush administration, instructed the Sandia National Laboratories to undertake a study of American education. Unlike *A Nation at Risk*, the findings of the Sandia Report (Carson, Huelskamp & Woodall, 1991) were more positive. The following are among the principal findings as reported by Daniel Tanner (1993):

1. Since the late 1970s every ethnic or racial group has maintained or improved SAT (Scholastic Aptitude Test) scores. The aggregate decline in SAT scores is largely a product of demographic changes, since a higher proportion of students are taking the test than ever before.

2. Performance on the tests for the National Assessment of Educational Progress (NAEP) has been improving. No declines were found in NAEP scores in science, mathematics, writing, geography, and computer skills from 1977 to 1986.

3. High school dropout rates are declining for all ethnic populations and community types with the exception of Hispanics. As many as half of all Hispanic dropouts, however, are immigrants who did not complete high school in the native countries even though they have never attended an American school.

4. Dramatic demographic changes have been occurring in our schools as a result of increases in immigration. Today, almost one-third of our students are minorities, principally from Latin America and Asia. These rapidly changing demographics led the Sandia researchers to conclude the schools must become more sensitive to the needs of their students. They cited the urban metropolitan schools in particular as problem areas.

BREAKING RANKS: THE CHANGING OF AN AMERICAN INSTITUTION

The National Association of Secondary School Principals and the Carnegie Foundation for the Advancement of Teaching joined forces in 1994 to create the Commission on the Restructuring of the American High School. The Commission, composed predominantly of practitioners and others directly involved in the improvement of high school education, produced the report, *Breaking Ranks: The Changing of an American Institution* (1996). Nine major themes framed the recommendations and established the Commission's vision for the nation's high schools. These themes are:

- High school is, above all else, a learning community, and each school must commit itself to expect demonstrable academic achievement for every student in accordance with standards that stand up to national scrutiny.
- High school must be a transition experience, getting each student ready for the next stage of life, whatever it may be for that individual, with the understanding that, ultimately, each person needs to earn a living.
- High school must be a gateway to multiple options.
- High school must prepare each student to be a lifelong learner.
- High school must provide an understanding of the requirements for good citizenship and for full participation in a democracy.
- High school must play a role in the personal development of young people as social beings who have needs beyond those that are strictly academic.
- High school must help prepare to participate comfortably in an increasingly technological society.

- High school must equip young people for life in a country and world in which they will be interdependent with others, however different those others may be from them.
- High School must be an institution that unabashedly advocates in behalf of young people (*Breaking Ranks,* 1996, p. 2).

While most of the eighty-two recommendations derived from these themes may not be new, their appearance together in one document is significant. Deborah McRae, the coordinator of the international baccalaureate program at Harding University High School in Charlotte, North Carolina observes, "It (the report) pulls together many ideas that have been floating around independently and gives them coherence" (Sommerfield, 1996, p. 9).

HIGH SCHOOLS FEATURED IN THIS BOOK

Some of the high schools cited in this book are implementing one or more of the recommendations independently. Others are affiliated with national projects such as the Coalition of Essential Schools, Outcome-based Education, or the NASSP High School Alliance. The data for this book were collected from over 150 high schools recommended by colleagues, national organizations, and the authors' personal experiences. All of the featured schools responded willingly to letters written requesting information about their innovative programs.

ORGANIZATION OF THE BOOK

Using the recommendations from *Breaking Ranks* and the specific examples provided by the participating high schools, ten chapters were developed. Chapter One takes a historical look at high schools: What began as public-supported schooling for college-bound youth has become a more comprehensive institution attempting to meet the needs of a multilingual population. Chapter Two examines trends in curriculum. Nationally developed standards frame the debate over a possible national curriculum. Resources such as the internet expand the availability of information dramatically. Chapter Three describes new approaches to instruction designed to meet the needs of widely different student populations. The instructional and administrative uses of technology are presented in Chapter Four.

Chapter Five presents ways to personalize schooling through advisement. Programs that provide each student with a personal advocate or adviser are described. Alternative methods of building student schedules and master schedules are discussed in Chapter Six, as are different approaches to block scheduling. Chapter Seven explores organizational structures, emphasizing learning teams for both students and teachers. The concept of school and community partnerships is explored in Chapter Eight. Chapter Nine describes the shifting role of the teacher in the new high school. No longer can we think of high school teachers strictly as specialists. They must be involved with students as mentors and coaches, helping them to see that a formal education adds quality to their lives. The final chapter, Chapter Ten, demonstrates the need for leadership at all levels. New standards for the principal-ship and the idea of teachers as lead managers are advocated.

THE NEW HIGH SCHOOL

Our vision for the new high school uses the present as prologue. Much has been written and said about the need for a paradigm shift as schools approach a new century. Using the assumptions of the traditional school paradigm as markers, one transformation might read as follows:

Assumptions of the Traditional High School Paradigm

1. Achievement in school follows a normal distribution curve. It is therefore logi-cal to label students as possessing high ability, average ability or low ability.

2. Intelligence is a unitary concept usually associated with language and mathe-matics. It can be measured by a standard test.

3. Achievement is related to time. All students should be judged on their ability to attain similar results in a fixed amount of time.

4. Failure is a profound teacher. Students learn from their failures and thereby im-prove performance. Combined with assumption #1, a certain amount of failure is to be expected.

5. The school is a service delivery institution. It provides students with a cafeteria of opportunities, and it is the responsibility of the students to avail themselves of those opportunities.

6. All students learn in similar ways. Similar learning environments, therefore, provide equal and fair opportunities for all students.

7. Learning is best achieved when it is undertaken individually in a competitive en-vironment.

8. Rewards, incentives, and punishments are the best way to motivate students to learn. Threatening students will get them to work harder and behave more re-sponsibly. By this reasoning, getting tough, raising expectations and assigning mandatory homework will make students learn more.

9. Memorization of information constitutes learning.

10. Chronological age is the best indicator of where a student should be placed in order to maximize learning.

Assumptions of the New High School Paradigm

1. All students, with the possible exception of the profoundly handicapped, are ca-pable of learning. It is the educators' responsibility to organize the school to fa-cilitate learning.

2. Intelligence is a multi-faceted concept. Educators should assume that all students are gifted in some way, and then organize the school to bring out each student's talents.

3. Time is a variable and not a constant when applied to learning. It does not measure achievement.

4. Success is a profound teacher, Students learn from their successes and improve performance.

5. The school should engage learners by making learning exciting and attractive.

6. Students learn in different ways. The learning environment directly impacts student learning. Students respond differently to different methods of teaching.

7. Learning should be cooperative as well as competitive. Instructors should help students to appreciate the value of community in learning.

8. Motivation that is intrinsic to the learning task is most effective. Instructors should organize learning around student strengths, not the remediation of weaknesses.

9. Memorization is only part of the learning process. True learning occurs when students are able to place new information in long-term memory and retrieve it as necessary to solve real-life problems.

10. Chronological age is only one way to group students for learning. Placement of students should be based on multiple criteria. The graded school is an anachronism that no longer supports student progress as it is now understood.

Translating the assumptions of the new paradigm into school practice results in an expansion of the high school from a single location to many different venues for learning. School facilities will be extended to include community placements, the home, travel to diverse areas, the Internet, museums, and institutions of higher learning, to mention just a few possibilities. The late educational innovator J. Loyd Trump recommended that the capacity of high schools should not exceed two-thirds of the student body so that the other one-third could be simultaneously placed in the community. Smaller learning communities where teachers and students know each other well and deliberate solutions to problems will dominate. We view the large high school of one to five thousand students as an obstacle to the goal of personalized instruction.

Time frames will be more flexible for teachers and students. Periods of time will be appropriate to the tasks to be accomplished. Students may spend entire school days, and perhaps even more time, investigating topics of interest, working on projects, engaging in cognitive apprenticeships, browsing the internet, or conducting research projects with university scholars. The senior slump, characteristic of the final semester of a senior's school year, will become a rarity. Similarly, teachers will have time to plan, confer with colleagues, prepare presentations, read professional literature, and serve as academic mentors to students. They will be generalists first and subject matter specialists second.

Curriculum will be based on the structure, methodology, and content of organized fields of knowledge. Each discipline will hold up as the ideal of accomplishment a person actively engaged in solving problems and adding to the body of knowledge—what Reich calls a symbol analyst and a symbol generator. Students will be able to begin the study of a discipline wherever they happen to be and to advance along a continuum toward mastery. Building on the work of David Feldman (1980), the curriculum will be defined as follows:

Phase One: The starting place (novice)

Phase Two: Beginning to learn how to apply knowledge (apprentice)

Phase Three: Applying knowledge in everyday situations (journeyman)

Phase Four: Applying knowledge creatively (craftsman)

Phase Five: Using knowledge to create new knowledge (expert)

Phase Six: Using knowledge to teach others (master)

Each phase will serve as a benchmark along the journey to mastery. Quality examples will be provided at each phase to give students a concrete picture of what a novice, apprentice, journeyman, craftsman, expert, or master is able to do in a given discipline. The examples will give students a picture of what is required to advance to the next phase. Culminating assessments tied to these examples will determine a student's readiness to end one phase of learning and begin another. If a student does poorly on a threshold assessment, the results will be analyzed, a plan developed, and weaknesses addressed.

Within each phase instruction will vary. Teachers and teams of teachers will devise or locate materials that personalize instruction. Students will work independently, in learning teams, and sometimes in larger groups. Each student's cognitive learning style will be diagnosed to enable teachers to accommodate student strengths and preferences in delivering instruction. Teacher advisers will oversee advisees' daily schedules, assigning them to appropriate learning environments based on need, desire, style differences, and academic progress. Electronic databases will connect teacher advisers to student progress records. Individual conferences will be held at regular intervals to monitor academic progress and develop personal plans for success. The traditional master schedule will be replaced by a student-driven schedule with some permanent group meetings and numerous opportunities for independent, paired, and team learning. The learning team will take precedence over the competition between individuals.

Staffing patterns will include professionals, paraprofessionals and volunteers. Community resources will be employed liberally. Teachers will be freed from the perfunctory duties of lunchroom, corridor and bus supervision. Their roles will encompass more professionalized staff development. The school calendar will be expanded so that student progress can be continuous through a full year. Emphasis will be placed on what students have accomplished rather than what they have failed to accomplish.

Technology will make available extraordinary information and communication resources for students and teachers. The proliferation of information will require that teachers take on the roles of structurer, stimulator, linker to resources, co-evaluator, and verifier of outcomes. Students will be expected to demonstrate learning through performances, exhibitions, portfolios, and similar devices. The Carnegie unit will be abandoned or modified.

Leadership will be broadened to include administration, faculty, staff students, parent and community members. Principals will return to their original roles as principal-teachers, signifying the best teacher in the school. Their primary duty will be to improve instruction.

This vision of a high school is limited by our own perceptions influenced by our current level of knowledge and experience. Whether our image of the new high school will come to pass is conjectural. When Bob Dylan observed in the 1960s that "the times they are a changin'," he was probably more prophetic of today's circumstances than he was of the circumstances over 30 years ago. One has only to recognize the rapidity of change in the personal computer field to gain a sense of this phenomenon. When predicting the future, one must be sure to allow for a significant margin of error.

The innovations taking place in some of today's most advanced high schools give reason for optimism. Many of the changes we predict are incipient in some high schools and refined in others. Readers should be mindful, however, that the practices represented in this volume are employed in a minority of high schools. There is still much to be done. But regardless of the direction that change in our high schools will take, one thing seems clear: The focus must be on success for all students—not just a few or some or even ninety percent. As W. Edwards Deming reminded us, "Everyone wins or everyone loses!"

REFERENCES

Breaking ranks: Changing an American institution (1996). Reston, VA: National Association of Secondary School Principals.

Carson, C. C., Huelskamp, R. M. S., & Woodall, T. D. (1991). *Perspectives on Education in America.* Albuquerque, NM: Sandia National Laboratories.

Feldman, D. (1980). *Beyond universals in cognitive development.* Ablex Publishing Company.

Kotlowitz, A. (1998, July 5). The high school at the end of the road. *The New York Times Magazine,* 32–37.

National Commission on Excellence. (1983). *A Nation at Risk.* Washington, D.C.: Author.

Sommerfield, M. (1996, February 28). Report calls for personal touch in high schools. *Education Week,* 1, 9.

Tanner, D. (1993). A nation truly at risk, *Phi Delta Kappan. 75,* 288–297.

Walberg, H. (1984). Improving the productivity of America's schools. *Educational Leadership, 41,* 19–27.

The Exemplary High School

Paul S. George
University of Florida

C. Kenneth McEwin
Appalachian State University

John M. Jenkins
University of Florida

CHAPTER 1

THE EVOLVING AMERICAN HIGH SCHOOL

WHAT YOU WILL LEARN IN THIS CHAPTER

Goals of the American high school
Early American high schools
The comprehensive high school concept

Reform efforts and other influences
shaping the high school
The contemporary high school

High school is, above all else, a learning community and each school must commit itself to expecting demonstrated academic achievement for every student in accord with standards that can stand up to national scrutiny.

High school must provide an underpinning for good citizenship and for full participation in the life of a democracy.

High school must lay a foundation for students to be able to participate comfortably in an increasingly technological society.

—*Breaking Ranks, p. 2*

THE AMERICAN HIGH SCHOOL: SERVING MULTIPLE MASTERS

Almost from the origins of the high school until the present, American high school educators have been engaged in a continuous and often frustrating attempt to achieve simultaneously three very different and potentially conflicting goals. American citizens, throughout the decades, have come to demand that high school educators offer programs that: (1) yield graduates who are ready to undertake the responsibilities of effective democratic citizenship; (2) produce young adults who are capable of filling necessary roles in the economy, and who are sufficiently skilled to promote economic growth; and (3) provide individual students with the educational opportunity and resulting credentials to allow them to get ahead, or to maintain their position, in the world they enter after high school graduation. Today every American high school attempts, says Labaree (1997, p. 39), to educate citizens, workers, and winners.

The goal of democratic equality focuses on the high school as the producer of democratic citizens, and on the provision within the school of equal access for all and equal treatment for all who attend. The high school should help, in accordance with this goal, to provide the citizens of the nation with a "common culture and a sense of shared membership in the community" (Labaree, p. 45). Those who see the high school as the agent of social efficiency stress the obligation of the high school to "prepare the young to carry out useful economic roles with competence" (Labaree, p. 42). Our lives depend, they argue, on the capability of all to contribute to a productive economy; this is the perspective of the taxpayer and the employer. Those who view the high school as an agent of social mobility see the school as providing a commodity for their children or the children who are of concern to them. The school, from this perspective, exists to provide a competitive opportunity to achieve, a chance to demonstrate one's fitness compared with peers, and further education and opportunity.

For most of the last 150 years, high school educators have struggled to organize and operate schools that effectively meet the perceived needs of students in the communities they serve in these three goal areas. Educators have responded reluctantly or frenetically to the emergence of goals or changing goal priorities, and to the pendulum swings in demands for reform that emerge from such changes. The evolution of the American high school, its earliest manifestations, its present structure and program, debate about its effectiveness, as well as current calls for reform and activity aimed at school improvement—all can be understood more clearly when viewed with an awareness of the incredible influence these three goals have exercised on the institution called "high school."

THE EARLIEST AMERICAN SECONDARY EDUCATION

The Latin Grammar School

The first colonial efforts toward secondary schooling illustrate the early primacy of the goal of social mobility, which was at the heart of what was to become

American high school education. Latin grammar schools were established as early as 1635 to provide a general and college preparatory education for the sons of the New England and other colonial elite, an education that would permit these children to maintain their place as adults in the upper class (Button & Provenzo, 1983). Conceived as preparation for leadership in church or political life, the curriculum of the schools drew heavily on classics that had been studied in European Latin schools for more than a century, and teachers were usually ministers who were not attached to a church at the moment.

Knowledge of Greek and Latin classics, even for those who did not go on to Harvard, Yale, or William and Mary, was "one of the identifying marks of the person of education and breeding" (Gutek, 1991, p. 98). With attendance limited by wealth and social class, because only the most affluent and influential could afford to "take a boy out of economic production for seven years" (Krug, 1966, p. 3), the numbers of students were small, but the influence of these first schools went far beyond their numbers. During the remainder of the 17th century, in the Latin grammar schools, the concept of education in the service of the goal of social mobility, as primarily a process intended to provide a competitive advantage in later life, especially for the elite, became deeply ingrained in the school. The goal of social mobility (Labaree, 1997), providing advantaged individual students with the credentials to maintain or improve their privileged position, had been established.

The Academy

An eminently practical man, Benjamin Franklin issued a proposal in 1749 for a new kind of secondary school. This proposal announced a new goal for education, a conception of secondary education as a resource for producing trained workers who could become effective participants in the new national economy. This was perhaps the first appearance of the goal of social efficiency in American secondary education. Though Franklin was not the first to propose or establish alternatives to the Latin grammar school, his *Proposals Relating to the Education of Youth Pensilvania* (sic) advocated for a school that educated all worthy students regardless of social class, and for a school program that helped to move the economy of the new nation forward. His proposal, thus, "stands as an eloquent landmark in the polemical literature of pedagogy" (Krug, 1966, p. 16). That is, Franklin articulated the desire of the many new middle-class citizens in the growing and prospering young nation, for a secondary school that did more than provide a classical education for the colonial religious and political elite. These new middle-class businessmen and professionals sought college preparation for their own children and training that would prepare a new generation of workers for the emerging industries of the nation.

Franklin sought to break the monopoly of the classical curriculum and broaden the role of the school beyond service to the youth of the aristocracy. He pressed for a school that would include arithmetic, accounting, geometry, astronomy, navigation, English, modern languages, gardening, and "good breeding," along with some of the classics and "every other useful part of learning"; but in Franklin's academy, no student would be compelled to study Latin or Greek. By the beginning of the Civil War, there were more than six thousand academies in existence, serving more than a quarter of a million American youths, both boys and girls (Butts, 1978).

The academy became the institution that attempted to meet the needs of a nation that was expanding its frontiers, expanding its concept of democracy, and establishing a new industrial and commercial base. Some academies offered courses in the classics for those who wished to attend for purposes of college preparation, but virtually all also offered practical training for those who intended to enter business or commercial life after leaving school. The academies also attempted to prepare students to participate more effectively in civic affairs (Gutek, 1991). An explosion of curricular possibilities, in addition to the classics, followed the spread of the academy: bookkeeping, surveying, geography, United States history, chemistry, drawing, algebra, geology, and agriculture, to name a few.

The most reputable academies were controlled by independent boards, and while a few received supplements from local or state governments, most were supported primarily by tuition fees paid directly to the school. Poor children were, thus, still unable to attend such schools. Reese (1995, p. 6) writes: "Colonial public schools were not created as potential avenues of opportunity for poorer boys or *any* girls or people of color." Only children who could already read and write well could be admitted to any of these schools—which effectively excluded most, if not all, poor children. What came to be known as "Sunday school" was really the first attempt to teach basic literacy and Christian morality to the local poor (Reese, 1997, p. 10).

Many religious denominations established their own academies; in fact, many small private denominational colleges were originally established as academies. Some academies were connected to state colleges, as preparatory schools. In general however, there was little organization, coordination, or commonality from one academy to another (Gutek, 1991).

The decades following the Revolution and prior to the outbreak of the Civil War saw increasing enthusiasm for democracy and social equality in the new nation, and witnessed the emergence of a third important goal for American secondary education, democratic citizenship. Some years after the academy proposed by Franklin, in 1779, Thomas Jefferson submitted a plan for a free school system in the state of Virginia. Jefferson's *A Bill for the More General Diffusion of Knowledge* was a clear and strong statement of the goal of education as a process for establishing a strong democracy based on meritocratic equality. Jefferson believed that social democracy and universal education went hand in hand. He stated that after the anti-democratic years of colonial rule and the disorder of the American Revolution, the needs of the new social order could best be met by establishing a virtuous citizenry through universal, free, public education (Button & Provenzo, 1983).

Jefferson proposed a free school system that would provide three years of education for all "free" boys and girls. The best of these students would be selected to attend further schooling in residential grammar schools. Further selection processes would produce a small group of the best and the brightest, regardless of wealth or poverty, who would attend the College of William and Mary (all expenses paid) and eventually form an intellectual elite who would lead the state of Virginia to a bright democratic future (Krug, 1966). In the years that followed, a great rush toward free universal public schooling for all white citizens spread from state to state (Button & Provenzo, 1983). The nation appeared to heed Jefferson's dictum that a nation could not be both ignorant and free.

THE FIRST HIGH SCHOOLS

On January 15, 1821, citizens of Boston voted to open a new school, to be called the Boston English Classical School, generally regarded as the first free and public high school in the United States. The boys-only school, which soon became known as the English High School, was a new school, indeed. No one even knows where the term "high school" came from. The English High School was a social and educational innovation unlike anything that had preceded it; it was no Latin grammar school, and it was not a church-supported institution (Krug, 1966; Reese, 1995).

The Boston Latin School, formed almost two centuries earlier, in 1635, had a very clear purpose—to send to Harvard a steady stream of students who would emerge to lead the nation. The Puritans did a good job of establishing a school program that fit the interests of their own social class very well. This new high school, however, was very different, and responded to the needs of a new class, merchants who needed a generation of clerks and other workers with the skills required by the new economy (Reese, 1995). The report that prompted the opening of the high school contended:

> . . . A parent who wishes to give a child an education that shall fit him for an active life, and shall serve as a foundation for eminence in his profession, whether Mercantile or Mechanical, is under the necessity of giving him a different education from any which our public schools can now furnish (Report of the Subcommittee of the Boston School Committee, October 26, 1820; cited in Krug, 1966, p. 46).

The English High School was a secular school established for students who were not from the ruling class. The school, intended for boys who did not plan to go to college (Pulliam & Van Patten, 1995) had a three-year curriculum: English literature, science, mathematics, ancient history, and American history formed the core, with navigation, surveying, bookkeeping, and other practical subjects also included. In 1826, the Boston School Committee also opened the High School for Girls, but the circumstances surrounding the school were so contentious that it was closed within two years (Krug, 1966).

Two schools—Boston Latin and English High—were now in operation, serving two different student populations and working toward two different goals. Even so, the students who were able to attend English High School were not from the ranks of the poor and were certainly not African-Americans. Students were admitted by examination only and had to know how to read and write prior to admission, which would have eliminated the children of the poor. Candidates from the new English High School were from the homes of relatively affluent merchants and other members of the new economic class the school was intended to serve.

On March 10, 1827, the Commonwealth of Massachusetts passed what became known as the Massachusetts Law on High Schools (Pulliam & Van Patten, 1995), requiring towns of more than 4,000 inhabitants to establish a free, public high school. By 1840, Massachusetts had 26 high schools, but elsewhere in America the spread of the high school movement was much slower, probably since so many unregulated private or semi-public academies were established at nearly the same time.

In many towns, two schools operated: an academy that offered a more classical education, and a free public high school. The high school movement, however, spread very slowly for the next several decades. By the time of the Civil War, there were about 300 high schools in America (Pulliam & Van Patten, 1995).

The Unheralded Birth of the American Comprehensive High School Concept

In 1851, the school committee of Lowell, Massachusetts took the dramatic step of incorporating two "programs of study" in their public high school. One program consisted primarily of the classics, and was intended for college-bound students. The other program of study followed the English High School model and was offered to students intending to enter the world of commerce, business, and industry. For the first time, two different groups of students with two different life plans began to study under the same school roof. A comprehensive high school was open (Krug, 1966), establishing an important precedent that actually may have been the first step toward the comprehensive high school of the 21st century. The growing presence of such schools after the Civil War may have been the cause of the virtual disappearance of private academies during that time.

Establishing a new high school was not a simple task, and the numbers increased very slowly at first. Everything about the new high schools was controversial. The expanding wealth of the new nation led to a willingness to take adolescents out of factories and place them in school, and made possible the increased expenditures required to construct new high school buildings. But spending the money on new schools and including girls in compulsory attendance alienated many. In one illustrative case, the working men of Beverly, Massachusetts, voted to abolish their high school in 1860; the fishermen, farmers, shoemakers, and laborers were convinced that the high school would benefit only the elite and the merchant classes, but that it would be paid for by simpler working people (Butts, 1978).

Even the rich were less than enthusiastic about the rising expenses for public high schools, and about the secularism that characterized high school programs of study. During this period, a number of exclusive, private, and denominationally oriented schools, such as St. Paul's in Concord, New Hampshire, were opened, in the belief that such schools could do a much better job of preparing the leaders of the nation than could public high schools, "because the mass of voters who elected school boards were too often swayed by passion, prejudice, and jealousy of the aristocrats" (Butts, 1978, p. 109). Education for social mobility was still an important goal for many, even though the common school movement became stronger and stronger as the years passed.

The years that followed the birth of the high school, leading up to and beyond the Civil War, saw tremendous economic growth and increasing social optimism in America. The presidency and perspective of Andrew Jackson typified the new political and educational support for the growing middle class. What had been basically a rural, agrarian nation was becoming more urban, commercial, and industrial. An education system was needed that produced graduates trained in the specialized vocations of the new, industrially dominated society. The basic skills of reading, writing, and 'rithmatic were no longer adequate for effective participation in the new America, nor was college preparation for the elite the only desirable option (Gutek, 1991, p. 102).

The new public high schools that developed during these decades came to resemble the factories for which they produced a generation of new workers. Large high schools with graded classes replaced the small one-room schoolhouse at about the same rate that factories replaced individual workshops. The graded classroom was actually a major innovation in the 19th century; without it the public school as we have come to know it would not have existed. Greater efficiency and more effective coordination, standardization and classification—hallmarks of the new factories—became the distinguishing characteristics of the new high schools (Reese, 1995).

The Kalamazoo Decision and Its Aftermath

The spread of the new American high school after the Civil War clearly was related to the goal of social efficiency. The educators and businessmen of the period hoped that such an education would "instill the values of ambition, hard work, delayed gratification, and earnestness—students would become sober, law-abiding, and respectable citizens" (Reese, 1995, p. 57). Eventually, the public comprehensive high school became the model for educating virtually all American youth, except the elite who attended and continue to attend exclusive, expensive, private college preparatory schools.

The dominance of the public high school was perhaps locked into place in 1874, when the Supreme Court of Michigan ruled that the state had a responsibility to provide a free public high school education, especially because the citizens had already endorsed both public elementary schools and a state university. It made no sense, said Chief Justice Cooley, to leave a large gap in the middle; to do so would unreasonably favor the sons and daughters of the wealthy who could afford their own private high school education. Only the rich, Cooley stated, would ever get to college under such absurd circumstances. Endorsing the concept of the comprehensive high school (unknowingly), Cooley wrote that it was entirely reasonable for communities to support common democratic high schools that had both classically oriented programs for college entrance and conventional "English" programs of study for those who sought to enter the world of business and industry at the end of their high school education (Krug, 1966).

Even though the aristocratic elite had departed for private boarding schools, "democratic schooling" still meant, narrowly, schooling for the sons and daughters of native born, middle class, white, Anglo-Saxon protestants: the children of merchants, small businessmen, manufacturers, and professionals. Regular attendance, punctuality, and proper "deportment" were essential virtues cultivated in the new middle class schools, and report cards gave equal space to achievement and behavior. Bible readings, prayers, and the singing of hymns opened the school day, and the classical program of study was still in place alongside the "English" course that prepared students for the world of work.

Virtually all but the most successful and most financially able dropped out by age 14 or 15; even in the best high schools, a 75 to 90 percent drop-out rate was common. Juniors and seniors were few indeed, and a great many children never even got to high school. In both the north and the south, most high schools were racially segregated, and public high schools for African-Americans were rare in any part of the country. Because attending school instead of working was still very expensive, only a tiny percentage of minorities attended high school, even in the north. Even one or two years of high school attendance, however, qualified many for jobs as clerks, salesmen, accountants, and even managers, jobs that were much better than those taken by unskilled laborers (Reese, 1995).

REFORMULATION OF THE HIGH SCHOOL CURRICULUM: THREE GOALS PERSIST

The arguments over the most appropriate curriculum plan for the comprehensive high school began almost immediately, creating a controversy that remains fresh approximately 150 years later. Curriculum developers tried, in the last decades of the 19th century, to fashion a coherent English curriculum for the many bound for the world of work, while preserving much of the classical curriculum that educated the few for college. The efforts to do so continue today.

Some pressed for a classical curriculum for all students, arguing that the "mental discipline" of the college preparatory curriculum would also be the best preparation for both the world of work and for the responsibilities of citizenship. Such a curriculum, it was contended, would serve all three goals of American high school education: social equality and democratic citizenship, social efficiency, and social mobility. Many shared Jefferson's dream that the high school would provide the nation with an aristocracy of intellect based on academic achievement, an aristocracy that would replace a rigid class system based on inherited wealth and status.

But momentous changes had occurred in America during the last half of the 19th century. Advances had been made in commerce, science, technology, and industry—advances that promised a land in which many more people could live lives of a high material standard, if not wealth. Under such circumstances, arguments for classical studies had great difficulty competing against the calls for an evermore practical curriculum. Textbooks appeared in large numbers for the first time providing common reading materials, and they were rightfully regarded as a major advance in education and a tremendous lift for the forces of democratic schooling (Reese 1995). Pulliam and Van Patten (1995, p. 90) describe the status of the high school curriculum near the turn of the century:

> High schools offered both traditional and practical programs, but the emphasis was usually placed on the college preparatory curriculum. In spite of the fact that only about one tenth of the students in high schools in 1900 expected to enter college, the "classical" course was taken by a majority of youngsters. Latin and algebra were the subjects which had the highest enrollment. Sometimes the college course was divided so that a student could elect an English or a scientific

major, but there was no free choice of subjects. Many schools had whole programs or courses such as "manual training or commercial," for the terminal student; many studied the "English" course even if they had no plans for higher education. A few high schools had specialized vocational courses and some offered preparation for teaching. Physical education, art, music, and religion were included in the subjects offered by many high schools at the end of the nineteenth century. There was very little standardization. Some high schools offered as a four-year course what others gave in one semester or one year.

Other now-familiar arguments appeared with the spread of the high schools in the latter half of the 19th century. In the 1870s, for example, high school teachers began to complain that the students they were receiving from the common elementary schools were not adequately prepared to do high school work successfully. Standards, said high school teachers, had once been high, but had now seriously declined. "Since the Puritans, Americans have bemoaned the failures of the rising generation," and parents then, as now, wanted their children to have a "competitive edge" over their peers, to be gained through education (Reese, 1995, p. 219).

All three of the goals that have dominated the course of the American high school were represented in late 19th century arguments about the high school curriculum; as a result, three major curriculum developments emerged. Butts (1978, p. 188) describes the situation:

> The efforts to achieve academic coherence dispersed in three different directions: mental discipline, social efficiency, and civic responsibility to democracy. Toward the end of the nineteenth century the purposes of education as well as the curriculums of the schools had become so scattered and fragmented that these three diverse programs for curriculum reform had the common objective of imposing some order, uniformity, and consistency upon the educational enterprise, although they took quite different directions to achieve this purpose. The dissonant voices of academic discipline and social efficiency created such a clamor that the political purpose to develop civic responsibility, which harked back to the Revolutionary era, was almost submerged in the tumult except when its ideals were distorted in a raucous call for "Americanization."

The Committee of Ten on Secondary School Studies

In the midst of this turmoil about the proper goals and curriculum for the high schools, the Committee of Ten on Secondary School Studies was appointed in 1892 by the National Education Association. The Committee was given the mandate to bring clarity and consistency to the high school curriculum. Composed primarily of college presidents and university professors, and chaired by Charles Eliot, the president of Harvard, the commission had one high school principal as a member, but no high school teachers. Not surprisingly, the recommendations of the Committee strongly reinforced the goal of social mobility, calling "the intellectual value of academic training . . . the prime purpose of secondary and higher education" (Butts, 1978, p. 188).

While recognizing that only a small fraction of high school students ever went on to college, the Committee asserted that the curriculum that was appropriate for college preparation was also the best curriculum to prepare high school students for life and work immediately after secondary school. The Committee based their recommendations on what has come to be identified as faulty psychology—the mental discipline approach. The report of the Committee contended that four years of "strong and effective mental training" would exercise and strengthen the mind as if it were a muscle to be worked. Naturally, the subjects identified as the best for mental discipline turned out to be those studied by the elite (Latin, Greek, and mathematics).

Many other academic subjects were also admitted to the curriculum, courses quite recognizable as the core of today's academic curriculum: algebra, geometry, and trigonometry; natural and physical sciences; English and modern foreign languages; and history. The recommendations did include one radical proposal for the time—that a student might go on to college without studying either Latin or Greek; although at that time few probably did. Vocational and commercial studies were completely ignored (Gutek, 1991). It should be clear that college educators, others who saw themselves as preparing students for college, and those who sought college entrance for themselves or their children were strongly supportive of the recommendations of the Committee of Ten.

In the years that followed, a number of developments strengthened the goal of the high school as servant of social mobility through college preparation. The establishment of the College Entrance Examination Board in 1900 added more uniformity to the high school curriculum through the influence of college entrance examinations, an influence felt dramatically in today's high school. The creation of the Commission on Accredited Schools, in 1901, and the North Central Association of Schools and Colleges established the practice of setting standards for high schools and ensuring their implementation through regular on-site evaluations. Both organizations, now with six regional accreditation units, continue to influence the scope and sequence of the high school curriculum.

One other permanent influence of the Committee of Ten was the recommendation that every subject should be studied for one period each day, five days each week, for a year. In so doing, every subject would carry equal weight. Eventually, the result of this recommendation came to be known as the "Carnegie Unit," the standard unit of credit for high school subjects. More than a century later, the Carnegie Unit continues to dominate the organization and operation of the American high school.

The Press for Vocational Education and "Socialization"

In the years that followed the Committee of Ten's report, an unanticipated explosion in high school attendance occurred, and the high schools became overwhelmed by vast numbers of youth. Increasing prosperity, child labor laws, and waves of immigration threatened to produce numbers of students that would swamp the American high school.

> Between 1890 and 1930 the secondary school enrollment leaped from 360,000 to nearly 5 million—from 7 percent of the group aged 14 to 17 years to more than 50 percent of that age group, no longer an "insignificant percentage." This

meant that an increasing number of educators and the public began to array themselves against a purely academic and disciplinary emphasis in school and college (Butts, 1978, p. 190).

Not surprisingly, new and reinforced efforts were made to dislodge the traditional academic curriculum, or at least to supplement it with education perceived to be more relevant to the lives of the great majority of high school students who would not be going to college. Not only Latin and Greek, but every narrowly academic subject came under attacks reminiscent of Horace Greeley's earlier criticism of the high school curriculum's lack of practicality. Greeley had stated:

> I am thankful that Algebra had not yet been thrust into our rural common schools, to knot the brains and squander the time of those who should be learning something of positive and practical utility (Reese, 1995, p. 111).

Vocational education was vigorously supported, perhaps surprisingly, by advocates for all three of the goals that have historically driven the American high school. Those in favor of the goals of social mobility and social efficiency, for example, stated that vocational education was needed to equip the millions of immigrants with the skills to make them useful to American industry and the "socialization" that would make them fit for an urban, industrial, capitalist society. In 1906, the Massachusetts Commission on Industrial and Technical Education concluded that the schooling of most, if not all, immigrant children should be "infused with industrial education." Even the traditional subjects were to be taught in a way that would directly show their applicability to the world of work (Preskill, 1989, p. 356).

In 1905, the National Association of Manufacturers reported that 97 percent of all high school students failed to graduate. This group suggested that all public school students be categorized into three groups: the small minority who would go on to college and to social, political, and economic leadership; those who were destined to be foremen and skilled laborers; and "the concrete and hand-minded children" who comprised more than half of all public school students and who could expect little more in life than to occupy a place in the great machinery of industry (Preskill, 1989, p. 355).

Charles Eliot, the president of Harvard who had earlier chaired the Committee of Ten, vigorously supported the idea of using the high schools to sort students into the categories for which they were destined in life, and stated that educational tracks and ability grouping be established to provide them with the education they required, one that matched the students' "probable destiny." Eliot stated that there was a tiny managing and leading class whose children required a classical education befitting the positions in life that they would assume after graduation from a New England college or university. There was a larger group that was "devoted to buying and selling, and a group of skilled artisans." By far the largest group were those Eliot described as the "rough workers," and for this group, said Eliot, vocational education should begin in elementary school (Preskill, 1989).

In 1915 and 1919, the Committee on Economy of Time in Education issued several reports that supported the notions of tracking and sorting students, and providing the great majority with a practical, vocational education. High school students should be, the committee stated, identified according to their likely futures, then placed in college preparatory, vocational, or general tracks, and provided with a properly differentiated curriculum. In 1917, the Smith–Hughes Act for Vocational Education solidified the national support for vocational education (Krug, 1966). Curriculum developers such as Franklin Bobbitt and W. W. Charters advocated an analysis of the major "activities of life" in the industrial world as the basis for the curriculum. Charles Eliot's vision of a three-tiered school system, a small college-preparatory track for the elite, and much larger vocational and general tracks for the rest had, for better or worse, been implemented.

Preskill (1989, pp. 357–358) summarizes:

> . . . and to this day we continue to feel its influence. Despite our democratic ideals, the structure of our schools reflects Eliot's vision of a differentiated America, where schooling prepares young people to assume their various roles in a stratified society. If we fail to understand this basic truth and the way it has shaped our educational history, we can never properly reform our schools and live out the true meaning of the pedagogical creed that all children should receive a stimulating and challenging education to help them achieve their fullest potential as human beings.

Commission on the Reorganization of Secondary Education

Advocates for the third goal—schools as the foundation of democratic citizenship and the guarantor of equal opportunity—were not totally silent during the activities of the Committee of Ten or the press for narrow vocational training. A whole host of thinkers (e.g., John Dewey) wrote about the necessity for the high school to continue to pursue the Jeffersonian vision. They vigorously opposed the mental discipline approach of the Committee of Ten and protested against the "social efficiency" of assigning children to a role in life that was predetermined by their parents' socioeconomic status. They believed in a much broader and more democratic role for the American high school. This advocacy led to the publication in 1918 of a document that was to influence American secondary education for the rest of the century. The Commission on the Reorganization of Secondary Education issued a report, a pamphlet really, entitled "The Cardinal Principles of Secondary Education."

The Commission addressed several critical issues in secondary education. One was the question of whether the relatively new vocational education should be provided in separate special schools or in the emerging comprehensive high schools. The second was the issue of tracking and curriculum differentiation—the extent to which students in separate tracks or programs of study should be isolated from each other, and at what grade level such tracking should begin. Influential educators like Charles Eliot stated that such differentiation should be extended downward as early as the seventh grade, a view that coincided with the emergence of a separate "junior" high school, containing grades seven through nine, in many parts of the country. The third major issue was connected to the argument that the place of any subject in the curriculum could be justified only by the degree to which the subject contributed to the ends of the goal of social efficiency (Krug, 1966).

The Commission's final report, *Cardinal Principles of Secondary Education,* was issued after three years of laborious effort; the succinct statement of seven principles became a reference point for most of the remainder of the twentieth century. Stressing the importance of democratic education that would benefit both the person and the society, these principles were what the members of the Commission believed should be the necessary conditions of quality secondary education:

1. Health
2. Command of fundamental processes
3. Worthy home membership
4. Vocation
5. Citizenship
6. Worthy use of leisure time
7. Ethical character

At a time when other educators were calling for schools that served the elite headed for college, or for a school system that operated primarily as the source of workers for the capitalist system, the work of the Commission worked boldly toward the goal of democratic equality and citizenship. It attempted to broaden the social role of education in a number of important ways. First, the report insisted that the core of high school education be conceived in terms of the needs of all students and the achievements required of them, rather than as a set of academic hurdles to be jumped or courses to be mastered; the needs of all students (instead of curriculum) were primary for the first time. Butts points out that the Commission emphasized the goal of democratic citizenship far more, perhaps, than anyone since Jefferson.

The authors of the *Cardinal Principles* took a firm stance for other programs that would contribute to democratic citizenship and equality. They reaffirmed a commitment to the emerging comprehensive high school instead of accepting separate academic, vocational, and commercial high schools. High schools were to become comprehensive, not simply by housing both academic and vocational education programs. The high school curriculum would also include health, citizenship, character education, and the worthy use of leisure time. Reflecting the dramatic effects of continuing waves of immigration, the Commission envisioned a high school comprehensive in a third way: a school where students of varying racial, religious, ethnic, and economic backgrounds would learn together in the same institution. After 1918, the comprehensive high school was a firm fixture in American education, and growth in the numbers of students attending high school was explosive.

The Commission also resisted the pressure to institute rigid tracking and ability grouping in the seventh grade. It stated, instead, that there should be a number of common subjects that every student would take, in common classrooms. Krug (1966, p. 120) says that "perhaps the most striking recommendation in the report was the one that called for universal secondary schooling."

All normal boys and girls, said the report, should be encouraged to stay in school until eighteen of years of age, and if possible, with full-time attendance. Finally, the report recommended compulsory schooling up to age 18, and reaffirmed that this should take place in a comprehensive high school, not a "continuation school." It is very likely that the Commission's stance on universal education through high school was the beginning of a national commitment, one that continues today.

The high school that exists today took shape during the 1920s and 1930s. The high school included grades nine through twelve, and offered a broad curriculum to an increasingly diverse student body. Typically, four curriculum tracks were present in those years: the traditional college prep program, vocational–commercial, general, and agricultural education. For various reasons, American students accepted the idea of a high school education. In 1930, there were approximately four million students attending high school, but by 1960, that number had grown to nearly ten million.

Progressive Education Reform Affects the Emerging High School

By 1920, American culture had been transformed in important ways, most importantly from a rural, agrarian society to one in which the industrialized city was dominant. Not only was city life radically different, but the cities of post–World War I America were teeming with a social diversity and a bustling industry never before experienced. Technological improvements on the American farm meant that fewer youths were needed to work there. The enforcement of compulsory education laws delivered millions of new students to the doors of the high school. "Assimilation of vast numbers of foreign immigrants nearly engulfed the schools and exhausted their energies" (Butts, 1978, p. 196).

In spite of the birth of the comprehensive high school concept, many educators believed that for the most part, the high school still served a predominantly college-oriented elite, and they consequently either ignored the masses of students or offered them an education appropriate only for a life of drudgery in office or mill. Like reformers attempting to improve conditions in other areas of life, such as the factory, educational reformers sought to improve the high school program. George S. Counts, for example, stated in *The Selective Character of American Secondary Education* that the high school was still too selective, and that the doors needed to be opened to all students, with effective educational programs for all (Gutek, 1991).

In 1919 the Progressive Education Association was formed, and for the next several decades it exerted an influence on American education that can still be felt, working toward the goal of democratic citizenship and equality. Krug describes the association as "a protest movement, not only against conventional teaching but also against the stern doctrines of social efficiency and social control being voiced by leading educators at that time" (Krug, 1966, p. 123).

The Progressive Education Association announced a platform of six points. They were:

- The child should be able to develop in free and natural ways.
- Intrinsic motivation should be primary in education.
- The teacher should be a guide, not a taskmaster.

- Educators should study child and adolescent development scientifically.
- Greater attention should be paid to the myriad factors that affect human development.
- There should be greater cooperation between home and school. (Krug, 1966, p. 122)

The most prominent member of the association was educator and philosopher John Dewey. Dewey stated that the changing society and culture required new educational strategies that were responsive to the needs of the new society (Button and Provenzo, 1983). Instead of lecture and drill, Dewey pressed for an educational experience that engaged the student in active learning, with a curriculum that was tied to the perceived needs of the student. The teacher, according to Dewey, should create rich and stimulating classroom environments and engage the students in active exploration of their world. Venturing out into the community to provide an education that was real was, at the time, a radical notion in education. Learning by doing made much more sense to Dewey than teaching by the book, lecturing, note-taking, memorization, recitation, and drill.

The Eight Year Study

At its annual conference in 1930, the Progressive Education Association launched an effort that culminated in one of the most famous educational experiments in the history of the American high school, the Eight Year Study. Having devoted a great deal of attention to the elementary school, the association now turned its attention to the high school. In the course of several days of discussion among conference attendees of ways to improve the American high school, virtually every suggestion was met with the reply, "Yes, that should be done in our high schools, but it can't be done without risking students' chances of being admitted to college. If the student doesn't follow the pattern of subjects and units prescribed by the colleges, he will probably not be accepted" (Aiken, 1942, p. 1). Eventually, someone suggested that the Progressive Education Association explore ways in which colleges and high schools could cooperate in ways that would permit high schools to implement many of the ideas of Progressive Education without penalizing the students who sought to go to college. The Eight Year Study was born.

The Commission on the Relation of School and College, established to conduct the study, issued after one year of initial work a comprehensive indictment of the high school of the day that readers may find familiar. Examples of the charges made include:

- The high school seldom challenged students of first rate ability to work up to their potential.
- The high school neither knew their students well nor guided them wisely.
- The high school failed to create conditions necessary for effective learning.
- The conventional high school curriculum was far removed from the real concerns of youth.
- The curriculum contained little evidence of unity or continuity.

- Complacency was characteristic of high school educators.
- Teachers were not well equipped for their responsibilities.
- The high school diploma meant only that the student had done whatever was necessary to accumulate the required number of units of credit. (Aiken 1942)

The members of the Commission decided to conduct an experiment with sufficient scope, significance, and credibility to determine and demonstrate the ways in which progressive education ideas might improve the American high school in the areas identified as unsatisfactory. Approximately 300 prestigious colleges and universities (e.g., Harvard, Princeton, Yale), practically all accredited institutions of higher education at the time, agreed to accept the graduates of 30 "unshackled" high schools, beginning with the graduating class of 1936. Educators in these high schools, 15 of which were public and 15 private, would be free to implement the theories of the Progressive Education Association as espoused by reformers such as John Dewey and William Heard Kilpatrick of the University of Chicago.

As the educators in the 30 high schools began to reconceptualize the educational experience in their locales, a number of common perceptions materialized. According to Aiken (1942, pp. 17–23), the reformers were agreed on several important points, including the following:

- The general life of the school and methods of teaching should conform to what is now known about the ways in which human beings learn and grow.
- The curriculum of the high school should deal with the "present concerns of young people as well as the knowledge, skills, understandings, and appreciations which constitute our cultural heritage."
- Educators must know each student well and guide each one wisely.
- They doubted that success in college depends upon the study of certain subjects for a certain length of time. There were, they asserted, many avenues of study and experience that could lead to success in college.

The importance that the members of the study attached to evaluation led them to solicit the assistance of Professor Ralph Tyler, head of the Bureau of Educational Research at Ohio State University, who insisted on including some "control" schools, so that the results would be more widely accepted as valid and reliable. This step added more credibility to the study, involving both the reformers of the Progressive Education Association and those who were most interested in making the study of education more scientific (Krug, 1972).

What happened in these project high schools during the eight years? While each of the 30 schools planned and implemented their new educational freedom in different ways, it appears that several common curriculum strategies were employed. Perhaps because of their common concern with curriculum unity and coherence, educators in many of the high schools implemented what came to be known as a "core curriculum," integrating several traditional subjects into a more thematic approach. Projects that involved students in active investigations were more common as was problem-solving aimed at developing the "habit of reflective thinking." Cooperative learning was there. The "common problems of American youth became the heart of the curriculum" (Aiken, 1942, p. 81).

Because of their commitment to the democratic process in human life, the schools may have engaged in a great deal more curriculum planning that included students, parents, and the community. Shared decision making was supposed to be the preferred way of solving problems, establishing policies, and making important decisions. Providing time for teachers to study and plan together was a priority, though it was difficult to accomplish. The home room appeared as a way to make it possible for each student to be known and wisely guided; school counselors became more popular and more numerous in project schools. The conviction that the curriculum should reflect the perceived needs of students may have led to greater student involvement in curriculum decisions. Parent involvement was sought in new and more vigorous ways: general parent–teacher meetings, parent conferences, small group discussions, and "individual teacher–parent interviews" (Kahne, 1995).

What were the results of the project? Generally, the meticulously conducted evaluation was able to document that students from the experimental, progressive, or "unshackled" schools did as well in college as the students from more traditional high schools; they actually earned a slightly higher grade point average, received slightly more academic honors, and were more likely to participate in artistic, theatrical, and musical extracurricular activities. Their grades in foreign languages and their participation in religious, social service, and organized sports activities were slightly lower. Moreover, when the "most experimental schools" were compared to the others, the results were strikingly positive in favor of the innovative schools (Kahne, 1995).

Proponents of the study stated that the results showed that the high school can afford to be more innovative and experimental, and that traditional college entrance requirements unreasonably restricted high school educators from the sort of flexibility they needed. Advocates agreed that high school educators could be trusted with greater autonomy. They wrote about what they believed they had established:

- Every student should achieve competence in the essential skills.
- Inert subject matter should give way to content that is alive and relevant to the lives of students.
- The common recurring themes of American youth should be the heart of the curriculum.
- "The life and work of the school should contribute, in every possible way, to the physical, mental and emotional health of every student."
- "The curriculum in its every part should have one, clear, major purpose. That purpose is to bring to every young American his great heritage of freedom, to develop understanding of the kind of life we seek, and to inspire devotion to human welfare."
- To prepare students for life in a world of freedom was "the supreme opportunity of the schools of our democracy" (Aiken, 1942, pp. 138–139).

Unfortunately, the Eight Year Study ended and submitted its report in the middle of World War II, and many of the findings—relevant then and now—disappeared with little attention or comment. If college educators heard the message of the study or accepted its conclusions they failed to put them into practice in their admissions programs. The Progressive Education Association, sponsor of the study, lost its own momentum during the years of the war and those immediately following. For 35 years it had been a powerful force in support of the goal of democratic citizenship and equality.

With the entry of America into World War II, the influence of advocates of the goal of democratic citizenship and equality quickly evaporated. Concepts like peace education, life adjustment, the inherent goodness of human beings, shared decision making—even if they had not been widely practiced—were quickly pushed aside as the nation geared up for war. Progressive education had never dislodged traditional schooling in practice, and now even the ideas of progressive education became unpopular. Krug (1972, p. 351) summarizes:

> When one was no longer supposed to reason why and when force again became a respectable approach to human affairs, progressive education had no choice but death. Humane culture had nothing that would be heard; its transmission through the schools in this context had little relevance or point.

High School Education in the 1940s and 1950s

Following the end of World War II, the nation and its schools experienced a decade of tranquillity and prosperity. It was believed that America had won not only the war but, in a sense, the world. American values, American steel, and American schools had provided what Europe and Asia had lacked and needed to defeat fascism in Germany and Japan. Graciously, Americans were willing to contribute their own resources to the rebuilding of Europe and Japan. Not surprisingly, this rebuilding was done, in many ways, in the image of those American institutions that now stood as the envy of the world. For example, the Japanese national school system, its economy, and its governmental structure were completely reorganized to resemble American models. At home, a variety of social and legal movements (e.g., *Brown vs. Topeka*) led to breakthroughs in racial desegregation that began to alter the schools in fundamental ways. During these years, Americans seemed satisfied with their world, and the schools within it.

For a while, the tenets of progressive education continued to receive widespread publication in different forms. In 1944, for example, the National Education Association published "Education for All American Youth," a lengthy document endorsing compulsory education until age 18, and advocating the implementation of progressive ideas relating to curriculum and teaching (Hampel, 1986). In 1945, "Life Adjustment Education" attempted to improve the education of the 60 percent of high school students who were neither headed for college nor clearly relegated to common labor. Arguing that the education of the majority of high school students was bereft of focus or meaning, Life Adjustment proponents sought a high school program that would equip "all American youth to live democratically with satisfaction to themselves and profit to society as home members, workers, and citizens," but with special attention to that forgotten 60 percent (Krug, 1966, p. 132).

With the exception of those relatively few high schools that had been influenced by various activities and philosophies of the progressive education movement, however, the American high school remained very much a formal, traditional institution. High school teachers were expected to be models of virtue, exceeding the standards to which parents and the community as a whole were held. A teacher's reputation rested as much on behavior at home and in town as it did on competence in the classroom. Most surveys of actual practice in high school classrooms during this period indicate a very formal classroom, with heavy reliance on lecture and textbook, content coverage, and the survival of the concept of mental discipline. Three or four curriculum tracks were present, and the larger the high school, the more pronounced the influence of the tracks on the climate and culture of the school. Then as now, track selection was strongly correlated with parent social class, and a great deal of social snobbery was in evidence, with schools maintaining organizational strategies that "openly classified students as inferior or superior" (Hampel, 1986, p. 11).

In the period from 1945 to 1955, most American high schools had remained relatively unchanged in spite of the various efforts by progressive education theorists. Except for the dramatic growth in vocational and general education tracks, traditional programs and approaches remained at the center of high school life and practice. Nonetheless, criticism of progressive education theories began to gain a momentum, suggesting that such ideas had permeated the American high school when in fact they had not. Hampel (1986) points out that the education journals may have been loaded with progressive education ideas for decades, but the effect of such ideas on the typical high school classroom was minimal.

Criticism of Life Adjustment Education and of progressive education in general charged that the curriculum and teaching that resulted from such theories was intellectually bankrupt, trivial, based on soft pedagogy, and insufficient to prepare high school students to make any contribution to American society. Vigorous attacks by writers such as Arthur Bestor's *Educational Wastelands: The Retreat from Learning in Our Public Schools* (1953, 1985) and Albert Lynd's *Quackery in the Public Schools* (1953) set the stage for a criticism of progressive education that was soon to take on dramatic new life.

Bestor, a college history professor, stated that "disciplined intelligence" was disappearing, and that the disappearance was largely due to "professional educationalists." He maintained that the essence of democracy was in the right of every individual to develop his or her intellectual powers to the maximum (squarely behind the goal of social mobility), and that progressive education had really been 'regressive education," the integrated curriculum foolish, and vocationalism a waste of time and talent, because the liberal arts was the best vocational education there could be. Life Adjustment was a "parody of education," and the idea that the school had to step in where other American institutions were failing was a "preposterous illusion."

Sputnik and American High School Education

On October 4, 1957, the USSR launched Sputnik I, the first man-made satellite, and the post-war tranquillity of American life and support for American schooling was destroyed. Within a month, Russia had launched a second Sputnik, this time with a live dog aboard. Americans shivered with fear; if Russians could launch a satellite, they could clearly also launch an intercontinental ballistic missile targeted anywhere in the United States. No one was safe and the "missile gap" also seemed to make clear an educational gap of enormous proportions. How could America have been caught so unprepared? The "immediate reaction throughout the country was that the United States had fallen behind because of life adjustment education" (Krug, 1966, p. 134) and other progressive ideas that had reduced the American schools to "wastelands."

A fusillade of criticism of perceived weaknesses of American education was now launched. Some stated that the schools had abandoned the classic essentials. Others condemned what they believed to be the abuses of progressive education. Still others voiced their concerns about the status of American education in science and technology. The most important spokesperson for reform was Admiral Hyman G. Rickover, naval engineer and atomic energy specialist (Rickover, 1963). Rickover was widely regarded as a military and scientific leader of the first order, a demanding commander satisfied only by perfection, if at all. Rickover stated, with great effect to a large national audience, that the primary purpose of education should be intellectual training, especially of the best and the brightest students, with the end being the production of a group of leaders who would help the nation to victory in any kind of war, hot or cold. The nation's safety, he stated, was "largely determined by the respect accorded its science and technology," and American educators turned their attention to these areas (Button & Provenzo, 1983, p. 289).

Through such programs as the National Defense Education Act, emphasis was placed on science, technology, mathematics, foreign languages, and especially on high standards and education for the most able. Natural, physical, and social scientists were invited to provide shape and substance to the high school curriculum. These scholars and scientists saw the school curriculum as an extension of their academic disciplines; the best way to learn an academic discipline, they reasoned, was to learn it the way that scholars learned it. The school curriculum and the methods of teaching it should be related to the unique structure of that academic discipline. High school students in a history course would, for example, approach their studies as historians would. Students in a physical science class would come to know physics best by acting as physicists. The discovery method of teaching became immensely popular in the educational literature.

The emphasis on the academic disciplines as the source of the curriculum and as the model for classroom teaching was reinforced by a brief but highly influential book, *The Process of Education,* by Harvard psychologist Jerome Bruner (1977). Bruner stated that virtually any subject could be learned, with integrity, at virtually any age, and that almost anything worth knowing had been discovered within one traditional academic discipline or another and should be studied in the context of those disciplines. Academically oriented students were obviously well served by such a curriculum; many other students were not so well accommodated by a "teacher-proof" curriculum developed by university scientists and professors.

The Contemporary American Comprehensive High School

The Conant Reports on the American High School

In 1959, James Bryant Conant, the highly respected former president of Harvard University, entered the world of high school education with the publication of *The American High School Today*. Conant posed, as the most important question to be answered, the following:

> Can a school at one and the same time provide a good general education for all the pupils as future citizens of a democracy, provide elective programs for the majority to develop useful skills, and educate adequately those with a talent for handling advanced academic subjects. . . ? (p. 15)

His answer was an unqualified "Yes," and from that point on, Americans have never seriously considered any alternative to the comprehensive high school for the education of adolescents and young adults.

Conant outlined what he believed to be the three main objectives of the comprehensive high school and, in doing so, summarized the three goals of education that high schools had been struggling to achieve for nearly 150 years. The first goal, he wrote, was to provide a general education for all future citizens (the goal of democratic citizenship and equality). The second goal was to provide "good elective programs for those who wish to use their acquired skills immediately upon graduation" (the goal of social efficiency); the third objective was to prepare a smaller group for their subsequent education in college or university (the goal of social mobility). Conant stated:

> If one could find a single comprehensive high school in the United States in which all three objectives were reached in a highly satisfactory manner, such a school could be taken as a model or pattern. Furthermore, unless there were some especially favorable local features which enabled such a school to attain these three objectives, the characteristics found might be developed in all other schools of sufficient size in the United States. (p. 17)

Conant (pp. 19–20) even provided a checklist to assist educators in determining if a high school had achieved the desired level of comprehensiveness. A glance at the list should indicate how much more successful Conant was in translating his vision into school practice than were the members of the Eight Year Study. This was Conant's specific delineation of the attributes of the comprehensive high school:

Adequacy of general education could be judged if the high school had:

1. Four years of offerings in English literature and composition

2. Social studies, including American history, government, and economics

3. Ability grouping in required courses (96.5% did, he reported later)

Adequacy in "nonacademic elective programs" could be assured if the high school had:

4. Vocational programs for boys and commercial programs for girls

5. Opportunities for supervised work experiences

6. Special provisions for very slow readers (grouped, with special teachers)

Adequacy of the third goal could be assured if programs for "academically talented students" had:

7. Special provisions for challenging the highly gifted students

8. Special instruction in developing reading skills

9. Summer sessions for the most able students

10. Individualized, flexible programs for the academically gifted

11. A school day organized into seven or more instructional periods

Several other features were important for a truly comprehensive high school:

12. Adequate guidance services

13. Student morale

14. Well-organized, heterogeneous home rooms

15. Effective social interaction among students of widely varying academic abilities so that mutual understanding was promoted

Conant offered further descriptions of those students he identified as "academically talented." He stated that it was "clear" that only a fraction of students are ready to study "effectively and rewardingly" a wide program of advanced mathematics, science, and foreign languages; about 15 to 20 percent of the students in a comprehensive high school would fit this model, he thought. These students should be able to be identified in the eighth grade, prior to their arrival at the high school, and be slotted for special programs at that time. He was convinced from his visits to high schools that such students were not being sufficiently challenged. Academically talented students should all have four years of mathematics, four years of one foreign language, three years of science, and three years of social studies. "This program will require at least fifteen hours of homework each week." He eagerly endorsed the new advanced placement course for the "highly gifted," and advocated reorganizing the mathematics curriculum in order to make it possible for these students to take calculus in high school (Conant, 1967, p. 42).

Conant was particularly committed to the elimination of small high schools where he believed that it would be impossible to offer comprehensive programs. Such schools could not provide the required curriculum, would be too expensive if they did, and would be an uneconomic use of the time and talent of administrators, teachers, and specialists. Conant suggested that the number of high schools in the country be dramatically reduced through consolidation to 9,000 from the 21,000 that existed at that time. He urged state departments of education to immediately undertake a program of reorganization and school consolidation to reduce the number of small high schools and increase the number of larger, comprehensive high schools (pp. 77–84).

In 1967, Conant returned with a second volume. *The Comprehensive High School,* documenting the expansion of comprehensive high schools in the United States. Relying on an earlier description by John Gardner, he summarized:

> The comprehensive high school is a peculiarly American phenomenon. It is called comprehensive because it offers, under one administration and under one roof (or series of roofs), secondary education for almost all the high school age children of one town or neighborhood. It is responsible for educating the boy who will be an atomic scientist and the girl who will marry at eighteen; the prospective captain of a ship and the future captain of industry. It is responsible for educating the bright and the not so bright children with different vocational and professional ambitions and with various motivations. It is responsible, in sum, for providing good and appropriate education, both academic and vocational, for all young people within a democratic environment which the American people believe serves the principles they cherish. (p. 3)

Conant described (albeit with a gender bias now outdated) how an American high school could and should be responsible for meeting all three goals of American secondary education; since that time, high school educators have been striving to do so.

James Conant contributed one other important work that has proved to be as prophetic, if not as influential, as his works on the comprehensive high school. In 1961, Conant published *Slums and Suburbs,* in which he alerted Americans to a serious shift in socioeconomic patterns. Alarming differences in the quality of the high school experience had developed, and were tied to the location of the schools. According to Conant, suburban high schools were providing the advanced curriculum needed for college entrance, and inner city schools had turned into a "holding pattern" for disadvantaged minorities who eventually dropped out or graduated but still were likely to be unemployed or underemployed. A dual school system was developing in America, Conant warned. Thirty-five years later, the works of Jonathan Kozol (1991, 1995) and Gary Orfield (1996a, 1996b) made it clear just how prophetic Conant's book really was.

The Comprehensive High School in the 1960s and 1970s

The 1960s were a period of cultural and political change unique in American history (Button and Provenzo, 1983). National attention in the 1960s did, in fact, turn to issues of racial and socioeconomic equality; a decade of reexamination of the influence of race and poverty on education followed. The goal, of course, was the expansion of democratic citizenship and equality. In 1964, for example President Lyndon Johnson declared "war on poverty" with the Economic Opportunity Act. This legislation created such educational ventures as the Job Corps, Head Start, and other efforts at what came to be called "compensatory education." Massive federal and state government efforts were aimed at desegregating schools at every level and in every area of the country. Civil rights militancy, teacher union activity, and the enforcement of the Civil Rights Act of 1964 had a substantial impact on community and school culture.

Toward the end of the 1960s, the nation's attention shifted toward those areas connected with youthful antiwar activism, distrust of government, and the "generation gap" that seemed to separate youth and adults. Youthful alienation, drug use, sexual experimentation, rock music—all seemed characteristic of a new youth culture. These things combined with the appearance of birth control pills, a dramatic rise in divorce rates, easy access to automobiles, and the presence of television as a permanent diversion and a new window on reality to create a whole new world for students outside the high school. The pace and drama of social change seemed to accelerate daily (Gutek, 1991). Throughout the 1960s and 1970s, the high school was jolted by the events of this time of turmoil. Political protest, Black pride, student rights, budget cuts, declining enrollment, teacher strikes, public skepticism, court orders and decisions on a variety of issues (e.g., hair length, locker searches, dress), and "pluralistic liberalism" in various incarnations all affected the communities in which the comprehensive high schools were located (Hampel, 1986).

J. Lloyd Trump

One of the most active and creative, some even say visionary, educators of the time was J. Lloyd Trump, Director of Research for the National Association of Secondary School Principals. Trump proposed and directed the NASSP's influential Model Schools Project, which incorporated a series of components not unlike those being touted today:

- Continuous progress education
- Teacher-based advisement for students
- Differentiated staffing
- Flexible scheduling
- Large and small group instruction
- Independent study
- New approaches to reporting student progress
- Team teaching
- Principal as instructional leader
- Community-based learning
- Shared decision making (Trump 1959, 1960, 1961, 1968)

Of the 36 schools in the Model Schools Project, 6 actually implemented all aspects of the proposed model: Bishop Carroll High School (Calgary, Alberta), Pius X (Downey, California), Chalmette High School (Challmette, Louisiana), Wilde Lake High School (Columbia, Maryland), Mariner High School (Everett, Washington), and Mercy Academy (Louisville, Kentucky). Some of these schools (e.g., Wilde Lake High School) remain at the forefront on high school improvement.

Trump's work was highly unusual and seminal, combining theoretical understanding with the practitioner's touch. Consequently, much of what now looks new actually has antecedents in work done 35 years earlier by educators like Trump. The authors of this book believe that the work of many contemporary reformers might be more effectively framed and more positively received if it consciously built on and acknowledged the important work of the educators like Trump who helped to shape it. The National Association of Secondary School Principals publication *Breaking Ranks* (1996), for example, and the central concepts of the Coalition of Essential Schools are, we think, clearly indebted to the creative efforts of J. Lloyd Trump.

Liberal Criticisms of the Schools

A number of liberal criticisms were eventually directed toward the high school, especially the inner-city high school. Among the earliest liberal critics of the high school of the time was sociologist Edgar Friedenberg, author of *The Vanishing Adolescent* (1959). A.S. Neill's book, *Summerhill School: A Radical Approach to Child Rearing* (1960) became immensely popular during these decades. Neill wrote that his experience as director of the school had persuaded him that all children were basically good and inherently wise; it was the perverted nature of the suffocating institutions in which they were placed that so often caused them to go awry. The best way to help children and youth grow and develop in a healthy way was to give them the maximum degree of freedom and love, and the minimum amount of restriction. Sociologist Paul Goodman (1962) agreed; he claimed that any motivated teenager could learn in 6 months what the school took 12 years to teach.

Author John Holt (1964, 1967, 1972, 1976, 1981) produced a series of popular books in these two decades, advocating alternative schools, home schooling, deschooling, and other ways of maximizing student freedom and integrity. Sociologist Ivan Illich's *Deschooling Society* (1971) charged that the American high school had become moribund and ought to be replaced with smaller, more humane organizations. George Dennison (1969) described a popular alternative school in *The Lives of Children,* a school where the daily violence and poverty of the students' lives could be counteracted by love and support. Perhaps the most well-known single volume was Charles Silberman's *Crisis in the Classroom,* published in 1970. Silberman stated that the typical high school offered a "repressive, almost prison-like atmosphere" (p. 349). The high school, said Silberman, needed to be freer and more humane, and unreasonable rules needed to be relaxed.

Carl Rogers (1969), the developer of client-centered therapy, joined in with *Freedom to Learn.* According to Rogers, if the most effective psychotherapy placed trust in the individual to find his or her own best way to mental health, surely high schools could do the same. If learning about one's psychological self was "facilitated" by a counselor who exhibited unconditional personal regard, empathy, and interpersonal congruence, surely high school teachers would be most effective when acting in similar ways with their students (Rogers, 1969). Maximum flexibility in the curriculum, multiple instructional strategies and an atmosphere of trust and freedom would help to transform what had become a restrictive and unstimulating high school environment into one that was person-centered and humanistic. A great deal of "holistic" education activity emphasizing student freedom and individuality continued throughout the 1970s.

Other critics, even more radical, fired additional volleys at the traditional high school of the period on behalf of the goal of democratic equality. Samuel Bowles and Herbert Gintis (1976), two radical economists, published *Schooling in Capitalist America,* in which they charged that the American high school was little more than the sorting tool of the elitist groups in charge of the capitalist society, an institution that legitimized the continuing status of those classes and groups who had money and power. Revolution, rather than reform, was the way to real change, they said. Once again, however, while the literature was full of reform, and a few alternative schools made startling changes, the organization and operation of most American comprehensive high schools continued, as the 1980s neared, along the lines laid down by Conant several decades earlier.

It was not that conditions within the high school had remained completely unchanged. There had been, Hampel (1986) notes, piecemeal changes like the addition of driver's education, attempts at team teaching, modular scheduling, English electives, career days, more guidance counselors, and bigger libraries that became known as media centers. B. Frank Brown (1963, 1972) and others attempted to implement more innovative programs such as the nongraded high school—a radical concept even then. Several high schools (Nova High School and Melbourne High Schools in Florida, and Middletown High School in Rhode Island) developed exciting nongraded programs.

Hampel states, however, that changes in the students who enrolled in high school, along with the social ferment outside the high school, produced far more upheaval than any planned changes in curriculum or instruction. Increased diversity led to the emergence of racial and language/ethnic issues (e.g., busing) throughout the period. Widespread curriculum tracking seemed to produce student cliques to match: preppies, druggies, dropouts, jocks, and so on. The number of students who spoke limited English and the number of special education students skyrocketed. In fact, the high schools were "full of students who, 25 years earlier, would have rarely even begun high school, let alone stayed until graduation' (Hampel, 1986, p. 126).

More importantly, perhaps, was the "pervasive disengagement" that began to characterize the attitudes of students, even in the so-called "good" high schools (Hampel, 1986). For a while, student passivity may have even been welcomed, as a respite from the rebellion and activism of the late 1960s. The American high school's assumption of the burden of getting and keeping all students in school, however, did not mean that either student or teacher worked hard at securing student engagement in the intellectual and academic life of the school.

Commitment to the egalitarian ideal of democratic equality seemed in many high schools only to mean a commitment to being there. This egalitarian ideal also meant, however, that there was an elective curriculum with a great deal of student choice; teachers were given the freedom to decide what they wanted to teach and how they wished to teach it (Cusick, 1983). Little agreement existed on the essential components of being a teacher: what to teach, how to teach, how to relate to students, or how to connect (or not) with one's colleagues. Beyond being assigned a set of courses and perhaps a few additional duties, teachers were subject to little regulation.

Little coherence or unity could be found in the high school curriculum during this period. Large numbers of students, growing student diversity, the absence of instructional leadership or supervision, the preferences of teachers, and the demands of colleges and the workplace—all conspired to create a curriculum that was "much broader, more varied, disparate, and fragmented that anyone realized or publicly admitted" (Cusick, p. 106). To summarize:

> The school's curricula were open to influence by any and all of those diverse elements, none of which were processed through faculty deliberations or added according to some larger scheme or set of educational ideals. The curriculum was the aggregate of the teachers' idiosyncratic approaches. (Cusick, p. 107)

High schools were full of students who would have rather been somewhere else, and the curriculum had little relevance or coherence. It is no surprise, therefore, that schools in the 1970s became preoccupied with classroom discipline and keeping order in the school. Even the appearance of disorder was of concern, because such appearances could stimulate parent investigations, media inquiries, and the failure of school bond issues. More importantly, wrote Cusick, disorder in the high school could cause the public to question the basic assumption of the goal of democratic citizenship and equality—the value of attempting to educate all future citizens to a level of effectiveness:

> Disorder in schools can serve as proof to those people that such students, particularly if they are from the lower classes, do not deserve the chance that society is attempting to provide for them and therefore the egalitarian ideal should be discarded. But if it is discarded, the public schools as we know them have no place in our society (1983, p. 109).

It was not that students were openly hostile or defiant, but that there was so much pervasive disengagement. Of this situation, Cusick noted:

> They are not particularly troublesome, but they do not attend class or they attend sporadically. They skip the tests, do not hand in the homework, and just do not care. School people are reluctant to admit this, because it makes them look bad and also because as hard as they try to correct it, the problem persists. But the teachers in these schools discussed it candidly, admitting they had many more listed on their class rosters than were there on any day. (p. 110)

> . . . the very legitimacy of the school rests with its obligation to preserve the egalitarian ideal. That means getting all students to come, even those that don't want to, getting them to stay, and attend class regularly, even if they would rather be somewhere else, getting those that are repeatedly disorderly to try again to see if they can complete the required work. If they can stay in their seats, learn to hand in their work on time, take and pass the tests, put up with the deferred gratification, they may through education make something of themselves and contribute to the larger society (p. 111).

As the decade of the 1970s came to a close, public confidence in every institution was shaken. The American corporate and industrial behemoth that had stood astride the world in the years following World War II had been humbled by the very nations (Japan and Germany) that were thought to be beaten once and for all time. America's dominant position in the worlds of automobiles, cameras, banking, steel—virtually anything complex, expensive, and fragile—had crumbled. The Viet Nam War demonstrated the nation's vulnerability in the area of military operations, the area in which Americans had felt the greatest confidence, and divisions over the conduct of the war had torn to shreds any consensus about national direction and focus. Trust in government was dashed by events surrounding Watergate and other government scandals. Drugs, divorce, and what was viewed as a general decline in morality persuaded many that the American family was in disarray.

The American school system was far from immune to such instability, and it should have come as no surprise that several decades of emphasis on equity, access, and freedom in education had had a leveling effect on overall school academic achievement. When every other American institution was in disarray, could it have been different for the high school? Rudderless schools, as described earlier by Cusick, with an expanding population of students that included far greater numbers of minorities, the poor, and those with exceptional needs, could hardly be expected to be at their best in terms of the goals of social efficiency and social mobility. Many began to question whether the American high school could be both equitable and excellent.

In fact, a number of educators and others had begun to call attention to what they saw as a substantial decline in academic achievement, marked not only by the perceived disorder and disarray in the schools, but in student scores on standardized tests of academic achievement. The accumulating evidence seemed to suggest that the academic preparation of high school students headed for college had been declining since the early 1960s. In particular, noted Gutek (1991), the concern focused on a 14-year decline in scores on the Scholastic Aptitude Test.

A panel was formed to investigate, and its findings substantiated the decline; the decline in scores received a great deal more attention than the panel's attempts to explain why such a decline had occurred. The report discussed the effects of the changing school population, the curricular drift of the past decades, the effect of substantial increases in television watching and corresponding decreases in time spent in reading and homework, and the devastatingly unsettling effects of two decades of social turbulence. The news media and the American populace, however, focused on the scores, anticipating "what would be a searching reexamination of American secondary education in the 1980s" (Gutek, 1991, p. 115).

A NATION AT RISK and Its Aftermath

Billed as an "open letter to the American public," the report of the National Commission on Excellence in Education, *A Nation at Risk* (1983), was an earthquake-size reaction to the liberalities of the previous two decades. The charges of educational inadequacy in the public schools rocked American confidence in public education, perhaps permanently, and shocked educators into a flurry of responses that lasted more than a decade. Chiefly in the service of the goal of social efficiency, the report charged that the nation was at risk from a "rising tide of mediocrity" that threatened to erode the foundations of the society. Even more seriously, it charged that:

> If an unfriendly power had attempted to impose on America the mediocre educational performance that exists today, we might well have viewed it as an act of war. As it stands, we have allowed this to happen to ourselves. We have even squandered the gains in student achievement made in the wake of the Sputnik challenge. Moreover, we have dismantled essential support systems which helped make those gains possible. We have, in effect, been committing an act of unthinking, unilateral educational disarmament (National Commission on Excellence in Education, 1983, p. 5).

The report cited an amazing array of statistics to document its charges of a loss of educational direction and increasing lassitude among students and educators. Unfavorable comparisons to the educational achievements of other countries, particularly countries in Asia and Europe, were highlighted. Large numbers of Americans were found to be "functionally illiterate." Academic achievement as measured by the SAT was determined to be lower than it had been 26 years earlier when Sputnik had been launched, and the decline threatened to continue. Gifted students were going unchallenged. Higher-order thinking skills were absent from the curriculum. Business and military leaders, as well as college educators, were complaining that they had to spend millions of dollars on remedial education in areas that should have been mastered in elementary school. All of this was happening, the report charged, at a time when the nation, especially the nation's business and industry, needed to be more competitive than ever before. A renewed commitment to excellence was urgently required.

The authors of the report made a number of recommendations. High school graduation requirements must be strengthened; all high school students must demonstrate achievement in what the report called the "Five New Basics." This entailed the completion of 4 years of English, 3 years of mathematics, 3 years of science, 3 years of social studies, and one-half year of computer science. Two years of foreign language were advocated for college-bound students. The report recommended that schools, colleges, and universities adopt much higher standards for academic performance, student conduct, and for admission to four-year colleges and universities.

The third recommendation of the report was the devotion of "significantly more time" to learning the New Basics. Schools should have longer days, perhaps a lengthened school year, more homework, and more rigorous discipline and attendance policies. Furthermore, "placement and grouping of students, as well as promotion and graduation policies, should be guided by the academic progress of students and their instructional needs, rather than by rigid adherence to age (p. 30).

The fourth recommendation was focused on improving the preparation of teachers. New high standards for teacher preparation programs should be introduced. Salaries should be raised, and teachers should be given 11-month contracts by their school boards—although no mention was made of where the huge funds for such recommendations might be found. Career ladder programs that would recognize teaching excellence were suggested, with new "master teachers" assuming greater roles in designing teacher education programs and supervising new teachers during "probationary periods." The last recommendation was that citizens across the nation should hold their elected officials responsible for providing the leadership to accomplish the other recommendations (National Commission on Excellence, 1983, pp. 30–32).

The report caught the attention of American educators, parents, and business and industry like few such reports ever have. In the years that immediately followed the report, for example, more than 30 additional investigations, reports, and recommendations came forth (Pulliam and Van Paten, 1995). Legislation in virtually every state responded to the recommendations for increased requirements and higher standards of all sorts; virtually every state formed its own task force to tailor the recommendations to their situation. Education was clearly back on the "front burner" of American consciousness. In particular, the business world joined the national debate in a new and substantial way, responding to the root cause of improving American economic competitiveness to which the report was dedicated. Much was written to suggest that business and corporate models of productivity and effectiveness could be applied to the organization and management of public schools.[1]

Independent Studies of the American High School in the 1980s

Adler's Paideia Proposal

A number of other substantial studies of the American high school appeared at about the same time as the *Nation At Risk* report, or shortly thereafter. Among them, Mortimer Adler's *Paideia Proposal* (1982) was one of the most popular, with an influence that, though limited in range, persists to the present. Adler and his group stated that the education that was appropriate for the best students was also the education that was best for all students. Advocating what has been known as a "perennialist" perspective, the proposal advanced a curriculum of classics, with no electives, that would focus on the life of the mind. Teachers would be coaches and supervisors who would help high school students to think more clearly; seminars and discussions would be more common.

Several of the reports were remarkable, in that the authors of each report actually spent time immersed in the high schools, on which they report. Their descriptions and recommendations, therefore, had a ring of authenticity about them. Each has, consequently, added to the current momentum to reform the American comprehensive high school. Ernest Boyer's *High School: A Report on Secondary Education in America* (1983) and John Goodlad's *A Place Called School* (1984) were careful and comprehensive examinations of the high schools of the time. Each affirmed the dreary picture painted by Cusick (1983).

---

[1]One of the authors of this text, Paul George, wrote a book called The Theory Z School, published in 1983 by the National Middle School Association, in which he illustrated how Japanese management tactics could be used to improve American education.

Boyer's High School

Ernest Boyer, head of the Carnegie Foundation for the Advancement of Teaching, investigated what he believed to be 15 representative high schools around the nation. Boyer criticized what he saw as the tendency to organize the high school in a way that isolated students in groups that were too narrowly representative of their members' socioeconomic status. He recommended a revitalization of an academic core curriculum that would be offered to the great majority of the students in every high school. He urged high schools to provide opportunities for service learning and to engage high school seniors in individually designed senior projects that would be the capstones of their high school education. Boyer believed that the teaching profession was in deep crisis, and that teachers knew it and were deeply troubled about their schools and their professional lives (Boyer, 1983).

Goodlad's Place Called School

Goodlad (1984) conducted an 8-year study of 38 representative secondary schools across the country. He found high schools to be dreary places where teachers and students plodded through a dull curriculum that was of little interest to either party; he found too much emphasis placed on acquiring knowledge in such a curriculum, at the expense of intellectual development. Virtually every class was taught in the same way; the range of teaching methods was far too narrow and constricting, and when this was combined with a curriculum that failed to touch the lives of the students, the result was a dull, dry, and deadly classroom climate. The high school, Goodlad stated, needed more than the knee-jerk reaction for higher standards of the *Nation at Risk* report. He, like Boyer, favored a core curriculum that would be studied in common by 70 to 80 percent of the students in the school; elimination of ability grouping was considered essential. And, like Boyer, Goodlad recoiled from the socioeconomic class divisions he saw; increased emphasis on equity and access were essential, he believed. Goodlad called for more teamwork among teachers, smaller schools, and more autonomy for individual schools and educators to make the changes at the local level.

Powell's Shopping Mall High School

Along with the writings of Theodore Sizer and Robert Hampel, Powell, Farrar, and Cohen's *The Shopping Mall High School: Winners and Losers in the Educational Marketplace* (1985) was one of three major analyses of the high school in the 1980s cosponsored by the National Association of Secondary School Principals and the National Association of Independent Schools. These authors reiterated what others had pointed out as the central purpose of the American high school: The high school should do whatever is necessary to ensure that nearly all students attend, stay until graduation, and find something of value there when they are in the high school. Something for everybody, with great variety and inclusiveness; it was this aspect of the high school, the authors wrote, that made it resemble a shopping mall.

Attendance and acceptable grades, resulting in a credential known as a diploma were the object, not learning or mastery of the curriculum. Students and teachers developed "treaties" with one another to ensure that the goal of attendance and graduation was met, even if this happened without significant learning or hard work on either side of the desk. All of this promoted a disappointing mediocrity, because Americans had come to accept the belief that real mastery was neither possible or necessary for most of the students in attendance. "High school attendance and graduation are nearly a social entitlement. They are things people take for granted" (Powell, Farrar & Cohen, 1985, p. 61).

Students who were "special" in some way got treated well in the shopping mall high school, in gifted and advanced placement "specialty shops" or in special education. The great majority of the "unspecial" (which Powell estimated to be about 70 percent of students) were in situations where little was expected, time demands were at a minimum, class time was used for "homework," worksheets substituted for pedagogy, and "treaties of avoidance rather than engagement" dominated (Powell, Farrar & Cohen, 1985, p. 184). By the 1980s, the high schools had done a "masterly job at selling the importance of high school attendance, but [had] failed in the attempt to sell to most students the value of working hard to learn to use one's mind" (p. 311).

Theodore Sizer, Horace, and the Coalition of Essential Schools: From the 1980s until Today

Theodore Sizer, we believe, stands alone among the authors of the 1980s and 1990s as having had a prolonged and widespread influence on the restructuring of the contemporary American high school. In *Horace's Compromise: The Dilemma of the American High School* (1984), *Horace's School: Redesigning the American High School* (1992), and *Horace's Hope: What Works for the American High School* (1996), Sizer echoed the observations and recommendations of Boyer, Goodlad, Hampel, Powell, and others. He charged that, on the whole, American high school students were being required only to attend, not to learn. Demonstration of mastery was rarely required of high school students in the 1980s.

Sizer stated that the focus of the high school program ought to be on the development of students' minds and on the refinement of cognitive skills, not on the memorization and regurgitation of meaningless curriculum. Sizer advocated a core curriculum, studied in depth, with a number of themes small enough to allow students to master them instead of passive absorption of curriculum that would be soon enough forgotten.

Agreeing with Goodlad, Sizer advocated a grass-roots type of restructuring that eschewed grand pronouncements from governments or policy groups in favor of shared decision making and autonomy at the local level in the service of a more noble vision of the American comprehensive high school. Experimentation rather than restriction and autonomy rather than mandated curriculum would be much more likely to lead to lasting reform. Out of this thinking came a vital and modern group of secondary school educators known as the Coalition of Essential Schools.

Founded in 1984 by Sizer, the Coalition has been an ambitious project in secondary school reform based on the ideas laid out by Sizer, Powell, Hampel, and others. Educators in member schools of the Coalition have pledged themselves to push for school reform and restructuring in accordance with nine common principles:

1. The focus of the school should be on helping students use their minds well.

2. Students should be guided toward mastery of less, rather than simply coverage of more.

3. The school's goals should apply to every student in the building.

4. Teaching and learning should be personalized to the greatest extent possible.

5. Schools should subscribe to the concept of "student as worker."

6. Intensive remedial work should be provided immediately for students who need it, and should continue until they no longer need it.

7. The high school diploma should be awarded for demonstration of mastery, not attendance.

8. High expectations, trust, and decency should characterize the school.

9. Educators should be generalists first, and specialists second, with a total school commitment. Common planning time for teachers should be instituted. Teachers' salaries should be raised, while costs in general for the school should decrease, meaning that some programs that are tangential to the school may be eliminated.

Thirteen years later, in 1997, approximately one thousand schools had become members of the Coalition. In addition, the generous support of the Annenberg Foundation in establishing an Institute to further promote effective school restructuring has provided continuing momentum to the Sizer-inspired efforts to improve the American high school. Whether the Coalition can stimulate effective and lasting improvement remains to be determined.

Breaking Ranks: Changing an American Institution

In 1996, the National Association of Secondary School Principals, in collaboration with the Carnegie Foundation for the Advancement of Teaching, issued a report envisioning the high school of the 21st century. *Breaking Ranks: Changing an American Institution* is the latest in a long line of attempts to restructure and improve the American comprehensive high school. Dedicated to the memory of Ernest Boyer, the report was based on the assumption that, ultimately, it must be the practitioners of high school education who do the work of reform and improvement. The focus on practitioners, rather than on college presidents and other luminaries, makes *Breaking Ranks* unique among such reports.

The authors of the report ask the question, "What goals ought today's high school to embrace?" (*Breaking Ranks,* p. 2). The answers encompass the three goals that have long been both the essence and the anathema of the high school in America: democratic citizenship and equality, social efficiency, and social mobility. The high school of the twenty-first century was described as an institution with nine purposes:

1. A community committed to demonstrable academic achievement

2. An experience in transition to the next stage in life for every student, with the understanding that "ultimately each person needs to earn a living"

3. A gateway to multiple options

4. A place to prepare lifelong learners

5. A provision of the necessities for developing good citizens for "full participation in the life of a democracy"

6. A place where students are helped to develop as social as well as academic beings

7. A place where students learn to be comfortable in a technological society

8. A place where students become equipped for life in an internationally interdependent world

9. A place that "unabashedly advocates in behalf of young people" (p. 2)

To accomplish such schooling, the report offered 82 recommendations within six main theme areas. To accomplish the objective of increased personalization, the high school must break into units of no more than 600 students so that teachers and students can get to know and become important to one another. Increased personalization could also be enhanced by providing teacher-advocates or advisers for each student, as well as more individualized curriculum planning. To accomplish the theme of coherency, high schools were urged to reorganize to produce more interdisciplinary effort, with fewer barriers between academic departments. A more integrated curriculum would assist students in seeing the coherence within the world of knowledge. A third theme, time flexibility, could be accomplished through modifications of the Carnegie Unit, longer school years, and a schedule that would provide more options for both teachers and students. The theme of technology called on high schools to infuse and integrate technology in all aspects of teaching and learning. A fifth theme focused on the professional development of teachers and school leaders. Finally, the sixth theme for schools in the new century stands in recognition of the fact that "sooner or later every school takes on the characteristics of its leadership."

Developments at the Turn of the Century

At least two separate developments in the organization and operation of American high schools emerged in the 1990s, offering challenges to the centuries-long hegemony of the comprehensive high school concept. The first was the re-emergence of the small high school in one form or another; the second was the appearance, mostly in urban areas, of large vocational schools or other special magnet high schools that made no attempt at comprehensiveness. In the years to come, educators will learn whether these two movements will dislodge, in any substantial way, the American commitment to the comprehensive high school.

The Small High School

In 1987, Gregory and Smith echoed, in *High Schools as Communities: The Small High School Reconsidered*, the argument made by Cusick (1983) and others: the large comprehensive high school with its commitment to educating everyone had become unmanageable. Able to offer a curriculum that made the local university pale by comparison, Gregory and Smith stated that such schools had lost sight of the need for a sense of community. In order to be effective, a high school had to balance the twin goals of curriculum and community, and the large comprehensive high school had failed to do so. Increasing the size of the high school had led to an intolerable increase in student misbehavior and the consumption of huge portions of resources to maintain control of students in the school and classroom (Haller, 1992).

Large high schools, Gregory and Smith agreed, were much better at confining adolescents than truly educating them. Contemporary high schools were too big, with a structure that no longer worked well enough to justify continuing, and lacked the genuine sense of community necessary for authentic education for the 21st century.

Among their criticisms of the large high school are these:

- Such high schools make adolescent identity development very difficult.
- The hidden curriculum of the large high school (e.g., tracking) undermined the lessons in the formal curriculum.
- The large high school is incapable of fostering self-discipline.
- Teaching well demands that the teacher and the student know each other well; this is virtually impossible in the large high school.
- The large high school makes the development of a healthy sense of community impossible.
- Comprehensive high schools foster a top-down hierarchical authority that prevents real faculty empowerment or shared decision making.

The small high school, by contrast, offered a number of very important benefits, they suggested, including:

- Authentic teacher collegiality
- Expanded roles for both teachers and students
- Expanded involvement for students in school activities
- Increased access to adults
- A true sense of belonging
- The development of a strong sense of teacher efficacy
- Increased instructional leadership from school administrators
- More democratic governance
- A decline in the importance of control and discipline
- Increased teacher and student identification with the school
- Increased capacity for flexibility and change

Deborah Meier (1996), celebrated leader of Central Park East schools in New York City, also stated that the small urban high school has "big benefits from smallness." She cited seven good reasons to consider reorganizing large high schools into smaller ones of three to four hundred students: improved governance; increased teacher–student respect; simplicity; safety; parent involvement; accountability; and belonging. Educators in New York City have, it seems, taken the lead in creating small high schools out of big ones.

Specialty High Schools

In the late 1990s many large school districts were moving in a different direction, toward the organization and operation of large vocational or academic schools that made no attempt to be comprehensive. Schools of "choice," these high schools are often competitive in their admissions and sharply focused in their curriculum. In the schools of Detroit, Michigan, for example, many such specialty high schools have been opened in recent years.

One unusual example is the Benjamin O. Davis, Jr., Aerospace Technical High School (ATHS), in Detroit. ATHS offers a narrow focus of study that includes aviation power plant and airframe programs that prepare students for careers in aviation mechanics, a program in avionics that prepares students for work in aircraft navigation and communications, and a program in flight training that actually permits high schools students to qualify for their private pilot's licenses while still in high school. In addition, ATHS offers a standard academic curriculum that meets the graduation requirements of the state, in addition to modest extracurricular offerings and reasonable support services. It is easy to imagine the excitement of adolescents who seek, qualify for, and attend such a program. Only time will tell educators whether this trend, already underway in hundreds of specialty schools in dozens of districts, will offer a permanent challenge to the now dominant comprehensive American high school.

SUMMARY

Many of the early forms of schooling in the United States helped mold high schools as we know them today. Latin grammar schools helped establish the concept of education for social mobility, and academies were created based on the key concept of providing all students a free public education. The establishment of comprehensive high schools, however, did not begin until the 1850s.

A number of significant events and circumstances that occurred in the 20th century have helped define contemporary high schools. For example, the Committee of Ten on Secondary School Studies made recommendations that strongly reinforced commitment to the goal of social mobility, and the Committee on Economy of Time in Education issued several reports that supported the tracking of students while providing the great majority of them with a practical, vocational education. The Commission on the Reorganization of Secondary Education released an influential report entitled *Cardinal Principles of Secondary Education,* which questioned many of the recommendations in earlier reports and advocated for a much broader and more democratic role for high schools. This report promoted the idea of the importance of comprehensive high schools that would contribute to democratic citizenship and equality. A report on the Eight Year Study, sponsored by the Progressive Education Association, also revealed many significant findings that had the potential to change high schools significantly. However, this report was published during the middle of World War II, and many of the findings were ignored and forgotten with little attention or comment.

The nature of high schools at the beginning of the twenty-first century took shape in the 1920s and 1930s. Many of the programs and practices of high schools during those years are still commonly found today (e.g., inclusion of grades nine through twelve, comprehensive range of curricular offerings, tracking plans for students). With some exceptions, such as the dramatic growth in vocational and general education tracks, high schools remained relatively unchanged during the 1940s and 1950s in spite of the efforts of progressive education theorists. However, the USSR's launch of Sputnik in 1957 brought on stinging criticism of American education. One result was a renewed emphasis on the importance of science, technology, mathematics, foreign languages, and high standards for the most able students. Another event that influenced the nature of high school today occurred in 1959, when James Conant issued a report entitled *The American High School Today*. This report strongly supported the concept of comprehensive high schools and listed the desirable attributes of such schools.

The cultural and political changes (e.g., racial and socioeconomic equality) of the 1960s also helped define the contemporary high school. Civil rights militancy, teacher union activity, and enforcement of the Civil Rights Act of 1964 impacted communities and school structures. Toward the end of the 1960s and into the 1970s, the nation's attention shifted toward areas connected with youthful anti-war activism, distrust of government, and the generation gap. Numerous other factors emerged (e.g., political protests, rapid social changes, student rights, budget cuts, public skepticism, court orders) that created a whole new world outside of school. This new environment profoundly influenced high schools throughout this period.

Liberal criticisms of schools also affected the nature of high schools during the 1960s. John Holt advocated alternative schools, home-schooling, deschooling, and other ways of maximizing student freedom and integrity, while Ivan Illich charged that the American high schools ought to be replaced with smaller and more humane organizations. Charles Silverman observed that high schools were repressive and "prison-like," and needed to be freer and more humane. Even more radical critics such as Samuel Bowles and Herbert Gintis charged that the high school was little more than the sorting tool of the elitist groups in charge of a capitalist society. However, while the literature was full of reform and a few high schools were making changes, the organization and operation of most comprehensive high schools continued along the lines of the recommendations made years earlier by Conant.

A Nation at Risk, issued by the National Commission on Excellence in Education in 1983, was in many ways a reaction to the liberalities of the previous two decades. The charges of educational inadequacy of public schools contained in this report greatly weakened confidence in public education and shocked educators into a flurry of responses. A number of recommendations were made that have influenced current programs and practices in public schools. The report also led to many other investigations, reports, recommendations, and legislative mandates that have exerted powerful influences on high schools.

A number of other reports and publications have been issued since *A Nation at Risk* (e.g., Adler's *Paidia Proposal,* Boyer's *High school: A Report on Secondary Education in America,* Goodlad's *A Place Called School*) that continue to influence high schools into the new century. Adler claims that the education that is appropriate for the most capable students is best for all students. Boyer calls for the revitalization of the academic core curriculum and urges high schools to provide opportunities for service learning and individually designed senior capstone projects. Goodlad favors a core curriculum that would be studied by 70 to 80 percent of students, and for the abolition of ability grouping.

The contributions of Theodore Sizer, whose series of books and other professional publications continue to be powerful positive influences on contemporary high school education, continue to shape programs and practices in high schools. His observations and recommendations (e.g., development of students' minds, meaningful curriculum, the "student as worker" concept), as well as his leadership in the establishment of the Coalition of Essential Schools, have provided guidance for those seeking to improve high schools and increase meaningful student learning.

One of the most recent major reports focusing on high school reform is *Breaking Ranks: Changing an American Institution.* This report, which was written by a group made up primarily of high school practitioners, includes nine major purposes and 82 recommendations. The report, which is utilized throughout this book, has the potential to provide much guidance for those seeking to improve educational opportunities for high school students.

In conclusion, the history of the American high school is one of tumult, turbulence, and growth as an institution, as educators have attempted to simultaneously achieve three important and disparate goals: to encourage democratic citizenship and provide equality; to respond to the needs of the community, the nation, and the marketplace; and provide opportunities for every willing individual to develop to the fullest, in a way that will enable that person to be as successful as possible as an individual, in further schooling and in life. As the new century dawns, two things are certain: Educators will continue to work to achieve those goals, and the community will continue to express its pleasure or its dissatisfaction with what it perceives as progress or the lack of it. The remainder of this book will chronicle current attempts of high school educators aspiring to organize and operate what they hope will be regarded by all as an exemplary high school.

CONNECTIONS TO OTHER CHAPTERS

You should now be able to read about new directions in the high school curriculum, as well as changes in other aspects of the high school program, and be able to think more clearly about the historical goals of the school to which these new directions are connected. You might be able to forecast the probable success of various reforms being discussed.

ACTION STEPS

1. This might be a good time to interview high school teachers or administrators about what they believe to be the mission of their school. Formulate several questions and invite a small group of educators to provide their affirmation or rejection of the goals you have learned about in this chapter. Ask them to rank the three goals in order of importance. You might want to find out which of the goals they believe their school most effectively achieves.

2. This might also be an appropriate time to conduct interviews of high school students, using the same questions. Ask about their sense of the importance of each of the goals for themselves as individuals, and for all the students as a group. Find out which goal they believe is most effectively achieved. You may be able to design some questions that get students to suggest what their school might do to improve its effectiveness in pursuing the goals.

3. Interviews of parents and community members can also provide some important insight into the struggle of the high school to achieve its mission. The sort of interviews suggested above would be appropriate for parents, members of the business community, and others.

4. One of the techniques used by "futurists" to forecast important emerging trends is to scan several dozen newspapers from various parts of the country. What might appear to be isolated and unimportant in one community could actually be part of an important national trend if it appeared in a number of newspapers at the same time. A trip to a local university, college, or community library should enable you to examine a number of newspapers or news magazines. Look for any mention of high school education. What you find, or do not find, might tell you something important about directions of high school change locally or nationally.

DISCUSSION QUESTIONS

1. Think about the high school that you attended. Can you describe the ways in which your school attempted to meet all three of the goals described in this chapter? How effective was your high school in doing so?

2. Identify and discuss the goals that influenced each of the major attempts at high school reform in the last 25 years.

3. Identify and discuss the goals motivating contemporary attempts at high school reform.

REFERENCES

Adler, M. (1982). *The Paideia proposal*. New York: Macmillan.
Aiken, W. (1942). *The story of the eight-year study*. New York: Harper and Brothers.

Bestor, A. (1953, 1985). *Educational wastelands: The retreat from learning in our public schools.* Urbana, IL: University of Illinois Press.

Bowles, S., & Gintis, H. (1976). *Schooling in capitalist America: Educational reform and the contradictions of economic life.* New York: Basic Books.

Boyer, E. (1983). *High school: A report of secondary education in America.* New York: Harper and Row.

Breaking ranks: Changing an American institution. (1996). Reston, VA: National Association of Secondary School Principals.

Brown, B. F. (1963). *The nongraded high school.* Englewood Cliffs, NJ: Prentice Hall.

Brown, B. F. (1972). *New directions for the comprehensive high school.* West Nyack, NY: Parker Publishing Company.

Bruner, J. (1977). *The process of education.* Cambridge, MA: Harvard University Press.

Butts, F. (1978). *Public education in the United States: From revolution to reform.* New York: Holt, Rinehart, and Winston.

Button, H. W., & Provenzo, Jr., E. (1983). *History of education and culture in America.* Englewood Cliffs, NJ: Prentice Hall.

Conant, J. (1959). *The American high school today.* New York: The McGraw-Hill Book Company.

Conant, J. (1967). *The comprehensive high school.* New York: McGraw-Hill.

Conant, J. (1961). *Slums and suburbs: A commentary on schools in metropolitan areas.* New York: McGraw-Hill.

Cusick, P. (1983). *The egalitarian ideal and the American high school.* New York: Longman.

Dennison, G. (1969). *The lives of children: The story of the First Street School.* New York: Random House.

Friedenberg, E. (1959). *The vanishing adolescent.* Boston: Beacon Press.

Goodlad, J. (1984). *A place called school: Prospects for the future.* New York: McGraw-Hill.

Goodman, P. (1962). *Growing up absurd: Problems of youth in the organized system.* New York: Random House.

Gregory, T., & Smith, G. (1987). *High schools as communities: The small high school reconsidered.* Bloomington, IN: Phi Delta Kappa.

Gutek, G. (1991). *An historical introduction to American education. (2nd Ed.).* Prospect Heights, IL: Waveland Press.

Haller, E. (1992). High school size and student discipline: Another aspect of the school consolidation issue? *Educational Evaluation and Policy Analysis, 14,* 145–56.

Hampel, R. (1986). *The last little citadel: American high schools since 1940.* Boston: Houghton Mifflin Company.

Holt, J. (1972). *Freedom and beyond.* New York: E. P. Dutton.

Holt, J. (1964). *How children fail.* New York: Pitman Press.

Holt, J. (1967). *How children learn.* New York: Pitman Press.

Holt, J. (1976). *Instead of education: Ways of helping people do things better.* New York: E. P. Dutton.

Holt, J. (1981). *Teach your own.* New York: Delcorte Press.

Illich, I. (1971). *Deschooling society.* New York: Harper and Row.

Kahne, J. 91995). Revisiting the Eight-Year Study and rethinking the focus of educational policy analysis. *Educational Policy, 9,* 4–23.

Krug, E. (1966). *Salient dates in American education: 1635–1964.* New York: Harper and Row.

Krug, E. (1972). *The shaping of the American high school, 1920–1941.* Madison, WI: The University of Wisconsin Press.

Kozol, J. (1995). *Amazing Grace: The lives of children and the conscience of a nation.* New York: Crown.

Kozol, J. (1991). *Savage inequalities: Children in America's schools.* New York: Crown.

Labaree, D. (1997). Public goods, private goods: The American struggle over educational goals. *American Educational Research Journal, 34,* 39–81.

Lynd, A. (1953). *Quackery in the public schools.* Boston: Little, Brown.

Meier, D. (1996). The big benefits of smallness. *Educational Leadership, 54,* 12–15.

National Commission on Excellence in Education. (1983). *A nation at risk. The imperative for educational reform.* Washington, DC: The Commission.

Neill, A. S. (1960). *Summerhill: A radical approach to child rearing.* New York: Hart.

Orfield, G. (1996a) *Dismantling desegregation: The general reversal of Brown v. Board of Education.* New York: New Press.

Orfield, G. (1996b). *Who chooses? who loses?: Culture, institutions, and the unequal effects of school choice.* New York: Teachers College Press.

Powell, A. G., Farrar, E., & Cohen, D. (1985). *The shopping mall high school: Winners and losers in the educational marketplace.* Boston: Houghton Miffin Company.

Preskill, S. (1989). Educating for democracy: Charles Eliot and the differentiated curriculum. *Educational Theory, 39,* 351–358.

Pulliam, J., & Van Patten, J. (1995). *History of education in America.* Englewood Cliffs, NJ: Prentice Hall.

Reese, W. (1995). *The origins of the American high school.* New Haven: Yale University Press.

Rickover, H. (1963). *American education, a national failure; the problem of our schools and what we can learn from England.* New York: Dutton.

Rogers, C. (1969). *Freedom to learn.* Columbus, OH: Charles Merrill.

Silberman, C. (1970). *Crisis in the classroom.* New York: Random House.

Sizer, T. R. (1985). *Horace's compromise: The dilemma of the American high school.* Boston: Houghton Mifflin.

Sizer, T. (1996). *Horace's hope: What works for the American high school.* Boston: Houghton Mifflin.

Sizer, T. R. (1992). *Horace's school: Redesigning the American high school.* Boston: Houghton Mifflin.

Trump, J. L. (1959). *Images of the future: A new approach to secondary education.* Urbana, IL: National Association of Secondary School Principals.

Trump, J. L. (1960). *New directions to quality education: The secondary school of tomorrow.* Urbana, IL: National Association of Secondary School Principals.

Trump, J. L., & Baynham, D. (1961). *Focus on change: Guide to better schools.* Urbana, IL: National Association of Secondary School Principals.

Trump, J. L., & Miller, D. (1968). *Secondary school curriculum improvement: Proposals and procedures.* Boston: Allyn and Bacon.

2

THE EMERGENT HIGH SCHOOL CURRICULUM

WHAT YOU WILL LEARN IN THIS CHAPTER

The current national status of the high school curriculum

A review of nationally-developed standards in common curriculum areas

Recasting nationally-developed standards at the state and local levels

Values education from a different perspective

A rebirth of the interdisciplinary curriculum at the high school level

Writing across the curriculum

Developing higher-order thinking in all students

The application of knowledge and skills through school to work, apprenticeships, applied academics, projects, and exhibitions

Each high school community will identify a set of essential learnings—above all, literature and language, mathematics, social studies, science and the arts—in which students must demonstrate achievement in order to graduate.

The high school will integrate its curriculum to the extent possible and emphasize depth over breadth of coverage.

Teachers will design work for students that is of high enough quality to engage them, cause them to persist, and, when successfully completed, result is their satisfaction and their acquisition of learnings, skills and abilities valued by society.

The content of the curriculum, where practical, will connect itself to real-life applications of knowledge and skills to help students link their education to the future.

Each student will have a Personal Plan for Progress to ensure that the high school takes individual needs into consideration and to allow students, within reasonable parameters, to design their own methods of learning in an effort to meet high standards

—*Breaking Ranks*, p. 11

HIGH SCHOOL CURRICULUM

The high school curriculum is in motion. Spurred by a plethora of recommendations from educational reform commissions, the bully pulpit of the elected officials, and the global nature of economic competition, a variety of curriculum changes is being tested. The emphasis is clearly on higher expectations for all, expanded academics, and higher-order thinking. The development of a core curriculum for all students places the responsibility on education professionals to devise ways to impart mastery of complex subject matter to students previously given brief introductions to the same content. Students must be taught habits that enable them to solve problems and apprehend new information and ideas. Vocational and technical education, once a dumping ground for students of lesser abilities, now integrates higher mathematics and science courses with on-the-job training. Magnet schools that focus on specific careers or specific academic areas have increased in number. International Baccalaureate programs are found in almost every medium and large school district.

Foreign language programs have multiplied. The traditional fare of Spanish and French is augmented by German, Russian, Hebrew, Japanese, Mandarin Chinese, Hindi, and Arabic. Even Latin has returned to prominence. Many high schools are requiring all students to study a second language, while others are increasing the number of required years of study. The number of immersion programs is growing as practical language use takes precedence over verb conjugations and vocabulary. Foreign exchanges enable students to spend time in a different culture learning the language and the customs. As the world shrinks and as our own country becomes more multicultural, knowing a second language may become a survival skill.

There is an increase in interdisciplinary course work. The traditional English–social studies and mathematics–science links have been joined by others. Teams of teachers plan units that integrate three and four subject areas. School-wide themes cross disciplinary boundaries. Realignments within disciplines create courses such as biochemistry, biotechnology, geophysics, and microbiology. Integrated mathematics focuses on problems rather than on the traditional Algebra I, geometry, Algebra II, trigonometry sequence. Teaching writing becomes everyone's responsibility. Theme weeks ("The Renaissance," for example) bring together art, architecture, political science, history, literature, science, medicine, and music. Projects challenge students to coalesce their knowledge and skills from different subjects to answer provocative questions. Applied mathematics and science courses help students see the relationship of school work to the professional world.

Performance, portfolios, and *projects* are words that describe the connection between curriculum and assessment. Traditional multiple-choice tests decontextualize assessment and at best have an artificial connection with the curriculum. New assessment techniques supplement, and in some cases supplant, the traditional measures of student learning. The aphorism that less is more implies that depth is more important than breadth. Traditional assessment tends to measure an array of skills and knowledge without really measuring depth of understanding. The best tests of student comprehension are embedded within the curriculum itself so that they become part of the act of learning.

The ability to identify and solve real-world problems seem a better measure of student learning than completion of true/false, matching, fill-in-the-blank, and multiple-choice test items. The new assessment is unobtrusive and integrated into the curriculum. When students present portfolios of their best work, undertake a community project, or complete an exhibition, they must *use* knowledge rather than simply display it. Apprenticeships, internships, and community service require students to apply knowledge to current issues and problems. They represent an acid-test of student learning. Moreover, central to the new assessment is the belief that students can learn to evaluate their own work effectively. The concept of quality is learned over time, as the result of much discussion and practice. One school reports that students responded to a letter to the editor of a local newspaper criticizing outcome-based education by creating scoring rubrics that they used in evaluating the quality of the critic's letter.

The school curriculum can mean different things to different people. Theoretically, it serves as a work plan that gives direction to the work of school-based personnel. It is often tied to textbooks published by one of the seven major textbook companies in the United States and/or to curriculum guides developed at the state or district level. With the growing movement toward local control, many decisions about what is to be taught have shifted to school districts, schools, and classroom teachers. The states develop standards for student achievement, and districts and schools are charged with implementing the standards while taking local conditions into consideration. In reality, curriculum decision making involves national, state, and local educational agencies, as well as other influential groups.

Some educators define *curriculum* as everything that happens to students under the direction of the school. Others adopt a narrower frame of reference and include selected subject-matter goals, objectives, and activities. Still others take a position somewhere in between. Regardless of the definition one uses, there is agreement that the curriculum should enable students to cope with the exigencies of a world that has become increasingly interrelated, and to become effective learners throughout their lives. Former Secretary of Labor Robert Reich refers to the need for high school graduates to recognize, identify, define, and solve problems in a global information society. He calls for students to become symbol analysts in order to make sense of the complexity of 21st-century living and to identify and solve real-world problems. Additionally, he sees an ever-increasing need for students to become not only consumers of knowledge but generators of new knowledge (Reich, 1991).

In response to the demand for higher student achievement, nationally developed standards have been completed for most subject matter fields. The *Goals 2000* document produced by U.S. Department of Education states that "All students will leave grade . . . 12 having demonstrated competency in challenging subject matter including English, mathematics, science, foreign languages, civics and government, economics, arts, history, and geography, and every school in America will ensure that all students learn to use their minds well so they may be prepared for responsible citizenship, further learning, and productive employment in our nation's modern economy." This document, its predecessor (*America 2,000*), and a legion of studies during the 1980s called for high standards of student performance, and prompted a trend toward the development of national standards in most of the subject disciplines.

A National Core Curriculum

The concept of a core curriculum was originally introduced by Harold Alberty of Ohio State University in Columbus, Ohio, in the early 1950s. Alberty's core curriculum was an interdisciplinary approach to curriculum that combined language arts, social studies, and sometimes science in two- and three-hour blocks of time. This approach was implemented at many junior and senior high schools in the United States, and appeared to be an outgrowth of the findings of the Eight Year Study (1933–1941).

Unlike Alberty's core, the new core curriculum focuses on identifying essential learnings in specific academic subjects. In 1989, the National Council of Teachers of Mathematics published the first attempt to define what all students should know from kindergarten to grade twelve. Their publication *Curriculum and Evaluation Standards for School Mathematics* details what mathematics students need to know, how students will achieve the curricular goals, what teachers will do to help students develop mathematical knowledge, and the context in which learning and teaching occur (National Council of Teachers of Mathematics, 1989, p. 1). The standards focus on a fundamental new set of goals for students in mathematics. Students will: (a) learn to value mathematics, (b) become confident in their ability to do mathematics, (c) become proficient mathematics problem solvers, (d) learn to communicate mathematically, and (e) learn to reason mathematically. Understanding mathematics appears to be the predominant theme for transforming classrooms to learning environments where all students can develop a deeper understanding of content. The mathematics report set the tone for subsequent efforts to define standards in other subject areas.

Standards in science appear in two primary efforts: *The National Committee on Science Education Standards and Assessment* (NCSESA) and *Project 2061*. The NCSESA report identifies "a . . . number of important concepts, principles, facts, laws and theories that provide a foundation for understanding any applying science" (National Committee on Science Education and Standards, p. 15). The standards are presented in four categories: Science Subject Matter, the Nature of Science, Applications of Science, and Contexts of Science.

Project 2061, named for the date in which Haley's Comet will once again appear, comes from the American Association for the Advancement of Science. The Project (1985) produced over sixty literacy goals in science, mathematics, technology and the social sciences. Later, the Project's principal investigators recommended what students should know by the end of grade twelve. In their book *Science for All Americans,* Rutherford and Ahlgren (1990) expressed the belief that "the scientifically literate person is one who is aware that science, mathematics, and technology are interdependent human enterprises . . ." (p. ix). The book presents content that all students must understand in order to function effectively today and in the future.

In addition to these efforts, the National Science Teachers Association produced *Scope, Sequence, and Coordination of Secondary School Science: The Content Core* (1993). It recommends that all students study science every year for six years, and advocates carefully sequenced instruction in all the sciences. This report challenges the traditional biology–chemistry–physics sequence and proposes that students should study each discipline every year.

The History Standards Project, released in November 1994 by the National Center for History in the Schools and later revised, includes standards for U.S. history and world history. U.S. history is presented in ten eras, focusing on subjects such as expansion and reform, immigration, and the Cold War. World history "treats the history and values of diverse civilizations, including those of the West, and addresses the interactions among them" (Diegmueller 1996, p. 31). Although the initial drafts of both the U.S. and world history standards were returned for revision, there was a deliberate attempt to involve groups and individuals with a variety of perspectives on the writing team. The standards are content specific. Another set of standards has been developed by the National Council for the Social Studies. These standards are less specific and draw from all of the social sciences. Ten standards are formed around key themes such as culture, time, continuity and change, and individual development and identity. Emphasis in the social studies is on the development of higher-order thinking skills.

The standards in geography call for students to be competitive in two aspects of geographical education: knowledge and performance. One document, *Geography for Life: National Standards* (1994) emphasizes the significance of geography in everyday life. Another publication of the Geography Education Writing Committee structures the materials around five themes—location, place, human-environmental interaction, movement, and regions. The National Assessment of Educational Progress (NAEP) has translated these five themes into specific outcomes for assessment.

English/language arts was the last major subject area to produce a standards document. The standards were a joint effort of the National Council of Teachers of English (NCTE) and the International Reading Association (IRA). The report lists twelve standards dealing with literature, writing, basic skills, diversity issues, and English for speakers of other languages, and stresses connections among reading, writing, and speaking. The standards are general and place responsibility on states, districts, and schools for developing curriculum and instruction. In fact, the NCTE states clearly that the standards are not prescriptions for curriculum and instruction. The standards have been criticized by several sources because of their emphasis on process rather than content. For example, one standard states, "Students read a wide range of literature from many periods in many genres to build an understanding of the many dimensions of human experience" (Smagorinsky, 1996). The other standards are written similarly. The NCTE has published four books describing how the standards might appear in practice.

Other professional groups have joined the standards procession. The Foreign Languages Council and the associations of French, German, Spanish and Portuguese teachers have produced a document calling for students to master at least one second language (Diegmueller, 1995). They view fluency in a language other than English no longer the province of the academic elite, but a survival skill for one's native land and beyond. The McLuhanesque global village seems to call for graduates with increased language skills. At the core of the new standards is the ability to communicate in a second language as opposed to a command of verb conjugations and vocabulary words. The Center for Civic Education has produced *National Standards for Civics and Government* (1994). Standards for dance, music, theater and the visual arts have been developed by the Consortium for National Arts Education (1993). The standards include art production, art history, criticism, and aesthetic education. The National Association for Sport and Physical Education published *Outcomes of Quality Physical Education Programs* (1992). Standards have also been developed for health education, as have standards delineating the knowledge and skills required for success in the world of work.

Many of the efforts at national models of standards have been funded by agencies within the federal government with supplemental funds from private enterprise or professional associations. In 1992 Congress chartered the National Council on Education, Standards, and Testing with a mission to create national standards and assessments in core subjects. The goal was a consensus for what students should know and be able to do in key subject areas. Carried to the ultimate, this effort could result in a national curriculum and a national testing program.

To date, the nationally developed standards have served each of the 50 states in creating their own curriculum standards and frameworks. The suggested standards articulate what students should know and be able to do. They emphasize more than the traditional acquisition of knowledge and skills. Among the common threads are the following: Depth seems more important than breadth. Memorization of content is deemed less important than the application of knowledge in the solution of problems. Social problems and issues are afforded more importance. Students are expected to develop habits of mind associated with a given discipline. Career education is viewed as an outgrowth of academic study rather than an alternative to it. Rigid boundaries between traditional subject matter are softened to enable students to consider relationships. The standards are usually accompanied by guidelines showing the content that students should master at strategic points in their education. Content and skills placed on a continuum give new meaning to the concept of remediation and have the potential to breathe new life into what tradition labels the lower track. Higher expectations in the form of standards and benchmarks are directed to all students, not just the academically elite. Technology is integrated into each of the disciplines.

Unfortunately, the standards come in a variety of formats, making them difficult to use when attempting to coordinate the curriculum at the state and local levels. In response, one group, the Mid-continent Regional Educational Laboratory (MCREL), synthesized the standards documents in several subject areas, providing a more usable format suitable for curriculum workers. (See *The Systematic Identification of Content Standards and Benchmarks,* 1994 and 1995.) Additionally, standards in any format only define essential learnings; they do not ensure achievement. Students still must perceive them as desirable and worthwhile. Student outcomes, and not the number or difficulty of standards, are the measure of a high school's success.

RECASTING STANDARDS AT THE LOCAL LEVEL

Standards can create a level playing field for students in the nation's high school. They must, however, be accompanied by a range of strategies that help all students reach them within a reasonable degree of time. Otherwise, higher standards may only widen the gap among students. For example, in an effort to increase achievement in mathematics, some states and high schools require that all students complete a minimum of one course in algebra to graduate. Students who previously enrolled in general math or prealgebra now must complete the more challenging algebra course. When the California legislature mandated that all students would study algebra, many high schools instituted a two-year sequence for students who were not thought to be ready for the traditional algebra course. By varying time and standardizing achievement, more students can succeed at a higher level.

At James Bowie High School in Austin, Texas, Algebra I is spread over two years rather than one for some students. Another way to offer algebra for all students is through a system called continuous progress. This approach is similar to what has been called nongraded schooling. Placing standards and benchmarks on a continuum allows students to begin the study of a subject at any point appropriate to their background and motivation. The continuous progress system focuses on understanding and applying basic and advanced properties of functions in algebra. These properties can be defined at various levels of difficulty, each building on the preceding level. Level I might focus on the identification of number patterns. Level II expects the student to interpolate and extrapolate simple number patterns. Level III leads students through coordinates and equations toward the solution of specific problems. Level IV includes trigonometric functions, inequalities, polynomial equations, polar coordinates, and the solution of more challenging problems. Each level would be expanded to include additional benchmarks. Each student could then progress at his or her own pace through the various levels of algebra. This approach is used more frequently in vocational programs in which curriculum modules are developed for various performance objectives. A few high schools offer continuous progress in all academic subjects as well. An excellent model can be found at the Thomas Haney Secondary Centre in Maple Ridge, British Columbia (Jenkins, 1994).

At Thomas Haney, the curriculum is divided into traditional courses based on the requirements of the Ministry of Education. Each course is then divided into units of study, with specific outcomes related to the overall course objectives. Units are supported by learning guides that establish the content and activities that students must complete in order to earn credit. Each students works at his or her own pace. Students' progress is monitored by teams of academic teachers and the students' advisers. Assessment is aligned with the objectives of the units and the learning guides.

At Central Park East Secondary School in New York City, students submit portfolios in 14 areas to a graduation committee of four people that determines their readiness to graduate. The portfolio requirements replace the traditional credit requirements for graduation. The requirements are written clearly in terms of what students must demonstrate. The 14 portfolio components are: (1) postgraduate plan, (2) autobiography, (3) school/community service and internship, (4) ethics and social issues, (5) fine arts and aesthetics, (6) mass media, (7) practical skills, (8) geography, (9) second language, (10) science and technology, (11) mathematics, (12) literature, (13) history, and (14) physical challenge. Students must defend their portfolios before the committee in seven of the fourteen areas. Among the seven required areas are science and technology, mathematics, literature, and history. The other seven portfolios are read and evaluated by the committee. Scoring grids are developed for the committees to assist with the evaluation.

The graduation portfolios establish high standards without standardization. The following description of the requirements for the literature portfolio supports this observation: "Students prepare a list of texts they have read in a variety of genres to serve as a basis for discussion with the graduation committee. They also submit samples of their own essays about literary works or figures demonstrating their capacity to reflect on and communicate effectively about literary products and ideas" (Darling-Hammond & Ancess, 1994, p. 15). The portfolio requirements are for all students. Some students complete them in the prescribed four years, but others may take additional time.

Graduation portfolios are also used at the Middle College High School in Long Island City, NY, where students prepare a Regents portfolio with entries in academics, the arts, and careers. In addition to the portfolio, seniors at Middle College complete a research project based on their interests and defend it before a graduation committee. At both Middle College and Central Park East, students must pass competency tests as part of their graduation requirements. The tests are included as part of the portfolio. The idea for graduation by portfolio originated at the Walden III High School in Racine, Wisconsin, where students must demonstrate mastery in 15 areas of knowledge and competence. The Rites of Passage Experience (ROPE) requires students to make presentations before a ROPE Committee in all 15 areas (Archbald and Newmann, 1988).

Littleton High School in Littleton, Colorado, replaced the traditional graduation requirements with 19 performance-based requirements. All students must demonstrate what they know and can do in English/language arts, mathematics, a second language, history, geography, personal health, ethics, and technology. They demonstrate accomplishment by writing letters to public figures, completing theater reviews, designing experiments in science, and completing community service projects (Westerberg, Thomas & Stein, 1994). The Cabot School in Cabot, Vermont, has identified twelve standards that students must complete for graduation. The standards are culminating benchmarks that define a graduate. The curriculum is then developed to enable students to achieve the twelve standards. Hico High school in Hico, Texas, has instituted a performance-based program focusing on traditional subject groupings. Their program resembles those implemented in several of the high schools involved in the Model Schools Project of the National Association of Secondary Principals (1968–1973).

The New Standards Project has published a three-volume set of draft academic performance standards for English/language arts, mathematics, science, and applied learning. The performance standards specify how students are to demonstrate their knowledge and skills at each level—elementary, middle, and high school. They build on the content standards developed by the nationally based groups. One part of the New Standards Project proposes a model for offering credit by performance. A certificate of mastery is awarded to students who successfully meet the performance standards. Several high schools have adopted this system. Valley High School Magnet-Career Academy in Louisville, Kentucky and the Cabot School are two examples.

VALUES AS BASIC EDUCATION

Teaching about values seems to have taken on new meaning in recent years. Once rejected as a form of indoctrination, values education is making a comeback. Whether it is the result of a growing dissatisfaction with the level of civility in the society, a realization that the global village brings people of difference in closer proximity, or a deepening interest in citizenship is speculation. Judging from the popularity of books like *The Book of Virtues* (Bennett, 1993) or the several editions of *Chicken Soup for the Soul* (Canfield, 1994, 1995, 1996, 1997) the importance of values resonates in the psyches of most Americans. While most would dispute the direct teaching of values, addressing them from different perspectives may well reflect an idea whose time has come several times over.

One approach to the presentation of values education can be found at Eastern High School in Louisville, Kentucky. Here, Socratic seminars are offered for credit to all high school students each month. Students in grades nine through twelve may elect to meet for one 50-minute period each month to discuss readings from the classics, modern works, historical documents, and current issues. The seminars are led by teachers who serve as moderators, preparing questions and facilitating discussion. At the Minnetonka High School in Minnetonka, Minnesota, Socratic seminars have become a part of a minority history course offered during the last quarter of sophomore American history (Holden & Bunte, 1995).

The Socratic seminar is one of the three modes of teaching found in the Paideia Proposals as described by Mortimer Adler (1982). Paideia schools include the Socratic seminars as part of students' regular school schedules. Students meet in seminar groups of 15 for 90 minutes each week. The method of the Socratic seminar is one of inquiry and challenge. Teacher leaders prepare thoughtful questions and encourage students to challenge each other in the course of the discussion. Students discuss values and great ideas with their peers.

William Bennett's *Book of Virtues* is an excellent resource for materials and ideas for the seminars. The book is divided into ten chapters, each focused on a different value—self discipline, compassion, responsibility, friendship, work, courage, perseverance, honesty, loyalty, and faith. Each chapter contains essays, stories, and poems related to the particular value. Although Bennett calls his book a "how-to book for moral literacy," its usefulness as a resource for Socratic seminars raises his pronouncement to a higher plane.

Using a different value as a theme each month is another approach to values education. In the text of *Breaking Ranks* (1996), the NASSP/Carnegie Commission on High School Reform writes that "schools must unabashedly teach students about such key virtues as honesty, dependability, trust, responsibility, tolerance, respect, and other commonly held values important to Americans" (p. 30). These virtues and others can serve as a list from which to draw the value of the month. Rather than address the values in a seminar, instructors would embed them in the regular curriculum in all subject areas.

Values are associated with what has been labeled character education. The primary question is not so much whether or not to support character education, but rather how to present values without creating a blind obedience to some or all of them. The judicious application of values associated with character education requires an ability to apply these values in appropriate situations. Some proponents of character education, such as Edward Wynne of the University of Illinois at Chicago Circle, believe that the great tradition of inculcating moral values in education was lost as a direct result of the misinterpretation of data from a study conducted by Hartshorne and May in the 1920s (Wynne, 1985–86). Others believe the decline was caused by an increasing pluralism, an emphasis on individualism, and a series of United States Supreme Court decisions that found school systems in violation of the Establishment Clause of the First Amendment (Vesels & Boyd, 1996). Wynne cites the social historians David and Sheila Rothman in support of a return to what he called the "great tradition" of inculcating moral virtue and right conduct in students. The Rothmans write that "the business of schools (in our early history) was not reading and writing but citizenship, not education but social control" (Wynne, 1985–86).

Other educators support character education but do so from a position of critical reasoning and judgment on ethical issues. They fear indoctrination will result in a nonthinking application of values at the expense of moral understanding. With the emphasis today on teaching academics for understanding rather than rote memorization, these proponents contend that a similar emphasis should be placed on character education. Thus the dividing issue seems to be whether or not students can learn basics in the context of application or whether learning content and skills must precede their application. A third position, represented by private, denominational schools, views character development as a matter of inculcating the norms of a particular religious behavior (Peshkin, 1985–86).

All high schools inculcate moral values of some type. There appears to be no way to avoid it. The hidden curriculum resides in all schools and reflects the values that administrators, teachers and the community believe to be important. The moral instruction can take the form of punishment for those who infringe on the rights of others, or the requirement of a reasonable explanation for being late to class or school. As a beginning, high school educators might uncover the values inherent in the school's hidden curriculum with the goal of deciding whether these are the best values to emphasize. Once the most important values are identified, it is a matter of deciding how they are to be presented. At the high school level, the decision may be easier than at the elementary and middle school levels. Here, the development of critical thinking skills seems to point toward the desirability of having students examine values objectively to determine their efficacy in adding quality to their lives and improving the larger society.

INTERDISCIPLINARY CURRICULUM

Like values education, the interdisciplinary curriculum represents an old idea whose time ostensibly has arrived. Judging from the curriculum publications of a number of high schools, grasping the interrelatedness of the disciplines is an important student outcome. Interdisciplinary curricula can take various forms. The simplest is presenting two disciplines (for example, English/language arts and social studies, or math and science) in a block of time. Another involves the creation of interdisciplinary units of two or more disciplines, while still another develops a generalized theme which cuts across several subject areas.

Many high schools are offering humanities blocks in which a team of two or more teachers present United States history and literature together. Humanities blocks can also include world history and literature. In addition to the humanities blocks, Eaglecrest High School in Aurora, Colorado, offers a ninth-grade interdisciplinary course combining environmental geography with environmental science. Ninth- and tenth-year students at the Central Park East High School enroll in two interdisciplinary programs as part of their common core, humanities and math–science. Several high schools offer humanities blocks for ninth-grade students to assist with the transition from middle school to high school. Ninth-grade humanities programs usually involve English/language arts with expressive arts, technology, some type of social studies program, and sometimes science.

The interdisciplinary curriculum may include more than two disciplines. When this occurs, three approaches appear to be common. The first is found in schools like Jefferson High school in Fairfax, Virginia, which integrates English/language arts, molecular biology and the principles of engineering and technology. It is organized around essential questions and real-world problems, as opposed to separate disciplines. The Twin Buttes High School in Zuni, New Mexico, offers a natural world course focused on the Grand Canyon that integrates social studies, science, and English/language arts.

At East Hartford High School in East Hartford, Connecticut, ninth- and tenth-grade students complete a minimum of three interdisciplinary units per year that combine content from English/language arts, social studies, science, and mathematics. A coordinated study of the rain forest involving biology, literature, and social studies helps students at Waukegan High School in Waukegan, Illinois, see how these subjects relate to each other. Biology classes concentrate on the workings of the rain forest ecosystem and the global, environmental, and scientific implications of its destruction. Literature classes read an array of Brazilian poetry, and social studies classes focus on the migration of Brazilians into the Amazon basin. The Academy, one of the six houses of the Cambridge Rindge and Latin School in Cambridge, Massachusetts, offers a three-year block of English/language arts, social studies and physical education. The tenth-grade core, "Project America," explores the American experience in terms of geography, history, literature, art, economics, social structure and personal perspective. "The Search for an American Identity" is a team-taught program for eleventh-grade students at Barrington High School in Barrington, Illinois, interrelating English/language arts with art, music, theater and architecture.

An interesting approach to interdisciplinary programs is offered by Howard Gardner and Veronica Boix-Mansilla (1994). They believe that the individual student is ultimately responsible to combine knowledge and skills. They pose several questions that can be addressed in any discipline throughout a student's high school experience. "Who am I?" "Who is my family?" "Which is the group to whom I belong?" "Who are the people around me, and in other parts of the world?" "How are they similar and different from me?" "How should I treat other people?" "What is fair?" "What is moral?" "How do you handle conflicts?" All of these questions illustrate the kinds of ideas that students and teachers can return to often. By the time students complete high school they should be able to draw from knowledge acquired in all their course work to answer these questions. Gardner and Boix-Mansilla are clear to note, however, that interdisciplinary work can only be carried out after students have become conversant in the relevant disciplines. They differentiate between disciplines and subject matters: "Subject matters are seen as collections of content while disciplines entail particular modes of thinking or interpreting the world" (p. 202).

Although mathematics and science are included in some of the interdisciplinary efforts, new developments in these disciplines integrate subject matter that traditionally has been taught in separate courses. Two specific trends are noted: the Interactive Mathematics Project (IMP) and STS (Science, Technology, and Society). These programs can be found in an increasing number of high schools. IMP has expanded from a small pilot project of four high schools in California to over 100 high schools. It is a four-year, problem-based mathematics program that replaces the traditional Algebra I, geometry, Algebra II/trigonometry, precalculus sequence. It is designed to meet the needs of both college-bound and non–college-bound students. The program consists of four- to eight-week units organized around a central problem or theme. During the first year students study problem solving, geometric and number patterns, the use of variables to express generalizations, and both algebraic and graphic equations. The second year includes the chi-square statistic, the Pythagorean theorem, and linear programming. The third year extends the understandings of the previous years and adds combinatorics, derivatives, and matrix algebra. The fourth year addresses the concepts of periodic functions, computer graphics, and statistical sampling.

Units with such provocative titles as "The Game of Pig," "The Overland Trail," and "The Pit and the Pendulum" pique students' interest in the study of IMP mathematics. "The Pit and the Pendulum" opens with an excerpt from the story by Edgar Allan Poe:

> In the story, a prisoner is tied down while a pendulum with a sharp blade slowly descends. If he does not act, he will be killed. When the pendulum has about 12 swings left, the prisoner creates a plan for escape and implements it. Students are

asked to determine whether the prisoner would have enough time to escape. To resolve the problem, students construct pendulums and conduct experiments to find out what variables determine the length of the period of a pendulum, and what the relationship is between the period and these variables. The students are introduced to the normal distribution curve and the concept of standard deviation as tools to determine whether a change in one variable affects other variables. The students make and refine conjectures, analyze data, and use graphing calculators to learn about quadratic equations and to explore curve fitting. After deriving a theoretical answer to the problem, the students build a 30 foot pendulum to test the theory" (Interactive Mathematics Program, 1994, pp. 3–4).

Some high schools, such as Grant High School in Portland, Oregon, give students a choice of the classical mathematics sequence or IMP. A recently conducted research study by the Center for Education Research at the University of Wisconsin, Madison, found that students who completed the IMP sequence did better on the quantitative section of the SAT than students who followed a traditional mathematics sequence. (Interactive Mathematics Program, 1994)

STS was recommended by a panel of the National Science Foundation (NSF) in 1983. Rather than a specific curriculum, STS is an approach to the teaching of science that acknowledges that science and technology are interwoven into current economic, political, and ethical problems. Traditional science is linked to problems of the everyday world. The textbook, *Logical Reasoning in Science and Technology* (1991) presents scientific facts in biology, chemistry and physics in a way that connects those facts with real-life problems. The book begins with the societal problem of drinking and driving and presents court cases in which contradictory testimony arises concerning the technology of breathalyzer testing. The social issue of drinking and driving creates a need to know: (a) the rules used when arguing over scientific evidence; (b) how science and technology interact with various aspects of society; (c) the technology of the breathalyzer; and (d) scientific content such as mixtures, concentration, chemical reactions, photometry, electrical circuits, and the biology of body cells and systems (Aikenhead, 1992).

The goal of STS is a scientifically and technologically literate citizenry. Learning science for its own sake or to perceive the world through the eyes of the biologist, chemist, or physicist may work well for a part of the student population, but it hardly impacts all students in a positive way. During the period of Biological Sciences Curriculum Study (BSCS) Biology, Chem Study, Chem Bond, and Physical Science Study Committee (PSSC) Physics, courses like "kitchen chemistry" and "shirt-sleeves physics" were offered as options for the non–college-bound student. The STS approach seems to expand the concept of practical science so that all students can learn together and see science as a means to understand the day-to-day world and improve their quality of life.

The Scope, Sequence and Coordination (SS&C) initiative of the National Science Teachers Association (1990) inspired the science faculty at South Gate High School in Los Angeles, California, to restructure the science curricula. Now, instead of the traditional cake-layer curriculum of earth science, biology, chemistry, and physics, students take a slice of each science each year. Coordination of the traditional sciences is accomplished by focusing on themes common to at least two sciences. Patterns of change is a theme integral to all sciences. Chemistry, biology, earth science, and physics all deal with patterns of change. Some changes are steady, some cyclical, and some irregular. Steady change involves the acceleration of falling objects (physics), radioactive decay (geology and physics) and growth of new island ecologies (biology). Cyclical changes include life cycles (biology), seasonal cycles, planetary cycles, water cycles, rock cycles, and plate movement (the earth sciences of astronomy, meteorology, and geology). Irregular cycles include the unpredictability of systems caused by random changes never repeated exactly, such as population cycles (Brunkhorst, 1991, p. 37). Systems, models, constancy, evolution, and scale are others suggested by Project 2061 (American Association for the Advancement of Science, 1989).

The science department at Santa Ana High School in Santa Ana, California, received a grant from the SS&C project to work with teachers in their feeder middle school to restructure the science curriculum for grades seven through twelve. They have begun the process of integrating the content of earth science, biology, chemistry, and physics. A new course, SS&C Biophysical Science, combines the life sciences and the physical sciences and is required for ninth- and tenth-grade students. It also aligns with the science curriculum in grades seven and eight. The content has been sequenced to cover concrete and descriptive topics during the early years, and theoretical and abstract topics during the later years (Atchley, 1993). Integrated science, though not a new idea (see the work of Victor Showalter in fused or correlated science during the 1970s), recognizes that the traditional sequence often bypasses large numbers of students who never get to chemistry or physics, and even those who do complete their study of biology in grade nine or ten do not encounter it again until they enter a university.

Integrated science is a two-year foundation program at Littleton High School in Littleton, Colorado, that introduces students to an integrated study of life science, physical science and earth science. It is organized around four themes: change, interactions, energy, and patterns. The culminating activity of the second year is a self-directed experiment. Working in teams or individually, students design, implement, interpret, and analyze an experiment of their choice.

WRITING ACROSS THE CURRICULUM

Writing is a form of human expression, and each subject in the curriculum offers students unique opportunities to express their ideas, perceptions, insights, and feelings in different ways. Formerly writing was thought to be the province of the English teachers. In social studies or science classes, students' ideas were more important than their grammar and syntax. There was little reason or opportunity to write in mathematics, physical education, the arts, or foreign language courses. Today this notion has been replaced by one that views the improvement of writing as every teacher's responsibility.

Early (1992) has refined what has been learned about writing and the teaching of writing to a few key propositions: (1) Students cannot develop ease in writing unless they write frequently; (2) students often discover what they know or don't know about a topic when they attempt to put that knowledge in writing; and

(3) students write differently—use different processes—depending on what they are writing. She concludes, "Since writing is a way of learning, a way of knowing, students should use it frequently in all disciplines where they are expected to assimilate ideas and make them their own" (p. 92).

Teachers at Barrington High School in Barrington, Illinois, have probably done more to generalize writing to all subjects in the curriculum than most high schools. They have presented their writing assessment program at the annual convention of the National Council of Teachers of English and at a regional meeting of the College Board. Their students have won numerous awards for the quality of their writing. At nearby Waukegan High School in Waukegan, Illinois, the English department teaches writing techniques, format, and mechanics. The social studies department assigns essays and shares errors or problems with the English teachers so that they might be corrected in the classes in which they occur. Grades are given in all writing assignments for themes, content and mechanics.

In the science classes at Minot High School in Minot, South Dakota, students explain principles, write reflections on environmental issues, and research biographies of scientists. Mathematics teachers at James Bowie High School in Austin, Texas, require students to explain in writing how they arrived at a solution to a problem. Students also complete logic problems and write expository essays on logic. The idea of students maintaining a mathematics journal has been accepted widely at the elementary and middle school levels. It would appear to be a logical step for high school mathematics teachers. The spread of writing across the curriculum may be slow. It is facilitated when it is encouraged by the culture of a school, and when opportunities to learn how to include writing in all areas of the curriculum are available.

LEARNING TO USE THE MIND WELL

Higher-order thinking appears in the goals and objectives of most if not all curriculum reform efforts. The Charlottesville Summit in 1989, convened by President Bush and attended by the governors of all 50 states, recommended that "every school in America will ensure that all students learn to use their minds well." In the aftermath of the Summit, higher-order thinking skills became an important ingredient for all students.

What does "use their minds well" really mean? Keefe's (1992) model of a continuum of thinking may provide an answer. He places thinking on a continuum of information processing beginning with cognitive skills (controls) and advancing through "learning to learn," content thinking, and reflective reasoning. The cognitive skills include analysis, focusing, categorizing, short-term memory, spatial reasoning, simultaneous processing, and sequential processing, and are the basics of higher-order thinking. Weaknesses in any of the skills limit access to higher-order thinking. Fortunately, the limitations can be overcome by practice. Keefe recommends that every high school employ a cognitive resource teacher and create a cognitive skills center where weaknesses are addressed. The cognitive skills center would be similar to a reading resource center. Students would be assigned to the center for one to two hours per week depending upon the nature and severity of their weaknesses and the flexibility of the overall school schedule.

Learning to learn involves applying the cognitive skills to the solution of real or simulated problems. Students must be helped to apply the skills to different situations. They will not do this on their own. Content thinking involves all teachers. It suggests the application of the skills to the formation of concepts and principles in a given subject area. It signifies synthesizing disparate bits of information and grasping big ideas. Students can integrate thinking skills in content areas when curriculum and instruction emphasize these skills.

Reflective reasoning is the highest form of thinking. It is usually the territory of advanced placement courses and gifted programs. In reality, however, such thinking need not be exclusive if Keefe's continuum is followed. This model makes such behavior as detecting bias, identifying points of view, identifying unstated assumptions, and determining the logic of an argument possible for all students. It is probable that students will have differing skill levels in each area of the continuum. For example, a student may have strong analytic skills and weak focusing skills, average learning-to-learn skills, very weak content application skills, and (because of his or her strength in analysis) good higher-order skills. Usually, however, a student's strength at the preceding level influences his or her strength at subsequent levels positively or negatively.

Thinking is often introduced into the curriculum through course content. Problem identification and problem solving require thought. When included in specific course content, thinking is commonly done without considering the prerequisite skills. Consequently, students are confined or challenged accordingly. In some cases, high schools adopt commercial programs to teach thinking. "Tactics in Thinking," "Cort," and "Cognetics" offer exciting possibilities for students. All have value, but like any course content, they impact each student differentially. The continuum of thinking offers a framework for developing strategies to incorporate a variety of approaches in a high school setting.

The Application of Knowledge and Skills

School to Work Transitions

The face of vocational education is changing. No longer are vocational courses for the non–college-bound student. In fact, some work-based programs combine the last two years of high school with two years at a community college. Closer connections between school- and work-based learning is taking place and redefining the relationship of the business community with the school community. Programs that were once located in area vocational schools are being transferred to high school magnet sites, and include job shadowing experiences and apprenticeships. Entering students in many high schools are being asked to select a career cluster to guide their program planning. At Lake Region High School in Polk County, Florida, all students choose a career cluster and are required to enroll in three courses related to the career choice prior to graduation. During ninth grade the students enroll in a wheel that includes a nine-week segment entitled "Career Research and Development." A career interest survey, *Florida View Interest Survey,* is administered to all students. The results are interpreted by a paraprofessional specially trained in the instrument with assistance from the teacher and the ninth-grade counselor. The counselor then works with the students for approximately eight days to help transform the students' interests into possible career choices. These tentative career choices are the basis for rethinking their four-year plan cards completed prior to entering the high school, and for choosing courses for the tenth grade. The text and workbook, *Career Choices, A Guide to Teens and Young Adults: Three Big Questions Are Who Am I? What Do I Want? and How Do I Get It?* provides additional information for the students. By the year 2002, all graduates will be required to complete a minimum of 20 hours of a business-related experience.

The changes in vocational/technical education reflect new demands on workers even during their first year on the job. Work in a high-tech, information society requires much more complex skills than were required 20 years ago. According to Gene Bottoms of the Southern Regional Education Board (1993), all modern workers need the following skills: (1) the ability to read, write, and use math to solve multi-step problems; (2) the capacity to apply knowledge from many disciplines to solving problems; (3) a broad academic and technical knowledge base and the good judgment to know when to use it and whether it has been used correctly; (4) creative and problem-solving skills associated with producing a variety of quality products; and (5) the organizational and communication skills necessary to work as a team member. These skills reinforce the findings of the Secretary of Labor's Commission on Achieving Necessary Skills (1991), popularly known as the SCANS Report. This report identified five basic competencies needed for successful job performance. They included working with others, allocating resources, acquiring and evaluating information, understanding systems, and using appropriate technology effectively. The Commission felt that the competencies must be built on the foundation of a sound academic education and the ability to apply higher-order thinking skills (The Secretary's Commission on Achieving Necessary Skills, 1991).

Youth Apprenticeships

Adapted from the highly successful German school-to-work system and given impetus by the National Youth Apprenticeship Act of 1992, this activity blends academic, technical, and worksite learning. Most apprenticeship programs last four years and combine high school with technical or community college. Students are paid while they study and learn. When students complete the program, it is expected that they will be ready for productive employment. There are essentially two models of the youth apprenticeship—the class-sized model, in which an entire class of students studies the same curriculum and is assigned to a common on-the-job training site; and a modified cooperative education program, in which individual students are placed at a variety of different work sites (Bottoms, 1993).

Craftsmanship 2000, based in Tulsa, Oklahoma, prepares students for jobs in the metalworking industry. The students become employees of Craftsmanship 2000, a nonprofit corporation. They commit to an 8-hour day, 47 weeks a year. In addition, they must complete a demanding academic and technical education. The academic program embraces four years of English/language arts, Algebra I and II, biology, applied physics, and applied chemistry. The program begins in the eleventh grade and continues through two years at Tulsa Junior College (Bottoms, 1993).

Alabama's Technology Plus Program connects academic and technical programs in high school with apprenticeship programs in industry. High school students in grades ten or eleven who have completed one year or more of technical training and who successfully pass Algebra I or higher can participate as student apprentices during their senior years. Each week students work 20 hours, which apply toward their total apprenticeship training program. After graduation, students are expected to enter a full-time apprenticeship program leading to a journeyman certificate. Individual placements in over 46 different occupations and 143 different companies have been achieved. Occupations include electronics engineer, computer technician, welder, dental assistant, nursing assistant, and auto body technician (Bottoms, 1993).

New Organizations

A number of high schools have adopted an academy model in which a large school is divided into several smaller ones, each with a career focus. Patterson High School in Baltimore, Maryland, has four career-oriented academies for 2,100 students—sports studies and health wellness, arts and humanities, transportation and engineering technology, and business finance. Students select one of the four academies after completing the academy exclusively for ninth graders. Johns Hopkins University researchers have noted that since the advent of the academies school attendance has increased, tardiness and vandalism have decreased, and students report that they are more focused on their academic studies (Viadero, 1996). The Cambridge Rindge and Latin School in Cambridge, Massachusetts, has six houses or academies for 2,200 students. The Fenway Middle College High School in Boston, Massachusetts, has three houses—pre-pharmacy, children's hospital, and crossroads house—to correspond with collaborative partnerships that connect school and work. South Miami Senior High School offers five different academies—the center for media arts, visual/performing arts, business and technology, an at-risk center, and liberal arts and sciences. These academies serve a multicultural student population composed of 74 percent Hispanics, 13 percent African-Americans, 12 percent Caucasians and 1 percent Asians.

Magnet schools were originally developed as an alternative strategy for desegregating schools. Academic magnets have gained in popularity. The International Baccalaureate is probably the best known. Other magnet schools, like Thomas Jefferson High School for Science and Technology in Fairfax County, Virginia, have focused on science and technology. This school has attracted national and international attention for its sophisticated programs. It has twelve technology laboratories with state-of-the-art equipment, each with a different focus—life science and biotechnology; computer systems; prototyping and engineering; energy systems; television production; computer-assisted design; microelectronics; industrial automation and robotics; microelectronics; chemical analysis; optics and modern physics, and aerospace and geoscience. Seniors complete mentorships in community laboratories. MAST Academy in Miami, Florida, is a magnet for the marine industries of South Florida. It is one of 56 magnet schools in the Dade County School System. At MAST students select one of three major fields of study: maritime studies and culture, oceanic and atmosphere technology, a maritime hospitality, and industry operations. The Valley High School Magnet Career Academy prepares students for careers in environmental and energy control, conservation, and preservation. As a capstone project, the students at Valley must demonstrate the capacity to engage in extended, in-depth work. Fairdale High School in Fairdale, Kentucky, is a public safety magnet. The school provides work-based learning and internships in fire science, law enforcement, legal/medical office technology, and radio/electronics communication.

The California Partnership Academies specialize in preparing students for jobs in business technology, electronics, health, print and media, hospitality, and agribusiness. They offer students who have dropped out or failed a second chance for success.

Applied Academics

One of the main differences between the newer vocational programs and older ones is the emphasis on academic studies. Students enrolled in vocational courses are no longer sentenced to less challenging content than their college-bound cohorts. Applied communications, applied algebra, and applied biology are course titles in the curriculum bulletin at Coloma High School in Coloma, Michigan. The content of applied communications includes report writing, expository writing, resume writing and memo writing. Applied algebra includes 36 modules prepared to help vocational students learn how algebra is used in the workplace. At the Area Vocational–Technical School in Drumright, Oklahoma, students take an applied physics course, Principles of Technology, that includes robotics, electronics, automation, commercial electricity, air conditioning, computer repair, and auto mechanics. The Thomas Haney Secondary Centre in Maple Ridge, British Columbia, requires all students to complete a core set of learning guides in technology. Applied academics help students learn content and skills in the context in which they are relevant. Although they originated as part of the new vocational education, they are just as appropriate for students who plan to attend a four-year university.

Projects and Exhibitions

These two curriculum innovations are gaining support as ways for students to demonstrate what they know. Projects are usually completed independently and are discipline- or multidiscipline-based. For example, at the Cabot School in Cabot, Maine, the senior project combines rigorous research built around a thesis of the student's choice, with related community service, career shadowing, an internship, and a senior symposium. Seniors at MAST Academy in Miami, Florida have a choice between completing a community internship or enrolling in a group research course, Thesis Production. The students select a topic, assign responsibilities based on interest, and complete a class project focused on a marine theme or problem. For example, the project for one school year was shipwrecks in the waters of South Florida. The students actually participated in a dive to explore a shipwreck off of Islamorada in the upper Keys.

Suncoast Community High school in Riviera Beach, Florida, requires a written thesis for graduation, while Crestline High School in Crestline, Ohio, emphasizes applications of knowledge by having culminating projects in each course that require students to demonstrate real-life applications.

The exhibition is a term often associated with high schools affiliated with the Coalition of Essential Schools (COE). Exhibitions are usually tied to a particular course but can cut across disciplines. Both approaches require students to make their knowledge public. The following exhibition was taken from the senior European literature course at Brookline High School in Brookline, Massachusetts.

> Instead of a final examine and project on Dante, you will demonstrate that you can read and understand a Canto from The Inferno which has not been discussed in class. You will present your Canto to a panel of three outside judges: one peer who is not taking the course, one adult from out of the school, and one adult from within the school. Your exhibition must include a brief check that your classmates have read the Canto you are presenting. Next, each of you will read aloud to the class a paper that you have written about the Canto on a subject of your choice. Finally, you will teach the class a major concept in the Canto (Podl & Metzger, 1992).

Note that the exhibition is structured. It gives specific directions to the students. They must apply what they have learned from the teacher's presentation of the first half of *The Inferno*. The assessment is built into the natural flow of the class rather than being an appendage at the end. It consummates the learning by requiring students to use what they have learned previously in a new and interesting way. In some respects, the exhibition is a distant relative of the merit badge system used in scouting.

Both projects and exhibitions often require a rethinking of curriculum and time. Compressing the curriculum is one way to find time for students. Central Park East High School students complete the regular curriculum at the end of the traditional grade ten. Their last two years are devoted to the Senior Institute, which serves as transition to the adult world. The school offers a variety of courses within the guidelines of the core requirements. Students participate in a work-related internship, and take at least two courses on a college campus. They also spend considerable time with a teacher-adviser who guides them through the experiences and assists with the preparation of their fourteen portfolios. Students at the Cabot School also complete the core curriculum by grade ten. The grade eleven and twelve experience is devoted to synthesis courses, which focus on real-life problems, vocational choice, and thematic interdisciplinary projects. Allowing students to complete the standard curriculum at their own pace is another way to compress the curriculum, thus freeing students to pursue more challenging work. Eaglecrest High School in Aurora, Colorado, allows students to test out of units or move more quickly so that they can work on projects.

Curriculum, like all learning, is cumulative. Reform at the high school level must be inextricably linked to other parts of the system. Quick fixes may be food for the daily newspaper and the television special, but they are hardly the remedy for a system in need of remediation. The promise of the efforts to define national standards depend on the acknowledgment that educational experiences K-12 are connected. What has been learned previously impacts the quality of present learning directly. Hence, the assessment of learning at grade ten or twelve is really an assessment of the entire educational system. Until the necessary reform of the pre-high school curriculum is in place, specific curriculum reform can soften the impact.

SUMMARY

High school curriculum is undergoing a period of significant change spurred by factors including recommendations from educational reform commissions, legislative actions, and global economic competition. Major areas of emphasis in this curriculum reform include higher expectations for student learning, expanded academic offerings, and efforts to teach higher-order thinking and problem-solving skills to all students. Vocational education programs are no longer dumping grounds for lower-ability students, and magnet schools focus on specific careers or academic areas. Foreign language programs have multiplied, there is an increase in interdisciplinary work, and new assessments of student learning are being used more frequently in today's high schools.

High school curriculum continues to mean different things to different people, and there are many different individuals and groups making decisions that impact it. Typically the pattern is one in which states develop standards for student achievement, and districts are charged with the responsibility of implementing the standards while taking into consideration local conditions. In the final analysis, however, curriculum decision making involves national, state, and local educational agencies and other influential groups.

A major influence on the current nature of high school curriculum is the concept of a core curriculum that focuses on identifying essential leanings in specific academic subjects. Professional associations such as the National Council of Teachers of Mathematics have published standards for all grade levels that outline what mathematics students should know and how students should achieve curricular goals. Standards published by NCTM and other groups are significantly influencing high school curriculum today.

Consideration of values as a part of basic education has taken on new meaning in recent years. A movement toward addressing values and/or character education in the curriculum, which in the recent past would have been rejected as a form of indoctrination, has emerged. Some possible reasons for this change include a growing dissatisfaction with the level of civility in society, a realization that the global village brings diverse groups of people together in new contexts, and a deepening interest in citizenship.

There is also a renewed interest in interdisciplinary curriculum at high schools. This trend is, at least in part, the result of the growing acceptance by educators and other stakeholders of the interrelatedness of the academic disciplines. Models of interdisciplinary curriculum found at high schools today range from the presentation of two disciplines in a block period to the creation of interdisciplinary units with generalized themes that cut across several subject areas. Writing across the curriculum serves as an additional example of curricular change in high schools. In past years, there were few expectations that students would engage in significant writing except in English classes. In recent years, however, teachers of nearly all subjects have been held responsible for improving student writing.

Special emphasis is placed on teaching students higher-order thinking skills in almost all curriculum reform efforts. Educators at schools committed to this goal typically focus on teaching cognitive skills such as analysis, focusing, categorizing, and spatial reasoning. One ultimate goal of such programs is to help students learn how to utilize reflective reasoning (e.g., detecting bias, identifying points of view). These, and other trends discussed in the chapter (e.g., school to work transition programs, new organizational formats, student projects and exhibitions) have caused high school educators and other stakeholders to reexamine the high school curriculum and to search for more effective ways to serve all students effectively. It remains to be seen if these new efforts will permanently alter the traditional high school curriculum.

CONNECTIONS TO OTHER CHAPTERS

New directions in curriculum are only part of the equation for the improvement of high schools. Tougher standards by themselves do not ensure learning. They only establish more challenging tasks. New research in cognitive psychology has all but eradicated the feasibility of a totally behaviorist approach to schooling. Students learn in different ways. It is the task of instruction to diagnose and accommodate the differences. The next chapter looks at new approaches to instruction.

ACTION STEPS

1. Select a subject area from the high school curriculum. Investigate the current status in writing national standards. What organizations are involved? If more than one, how are they alike? How are they different? Consult Marzano and Kendall's (1994) attempt to synthesize standards in several areas. What changes, if any, did they make in the original standards?

2. Investigate the topic of Socratic seminars. Select an essay, story, poem, speech, editorial, etc., for the class to read. Consult *The Performance Assessment Handbook,* Volume I: Portfolios & Socratic Seminars by Bill Johnson (Eye on Education), Chapter 4. Prepare and execute a plan for a Socratic seminar with the class.

3. Investigate the concept of learning expeditions as developed by Expeditionary Outward Bound (http://hugse1.harvard.edu/-elob/); 122 Mount Auburn Street, Cambridge, MA 01218. How are the learning expeditions like exhibitions? How are they different? What are the implications for high school curriculum?

4. Conduct a class debate exploring whether or not the establishment of a national curriculum and a national testing program will improve the quality of high school education throughout the nation.

DISCUSSION QUESTIONS

1. How does the current emphasis on "habits of mind" associated with a given discipline differ from the programs of the late 1950s and 1960s? (For example, SMSG Mathematics, BSCS Biology, Chem Study, Chem Bond, and PSSC Physics)

2. What are some strengths and shortcomings of the current "School-to-Work" initiative? How is the current status of vocational education different from previous vocational programs?

3. Discuss the feasibility of portfolio graduation requirements in all high schools. How do you predict colleges and universities will respond to such a change?

4. How is the concept of students completing exhibitions connected with the trend toward alternate forms of assessment?

5. What are some drawbacks of implementing a writing-across-the-curriculum program? What are some of the advantages?

6. What kinds of experiences would you include in a high school curriculum to enable all students to develop higher-order thinking skills? What are the implications of Keefe's continuum of thinking?

REFERENCES

Adler, M. (1982). *The Paideia proposals: An educational manifesto*. New York: Macmillan.

Aikenhead, G. (1992, Winter). The integration of STS into science education. *Theory into Practice, 31* (1), 27–33.

American Association for the Advancement of Science (1989). *Science for all Americans*. Washington, DC: Author.

Archbald, D. A., & F. M. Newmann. (1988). *Beyond standardized testing*. Reston, VA: National Association of Secondary School Principals.

Atchley, D. (1993). Curriculum reform in California. *The Science Teacher,* 60: (4), 37–39, April.

Bennett, W. J. (1993). *The Book of Virtues*. New York: Simon and Schuster.

Bottoms, G. (1993). *Redesigning and Refocusing High School Vocational Studies: Blending Academic and Vocational Education, Connecting the School Site to The Worksite, and Linking Secondary and Post Secondary Education*. Atlanta, GA: Southern Regional Education Board.

Breaking ranks: Changing an American institution. (1996). Reston, VA: National Association of Secondary School Principals.

Brunkhorst, B. (1991). Every science, every year. *Eductional Leadership, 49* (2), 36–38.

Brunkhorst, B. (1991). The national science teachers association and geoscience education. *Journal of Geological Education. 39,* 108–110.

Darling-Hammond, L., & Ancess, J. (1994). *Graduation by portfolio at Central Park East Secondary School.* New York: NCREST.

Diegmueller, K. (1995, November 22). 14-State reform project releases draft standards. *Education Week, 15* (12), 1, 6.

Diegmueller, K. (1996, April 10). History center shares new set of standards. *Education Week. 15*(29), 1, 14, 31.

Early, M. (1992). Can we move writing across the curriculum? In J. M. Jenkins, & Tanner, D. (eds). *Restructuring for an interdisciplinary curriculum.* Reston, VA: National Association of Secondary School Principals.

Gardner, H., & Boix-Mansilla, V. (1994). Teaching for understanding in the disciplines-and beyond, *Teachers College Record. 96,* Winter.

Holden, J., & K. Bunte. (1995, January) Activating student voices: The Padeia seminar in the social studies classroom, *Social Education. 59* (1), 8–10.

Interactive Mathematics Program (1994). *A Core High School Mathematics Curriculum.* Emeryville, CA: Author.

Interactive Mathematics Program (1995, Spring). Wisconsin center for education research five-year evaluation: An outline. *Evaluation Update. 1,* 1–4.

Jenkins, J. M. (1994). Thomas Haney Centre: A school for all seasons, In Jenkins, J. M., Louis, K. S., Walberg, H. J, & Keefe, J. W. *World class schools: An evolving concept.* Reston, VA: National Association of Secondary School Principals.

Keefe, J. W. (1992). Thinking about the thinking movement. In Keefe, J. W., & Walberg, H. J. (eds). *Teaching for thinking.* Reston, VA: National Association of Secondary School Principals.

Kendall, J. S., & R. J. Marzano (1994). *The systematic identification and articulation of content standards and benchmarks.* Aurora, CO: MCREL.

National Assessment of Educational Progress Science Consensus Project. (1993). *Science Assessment and Exercise Specifications for the 1994 National Assessment of Educational Progress.* Washington, DC: National Assessment Governing Board.

National Association for Sport and Physical Education. (1992). *Outcomes of quality physical education programs.* Reston, VA: Author.

National Committee on Science Education Standards and Assessment. (1993). *National science education standards: An enhanced sampler.* Washington, DC: National Research Council.

National Council of Teachers of Mathematics (1989). *Curriculum and evaluation standards for school mathematics.* Reston, VA: Author.

National Science Teachers Association (1993). *Scope, sequence, and coordination of secondary school science, The content core: A guide for designers.* Vol. 1, Washington, DC: Author.

Peshkin, A. (1985–86). God's choice: The total world of a fundamentalist Christian school. *Educational Leadership. 43* (4), 36–41.

Podl, J. B., & Metzger, M. (1992). *Anatomy of an exhibition.* Providence, RI: Coalition of Essential Schools.

Reich, R. (1991). *The work of nations.* New York: Alfred Knopf.

Rutherford, E. J., & Ahlgren, A. (1990). *Science for all Americans.* New York: Oxford University Press.

Smagorinsky, P. (1996). *Standards in practice grades 9–12*. Urbana, IL: National Council of Teachers of English.

The Secretary's Commission of Achieving Necessary Skills (1991). *What work requires of schools: A SCANS report for America 2000*. Washington, DC: U.S. Department of Labor.

Vessels, G. G., & Boyd, S. M. (1996). Public and constitutional support of character education. *NASSP Bulletin, 80* (579), 55–62.

Viadero, D. (1996, June 12). Environmental studies. *Education Week*.

Westerberg, T., Thomas, R., & Stein, T. (1994). Littleton high school: Direction 2000—rethinking the American high school. In Jenkins, J. M., Louis, K. S., Walberg, H. J., & Keefe, J. W. *World class schools: An evolving concept*. Reston, VA: National Association of Secondary School Principals.

Wynne, E. A. (1985–86). The great tradition in education: Transmitting moral values. *Educational Leadership, 43* (4), 4–9.

3

New Directions
For Instruction

What You Will Learn in This Chapter

Strategies to modify traditional teacher-directed, whole-class instruction in response to increasing student diversity and schedule changes that provide teachers with longer blocks of class time.

The basic technique of thematic unit planning.

Where to begin with cooperative learning.

An overview of two effective but little-used methods: case study teaching and simulations.

A bird's eye view of other major methods for differentiating instruction and teaching in the long block schedule: mastery learning, independent study, learning centers, learning activity packs, and the workshop approach.

Teachers will know and be able to use a variety of strategies and settings that identify and accommodate individual learning styles and engage students.

Teachers will be adept at acting as coaches and as facilitators of learning to promote more active involvement of students in their own learning.

Teachers will teach in ways that help students to develop into competent problem solvers and critical thinkers.

Teachers will convey a sense of caring to their students so that their students feel that their teachers share a stake in their learning.

Teachers will integrate assessment into instruction so that assessment does not merely measure students, but becomes part of the learning process itself

—*Breaking Ranks*, p. 21

Today's high school teachers face many challenges: student misbehavior and lack of motivation; angry parents; declining resources; an overflowing curriculum; crowded classrooms; increasing diversity in the student body; and the challenge of planning and teaching in the much longer periods of the block schedule. But instructors in contemporary high school classrooms must respond effectively to the public's demands for higher achievement, in spite of the many circumstances that make this difficult. Increasingly, as the popularity of the long block schedule sweeps across America, high school teachers must respond to these challenges in the context of a much different and more complex daily schedule. This chapter profiles instructional strategies that will help teachers raise the level of academic achievement in their classes, while simultaneously attending to the increasing diversity of the students and an entirely new time frame.

MODIFYING TRADITIONAL TEACHER-DIRECTED WHOLE-CLASS INSTRUCTION

Modifying Traditional Instruction in Response to the Long Block Schedule

Teaching strategies in many high school classrooms are not likely to be transformed overnight, in spite of the challenges teachers there constantly face. Instead, many teachers will probably continue to use whole-class, teacher-directed instruction until time and training make it possible for them to use new techniques with ease and confidence. So it is in the best interests of high school students that their teachers be encouraged to modify those traditional strategies.

One highly regarded researcher who has studied effective teachers for many years, Barak Rosenshine (1987), recommended an ideal sequence for active teaching in high-achieving classrooms. This sequence is probably used by effective teachers most often, even when they are teaching in a block schedule. According to Rosenshine, research on increasing academic achievement suggests that regardless of the subject matter or the length of the class, an effective teacher tends to begin any lesson by outlining the content and making motivational comments about its importance and relevance in the lives of the students. Throughout the lesson, whatever the content or method being used to teach it, the teacher repeatedly calls attention to main ideas and summarizes sub-parts of the lesson.

In the new long block schedule, a teacher's presentation might move, according to Rosenshine's format, in the following six-step cycle. Each step in the process should last from 15 to 20 minutes:

First, the teacher calls the class to order, reviews the previous work or lesson, collects and quickly reviews the homework with the class, and re-teaches, if necessary, as time permits.

Second, the teacher presents the new content, or introduces it through another teaching strategy such as a student presentation, video, or other method. The teacher phases in the new material so that it dovetails well with what has been learned. If the new content is presented through teacher-directed whole-class instruction, the teaching occurs in small, rapid steps, with detailed and redundant explanations.

Third, the teacher engages the class in guided practice and checking for understanding through careful questioning. This is the time for a small group activity, an application problem, or other similar tactics.

Fourth, after the period of guided practice, the teacher again engages in re-teaching if it is necessary, and it often is. The concept or skill is reviewed and re-explained, and student mistakes or misunderstandings are corrected. Within the constraints of time, the teacher sticks with it until the largest portion of the class is firm, with a success rate of at least 80% in answering the teacher's questions.

Fifth, when the teacher is certain that the new material has been grasped by the largest group of the class, the students are placed in an independent practice phase. High school students call this homework. Automaticity, or over-learning, is the objective of this phase of the lesson. Although this seatwork time may seem to be an easy time for the teacher, the effective high school teacher realizes that this is a very important, and equally vulnerable, activity, with almost guaranteed losses in student attention and engaged learning unless it is carefully structured and closely monitored.

Independent practice via seatwork appears to be the most common instructional strategy that American high school students experience, especially in the new long block schedule; it must be conducted carefully if academic achievement is not to suffer. Simply extending the amount of independent practice to take up the time offered by new long block schedules would be highly inappropriate.

Sixth, following the independent practice, the teacher pulls the class back to a single focus for a brief review each day; major reviews are repeated at weekly and monthly intervals as well. Any additional homework is then assigned.

Total-class instruction of this type has always been and may always be a mainstay of high school teaching; it remains particularly appropriate when the focus is academic achievement in basic content or skills, especially with lower achieving and more dependent students. For teachers and administrators interested in raising standardized test scores, teacher-directed total-class instruction of a fairly traditional nature is often superior to either discovery approaches, traditional small group teaching, or individualized instruction as it may have been practiced in schools of the 1990s. In 1979, Jere Brophy summarized the effective process of total-class, teacher-directed instruction; research in the 1980s and 1990s adds little to his conclusions at that time:

> The instruction that seems most efficient involves the teacher working with the whole class . . . Presenting information in lectures/demonstrations and then following up with recitations or practice exercises in which the students get opportunities to make responses and get corrective feed back. The teacher maintains an

academic focus, keeping the students involved in a lesson or engaged in seatwork, monitoring their performance and providing individualized feedback. The pace is rapid in the sense that the class moves efficiently through the curriculum as a whole (and through the successive objectives of any given lesson), but progress from one objective to the next involves very small, easy steps. Success rates in answering teacher questions during lessons are high (about 75 percent), and success rates on assignments designed to be done independently are very high (approaching 100 percent) (Brophy, 1979, p. 34).

Because it is so important, we repeat that unmodified teacher-directed whole-class instruction is not preferred over other methods for the high school classrooms of the new century. Teacher-directed instruction is an important part of every high school teacher's repertoire, but it should not be the only, or ideally even the main, arrow in the instructional quiver. It is likely, however, that traditional teacher-directed instruction can be conducted more effectively, without the need to race that teachers often feel. Teachers in the block schedule can move through the cycle with confidence, certainty, and at a reasonable pace for both teachers and learners.

MODIFYING TRADITIONAL INSTRUCTION TO ACCOUNT FOR GROWING STUDENT DIVERSITY

At the beginning of a school year many high school teachers discover that achievement levels in a single classroom range across as many as four to five or more grade levels no matter how carefully grouped the students have been. As the students grow older, achievement gaps increase, so that by the time the students get to the high school level, the differences are truly substantial.

In the best possible situations, the teacher may be able to meet a wide variety of needs, interests, learning styles, and achievement, but in the real world of many high school classrooms, the teacher-student ratio makes such individualized instruction either difficult or impossible. Under these circumstances, many teachers find that the traditional model of direct whole-class instruction is the most efficient, practical, and comfortable. But in many classrooms, especially those without tracking, large group instruction may be boring and unchallenging for some of the students, and at the same time too difficult for others in the same class.

Here, then, is a dilemma faced by many high school teachers, not just by those who might be called experts. Individualized instruction or other models of instruction may be so complex and time-consuming to design, and so many necessary materials may be unavailable, that even an expert teacher may become discouraged. Then, too, not every teacher is capable of managing alternative methods easily; such models may require exceptional skill, energy, and talent to conduct successfully. But the traditional whole-class approach used without any modifications may leave many students, and the teacher, unsatisfied.

What is a teacher to do? Given a sizable group of students with some degree of heterogeneity, the usual limited resources and assistance, and only a human level of energy and time, is there any hope of achieving success? Here again, the research on the practices of many expert teachers who face similar situations does give some reason for optimism. Although there are no perfect solutions in the real world, research tells us that many effective teachers, when faced with these situations, attempt to differentiate instruction in similar ways.

First: Preassessment

Teachers who respond flexibly to varying needs and abilities in the classroom assess entering students' achievement levels and learning styles. They anticipate that some students will not need to participate in every learning activity, whereas others may need extra time to master basic concepts or skills.

Second: Flexible Classroom Systems

Expert teachers design their classroom systems with diversity in mind. They plan the seating carefully, so that classroom physical arrangements do not represent ability groups. They design and use flexible grading systems and assignments that do not overemphasize competition between students. They opt instead for systems that stress individual student progress toward a set of objectives, rather than comparison with other students. The normal curve may be abandoned. The teacher may establish a system of peer tutoring or student team learning that encourages learners to assist each other. The teacher uses achievement-based subgroups, but only temporarily, such as after a test, or in restricted situations such as vocabulary.

Third: Compacting

They design lessons to reach the greatest number of students in the class, using a direct whole-class model. However, they also plan ways to adapt that direct whole-class instructional model to fit a diverse group more effectively. The effective teacher may use what has come to be called "curriculum compacting" or "curriculum telescoping," a practice of assessing and grouping students for instruction within the class so that those who have already mastered blocks of content are given alternative assignments instead of being expected to sit through lessons they have already learned. This is especially effective with gifted or other high-achieving students. These students may be involved in alternatives like independent study, work in the media center or computer lab, different patterns of recitation, extra credit projects, and so on.

Fourth: Alternative Responses and Assignments

The teacher designs a basic assignment for all students, adding options based on the needs of individual students. High-achieving and lower-achieving students may work on different problems involving the same content or skills; there may be choices in homework and other class assignments, and teachers involve themselves in helping students make choices in line with their interests, styles, and ability levels. The teacher avoids overemphasizing seductively attractive free-time activities that make slower students feel left out or cause them to race through their work to get to the "good stuff."

Working with less successful students, the effective teacher is likely to employ a number of different strategies that are not used with more successful students, and vice versa. The teacher makes certain that less successful students are asked shorter and simpler questions than those asked of high-achieving students during classroom recitation sessions. Focusing on the lower levels of the taxonomy of mental operations is appropriate. Easy questions, in this case, are those that the students are able to answer successfully, 80 to 90 percent of the time.

The teacher works hard to get at least some response from the low-achieving students during class discussion, and may provide clues, prompts, and other encouragement to get students to try. The teacher may rephrase questions for the low-achieving student. He or she may even back up and ask a different question or one that has already been answered. Sometimes a teacher may redirect a question from another student who has answered incorrectly or partially, getting the less successful student to supply the rest of the answer or agree or disagree with the answer the first student provided. It is also possible to establish classroom norms that permit low-achieving students to "call out" answers when they are certain they are correct. The teacher does not give up easily. Nor does the teacher accept silence in exchange for peace.

This is not to say that the teacher treats the lower-achieving high school student unrealistically. The expert teacher will, for example, disagree with a low-achieving student if an incorrect answer is given. As was discussed earlier, the expert teacher will not engage in gratuitous praise that everyone knows is undeserved. He or she will, however, remain warm and friendly, because warmth and friendliness do not have to be earned.

The expert teacher knows that the principle of "wait time," also discussed earlier, is even more crucial with low-achieving students. The teacher is aware that, as foolish as this may sound, sometimes teachers give slower students even less time to think. When a particular class contains a larger group of low-achieving students, the teacher may make a special effort to provide more structure and direction than usual. Instruction moves in smaller steps, and with greater degrees of structure than in other classes, and the teacher uses more examples, explanations, and overt practice.

Fifth: Support Tactics for Slower Students

The teacher takes advantage of every opportunity to provide special attention and help to less successful students. He or she might use limited within-class groupings to accomplish this, or use a differential grading system that considers effort and relative progress as a part of the formula. Limited peer tutoring may be employed. Frequent monitoring of and feedback to all students, but especially those who are having difficulty, is accepted as part of the teacher's responsibility.

Effective high school teachers modify teacher-directed instruction by using strategies that support slower students without holding back more successful ones. Study guides, given to all students at the beginning of a unit or before a test, will help slower students without penalizing the faster learners. Similarly, the use of clear grading rubrics that spell out the teachers' expectations for assignments or projects do not hold back fast learners who always know what the teacher wants. But rubrics that provide a clear "view of the target" may help students who have difficulty understanding exactly what the teacher expects. Effective modification of teacher-directed instruction can also include the use of "graphic organizers" like the ladder, web, or fish bone design that allow slower students to organize the teacher's lecture effectively without adversely affecting more able students.

High school teachers know that a frequent cause of low report card grades is the failure of students, particularly ninth grade students, to complete or turn in homework. The teacher is sure to encourage student participation in class and the completion of assignments. Recent experience with the long block schedule indicates that one of the most important outcomes of the use of such schedules is that students have more time to complete work that would not usually be completed if left until after school.

Sixth: Challenging More Able Students

In the same classroom, but with high-achieving students in mind, the teacher employs other strategies. He or she will choose more difficult questions for these students. An answer from a high-achieving student may be followed with more probing for the best answer rather than just for a correct one. The teacher may use what can be called "positive criticism," explaining that the high-achieving student's answer was correct, but that he or she can do much better. The teacher may ask the student to elaborate upon or justify an answer. Likewise, the teacher uses seatwork, homework, and other assignments to enrich and challenge the high-achieving students in the class. This can mean different assignments, extra work, more challenging work, or more creative opportunities.

Many textbooks and supplementary materials in most subjects offer a wide array of suggestions for different assignments and projects that high-achieving students will find stimulating. Using the class textbook for common assignments, and offering optional assignments from different sources to high-achieving students is particularly effective for many high school teachers. It is also possible to offer high-achieving students special opportunities for leadership.

Seventh: Remember Reviews

Finally, another word about periodic reviews and the extension of learning, one that applies well to both low-achieving and high-achieving students. No matter what the ability levels of the students in the class, the effective high school teacher rehearses for lasting learning by including reviews at every appropriate point in the year. Each day begins with a quick review of the previous day's work. Each week begins with a review of the previous week's work. Every grading period or new unit should begin with a review of the previous period or unit and discussion of how it fits into what is to be studied at this new point. An effective review is not just a quick mention of the preceding work, but an honest attempt to connect what is happening with what has gone before, and an attempt to check for understanding and to reteach to the extent necessary, as time permits.

Nicholas Hobbs, a wise teacher of teachers and an expert teacher himself, wrote long ago that "It is the job of the teacher to precipitate the student into just manageable difficulty." In plain talk this means that regardless of the ability level of the student, the truly expert teacher knows the students so well and plans so carefully that students are asked to stretch to exactly what they are capable of doing—no more, no less. That is personalizing instruction in a way that recognizes the difference between anxiety and challenge. Hobbs understood that students grow best when what they are asked to do matches what they are capable of doing. Our strength increases when we get in deep, but not in over our heads, in any life situation. The expert high school teacher helps students discover their strengths and build upon them this way.

RECOGNIZING THE LIMITATIONS OF TEACHER-DIRECTED INSTRUCTION

Traditional methods of teaching match traditional goals, so when the goal of instruction is to prepare students to perform well on standardized academic achievement tests, the teaching method chosen will often be traditional large-group, teacher-directed instruction. There are, however, many circumstances in which this method of instruction is inappropriate, and in which using traditional methods might actually work against the goals of the lesson. Research on teaching also suggests that teachers have preferred styles of teaching, ways that work best for them, in spite of what might work best for others. Some teachers, therefore, might find that they reach higher levels of time-on-task with their students by using small-group methods or project strategies.

It must also be recognized that when the goal of instruction is not performance on traditional standardized tests, but rather retention of learning beyond the test, or the application of concepts and principles to real-world problems and situations, traditional methods may even hinder learning. Recent research by Brooks & Brooks (1993) suggests that when it is important for the student to remember and apply classroom content, instructional strategies must range far beyond traditional lecture and whole group instruction. Problem-solving strategies, collaborative inquiry, and other techniques that help students make permanent meaning for themselves from what they are learning are the teaching techniques that seem to be more effective.

At Salem High School in Conyers, Georgia, principal Bob Cresswell described the classroom learning environment for which Salem teachers strive:

> Classrooms are student-centered, meaning that students take ownership of their learning. On any given day, one would find classes in which students are working in cooperative groups, preparing exhibitions, debating issues, persuading jurors in mock trials, critically thinking and listening in Socratic seminars, planning portfolio entries, or making presentations in a convention setting. In other words, students are engaged in *active* learning. The teacher serves as facilitator or coach, not a deliverer of facts.

Two other factors also contribute to the need for high school teachers to explore and develop skill in alternatives to the traditional lecture-discussion format. As public high schools become increasingly diverse demographically, it becomes clearer that assuming all students are equally capable of success in a large group lecture setting will produce higher levels of failure and frustration for both teacher and learners. Curriculum tracking, also known as ability grouping, is an increasingly less and less attractive solution to this diversity, because it often leads to inequitable distribution of the school's resources and fosters in-school segregation and isolation of students on the basis of race, ethnicity, or socioeconomic status (Brewer, Rees & Argys, 1995; Oakes, 1985). High school teachers are therefore likely to face increasing pressure to somehow differentiate instruction within more heterogeneous classrooms.

Good high school teachers have always recognized that every student is unique, and deserves and requires special attention and adaptation of the learning experience. As the 21st century approaches, however, teachers are being asked to work with ever more diverse groups of learners. Providing differentiated classroom instruction that responds effectively to this diversity is absolutely essential.

DIFFERENTIATING INSTRUCTION

What is "differentiated instruction?" In this chapter, the term *differentiated instruction* is used to mean the adaptation of classroom strategies to (1) accommodate students' different learning needs so that all students experience challenge and success, and (2) allow teachers and students to teach and learn more effectively and pleasantly in the long block schedule. Differentiated instruction leads to the development of classrooms in which students sometimes work at different paces, on varied tasks, assessed with a variety of indicators appropriate to their interest and needs. Differentiated instruction, then, can involve the alteration of what is taught (content), how it is taught (process), and how it is assessed (products).

The authors of the ASCD program "Challenging the Gifted in the Regular Classroom" argue that differentiated instruction is especially important if able students are to be placed in the heterogeneous classrooms increasingly found in American high schools. Gifted students may otherwise be overlooked in course planning because they are perceived to do well in class, frequently make good grades, and cause few discipline problems. In classrooms where a single curriculum is covered by all learners, however, many of these students may find school restrictive, frustrating, and uninspiring.

In traditional classrooms, some able learners receive good grades with minimal effort and can come to see themselves as impostors who are not really as capable as people believe them to be. Other able learners become addicted to high grades, rather than focusing on learning itself. Many fail to develop study and production skills appropriate for their learning capacities. Others decide that high school is a place to be tolerated and that real learning takes place elsewhere. Some lose interest in developing their abilities altogether. Some cause discipline problems, and as a result, school staff are less likely to perceive these students as highly able.

In classrooms where instruction is appropriately differentiated for learners, able students are more likely to feel challenged, to encounter both struggle and success, to be encouraged to develop advanced study and production skills, and to incorporate their individual interests into the context of the classroom. Differentiating instruction is key to creating learning environments that accommodate the diversity typical of today's high school classroom.

There is an equally compelling reason for differentiating instruction in today's high school classrooms. Many educators are increasingly uncomfortable with what they perceive to be incompatibility of the traditional classroom experience with the needs of tomorrow's citizens, especially those students who should reasonably be expected to assume positions of leadership. The traditional authoritarian classroom may create a culture in which students depend on the teacher for everything, do nothing on their own, and strive to keep up (or back) with the rest of the class.

Unfortunately, this can happen even in many advanced, honors, and gifted classes where the objectives of learning more and learning faster are still out of synch with the needs of students who will be tomorrow's leaders, independent thinkers, researchers, professionals, and artists. Such classrooms can reward conformity when nonconformity may be a more positive outcome. They may reinforce other-directedness when self-direction is the key to increased motivation and a broadened sense of personal and social responsibility.

The final motive for implementing alternative instructional strategies has to do with the knowledge explosion and the information revolution that has accompanied it. All of us are familiar with the impact of both of these on every facet of American life except the classroom. It has been said that if Rip Van Winkle woke up today, one of the few things he would recognize would be the type of teaching going on in today's schools. In the face of an incredible information overload, high school classrooms remain places where many teachers continue to think their primary duty is to provide information by talking.

Theodore Sizer tells the story of a Martian spy sent to learn about high school education on Earth. After spying on many classrooms, the Martian returns home, where the spymaster asks for a succinct report. "American high school classrooms," reveals the Martian spy, "are places where the relatively young sit and watch the relatively old work hard." High school education, argues Sizer, ought to be an experience where the student is the worker. (Sizer, 1992)

There simply is very little reason to continue to support or accept the traditional concept of teaching as primarily the provision of information. High school teachers can and should assume the important new roles of classroom manager and facilitator of learning (Sizer, 1992). Differentiation of instruction becomes an important strategy for achieving new roles and relationships in the classroom. Combine all of these important points with the reality of the long block schedule, and a pressing need to move away from the traditional lecture/discussion model becomes clear.

The widespread popularity of the long block schedule may make the teacher lecture less useful than it once was. When teachers and students are in class together for 85 to 110 minutes or more, it may be physically impossible for teachers to lecture for an entire period, and equally difficult for students to sit still and listen carefully. Clearly, the success of the block schedule is closely tied to the ability of teachers to change the way they teach in those classes; simply lecturing for shorter periods and alternating with seatwork is an insufficient response to the opportunities offered by the new long block schedule. Canady and Rettig make a persuasive case that teacher success and the effectiveness of the block schedule both depend on the capacity of the high school teacher to employ alternatives to traditional whole-class teacher-directed instruction:

> We predict that the single most important factor in determining the success or failure of block scheduling programs will be the degree to which teachers successfully alter instruction to utilize extended time blocks effectively. If instructional practices do not change, the block scheduling movement of the 1990s, like the flexible modular scheduling movement of the 1960s and 1970s, will be buried in the graveyard of failed educational innovations (Canady & Rettig, 1995, p. 22).

But changing one's instructional style is much easier to talk about than it is to do. Many teachers are uncomfortable with total reliance on the traditional teacher-directed, whole-class instructional model, but few teachers have the time, energy, or support to make revolutionary changes in the ways they teach. This is a real professional dilemma. On one hand, educators know that diverse classrooms are best, but that they only work well when all students, including the most able learners, experience challenge and success. Educators also know that few teachers and even fewer learners are satisfied with simply continuing with traditional models in the new long block schedule. On the other hand, educators also know how hard it is to make major changes in teaching strategies or to do a better job of differentiating instruction.

The second section of this chapter focuses on instructional strategies that offer teachers greater opportunities to meet the needs of different learners, adapt to the long block schedule, and respond to recent research on teaching and learning.

ALTERNATIVE INSTRUCTIONAL STRATEGIES FOR THE NEW HIGH SCHOOL CLASSROOM

Planning for Teaching

High school teachers in the field have an important message for teachers who are involved in a move to a new long block schedule. Moving to a block schedule, they say, means that for most teachers it will be necessary to make important decisions regarding *what* will be taught as well as *how*. That is, many teachers have discovered that the move to the long block schedule has meant that there are fewer hours of instruction for each course over the span of a semester or year. Teachers are therefore faced with the need to examine the content of their courses and to prioritize and concentrate the content of their courses in terms of (1) content that is absolutely central and essential to the course; (2) content that would be desirable to include, time permitting, but is not absolutely essential; and (3) content that is primarily enrichment and that cannot reasonably be considered essential in terms of its effect on student achievement or success in future work, school, or life. Teachers who are currently teaching in a block schedule argue that, as difficult as the decision may be, it is absolutely necessary for the teacher to prioritize the content of each course.

Having decided what will be included and what must be excluded in the course curriculum, it is somewhat comforting to learn that there are realistic strategies for creating classrooms where all students are successfully challenged without asking teachers to make impossible changes in their instructional styles along with sacrifices in the content they care about. It should be obvious, however, that each strategy is complex, and it is therefore beyond the capacity of a single chapter to provide readers with even the fundamentals in each case, let alone the requirements for mastery. More than one book has been written about each strategy. Here the authors briefly profile and describe each strategy.

Unit Planning and Teaching

The long block schedule forces teachers to think in terms of more time than what is contained in one traditional class period (Kauchak & Eggen, 1998). In doing so, the teacher thinks in terms of units and curriculum and instruction. A curriculum or teaching unit is a set of knowledge, attitudes, and skills that represents a logical whole, a subset of an entire course. A social studies teacher, for example, might teach a two-week unit on the culture of Japan in a world cultures course; a science teacher might teach a unit on simple machines as a part of an introductory physics course; in English 3, a teacher might offer a unit on modern American poetry; and a computer teacher might teach a unit called *Welcome to the Web* in a basic course on computer literacy. Unit teaching organizes the curriculum into meaningfully structured wholes for teaching and learning.

Units help students see the connections in the curriculum—how it all fits together—rather than presenting students with a seemingly endless series of single, unconnected lessons. An 18-week course might be made up of a series of one, two, and three-week units, or even longer periods, depending upon the importance of the content. Schurr, Thomason, and Thompson (1995, p. 126) describe units this way:

> Learning units are *thematic*. They tie many concepts and skills together around larger, central themes. These themes provide learners with connections and relationships which give meaning to the concepts and skills, being taught, in contrast to the traditional series of lessons strung together with apparently unrelated content. The theme is the thread that holds concepts together to facilitate learning.

The most effective units typically contain a number of common elements. The theme, of course, is the most obvious element, representing an important set of concepts, a vital topic, a significant problem, or other central thesis that draws the separate curriculum elements into a coherent, meaningful whole. Clear objectives or outcomes flow from the central theme or topic of the unit. The best units often seem to begin with an introductory "launching" activity that motivates students to move into the unit; effective units also conclude with a culminating activity that helps students bring closure to their study. Units typically conclude with an assessment of student progress that translates into a grade for that unit; evaluation of the unit itself can also be an important activity.

Learning activities (i.e., instructional strategies) are the heart of any unit, working to bring the students to the point of mastery of the unit's objectives or outcomes. The list of such activities is virtually endless: lectures, videos, independent projects, cooperative learning, field trips, simulations, case studies, debates, research papers and projects—all of the ways from which teachers and students might choose to teach and learn about the content of the unit. Teachers with experience in unit planning and teaching often say that this approach helps them to see the necessity for planning to teach in ways that offer variety and activity to students. Planning a unit that consists of the same teaching methods day after day quickly shouts out its inadequacy. The learning strategies that are described in the remainder of this chapter are all appropriate for adding variety, providing choice, and responding to student diversity in units developed for teaching in the long block schedule.

Unit teaching has a long and popular history in high school education (see, for example, Jackson, 1942; Jones, 1939; Stewart, 1983; Armstrong & Savage, 1998). Virtually every methods textbook in secondary education gives at least some attention to unit planning and teaching. For teachers interested in contemporary applications of unit teaching, numerous examples can be found in university libraries.

Cooperative Learning

Virtually every high school teacher involved in teaching in a long block schedule has investigated the utility of cooperative learning (CL) in his or her classroom. Cooperative learning is "the instructional use of small groups so that students work together to maximize their own and each other's learning" (Johnson, Johnson, and Holubec, 1991, p. 21). Cooperative learning is a generic term for many different techniques of small group instruction, and it is certainly not a new idea, because teachers have been using small groups for learning purposes for many years. Recently, however, CL has undergone a great deal of refinement, and research has confirmed many benefits associated with its correct use. Consequently, it is probably the most discussed teaching method today.

The CL classroom exhibits very different features from the traditional one. The teacher is not always the source of information and knowledge; students work together to discover what they need to know. Instead of eyes front and backs to the rest of the class, students in cooperative learning classrooms are often placed desk to desk, eye to eye, and knee to knee. Students are expected to talk to each other, listen to each other, teach each other, and learn from each other. They make decisions, work with others, discover information important to them, engage in productive talk, and are generally more active in learning. These are classrooms where the students are workers, as Sizer suggests, with teachers often acting as coaches, motivators, assessors, and facilitators rather than purely as sources of information.

Small group work does not always result in effective cooperative learning. Combining the insights of several major cooperative learning theorists (Johnson, Johnson, & Holubec, 1992; Slavin, 1995), reveals some basic elements (beyond what is required in traditional classrooms) involved in most effective cooperative learning situations. Several of them are absolutely critical:

- Students must agree that no one is successful unless all have succeeded.
- Positive interdependence must prevail; individual students should recognize that all students must contribute if the group is to be successful.
- Students must be seated in small groups, not in traditional arrangements.

- There must be individual accountability, without "hitchhikers." Individual performance and achievement must be identified and evaluated.
- Public recognition and reward must be provided for the group success and improvement as well as for individual accomplishments.
- Small groups must be as heterogeneous as the class as a whole.
- Students must be taught to use positive social skills in their interactions.
- Time must be allocated for debriefing and group reflection at the conclusion of a cooperative learning experience.

Of these components, there appear to be two essential elements in all cooperative learning experiences: positive interdependence and individual accountability. Cooperative learning will not work well without groups of students who are committed to a common task, nor will it prosper in classrooms where individual students are not held accountable for their particular efforts and evaluated accordingly. There is also some interesting research (Webb & Farivar, 1994) indicating that cooperative learning works best to raise academic achievement when a condition called "elaborated helping" is in place. When a student simply supplies another student or their group with an answer to a question or provides a solution to a problem, academic achievement is not affected as positively as when students are involved in explaining, teaching, persuading, resolving disagreement, and other forms of interaction that go beyond merely giving someone an answer.

Teachers who are ready to try cooperative learning in their classrooms will discover a series of steps associated with successful implementation:

- Begin with equal measures of humility and determination. Effectiveness comes only after a great deal of practice, as with any difficult endeavor.
- Prepare the students for cooperative learning by discussing why it is important, how it is different, and what they will need to do in order to be successful. Do not "just do it."
- Think big; start small. Begin with some simple cooperative learning structures and practice using those effectively with your students. Try those recommended by Kagan (1994).
- Practice grouping and regrouping in your classes for other purposes (e.g., checking daily homework) so that students get used to the process of moving in and out of groups.
- One at a time, begin teaching the social skills essential to cooperative learning. If you are unwilling to take this time from your other obligations, cooperative learning is probably not a good choice for you.
- Place students in heterogeneous groups, and take time for team building, helping students in each group to get to know each other a little better. Perhaps it will be appropriate for different students to be assigned different roles for their work together.
- Try using a more complex cooperative learning activity (e.g., Jigsaw) regularly in some constant area of your classroom life (e.g., a problem for the day, checking homework, vocabulary work) so that students become more and more familiar with its use.

- At this point it may be time to select and implement a more formal cooperative learning structure like Group Investigation, Pro-Con Coop, STAD or TGT. Study the strategy carefully, make certain that it fits the topic, and ascertain that the students are ready for this step.
- Before moving on to a more complex method, review with students the specific social skills that they will be using, and hopefully improving, in this activity.
- Establish, post, and discuss the modifications in classroom rules and procedures that will be necessary during the cooperative learning exercise.

There are a number of simple cooperative learning exercises to get a teacher started on the right track. We recommend those described by Kagen (1994). When a teacher is ready for the more complex, major cooperative learning structures, several exist that are well-known, carefully researched, and developed to the point that most interested teachers can implement them in their classrooms. Among the major structures, the most popular are:

Jigsaw
Originally developed by Elliot Aronson (1978) and refined by Robert Slavin (1995), Jigsaw uses small groups to divide the labor on learning tasks. It can be either short and simple or complex, covering many hours of class time. In jigsaw, each student develops expertise in an area that is then taught to the other members of his or her home base group or team. It is amenable to virtually every subject area at every level of ability or maturity.

Group Investigation
Sharan and Sharan's (1992) process begins with a provocative, intrinsically motivating central question based in the content of a course (e.g., "What do Americans need to know about Japan in order to develop a permanent, peaceful relationship between our two nations?"). It works best when students have a natural—or at least honest—motivation to pursue the topic. Following the acceptance of a topic, students focus on what they do not yet know about the topic to develop sub-questions. Students form subgroups according to the questions of most interest to them; each student determines, within the subgroup, a subtopic that he or she will investigate. These individual inquiries may last from a few class periods to several weeks. Eventually, the members of each small group reconvene, integrate their findings, and prepare a group report on their subtopic. Presentations are made to the rest of the class. Evaluation of the project and individual assessment conclude the investigation.

Student Teams Achievement Divisions (STAD)
More highly structured than some of the other models, STAD is complex and lengthy, but rewarding for both students and teacher when done effectively (Slavin, 1995). A typical cycle of STAD may be as short as several class periods or as long as a month or more. In STAD, the teacher identifies the learning outcomes, designs heterogeneous small groups, and pretests all students on the unit. The teacher then presents the content in whatever way is desired; following these teacher presentations, students convene in their small groups to make certain that every member of

the group has mastered the content. An assessment of individual learning follows, with individual scores contributing to a group score. Rewards are distributed on the basis of improvement in scores.

Teams–Games–Tournaments (TGT)

TGT is virtually identical to STAD, except that in TGT the assessment comes via a highly structured series of games and tournaments instead of individual quizzes. Instead of preparing each other to do well on a quiz, the members of each small group coach each other prior to the game or tournament that will determine their grades and team recognition. Tournaments are organized so that students at similar levels of achievement will be competing with each other, for the benefit of their heterogeneous home base groups. During tournament time, students leave their home base groups to go to game tables (groups of desks) arranged by prior level of achievement. This mixed ability and multiethnic arrangement is designed and introduced without comment by the teacher. To keep the competition between groups high, it is recommended that students be reorganized so that new, but still roughly equal, groups play games against each other in the next tournament. Elaborate explanations and materials are available from the developers at Johns Hopkins University.

Pro/Con Co-op

David and Roger Johnson believe that students formulate meaning and purpose in their lives, as well as notions of right and wrong, as part of a process of wrestling with controversies that are of deep interest to them. The resolution of controversy requires that students clarify issues, investigate cause and effect, consider advantages and disadvantages, reflect on initial positions they have taken, examine new data and the perspectives of others, take on those perspectives, and propose novel solutions. It is through this process of working with content, rather than just acquiring it, that real learning takes place.

In Pro/Con Co-op, students confront a controversy, problem, or dilemma, and work through to a new or reconceptualized position. Students work in pairs to research one side of an argument or one response to a difficult dilemma. Two pairs then take turns presenting a position to each other, obligated to understand the perspective of the presenting pair. Challenge and critical analysis are a part of the process. Pairs experience further disequilibrium by exchanging positions and taking the stance of their opposition. Then the group of four drops all advocacy and is required to develop a report that synthesizes the best evidence and arguments from both sides; reports are presented to the whole class. Individual assessment follows, through a quiz, essay, or other appropriate mechanism. As always in cooperative learning, debriefing provides closure.

Case Studies and Simulations

Case Study Methodology

A case study is a written document, usually in the form of a story, that describes a situation or predicament confronting the reader, who is called upon to make decisions, solve problems, and recommend or take action. It is a special type of problem-solving technique that requires students to study what could be real events. Case study teaching formally began at Harvard University School of Business half a century ago. The use of case study methodology is one whole-class instruction technique that possesses sufficient freshness and variety to permit both slower and more able learners to profit from its use, and it adapts well to the long block schedule. By now, hundreds of cases have been written for teachers and for the education of teachers.

Case study methodology, like some forms of cooperative learning, works well in diverse, heterogeneous high school classrooms. Cases provide opportunities for the class to learn as a group, but also challenge students who learn at different speeds and on different levels. This method is especially valuable for able high school students, because their status in the class often provides them with many opportunities to have their ideas examined by others, to reflect on their own thinking, to challenge and be challenged, and to practice seeing issues through the eyes of others. Done correctly, case study methodology avoids placing able learners in the role of tutor (Armstrong & Savage, 1998).

According to Wasserman (1994), a leading authority on case method teaching, it involves five phases:

The Case

The best cases (Schurr, Thomason, & Thompson, 1995) have a dramatic, attention-catching beginning, describe events and characters with authentic details, and include provocative ideas or circumstances that make students want to think and argue about them. In studying a case, students analyze details, try to get into the minds of the characters, assess the values involved, forecast consequences of various actions, respond to questions, recommend actions, and make decisions. The best cases present students with a problem focused on a "big idea," leading to a dilemma and forcing a choice between a variety of legitimate solutions to a central problem. Writing cases takes time, but the same case can be updated and used for years.

Study Questions

At the end of each case is a list of study questions that stimulate student thinking at several levels beyond mere recall: application, analysis, synthesis, and evaluation. This thinking results from requiring students to examine ideas, values, concepts, and issues presented in the case. Questions do not ask for the regurgitation of facts, names, or dates—they ask students to apply these data to solve problems and resolve dilemmas.

Small Group Work

Students initially work individually on the case, becoming familiar with the details. Ultimately, however, the value of case studies for all students, regardless of their ability level, comes in the opportunity to discuss their responses to the study questions in small groups. Students must have small group time, says Wassermann (1993, 1994), prior to having the whole class discuss the case. The small group session is preparation for the whole class discussion, giving all students an opportunity to try out ideas in a safer, smaller forum.

Guidelines and rules for small group discussion of case studies are important just as they are with cooperative learning experiences. The social skills that make for good interaction in cooperative learning and case study discussions are similar: six-inch voices, criticizing ideas and not people, listening carefully, paraphrasing prior speakers, and so on.

When students have had little or no practice working in small groups, teachers may find that the students' natural restlessness makes case study methodology difficult at first. Students who come from homes where harmonious interaction and discussion do not exist may be unprepared for this sort of interaction in the classroom. Students from widely varying racial, ethnic, and socioeconomic backgrounds may be apprehensive about working together on a case. Introducing case studies without first establishing the basics of cooperation in the culture of the classroom will lead to frustration, failure, and rejection of case study methodology for reasons that have little to do with the essence of case study teaching itself.

During the small group sessions, the teacher is up, monitoring the classroom, moving in and out of the small groups. The teacher observes the groups for both content and process. Noting the ideas that are discussed and the issues that are raised will help the teacher conduct the whole class discussion. Noting which students are adept at small group work and which are not will help the teacher plan for skill development and regroup students for the next case discussion.

When small group work is effective, substantial academic and affective benefits accrue. Students, especially the most able, learn more when they have the opportunity to wrestle with ideas and construct their own mindsets about important and complex issues. Other benefits include increased racial and inter-ethnic harmony, and improved interpersonal skills.

Debriefing

When each small group has concluded its discussion of the study questions and reached the level of agreement that was possible, or when time available for discussion has expired, the teacher reconvenes the whole class. Debriefing at this level is a critical aspect of case study teaching and should be conducted at two levels: content and process.

The teacher can make or break the case study method during the debriefing process (Wasserman, 1993, 1994). Here, the best teaching is done when the teacher takes the role of facilitator rather than the role of interrogator. Students must feel secure enough to share their thinking with the class and the teacher, not worrying about whether their ideas and feelings will be trod upon by either the teacher or other students. This does not mean, however, that the teacher fails to demand the students' best thinking, or that any and all ideas are accepted equally.

The best whole-class discussions follow some additional guidelines. Perhaps most important, all students must know that their participation will likely be required at some point in the discussion. Teachers must avoid calling on volunteers more than 10 to 15 percent of the time. Involve everyone, but adjust the questions to the ability levels of the students; probe and challenge the most able learners, support and encourage the timid and insecure. Some teachers use a systematic method for calling on students so that they are certain to get beyond volunteers. There are, of course, alternative strategies for bringing the discussion to the whole-class level. The teacher might ask a beginning question of the whole class and conduct the discussion that follows as a group. Alternately, the teacher might ask spokespersons from each small group to present the consensus that each group reached regarding the study questions. Other strategies, such as those suggested by advocates for cooperative learning, can stimulate discussion and student insight. Understanding the significant issues of a case, perceiving the dilemma involved, being aware of the options, and making a logical judgment are the tasks to be accomplished in the large group discussion. Final and unanimous agreement on a case is not only unlikely, it is often undesirable.

The second aspect of the debriefing session focuses on the process as perceived by students and teacher. Here the teacher leads students in an examination of individual and class behaviors, an evaluation of how well they used the essential cognitive and social skills that make case study work rewarding and productive. Students think and talk about how they and their peers might improve their work in the next case study.

Follow-up

In the best situations, the debriefing process will not be the end. Student interest and curiosity will be heightened. Follow-up activities might be conducted by individual students or small groups. Contracts and independent studies are perfect for this activity.

Several authors provide suggestions for the design of effective cases:

- Before you try writing your own, search textbooks and other sources for others already developed for your subject and grade level. These cases can save you the trouble of developing your own, and also help you get a handle on factors such as: how cases begin and end; how long they are; how much background is provided; how they are divided into sections, and so on.
- Select an important piece of your curriculum that you judge to be amenable to the case study format. Write out a story about that content, one that has realistic characters and actions, and ends with a dilemma for the reader.
- Give the characters names that might be fun or interesting. Puns as names can help.
- Be precise about details, rather than offering only generalities. If, for example, the case is about toxic waste, be sure to include the names of chemicals involved. The case must be believable.
- Highlight or underline particularly important details.
- Try to open the case with a sentence or situation that is an attention-grabber.
- Make certain that conflicting opinions can result from examination of the case.

Simulation

Simulation is an instructional strategy that brings simplified elements of the real world into the classroom in the form of models or scaled-down versions of actual or contrived situations. As such, simulation takes the process of experiential learning a giant step beyond the case study. Instead of allowing students to read about and discuss a case involving real or fictional characters and settings, the simulation technique plunges the learner into role playing and game-like group activity. In a simulation, learners play the roles of persons engaged in real-life situations, interact with others, and develop realistic solutions to complex problems.

Like the case study, simulation is valuable in the heterogeneous high school classroom because it challenges and involves able students while they work with others like themselves and also with those who may be less academically gifted. Simulations appeal to able learners because they tap the learner's curiosity, intuition, imagination, insight, enjoyment of competition, and problem-solving abilities. In a simulation, students will have different experiences and perceptions of the same situation, and the teacher can place students in roles according to what the students need to learn.

Almost everyone has taken part in simulations, even if they weren't called simulations at the time. If you played "cops and robbers" or similar games as a child, you have been involved in a simulation. If you have been involved in military or business training in recent years, you probably were unable to escape involvement in a simulation of some kind. If you are acquainted with contemporary techniques in driver education or pilot training, you have a sense of the simulation process.

Monopoly is another example of a simulation, because it represents a real-life situation with a scaled down "model." As America's favorite board game, it taps into values and goals that energize many of us throughout our lives, and it does so in a manner that involves us in a simulated clash of economic titans. Little wonder that the 60-year-old game is now played all over the world. Simulations can be just as exciting when brought into the classroom for academic purposes. Consequently, in the last 50 years simulations have been developed for virtually every area of the school curriculum. Simulation is now the method of choice in graduate schools attended by the most able learners: law, medicine, and business. In recent years, computers have made simulations a readily available educational tool.

Virtually all educational simulations share certain characteristics. Those involved ("players") take on roles representative of someone in the real world, act out lifelike situations, and make decisions on the basis of their assessment of the situation in which they find themselves. Activity is central. Players experience simulated consequences based on those decisions and on their individual or group performance. Problem solving is usually at the heart of the simulation; often a competitive situation must be resolved. Participants observe their actions and associated outcomes, and those of other players, in a way that causes them to reconstruct the experience, reflecting on their decisions and the consequences of those decisions. The ultimate goal of an educational simulation is the development of concepts, skills, and principles which can be retained and transferred to other situations and problems.

In comparison to other strategies for differentiating instruction, simulation probably requires more preparation and planning from the teacher. Most simulations require the development of what today might be called "software," the equipment that makes the game possible. They also require that students possess or develop the attitudes and social skills that make any cooperative enterprise possible.

Even when using a commercially developed simulation, there are important tasks for teachers to perform. Joyce and Weil (1996) point out that even well-designed simulations cannot operate without the effective facilitation of the teacher. Because students tend to become intensely involved in the activity of the simulation, they may not be conscious of the objectives of the learning experience.

It is the teacher who must raise the students' awareness of these goals, help the students develop insight into their own behavior, and generalize beyond the game. In a simulation, the teacher explains the rules, monitors and referees the interaction, coaches students to improve their play (without favoring anyone), and leads the debriefing process that solidifies the intended educational outcomes.

The simulation process, as described by Joyce and Weill (1996, p. 363) moves through four phases:

Phase One: Orientation

The broad topic of the simulation and the concepts to be incorporated into the simulation activity are presented.

Simulation is explained to the students.

An overview of the simulation is given.

Phase Two: Participant training

Scenarios are set up (rules, roles, procedures, scoring, types of decisions to be made, goals).

Roles are assigned.

Abbreviated practice sessions are held.

Phase Three: Simulation Operation

Activities are conducted.

Feedback and evaluation are provided.

Misconceptions are clarified.

Simulation is continued.

Phase Four: Participant Debriefing

Events, perceptions, difficulties, and insights are summarized.

Difficulties and insights are summarized.

The process is analyzed.

Simulation activities are compared to the real world.

Simulation activity is related to course content.

Simulation is appraised and redesigned.

As is true with the case study and other cooperative experiences, the debriefing must be handled effectively by the teacher if the simulation is to come to a productive conclusion. It is crucial to examine how decisions were made and how players felt about them. It is equally important to tease out generalizations and principles that have transfer value and illustrate how these concepts are important in areas beyond the simulation. Finally, the debriefing must focus on the development and refinement of the social skills that are involved, and produce suggestions for playing the simulation more effectively another time. Because simulations represent reality, they may become emotionally charged; effective teachers must know when to intervene during a simulation and how to process those experiences at the termination. In answer to the question, "How do I get started with simulations?" Schurr, Thomason, and Thompson (1995) suggest four possibilities: (1) acquire a commercially produced or professionally developed game that fits the content of your class; (2) adapt an available game or simulation for your own purposes; (3) design and develop your own game; and, (4) have students (usually able learners) design and develop a game for use by the class. One of many sources for existing simulations to use in your classroom is *Interact (Learning Through Involvement),* El Cajon, California.

There are many other sources of pre-packaged simulations. A trip to the nearby university library will reveal sources of literally hundreds of simulations in virtually every possible subject area. One source of simulations also available at a university library is a professional journal devoted solely to simulations. *Simulation and Gaming, An International Journal of Theory, Design, and Research* is used primarily by trainers in business, law, and medicine, but offers other possibilities to teachers who are really serious about simulations. Every issue contains a free simulation that readers can try in their own educational settings; many can be adapted to high school classrooms.

Teachers who attempt to develop their own simulations should include the following in their plans:

1. Decide on the goals and objectives of the simulation.

2. Develop a concise statement of a situation or problem that would be the focus of the simulation (e.g., feudal Japan).

3. Write a scenario that includes past events, background information, the present time and situation, and the other conditions that will frame the activity at the center of the simulation.

4. Identify the characters and roles to be played by the students. These role descriptions give direction to the students, but leave open the opportunity for able students to use their creativity, and perhaps their research, to embellish their roles.

5. Provide the characters with the objectives and resources. Students must be given directions as to what their character seeks from the activity and the resources they can bring to bear.

6. Provide rules that govern how the simulation is played, the time available, the external constraints that govern the situation, and the scoring that might be involved (because good simulations are often competitions between conflicting interests).

Major Methods for Differentiating Instruction

Learning Contracts

Learning contracts are agreements between one or more students and the teacher regarding specific learning objectives, activities, and/or assessment procedures. There are many situations in which contracts can be valuable for every student, or for an entire class, and the contract concept fits well into the extended classroom of the long-block schedule. Some educators might even argue that learning contracts and independent study are essential elements of an effective classroom.

Contracts are also effective for differentiating instruction to challenge gifted and other able learners in the regular classroom. Contracts are particularly useful as a follow-up to the curriculum-compacting process when the teacher has found a way to eliminate the repetition of content for one or more students who have already learned it. When one or more learners have demonstrated that they have mastered at least a substantial portion of an upcoming learning unit, they can be engaged in in-depth enrichment activities through the use of the learning contract. The contract usually lasts for the duration of the learning unit, from several days to several weeks.

The contract is typically used to engage the student in enrichment activities related to the learning unit in which other students are involved. The components of the learning contract include:

1. The objectives the students will pursue; learners know exactly what they have to accomplish.

2. The particular resources to be used in the learning process: books, media, computers, or human resources.

3. The learning activities in which students will engage: reading, writing, viewing, creating, researching, interviewing, experimenting, and other activities the student will pursue to fulfill the terms of the contract.

4. How the learning experience will be assessed, how the students will demonstrate what they have learned, and to what degree of quality. Tests, conferences, papers, portfolios, worksheets, demonstrations, models, and other conventional and innovative assessment strategies might be involved.

Winebrenner (1992) and others suggest the following steps in the contracting process:

1. Pre-plan the enrichment activities and identify materials that students will need. Check the library, consult teacher's manuals, talk with potential resource people, and so on.

2. Design a master contract form. It might include activities or assignments that are non-negotiable and those that involve student choice. Non-negotiable items could include components of the learning unit that were not completely mastered, new content that can be quickly mastered by the student, and so on. Negotiable items

would include activities that are more complex, more challenging, and thus more interesting to the student.

3. Pretest students who seek to move to learning contracts while you provide enrichment activities for students who opt to work through the unit with the teacher as a group.

4. Confer with students who are able to move to learning contracts for this unit, while other students continue to engage in enrichment activities. At this meeting, explain your expectations, describe the options available, and make certain the students understand the special rules that apply to them during this process.

5. Have the students sign the contracts and take them home for parent scrutiny. After the parents sign the contract, the teacher also signs it.

6. Provide a space in the classroom or some other place for materials, where the students pursuing learning contracts can work without interrupting you and the rest of the class, but still remain under your supervision.

7. Meet regularly with contract students to check on their progress and provide them with the teacher contact, feedback, and guidance that all students require.

8. Evaluate student work at the end of the learning unit.

Winebrenner recommends that all enrichment work be self-correcting and ungraded. When it is self-correcting, the teacher isn't submerged in even more paperwork. When it is ungraded, students need not fear that independent work will cause them to work harder for what might end up being a lower grade than they would have earned if they had simply moved at a slower pace with the rest of the class. They get the grade (A) that they earned by testing out of the regular curriculum.

This does not mean that the teacher ignores the products that students generate. The students may be asked to make presentations to the rest of the class, meet together in a small group to share with each other, or deposit their work in a continuously developing portfolio. They require the same praise and recognition for this work as for anything else they do.

Grading Contracts

Contracts can be used in a very different way. They can also be used to differentiate instruction by presenting the whole class with grading options related to a learning unit that is taught using other methods. The contract, in this case, presents student with a choice of grades (A, B, C, D, etc.) based on the amount and quality of the work that each student completes during the unit, grading period, semester, term, or course. The most able students, along with others who seek to attain a favorable grade, are encouraged to choose "A" contracts.

Students in a ninth grade World Cultures classroom, for example, might become involved in contracts during a three-week unit on China. The contract for the unit might present all of the students with certain options at each of four levels:

The "D" Contract: Students attend class regularly and punctually, behave well, listen carefully, and give evidence of having read the textbook by correctly answering questions when called on by the teacher.

The "C" Contract: Students meet the terms of the "D" contract and summarize in writing ideas from four written sources about life in China, only one of which can be an encyclopedia.

The "B" Contract: Students meet the terms of the "C" contract and receive at least an 80% on the unit test.

The "A" Contract: Students fulfill the terms of the "B" contract and complete an independent project dealing with life in China, choosing from the possibilities assembled by the teacher or a student idea approved by the teacher.

It would also be possible to offer students a contract that would give them the following choices:

For a "D": Successfully complete one of the four options (unit test, independent project, etc.).

For a "C": Successfully complete two of the four options.

For a "B": Successfully complete three of the four options.

For an "A": Successfully complete all four of the options.

In the above examples, the teacher retains the right to exercise judgment regarding the quality of student work. If a student completes all four options, for example, but does so with less than A-quality work, the teacher can move the grade down to a B+ or B. By the same token, if a student chooses a "B" option and does it exceptionally well, a B+ would be in order. Using grading contracts allows the teacher to guide able learners into more challenging and complex learning experiences while keeping the class together in the study of a particular unit. Individual teachers should, of course, adapt grading contracts to their own uses and preferences.

Independent Study

Independent study (IS) is a strategy in which students assume greater responsibility in: (a) selecting topics to investigate on their own, (b) designing procedures for learning about the topic, (c) conducting the inquiry, (d) sharing the findings, and (e) evaluating the process and products of the work. IS can also be a special course option external to the regular classroom. Such programs usually have a professional staff member designated to coordinate the program. This person helps students identify and delimit a topic for study, arrange community-based learning experiences, and find a place in the school to study and work. In this chapter, however, we are examining IS as an option *inside* the regular classroom.

Tomlinson (1993) argues that IS is especially valuable for able high school students. It builds on a recognition of student differences and allows the teacher to expand the dimensions of learning units beyond what the whole group will study. It encourages active learning and flexible grouping, two goals of contemporary high school education. And, she says, it leads to a more student-centered classroom—an important part of the rationale for *Breaking Ranks* (1996), the publication that sets the tone for each chapter in this book.

Topics appropriate for IS are usually those that would be unsuitable for the class as a whole. IS topics would be related to the main theme of the learning unit, but might be much more complex, or explore a tangent that would not be interesting to or appropriate for all students. Winebrenner (1992) suggests that IS can help selected students develop expertise on a topic that is a part of the learning unit, a topic that the student can eventually help the teacher present to the rest of the class.

To be eligible for IS, the student must agree to master the regular basic content of the unit on his or her own. For many able learners, the ability to learn school subjects more quickly than other students makes this an attractive prospect. Students thus satisfy the teacher's need to be sure that they know the basics and satisfy their own need to avoid the boredom of trudging slowly through material they could learn in a flash. Once such an arrangement is agreed upon, the student is freed from regular class time to pursue an IS project that he or she will eventually share with the rest of the class.

Winebrenner believes that, ideally, the IS project would not be a written report, and it would be done during school time. This helps to ensure that the student has something interesting to do during class time, when he or she might otherwise be bored. It also provides the student with the opportunity to contribute to the class in meaningful ways. Work must be done in the classroom or at another site in the school, and it can't be taken home until it is shared with the class.

The steps in the IS process include the following:

1. Provide an overview of the curriculum unit to all students, so that the domain of IS options is clear.

2. For students without much prior experience in the IS process, provide a list of "starter" suggestions for projects. In a recent learning unit on Japan, one of the authors of this textbook gave students a list of twenty-five possible projects, including the following:
   - Make a timeline on butcher paper of important events in the history of Japan.
   - Illustrate a trip to Japan by constructing a map and describing the parts you would like to visit, the proposed itinerary, preparations you should make, modes of transportation you would take, and stops you would make along the way.
   - Put up a bulletin board display entitled "Japanese Products in America."
   - Conduct a survey of ten adults, asking how they interpret famous Japanese sayings, like "Words are silver; silence is golden," and "The nail that sticks out shall be hammered in." Present the results to the class in graphic form.
   - Draw up ten true–false questions about important aspects of Japanese culture and quiz ten students who are not a part of your class. Report your findings to your class.
   - Pretend you are a Japanese radio broadcaster following World War II. Prepare and broadcast (to our class) a story based on fictitious interviews with five Japanese citizens about their lives and how they feel about the United States.
   - Draw a series of at least five cartoons depicting important events in the history of Japan, or five pictures portraying important aspects of Japanese culture today.

- Develop a photographic essay about life in Japan. Find seven to ten pictures about Japan and describe what they tell us about life there.
- Construct a detailed model of a traditional Japanese home. Label important parts from inside and outside the home. Take class members on a tour, explaining the meaning and importance of different areas.
- Imagine yourself a ninth grader in Japan during World War II. Write several poems expressing (a) your admiration for the emperor, or (b) your bitterness toward the enemy.

3. To avoid leaping into a topic prematurely, arrange for the students to explore the content area of this curriculum unit broadly. Students choose a topic, preferably one they really care about, instead of one assigned by the teacher. Topics must have plenty of available resources and references to use in the study process. Topics should be designed so that the students go beyond merely collecting information and reporting it. Answering intriguing questions, solving challenging puzzles, confronting difficult issues, or requiring the creative use of findings—all of these will help move the student to a different level of challenge and satisfaction.

4. Communicate with parents about the goals of the IS, the procedures to be followed, and what parents should and should not do to help their child.

5. Meet with the IS students as a group. Use this time to communicate all the rules, guidelines, and conditions attached to the IS privilege. Present each student with an IS contract that requires three signatures: yours, the student's, and a parent's.

6. Work with students to develop criteria for evaluating the IS project. Create a "rubric" that provides a clear description of what an "A" quality project would look like. This might include options for the final product for cases in which the project itself does not require a specific outcome such as those in the examples above. Students who conduct a project that is mainly research-oriented might opt to bring it all together in a computer program, a video, an art display, an oral presentation, or in some other way.

7. Help the students investigate a variety of resources.

8. Require each student to develop a schedule for initiating and completing the IS project, and to keep a calendar for his or her effort. High school students, no matter how gifted, are still occasionally unable to manage time as wisely as adults would prefer. Helping them make a choice in a timely fashion will be an important start. Supporting the student by requiring a regular "check-in" with the teacher will help overcome a tendency toward procrastination.

9. Tomlinson (1994) suggests that students be required to keep a "process log" of their thoughts and actions as they work through the project. The student records new ideas, difficulties encountered, and feelings at different points of the IS project.

10. Ask the student to share the final product with the class, as the "resident expert" on that topic, co-teaching it with the teacher for that day. Or, the student might make a presentation to another audience—his or her peers, another class, the school administration, or a group of parents.

Students who fulfill the expectations associated with the IS project during one learning unit may qualify to participate in a later project. This would require that, in addition to successfully completing the IS, the student:

- Learned the basic content of the unit independently, to at least the level of a "B" grade.
- Consistently remained on task, without disturbing the teacher when the teacher was teaching, and without disturbing the rest of the class in any way.
- Followed all classroom rules and acted appropriately when working in other locations, such as the library or another classroom.
- Did not brag or demean the work of the remainder of the class.

Winebrenner (1992) argues that IS projects should not be graded; the reinforcement should come from the satisfaction of delving into topics of interest, relief from boredom, and the opportunity to share with others.

Mastery Learning (ML)

ML is an attempt to combine whole class instruction with follow-up enrichment and remediation. When successful, it gives slower students more time to keep up without holding more able students back. ML moves the class in cycles between two phases—large group teacher-directed classes, and small group remediation and enrichment. These cycles fit well into the longer time period of newer block schedules.

ML is most often found as a unit-based, group-focused method of differentiating instruction. It begins with a series of teacher-directed whole-class presentations on a unit of curriculum objectives, quickly followed by an assessment (quiz, test, or otherwise). Based on the results of this first assessment, less successful students undergo remediation and correction until they reach mastery. At the same time, more able learners who successfully complete the assessment engage in enrichment activities that extend and enrich their knowledge of the subject beyond the minimum required for mastery. After the period of correctives and enrichments, a final assessment brings the unit to a close and a new unit with new objectives is launched.

The Rationale for ML

James Block (Block, Efthim & Burns, 1989), long one of ML's most prominent and thoughtful advocates, writes that ML differs from traditional instruction in several ways. All students study a common curriculum, and all students move through this course at the teacher's pace, not their own. Once every 10 to 14 days, however, the teacher checks the progress of the class with an assessment of some sort. Students who are not progressing well are provided with supplementary, personalized instruction. They are offered a variety of alternative learning materials and activities and additional learning time to address their particular learning difficulties. Students who are progressing quickly are provided with additional instruction too, to enrich their learning; independent study fits well here. After this correction and enrichment occurs, all students return to the root course of study and the cycle of teacher presentation–assessment–follow up alternatives begins again.

ML takes into account that most high school teachers already have a relatively fixed curriculum that must be covered in a certain length of time, and that unlimited amounts of time cannot be spent on diagnosis and prescription of individual learning. ML also recognizes that evaluation must occur and grades must be given. ML is holistic in that it deals with all major elements of classroom teaching and learning: curriculum, teaching, testing, and managing.

ML is philosophically based. It rejects the idea that there are good students and bad students, that only the good learners can learn more complex, abstract, and difficult concepts, or that poor learners are condemned to learning only the simplest and most concrete ideas. These false assumptions, say ML advocates, have led school systems to organize their curriculum, their instruction, and their grouping in ways that have been ineffective for many students.

ML was the first approach to argue that there are just faster and slower learners, not good and bad ones, and that all students could learn, retain, and apply most of the same concepts and skills if they had the time they needed. And when slower learning students succeed, their attitudes toward school are as positive as those of the faster learners. Think of yourself—you know that there are some subjects that you learn quickly and some that you learn very slowly. Given the time, effort, and correct instruction, though, do you not believe you could be successful at least at the minimum level in even those challenging areas? ML believes that when students are presented with unfavorable learning conditions, they separate even further with regard to learning, rate of learning, and motivation.

Advocates of the ML approach make a number of very bold claims about teaching and learning. For example, they believe that when using ML, from 75 to 95 percent of the students in school can achieve the same level of excellence that the best students attain in a traditional school environment, without holding back the gifted students. These advocates also assert that ML is more efficient, takes less time, and produces higher levels of motivation and better attitudes in students than traditional methods in the regular classroom (Guskey, 1988).

The startling contention of ML is that if each pupil is given the necessary time to learn to the level of mastery, then progress will be almost inevitable. When students are not allowed the time they need, failure is almost automatic; when students learn quickly and are held back with the rest of the class, boredom and disruption are likely. Mastery learning stresses the direct relationship between time spent on task and the level of achievement.

Basic Components in ML

There are four primary variables that influence achievement and that are involved in the ML approach.

First, the idea of an 'ability to learn" must be thought of in terms of an amount of time required for a person to learn a task, and not as an innate ability (such as an intelligence quotient). Some students need more time and help, and may need to expend more effort, but almost all are capable of learning what the school demands.

Second, the quality of instruction must be adjusted to provide students with learning activities geared to their individual learning styles. Having several learning activities from which to choose is crucial.

Third, individual perseverance (and motivation) in the learning task is significant. If a student needs twenty-five hours to learn a particular skill, but is only willing to spend ten, learning will not occur.

Fourth and most important is the time allowed for learning. An effective ML strategy provides a time framework flexible enough so that individual students are able to spend the time they need—no more or less. This demand for flexible time makes ML appealing for teachers in a long block schedule.

In addition to these four primary factors, several other items of concern give shape to ML. One is an insistence that all learners complete the necessary prerequisites before attempting to learn something new. Moving on to a new task before learning well what has been left behind is seen as a primary cause of academic failure. Mastery learning also places great significance on the role of formative and summative evaluation in facilitating learning. Quizzes help teachers decide whether the learner should move on to a new task or review a previous or current task. Summative evaluation helps to determine how much students have learned, and forms the basis for grading. If ML is implemented, say proponents, there will be far more "A's" and far fewer grades at the "D" and "F" levels.

Implementing ML

The process of implementing ML, while considerably more complex than the present space permits, generally follows a series of steps:

- Teachers review their curriculum requirements and instructional materials to determine which content should be learned by all students, and what level of achievement will be required for each grade (e.g., 90% for an "A").
- Teachers divide up the course content for the year into units of instruction with clearly specified outcomes or objectives. Each unit has objectives, quizzes, instruction, and tests. The teach–test–reteach cycle is repeated throughout the year until all units have been covered.
- The teacher selects the type of instruction that will be used for each unit. This involves the use of a variety of whole-class, small group, and differentiated approaches to the subject. It is not the teaching strategy that matters as much as the way the teacher uses class time for the four-phase cycle of teach–quiz–reteach/enrichment–test.
- The teacher implements instruction as it was designed.
- Each learning objective embedded in the instruction is matched with a diagnostic instrument (e.g., a quiz) used by the teacher to check on the level of learning reached after the first major instructional effort. From this formative assessment, the teacher learns who has learned how much, what major errors need to be corrected, and which students can be released for enrichment.
- The teacher implements corrective and enrichment activities. The corrective activities are designed as remedial efforts to bring slower students to the point of mastery. Enrichment activities challenge those who attained mastery initially, liberating them to pursue independent projects or other extensions of the learning unit.

■ Finally, after the corrective and enrichment time, the teacher administers a test or other more authentic assessment to assign grades for the unit.

Learning Centers And Learning Guides

Learning Centers

A learning center is an area for study and activity, in or near the classroom, that has been specially designed for teaching or investigating a particular topic or skill. It is a place to use and store materials that relate to a special interest or content area. It may be in a corner, on a wall, next to a bookcase, or on a table, but it exists somewhere in the physical space of the classroom. Although used primarily in elementary and middle schools and rarely seen in the high school classroom, learning centers seem perfectly suited for the long block schedule in the exemplary high school, and thus they are described here.

The term "learning station" is sometimes used as a synonym for learning center; the name used is not terribly important. What matters is the way in which learning centers or stations can provide opportunities for differentiating instruction and adapting to the longer block of time. Learning centers can be organized and placed in ways that appeal to the imagination of students. Teachers have put learning centers on lampshades, clotheslines, appliance boxes, tents, shoe boxes, groups of manila folders, cork boards, wine racks, coffee cans, terrariums, picnic baskets, window shades, picture frames, blankets, shower curtains, suitcases, coat racks, tables, sides of filing cabinets, in loose-leaf notebooks, on pizza boards, egg cartons, venetian blinds, and many other creative spots.

A complete and comprehensive learning center has five major parts. First, every complete learning center has an introduction, where in very few words students learn or are reminded of the purpose of their participation in that center. The introduction also tells them about any prerequisites that may have to be completed before they begin work. Since the best learning centers are highly structured affairs, the introduction must give clear and thorough directions for completing the center. A flow chart is often helpful. The introduction can be posted on the center. When the teacher is using as many as a half dozen different learning centers to teach a unit, directions probably should be given out to students in a small manual or packet.

Second, learning centers should have clear and precise outcomes, spelled out as objectives. Ideally, the students should be told exactly what they have to accomplish in order to complete the center successfully. Third, the best learning centers have a built-in pre-assessment. This pre-assessment is used to help students determine whether they will profit from a particular activity. If students pass the pretest at a certain level, they may proceed to another center or other predetermined activity (e.g., independent study). Or, they may be asked to skip directly to the post-assessment. In this way, the pre-assessment enables the brightest students to skip work that they have had before or that they already know and to move on to more challenging activities.

At the heart of the process, every learning center must have specific learning activities for each objective. There should be several alternative activities for each objective. It is also important to include what might be called "quest," "challenge," or "enrichment" activities that stretch and deepen the work of all students, but especially the work of those who are ready to go beyond the basics in a particular area or topic.

The fifth part of every learning center is the post-assessment. Ideally, this is a self-administered device that tells students how successful they have been. The results of the post-assessment might be a simple grade, or might suggest which parts of the center the student should revisit. Finally, all materials necessary to complete the center should be in the immediate area. Books, videos, exercises, papers—whatever is involved with the activity of the center—should be there. If they aren't, directions on where to get them should be clear, or else teachers will be overwhelmed with requests for help from students.

A wide variety of uses for learning centers in the high school classroom have now evolved. Teachers can use learning centers for a single purpose or for a variety of tasks. One of the more traditional uses of the learning center has been as an interest center where students may go when their regularly assigned tasks are completed. Usually the experiences of the interest center have little direct relationship to the major instructional objectives.

The learning center can be a place where faster working students use their time productively while others catch up on the basics of a lesson. This can be done in ways that become quite challenging for gifted and talented students in the regular classroom. Learning centers can be used as enrichment areas where students may go for additional work on a particular topic or skill. This use of the learning center need not be restricted to only the brightest students in the class. It can serve as an excellent change of pace for students working at any ability level. In this way learning centers can be used in conjunction with mastery learning in the block-scheduled high school classroom.

A related use of the learning centers approach is its employment as a reinforcement center. In mastery learning classrooms, for example, it may be termed a corrective center. This center usually operates as a supplement to small- or large-group teacher-led activities. Students might go to a reinforcement center in grammar, for example, after a small-group lesson with the teacher in which they haven't quite mastered the content. At the center students find a variety of games, problems, readings, and so on that reinforce the concepts introduced by the teacher in the larger group. While faster students use other centers, students in need of more time find it at the reinforcement center.

Another part-time use of the learning center is as a motivating device attached to upcoming topics of study. Here teachers introduce new units of study and new topics for investigation. The center may serve as a kick-off, or introductory device for a new unit. Teachers, if they choose, may also use this learning center as a culminating activity, looking back at what has been accomplished and forward to new ideas and implications.

The learning center can also function as a remediation and self correction center. Here students come when they need a booster shot in some subject or skill. They may come to the center on their own, at the teacher's direction, or as a result of making particular choices at another learning center. They may, for example, choose an activity or experiment that demands certain skills as prerequisites. The directions of that particular activity should clearly specify that prerequisite skill and the source of remediation at the self-correction center. The learning center can also assist in the development of those skills of continued learning that teachers rarely find time to deal with in the course of the regular day. A center may, for example, be used to teach the skills and responsibilities of cooperative learning.

The most important and far-reaching use of the learning centers approach for the high school classroom is as the major method of instruction. Learning centers offer help to teachers faced with heterogeneous classes by allowing them to move away from teaching the class as a single group in a teacher-directed lesson. It is often possible to design a unit of study lasting anywhere from three to six weeks that utilizes learning centers as a major supplement to traditional instruction. For example, a teacher in a biology class might use a group of learning centers as a major method to teach a unit on the cell. In such a situation, there might be separate centers on individual aspects of cells, perhaps a center on mitosis, one on the history of cellular exploration, another on the chemistry of the cell. Even a center on the literature of the cell might not be too "far out."

A talented English teacher known to the authors has taught an entire unit on mythology using learning centers as the central methodology. The unit included separate centers on the gods of Mount Olympus, and a major center introducing important myths that are familiar to many adult Americans. In addition to the centers, the teacher's ongoing activity was a teacher-directed study of the Odyssey.

One of the authors also recently taught a two-week unit on Japan in a ninth-grade World Cultures class, using learning centers as a core methodology. There were five basic centers: history, geography facts, culture, school life, calligraphy, and origami. There was also an enrichment center composed of Japanese items of interest brought in by students in the six different classes.

In situations such as these, the teacher spends a great deal of time preparing the centers prior to the beginning of the unit, but little or no time in daily preparation once the unit is underway. So although it may look like a great deal of work, it is actually no more preparation than is required for any good teaching. The first step in creating learning centers to supplement the teacher-directed classroom involves some decision-making by the teachers involved.

Teachers must first decide what role the learning center will play in their instructional program. Will they be used for remediation, enrichment, motivation, short courses, or as the major instructional strategy? Will centers be used throughout the day, for an entire class period, or for a shorter portion of the day? Will they be used for all subjects (as in an elementary classroom), a few, or only in an interdisciplinary unit? There must be some basic procedural decisions made before the first move toward construction of centers. The same detailed planning required for any other method of instruction must also take place if learning centers are to be successful.

The authors recommend that teachers interested in using learning centers begin by using this approach for only one subject area or for a few hours out of the day or week. In this way the teacher can slowly supplement the standard instruction with the least amount of disruption and confusion. It is also possible to work with another teacher or small group of teachers to develop and share learning centers, so that the burden of creating centers does not fall on one person.

Having determined the extent to which learning centers will be used, teachers may decide on the focus of the centers, using student input if it is appropriate. Such teacher–student planning can be crucial to the use of learning centers, as in every method. It is very important that learning centers are appropriate for the intended population. Centers may focus on a subject area (e.g., balancing equations), a problem or issue (e.g., censorship), a "process" such as cooperating, or a variety of other topics. The most important consideration, however, is that they be planned with the student's diverse interests and achievement levels in mind.

There are a number of questions a teacher should ask when planning a learning center.

1. How many centers will be used to teach this topic or unit?

2. What will be the theme or focus of the center?

3. What specific objectives for students' learning should the center's activities achieve?

4. What activities and materials might be most appropriate to the achievement of the objectives?

5. How will records of students efforts be kept? Who will keep them? Where?

6. What assessment procedures will be used to determine student achievement?

7. How well will the center work?

8. How will I introduce centers to students who have never used them before, and what rules and procedures will make them all run smoothly?

9. How will I accommodate various learning styles and differences?

It is important to have a procedure that permits students to move in a quiet and orderly fashion to a center of their choice. One teacher, for example, gives a different row of students their first choice of which centers to visit each day. It can help to give each student a packet that includes precise directions for working in the centers and a contract that describes grading options connected with different centers and activities within the centers, all of which fit the heterogeneous high school classroom.

While the scope of a particular learning center will vary greatly with topic and age level, experienced high school teachers offer the rule of thumb that from beginning to end, the student should be able to complete the activity in no less than three class hours and absolutely no more than ten. When a center offers an activity that requires less time than this, creation of new centers becomes a pressing burden on the part of the teacher. When the activity demands more than ten class periods of effort, students tend to lose sight of the original objectives and become less interested in completion of the task.

With the first centers, the teacher must be very directive. Taking students step by step through the centers may be wise. If centers are being used to teach major portions of an entire unit, it might take most of a period to work through this with the class before they start in the centers. There must also be directions governing how many students may work at a center at one time, how and where completed work is turned in, and many other nuts-and-bolts details of classroom life when the teacher is not "up front teaching."

When a student completes work at a particular center, a post-assessment should be submitted for the teacher to examine later. For situations in which a teacher is using learning centers in all classes (perhaps as may as six), it will be helpful to have class boxes where students can deposit finished work. When work at a center has been completed, the student proceeds to a new task or center, in line with the terms of the contract or directions for the unit. At the earliest opportunity the teacher evaluates the post-assessment and decides, perhaps in conference with the pupil, where the pupil goes—to a new center, to small group instruction, back to the first center for remediation, and so on.

When students are at work in learning centers, the teacher uses time in several ways. One of the most important of these is, of course, to supervise the work in the centers. For learning centers to produce high levels of academic achievement, the teacher really needs to monitor the process closely. This is not the time to retire to the teacher's desk and become involved in activities that will take attention away from the classroom activity. The teacher must also be available for individual conferences and for introducing new concepts and skill work to small groups. In addition, the teacher continues evaluation of class progress and plans new centers or activities in anticipation of future student needs or interests.

Learning Guides (Learning Activity Packets or Unipacs)

Learning guides or activity packages (LAPs) are teacher-made booklets duplicated for classroom use; they are similar in some ways to the larger, more complex learning center. The basic components of each learning guide or LAP are quite alike: introduction, objectives, pre-assessment, learning activities, post-assessment and, for the purpose of differentiating instruction, extra credit or enrichment activities. LAPs can be inexpensive, relatively simple, adaptable to many uses, and interesting to students if not overused. But the LAP is also different from learning centers in some important respects.

The LAP has also been known as a "unipac," referring to its characteristic feature, a design intended to cover a single objective. If it is written well, the LAP is like a sentence in that it should cover one complete thought, concept or skill. It might also be thought of as a road map to various learning activities designed to meet specific objectives. Often, they can be found in learning centers and as part of independent study efforts.

The ability to recognize how much content to cover comes from experience, but one rule of thumb is that an effective LAP should involve approximately one to five hours of work for the average student. Because an LAP is almost always a paper and pencil learning activity, anything longer than five hours tends to become tedious for the student; anything shorter than an hour requires too much management and design work for the teacher.

One way to conceptualize the length and complexity of a typical LAP would be to consider that if this were the only teaching method used by a teacher (which is not, of course, recommended), 30 to 35 LAPS or unipacs could cover the entire school year. LAPS can be used as an effective learning activity in a class unit, or as a part of a larger learning center. Instead of the multiple objectives found in a learning center, the much shorter unipac has only one. If your textbook has 36 chapters, a unipac might be thought of as about the same complexity as a chapter.

Suggestions for the successful use of LAPs (unipacs) include the following:

- Include in the introduction a brief motivational rationale telling the student why this objective needs to be completed and why it is important to the student. Follow this with an overview of the purpose and activities of the LAP. Wind up the introduction with some clear, step-by-step directions for completion of the LAP.
- List the objective separately, spelling out exactly what the student will be able to do upon successful completion of the activities that will follow.
- The pre-assessment should be brief, and if successfully completed should lead directly to the more comprehensive post-test.
- There should be at least five activities for the objective being learned. The activities should present some opportunity for success and challenge to each student. Such activities should relate directly and clearly to the objective of the LAP, and the student should be able to complete most of the activities at his or her seat, with little or no help from the teacher.
- The post-test should relate directly to the objectives. It may be contained in the LAP, or the teacher may administer it after successful completion of the post-assessment in the LAP. It should be easily scored, and available to the individual students when they are ready.
- There should be a part that permits the students to evaluate the LAP.
- Try using a different color paper for different sections of the LAP, or for different LAPs.
- Keep consumable materials separate, or have students use their own paper for completion of the activities.
- When designing the LAP for use in a heterogeneous class, develop the vocabulary at a level that aims at the low average students in the class. Because the LAP is designed to be a road map for individual learning trips, it should be clear to as many students as possible.
- As with learning centers or any other method in which students are expected to learn on their own, students should be given an appropriate orientation and training period at the beginning of the process.

Learning guides can be used to boost the differentiation of instruction in several ways. A teacher can design one or more guides or unipacs to serve solely as an enrichment process, available only to students who have had other content compacted. A unipac could be a basic part of a learning unit, completed by all students except those who move quickly from pretest to enrichment activity in or beyond the unipac. Enrichment activities should be challenging, complex, and interesting for those who move to them. Bright, well-prepared students should be able to skip much of the unipac's requirements. Unipacs can be used to teach the skills and process of independent study, and can be an integral part of a learning center. The possibilities are unlimited.

The role of the teacher using unipacs is significantly different from the teacher's role in total class instruction. The teacher sheds the roles of presenter, demonstrator, driller, and questioner, and adopts the mantle of decision maker, planner, evaluator, facilitator, initiator, monitor, coach, and coordinator. The manner in which the teacher relates to the students in these styles of differentiated instruction is much like the way in which the teacher must respond to the small group learning situation.

Excessive use of either learning centers or unipacs carries with it the same dangers that accompany overreliance on any other major instructional strategy. When correctly understood and used, both methods can be powerful instructional alternatives. In classrooms where more student involvement and greater personalization of the learning activity are major objectives, and where the long block schedule is in place, these modes offer attractive opportunities to teachers and students alike. This is why the authors predict that in the decade ahead these methods will attract more interest and use in the high school classroom than they have in the last ten years, provided that they are used as intended.

The (Reading/Writing) Workshop Approach

Popularized at the middle school level by Nancie Atwell (1998), the workshop approach promises to be an important addition to the repertoire of many high school teachers seeking to differentiate instruction and to adapt effectively to teaching in the long block schedule. Following the lead of reading and language arts teachers, math, science, and social studies teachers are now attempting to adapt the workshop approach to instruction in their fields. One of the authors of this text has used this model successfully for differentiating instruction in a graduate level course, The School Curriculum. Since the workshop approach is most fully developed in language arts, the explanation that follows will focus on that area. Teachers of other subjects will profit from attempting to work out a way that this approach might be applied to their subjects and course structures.

The workshop approach is based on several important assumptions explored earlier in this chapter. First, *students need to be workers;* learners need to spend much more of their time engaged in the "doing" of their subject, rather than in passive activity like listening to lectures. The basic philosophy behind the workshop classroom is that concepts and skills in virtually all high school subject areas are developed best by regular use. Reading and writing, for example, are acquired most effectively through language use. The scientific method is learned best by "doing science." Mathematics knowledge is best acquired by involvement with mathematics in a workshop approach that permits students to "construct" their own mathematics, through real world applications, problem-solving activities, and regular, frequent interactions with other students in which math is used.

In English, students of all ability levels need time to "do" English, to read and write in school. Regular and frequent time, as much as a 50-minute session every school day, is critical. This school time is important, among other reasons, for establishing the momentum that will permit students to overcome outside distractions that usually hamper their attempts to read and write in other settings. Advocates of this approach in the English classroom firmly believe that it is more important to teach students to love books and enjoy literature than it is to teach them to analyze literature in traditional ways. They believe that loving to read and write will lead to mastery of the skills and continuation of the behaviors involved, but that the reverse is not necessarily true.

It is very important to remember, however, that there is no attempt to completely abandon spelling, vocabulary, grammar, or traditional approaches to the study of literature in the workshop approach. Teachers take time to provide whole-class instruction in all of these, but the time involved is considerably less than in other methods. In a mathematics workshop classroom, as well, there would be plenty of whole-class attention to new skills and concepts. Second, adolescents increase their enjoyment of reading and writing, and improve their efforts in both areas, when they take *ownership* of their reading and writing. This means that students must be given extraordinary freedom in the choice of what they read. Classrooms and media centers must be equipped with high-interest reading, including dozens if not hundreds of paperbacks—even comic books and periodicals. Ownership also means that choice extends to the selection of writing topics as well. A common assignment that all students would pursue simultaneously might be valuable, but must be balanced by sufficient opportunities for individuals to choose their own vehicles for expression, whether they be short stories, personal narratives, editorials, or anything else.

Observation of the workshop approach in action at one school revealed a distinct and coherent structure:

- In many of the traditional English topics, total class instruction comes in the form of *mini-lessons*. Students receive direct instruction in punctuation, vocabulary, technique and style, and so on.
- Actual *workshop time* in both reading and writing workshop approaches is frequent and lengthy. Sustained silent reading and writing are integral parts of the daily schedule. Time is devoted to silent reading and to silent writing during every class period. Students are expected to come to class ready to read, or write, and to begin doing so as soon as they arrive. The message is that reading and writing are important enough to take place on their own in school, not just as homework.
- The workshop approach relies on a great deal of teacher–student and student–student *interaction* focusing on their writing and reading. Teachers hold brief conferences with as many as a dozen students during a block of time. Students help each other edit their work. Group-share sessions at the end of the workshop period are settings for many listeners to respond to a writer's work. Computer labs now allow students to critique each other's work almost as it is written. Teachers underline the importance of finding many ways for students to receive feedback and other responses to what they read and write. This happens in the workshop classroom through what Atwell calls the "status of the class conference," through conferring briefly with students as the teacher moves about the class during reading or writing time, through longer individual conferences at the teacher's desk, through group sharing sessions, through written responses to student writing by both teacher and peers, and in many other ways.

- The teacher's role in the workshop approach constantly shifts from direct instruction, to one-on-one conferences with students, to facilitating group discussions. Teachers are active, but not in the sense of making endless presentations to students.
- Students work a great deal on their own, but not filling in work sheets or other common assignments made by the teacher. Time-on-task can be extraordinarily high.

The classroom process, while student centered, is highly structured. Teachers have planned the placement of furniture, the location of student desks, resources for the workshop time, evaluation procedures, and teacher stations. The grouping of students, the nature and flow of the daily class period, the time allocated to each activity, and time for students to share and present what they are accomplishing—all of these things are planned carefully in the effective workshop classroom. While moment-to-moment activity is fluid, the long-term goals and activities to meet those goals are thoughtfully planned and structured.

The first phase of the workshop is noticeable at the very beginning of each class. Students are expected to be involved in reading or writing as soon as they arrive in the room, instead of waiting for the bell to ring or for the teacher to formally begin the class. In the workshop, students are expected to come to class with a book in hand, or to have one by the time the bell rings. They may be seen reading quietly or engaged in the process of selecting a new book. They cannot choose to do homework or to read a book from another class, because the workshop is not a study hall. Students who have been absent can, however, make up their reading time by reading at home, in a study hall, between classes, at lunch time, or at other times.

Students must choose a book; they may not choose a magazine or newspaper in which pictures compete with words. The emphasis is on the kind of book that will help the students build up speed and fluency. Teachers point out how crucial it is for students to be able to choose the reading they wish to do, and to select the writing projects that are most meaningful to them. A wide range of literature must be available and students need opportunities to choose books to read. During the writing workshop time, students are encouraged, step by step, to develop their own writing ideas and projects. Students may choose to read or write virtually anything they want for their own enjoyment. This is especially important when classes are heterogeneously mixed, with a wide range of achievement and interests.

Often, however, one book is read and discussed by the entire class. Since reading aloud to students has been shown to be beneficial to student learning, this has a very special place in the workshop classroom. It is from the common book that most of this reading aloud is drawn. It is also true that sometimes a common writing assignment is chosen to introduce or polish particular writing skills. Teachers using the workshop approach are not dogmatic about things like this.

Students must be quiet—no talking or disturbing others is allowed during the first few minutes or during any other part of the reading time. After the class has begun, there is a period of sustained reading, perhaps as long as 30 minutes. A look around the classroom would indicate that students are definitely not reading the same book, on the same page. They would instead be reading many different kinds of books at many different reading levels, and producing written reactions of many different types.

During this time some students will be found writing about what they have been reading. They might be writing in a journal, writing to other students, or to the teacher or to someone else. This writing about reading involves the student in an analysis of the reading. They might write about what they like or dislike about the book, describe character development or plot, or a number of other possibilities. This writing is also intended to help students think about their own progress as readers and what makes them successful or unsuccessful.

Following this extended period of reading and writing, the teacher usually asks for the attention of the class in order to present a brief "mini-lesson." In the early days and weeks of the year, this mini-lesson might focus on procedural matters, such as rules and routines of the workshop. Other early mini-lessons might focus on how to write about what one is reading, how to choose books, the grading system, and so forth. Later on, as Atwell says, mini-lessons examine different genres, real-life information about specific authors, and the elements of literary works. Always, reading aloud is a central part of this process, especially with things like poetry. Certainly, many mini-lessons during the year focus on specific skills. The particular skills chosen for the mini-lessons depend on the age and skill level of the students.

The other critical component of the workshop comes into play before and after the mini-lessons. In the workshop, the teacher uses many workshop approaches to allow students to personally respond to what they are reading. This also means interacting with others about the reading process and the reading they and others have done. Atwell likens this process to the environment that exists when family and friends gather around a dinner table to engage in congenial talk about books, authors, reading, and writing. (Atwell, p. 18). Classrooms are at their best, she says, when they come as close as possible to recreating this sort of environment in the schoolroom. The extension of this concept to other subjects would, for example, have history students engaged in discussions, debates, and the conduct of research in history class, rather than learning dates.

To accomplish this in English, the teacher may ask students to engage in written dialogues about literature with themselves and others through journals. Journal dialogues, back and forth between the teacher and the students, might focus on plot, character development, theme, and other traditional topics. Alternately, the topics might be on areas like the connections between books and the reader's lives, to their own thoughts and feelings about life, and other more personal responses and reactions to reading. Journals are also effectively used in mathematics, science, and other subject areas.

A vital task for the teacher under these circumstances is to write back to the students in individual and specific ways. Sometimes this involves asking students thoughtful questions about what they have read and written. Student-to-student dialogues are just as important. Of course, students will need help in beginning these dialogues and in structuring them so that they stay within the bounds of appropriate classroom and school interaction.

Evaluating student participation in the workshop generally involves three different areas. Students are expected to read every day, and to follow the regulations for the reading workshop. They are asked to write at some length about their reading at least once a week. Finally, they are expected to demonstrate substantial progress over the grading period toward goals they have established in the important areas of reading. This includes their skills, their speed, their personal involvement, the amount they read, and other important factors. Typically, report card grades reflect an average of the three grades students receive for these activities.

As one would expect, the activities of the writing workshop are similar in many ways to the structure of the reading workshop. Students enter the classroom and are expected to begin their work immediately. In a few minutes, the class may convene with a very brief drill, lasting perhaps 5–10 minutes, on some specific aspect of grammar or the mechanics of writing. Often his is an exercise similar to what one would find in a grammar book or traditional writing class. For example, students might be expected to examine a sentence or a quotation for spelling, punctuation, and other problems. When they are finished, the teacher leads the class through a brief correction of the sentence. This is often followed by a 10 to 15 minute mini-lesson directly teaching a specific concept or aspect of the writing process.

As Atwell (1998) notes, the point of the mini-lesson is for the teacher to share things about writing that he or she knows will help the students. Real solutions to real problems are the most helpful mini-lessons. Such lessons might focus on how to select a title for a written piece or how to choose a topic to write about. But they might also hone in on some of the troublesome aspects of grammar or spelling that plague all writers. The teachers often use their own writing as a model.

Following the mini-lesson, the teachers conduct what has come to be called a "status-of-the-class check." In a quick check with all students lasting only a few minutes, the teacher asks each one to explain where they are in the writing project on which they are currently working. Students might respond in several ways: They might be editing, working on a first draft, and so on. At this point, the writer's workshop really begins. In a typical period, this workshop activity might consume two-thirds of the class time. Atwell recommends several rules be followed:

- No erasing, because the teacher wants to be able to see how the student's thinking and writing change.
- Write on one side of the paper only, because writers often cut and paste, and this can be hard to do if you write on both sides.
- Save everything, because progress is what is most important, and demonstrating progress requires a history of the student's writing.
- Label and date everything.
- Speak in six-inch voices.
- Work really hard.

During the writer's workshop, the teacher moves among the students and quietly confers with individuals, or sits at the desk while students take turns coming up for one-on-one conferences about writing they have done or are planning to do. It is also during this time that students may be working with each other in conferences about their writing. One student may read a portion of his or her writing to another. A student may have read and responded in writing to another student's written effort, and they would now be talking about it. Usually these student conferences take place in a quiet corner of the room.

When there are perhaps eight to ten minutes left in the period, the teacher asks the students to quickly bring a temporary finish to what they are doing and to join her in a circle at the front of the classroom for the "group share" session. As another form of responding and reacting to one's own writing and that of others, the group share session invites students to share something new, something that has worked well for them, perhaps a problem they need help with in their writing. Perhaps they are just looking for general but honest reactions to something they have composed. Just before the bell, the teacher brings closure to the period with a suggestion for tomorrow, a generalization from the results of the group sharing session, or perhaps a helpful, encouraging comment.

There may be questions about the applicability of the workshop approach to some subjects, and to special populations of students. There may also be concerns about the adequacy of instruction in specific reading skills and about reading comprehension, for students other than able learners. There appears to be little doubt, however, about the impressive amount of reading and writing that students eagerly accomplish, especially those able learners unleashed to pursue the interests that motivate their reading and writing. If one must choose between preparing students who can read and write well but really hate to do either, and taking a chance on missing a few skills but developing adolescents who eagerly read and write, we think the choice is clear.

Perhaps the main attraction of the workshop approach is that it is perfectly adaptable to the heterogeneous, block-scheduled classroom. All levels of readers and writers can be accommodated in the same classroom, as easily as in highly tracked classrooms. Students, especially able learners, can be turned loose to pursue the interests in reading and writing that drive their excitement and enthusiasm.

SUMMARY

Teachers in the nation's high schools face many challenges in the area of instruction (e.g., student misbehavior, overflowing curriculum, teaching in the block schedule). They must find ways to meet these and other challenges as public expectations for high achievement increase. It is unlikely that teaching strategies will be transformed quickly in most classrooms, so it is essential for high school teachers to modify traditional strategies so that they can be used effectively with increasingly diverse student classroom groups and within the context of the block schedule.

Typical teacher–student ratios in most high schools make individualized instruction very difficult or even impossible. Because of these ratios and other conditions commonly found in high schools, many teachers find that the traditional model of direct instruction is the most efficient, practical, and comfortable. Students in many classrooms, however, may find large-group instruction boring and unchallenging, while other students find it too difficult and do not learn well when taught in this manner. Strategies presented in this chapter to help teachers succeed with larger numbers of high school students included: (a) preassessment; (b) flexible classroom systems; (c) compacting; (d) alternative responses and assignments; (e) support tactics for slower students; (f) challenging more able students; and (g) remembering reviews.

High school teachers should realize that although traditional whole-group instruction may be the most effective way to prepare students to score well on standardized tests, some teachers may be more successful using small-group or project strategies. It should also be clear that when the goal of instruction is not solely performance on traditional standardized tests, but rather the retention of learning beyond the test or the application of concepts and principles in the real world, traditional methods of instruction sometimes interfere with learning effectiveness. Problem-solving strategies, collaborative inquiry, and other techniques that help students make permanent meaning for themselves from what they are learning are the teaching methods that seem more effective.

An additional reason for using teaching strategies that go beyond traditional whole-group, lecture–discussion format is to better serve the growing diversity found in today's high schools. Effective teachers have always recognized that every student deserves and requires special attention and adaptation of learning experiences to meet his or her needs, interests, abilities, and attitudes. The increasing diversity of students in today's high schools makes it essential to provide differentiated instruction that responds effectively to that diversity. Some examples of strategies discussed in this chapter that add variety, provide choices, and respond well to student diversity include; (a) unit teaching and planning; (b) cooperative learning; and (c) case studies and simulations. Additionally, major methods for differentiating instruction were presented which included: (a) learning contracts; (b) grading contracts; (c) independent study; and (d) mastery learning.

If these and other strategies are to be effectively implemented, high school teachers will have to change their teaching styles significantly. This may be particularly difficult for high school teachers if the primary model for developing a teaching style depends upon how a person was taught when he or she was a student. Models for high school teachers tend to be college professors, who themselves are often less than effective exemplars of differentiated instruction. Nevertheless, moving away from teaching as talking, and incorporating alternative strategies that move students into the role of the classroom "worker," have become increasingly popular with high school teachers wrestling with dramatic changes in their students and in the time frame that shapes their teaching. We predict that methods described in this chapter, and others, will become increasingly visible in high school classrooms as the first decade of the 21st century unfolds.

CONNECTIONS TO OTHER CHAPTERS

As new technology floods the typical high school classroom with information, the impact on teaching strategies and classroom life should be immense. Teaching as primarily the provision of information will be passé. Alternative instructional strategies that focus on investigation, application, and problem-solving will flourish. These two chapters, then, are really one.

ACTION STEPS

This might be a good time to investigate the extent to which practicing teachers are willing or able to implement modifications to their classrooms that accommodate increasing student diversity. Ask five high school teachers the following questions, collect and analyze their comments, and prepare a brief essay on the topic of "Personalizing the High School Curriculum: Fact or Fantasy?"

Questions for teachers:

1. How much academic diversity is there in your classes? That is, what range of achievement exists in the classes you teach?

2. Does the way students are seated in your classroom reflect these achievement differences? Do you determine where students sit, or do you permit them to decide for themselves?

3. Do you use the "normal curve" when issuing grades in these classes, or do you use some system that focuses on individual progress?

4. Are the really smart kids in your classes ever bored?

5. Are the slow students in your classes ever frustrated because they have difficulty keeping up?

6. Do you ever excuse high-achieving students from lessons that the rest of the class pursues? If so, what alternatives do you give these more advanced students?

7. Have you found ways to assist and support slower learners so that they can achieve at least the minimum you expect? If so, what strategies have you found useful?

8. Do you ever provide alternative homework assignments? If so, what are some examples you could share?

9. Do you ever use any type of peer tutoring or team learning that might involve students assisting each other? If so, how well does it work for you?

10. Have you ever used subgrouping in your classes? If so, for what purposes and for what length of time?

11. How do you keep all the kids involved during class discussions?

DISCUSSION QUESTIONS

1. High school students say that the key to their contentment with the block schedule is the extent to which their teachers change activities during the period. How would you modify a traditional classroom in order to keep students involved and engaged?

2. Which modifications to teacher-directed instruction are most likely to be effective in accommodating student diversity?

3. Which of the alternative instructional strategies seems easiest to implement? Which seems to fit your style best?

4. What is your best guess about the extent to which teachers will be able to utilize one or more alternative instructional strategies on a regular basis?

REFERENCES

Atwell, N. (1998). In the middle: New understandings about writing, reading, and learning. Second Edition. Portsmouth, NH: Heinemann/Boynton/Cook Publishers.

Armstrong, D. G., & Savage, T. V. (1998). *Teaching in the secondary school.* Fourth Edition. Upper Saddle River, NJ: Prentice-Hall.

Aronsen, E. (1978). *The jigsaw classroom.* Beverly Hills, CA: Sage Publications.

Block, J. H., Efthim, H. E., & Burns, R. B. (1989) *Building effective mastery learning schools.* NY: Longman.

Breaking ranks: Changing an American institution. (1996). Reston, VA: National Association of Secondary School Principals.

Brewer, D. J., Rees, D. I., Argys, M. (1995). Detracking America's schools: The reform without cost? *Phi Delta Kappan, 77*(3), 210–216.

Brooks, J. G., & Brooks, M. G. (1993). *In search of understanding: The case for constructivist classrooms.* Alexandria, VA: The Association for Supervision and Curriculum Development.

Brophy, J. (1979). *Teacher behavior and student achievement.* East Lansing, Michigan: Institute for Research on Teaching, Michigan State University.

Canady, R. L., & Rettig, M.D. (1995). *Block scheduling: A catalyst for change in high schools.* Princeton, NJ: Eye on Education Inc.

Guskey, T. (1988, Mar-April). Research on group-based mastery learning programs: A meta-analysis. *Journal of Educational Research, 81,* 197–216.

Jackson, D. (1942). *The unit method of teaching and learning.* New York: John S. Swift Company.

Johnson, D., Johnson, R., & Holubec, E. (1993). *Advanced cooperative learning.* Edina, MN: Interaction Book Company.

Jones, A. (1939). *Principles of unit construction.* New York: McGraw-Hill.

Joyce, B., & Weil, Marsha (1996). *Models of Teaching.* Fifth Edition. Boston: Allyn & Bacon.

Kagan, S. (1994). *Cooperative learning.* San Juan Capistrano, CA: Kagan Cooperative Learning.

Kauchak, D., & Eggen, P. (1998). *Learning and teaching: Research-based methods.* Third Edition. Boston: Allyn & Bacon.

Oakes, J. (1985). *Keeping track: How American schools structure inequality.* New Haven: Yale University Press.

Rosenshine, B. (1987, May-June). Explicit teaching and teacher training. *Journal of Teacher Education, 38,* 34–36.

Schurr, S., Thomason, J., & Thompson, M. (1995). *Teaching at the middle level: A professional's handbook.* Boston: DC Heath.

Sharan, Y., & Sharan, S. (1992). *Expanding cooperative learning through group investigation.* New York: Teachers College Press.

Sizer, T. (1992). *Horace's school: Redesigning the American high school.* Boston: Houghton Mifflin Company.

Slavin, R. (1995). *Cooperative learning: Theory, research, and practice.* Boston: Allyn & Bacon.

Stewart, W. J. (1983). *Unit teaching: Perspectives and prospects.* Saratoga, CA: R & E Publishers.

Tomlinson, C. (Summer, 1994). Middle school and acceleration: Guidance from research and the kids, *Journal of Secondary Gifted Education, 5,* 42–51.

Tomlinson, C. (September, 1993). Independent study: A flexible tool for encouraging academic and personal growth. *Middle School Journal, 25,* 55–59.

Wasserman, S. (1993). *Getting down to cases. Learning to teach with case studies.* New York: Teacher's College Press.

Wasserman, S. (1994). *Introduction to case study teaching.* New York: Teacher's College Press.

Webb, N., & Farivar, S. (1994). Promoting helping behavior in cooperative small groups in middle school mathematics. *American Educational Research Journal, 31,* 369–395.

Winebrenner, S. (1992). *Teaching gifted students in the regular classroom.* Minneapolis, MN: Free Spirit Press.

CHAPTER 4

TECHNOLOGY IN THE EMERGENT HIGH SCHOOL

WHAT YOU WILL LEARN IN THIS CHAPTER

Why the use of technology is important to all high schools

How to develop a school plan to use technology

The coordination of technology in a high school setting

Instructional uses of technology for personalizing learning

Distance learning and collaborating for research

Administrative uses of technology

Technology and the future of high schools

School leaders will work with others to develop and implement a long-term strategic plan for use of technology in the school. The plan . . . will allow for ongoing changes in technology and adapt itself to continual changes in the school program.

Schools will make technology integral to curriculum, instruction and assessment . . . Helping teachers to individualize instruction.

High schools will equip classrooms with technology necessary to prepare students for life in the 21st century.

Every high school will designate a technology resource person to provide technical assistance and to consult with staff to assist them in finding the people, information, and materials that they need to make best use of technology

—*Breaking Ranks,* p. 37

THE IMPACT OF TECHNOLOGY

An announcement in *Education Week* for summer offerings at Teachers' College, Columbia University, listed the following three course titles: "Designing Educational Activities using the Internet," "Models of Cooperative Learning with Computers," and "Using Computers to Teach Problem Solving and Critical Thinking." Connecting every classroom and library in America to the Internet was one of the ten points in President Clinton's "Call to Action for American Education" that followed his State of the Union speech given in January, 1996. Bill Gates of Microsoft sees a world of powerful, high-speed networks stretching across the information superhighway and shifting the computer industry's center of gravity from the desktop. Says Gates, "The advances in communication . . . will create news ways of communication for learning, education, and commerce that go far beyond anything done to date" (Brandt & Cortese, 1994).

Technology has always been a part of public education. Broadly defined, it can include everything from radio, tape recorders, overhead projectors, and television, to a piece of chalk in the hand of a creative teacher. Computers are simply the most recent development. A humorous account of the new technology listed "B.O.O.K." as one technological advance that is being overlooked in the haste to modernize the classroom. The late Marshall McLuhan ventured that all technology was an extension of some part of the human organism. He observed that the wheel is an extension of the foot, as the computer is an extension of the nervous system (McLuhan & Fiore, 1968). Extending his metaphor, the communication satellites which now encircle the earth may turn the central nervous system back onto itself, making manifest the interconnectedness of all life.

The impact of technology on high schools is inescapable. Every school uses technology in some form or another. The effect of new technological advances, such as the computer and its peripherals, is much less universal. David Thornburg, a leading proponent of integrating new technology into formal schooling, reflected that "while technological advances have changed our society into a global village, today's classrooms continue to function as microworlds isolated from the real world" (Thornburg, 1991). While his remarks can be tempered by progress made in the last five years, it is still true that many high school classrooms do not have the technology found in the homes of many of the students. In his book, *Endangered Species: Children of Promise* (1989), D. P. Doyle perceives a more substantive problem. He writes:

> There are no limits to educational technology; there are only limits to school organization that limits its uses. As long as schools are organized like factories of the late 19th and early 20th centuries, educational technology will only be a flickering hope (p. 3).

Obviously, the use of technology is not an end in itself. The goal of education is and has always been to use technology as a tool to teach content. Decisions about what technology to purchase, where to place it, and how to use it for the improvement of teaching and learning are critical. Where technology plays a major role, both instructionally and administratively, high schools begin with strategic planning.

PLANNING FOR TECHNOLOGY

A strategic plan for the short- and long-term use of technology is an outgrowth of the overall plan for school improvement. The purchase and use of technology must be based on the outcomes that the school leadership desires. What are the school's aspirations for its graduates, and what does the school want to accomplish that can be enhanced by the use of technology? These questions must be answered before finite resources are invested in the latest technological advances. A large number of computers housed at a school site is not prima facie evidence that technology is integrated in the curriculum.

The strategic plan can be part of a district-wide plan or simply a plan for an individual high school. Because of budgetary constraints, school leaders should maintain open communication with the district personnel who have an overview of the status of the total system. At the building level, the technology plan can be developed by a task force of teachers and administrators with input from all staff. The plan should be consistent with school and district goals, and acceptable to all parties who are implicated in its realization. At Presque Isle High School in Presque Isle, Maine, the technology plan was developed by a committee of both technical and non-technical personnel who presented a draft of the plan to the school board for information and approval.

As the plan was under development, outside consultants were used to help determine what was to be done with new technology. Committee members also visited schools to see technology in operation, and attended trade shows to learn about new developments in hardware and software. They learned that in the long run, more money would likely be spent on software than hardware. Thus they decided to make software decisions first.

Carter (1996) suggests a systems theory approach in developing a technology plan. Her approach has five major stages: awareness, understanding, commitment, implementation, and assessment. She recommends that a task force or a committee of interested school personnel be appointed to determine useful technologies and funding strategies. These decisions must be based on an awareness of new technologies, an understanding of the potential of specific technologies to improve learning opportunities for students, and the availability of funding to support specific efforts. If a school employs a technology person, certainly he or she should be a member of the technology committee. Awareness is similar to a review of the salient literature in a research study. It means finding out what others have done in order to build on their successes and avoid pitfalls. Similar to what was done at Presque Isle, the awareness stage might involve outside consultants and visits to technology expositions.

Awareness should help the committee understand the instructional applications of various technologies and how to integrate them into practice. The more accurately the plan reflects the current thinking of the faculty, the more likely it is to be accepted. The plan must resonate with the people who are going to implement it. If it does not, it will likely suffer the fate of so many educational documents, written in sincerity, that occupy shelf space in many high schools. When the plan also proposes using technology to reduce the amount of paperwork, its appeal increases.

In the commitment stage, all people impacted by the plan agree to carry it out. Commitment is enhanced when the people affected are consulted, especially if those people are asked to sign a statement indicating their willingness to help implement the plan. Posting a plan signed by all faculty and staff increases motivation to implement the plan. Implementation, however, requires more than commitment.

Certain factors seem especially important to implementation. Communication is essential. Newsletters prepared for faculty and staff are an excellent way to share decisions, explain resource allocations, announce staff development opportunities, and update stakeholders on the plan's progress. Offering opportunities for the community to use existing technology and to plan to use new technology are excellent ways to increase their awareness and support. Some high schools invite community members to enroll in training sessions in the late afternoon or evening, or on Saturdays. For the faculty and staff, inservice is the key, and it can take many forms. It may involve formal workshops or mentoring, or time at a faculty meeting for someone to share an idea or a project. Sometimes placing students in leadership roles with technology can pay rich dividends both for teachers and students. Knowledgeable students can plan new programs or teach teachers about the nuances of the computer.

An implementation factor often overlooked is a calendar of events including assigned responsibilities. A plan must have vision. It should establish the course for several years in advance. The calendar of events places the implementation of the plan in perspective and provides an achievable set of short-term objectives. The calendar of events is revised each year based on an assessment of the previous year's accomplishments.

The final stage of the systems approach is assessment. It is the means by which school personnel determine the degree to which the technology plan was implemented. It may be helpful to track the use of different forms of technology by faculty. Reviewing sign up sheets for computer labs, tracking software purchases, and examining short- and long-range plans are examples of tracking strategies. High schools that use some form of teacher-developed learning guides can reveal the degree of technological integration. Teachers can be asked to respond to questions about the adequacy of technology for achieving instructional goals, the adequacy of the equipment for the numbers of students served, and the adequacy of technology for meeting the instructional needs of various students. Teachers and students can be asked to assess different software packages. The information provided will serve as the basis for modifying the technology plan annually.

Once the technology has achieved a certain momentum, it is important to maintain the committee for professional development activities and exploration of new technologies. Many technologically adroit high schools rotate committee members each year to keep ideas flowing. Carter (1996) suggests some topics for continuing consideration:

- Developing policy recommendations for copyrights and acceptable use of the Internet.
- Leading curriculum development by gathering models of curricula reflecting technological implications, increasing awareness and understanding of the value of curriculum change, and facilitating discussions and development of new curricula that integrate technology effectively.
- Looking for grant opportunities by maintaining a database of possible grantors and generic grant proposals.
- Facilitating liaisons with the business community.
- Sponsoring meetings to discuss the impact of technology on student learning and engaged time.

COORDINATING THE USE OF TECHNOLOGY

High schools that have effectively implemented a technology plan are staffed with at least one person who is directly responsible for coordinating the use of technology. In larger schools, such as the Lake Region High School in Polk County, Florida, the technology resource person is a full-time employee. As a member of the school's technology task force, he works directly with departments and teaching teams toward the selection of hardware and software, conducts inservice meetings, mentors individual faculty members, prepares administrative information for teachers, and troubleshoots malfunctioning equipment. In a smaller school, the technology coordinator can work part-time, depending on staffing resources. The main concern is the designation of a staff member with expertise to serve as point person for the school's use of technology. One alternative approach to a full time or part time coordinator is the establishment of a tech team of teacher technology experts to help other teachers to understand and use technology. Having both a coordinator and a tech team is even better.

The lack of technical and administrative on-site support is often cited as a major barrier to teachers' willingness to experiment with technology to improve instruction.

INSTRUCTIONAL USES OF TECHNOLOGY

Instruction is often regarded as a technology that hopes to focus student attention on particular content and skills. Because individual students respond differently to various forms of instruction, the way information is presented is a crucial aspect of instructional design. Analogous to the work of an architect, instruction involves articulating the specifications and then designing a way to get there. The key is for the teacher to consider what is to be learned, by whom, and for what purpose. The more variegated the learning environment, the more responsive students will be.

Personalized Learning

The skillful use of technology expands learning opportunities for more students. Students are able to work individually at computer stations and proceed through predetermined curricula at their own rate. Coloma High School in Coloma, Michigan, has developed a business curriculum consisting of 42 foundational skills and 30 common business skills. Students begin study at a point commensurate with their background and proceed at their own rate. A simulated office facility at Winter Park High School in Winter Park, Florida, has students check in with a receptionist upon arrival at the facility and then proceed to a work station where they can log on to one of seven different courses. The software enables the business teachers to expand offerings while providing a schedule flexible enough to meet the needs of students. Students can stop and start any course at any time without disrupting students or teachers.

Personalized learning systems begin with collecting salient information about individual learners, which is used to plan and implement learning environments. In essence, each student is provided with a personalized educational plan. Self-paced learning is one way to adjust instruction to individual students. The use of learning guides that include several different activities to reach common outcomes is another. The learning activities can be designed to accommodate different learning styles. The adoption of mastery learning would emphasize the mastery of educational objectives, not the amount of time spent working. Computer technology enables high schools to rethink conventional scheduling and make adjustments to fit the learning activities. Few if any authentic learning activities match the conventional schedule of 50- to 55-minute periods.

Computer-assisted Learning

Formal instruction establishes a climate for learning. Real learning occurs when students can integrate new knowledge into existing cognitive structures and apply the results to real-life problems. The Cambridge Rindge and Latin School in Cambridge, Massachusetts, integrates technology with American history using CD-ROMs and laser disks. At the Center for Applied Technology, a part of Wheeling High School in Wheeling, West Virginia, students use computers in combination with laser disks, video cameras, and VCRs to solve problems. Students at the Mayfield High School in Las Cruces, New Mexico, apply interactive simulations to recreate history. In their supercomputing lab they investigate scientific problems that can only be solved by computer simulations.

The use of CD-ROMs and the Internet allow high schools to reinvent the concept of student research, upgrading the level of questioning and increasing the required level of reasoning. Working alone, in pairs, or in teams, students in Bellingham, Washington, are taught to move through each step of the research cycle: questioning, planning, gathering, sorting and sifting, synthesizing, evaluating, and reporting (McKenzie, 1996). High school teachers in Bellingham emphasize research questions that require either problem solving or decision making. Students then try to determine where they can find the best information, and what sources are likely to provide the most insight with the most efficiency. Sometimes the students interface with university professors or graduate students via e-mail to sharpen their research questions and subquestions. The students learn when and when not to access the Internet. In many cases, books and CD-ROMs will prove more appropriate. When the students believe they have solved their problem, they then proceed to the reporting stage. Using multimedia, the students report their findings and recommendations to an audience of decision makers (simulated or real).

A joint project involving Northwestern University and New Trier High School in Winnetka, Illinois, provides on-line mentoring opportunities for science students as they work on long-term projects. The idea is for real scientists to offer advice and criticism to the high school students. In an earth science class, students investigate topics ranging from earthquakes to avalanches for approximately seven weeks. The on-line mentor helps them sharpen the focus of their investigation and sometimes even helps them obtain and analyze data (O'Neill, Wagner & Gomez, 1996).

The creation of a school Web page breathes life into composition classes. Using Pagemaker, ClarisWorks, or Front Page, students at North Rockland High School in New York create an electronic newspaper on the Web. The school's Web page is linked to the two feeder middle schools and the county's home page. Both the newspaper and the Web page give students the opportunity to test their writing skills on audiences outside of the school (Monahan & Tomko, 1996).

Distance Learning

The Web is an example of distance learning. It enables students to communicate with other students without regard to time and distance. Technology removes such barriers, permitting students from remote communities or from communities without adequate resources to access experts and information found only in larger centers. Many small high schools have limited curricula because of their size. In these schools, students often miss opportunities to complete advanced placement courses and other challenging courses because few students are interested in enrolling or because the courses are not relevant to enough students' post-secondary aspirations. Sometimes the school lacks facilities or qualified faculty to offer the advanced courses. Moreover, singleton courses, which advanced placement courses usually are even in larger high schools, often disrupt the master schedule.

A distance learning initiative can bring advanced courses to even the most remote areas. In British Columbia, the Ministry of Education, in cooperation with the Open Learning Agency and nine distance education schools, provides advanced course offerings to students in small high schools throughout the province. Over 350 students are enrolled. Available courses include biology, calculus, chemistry, law 12, English 12, science and technology 11, writing 12, communications 11, and career and personal planning 11/12. School districts and schools can purchase seats for each course for $350 per seat. New Directions in Distance Learning (NDDL), as this project is named, also offers courses to adult learners who want to complete secondary requirements (Hufty, 1996).

NDDL requires a teacher at each high school to serve as a course facilitator responsible for providing technical assistance, advice, and encouragement to the students. The facilitator's role is usually a part of the teacher's regular assignment, although sometimes it is assigned to a librarian or a counselor (Hufty, 1996).

A mentor serves as the course instructor, and provides guidance and advice in addition to teaching the course. "NDDL combines the traditional correspondence course with a range of technology tools that support a variety of learning . . . styles" (Hufty, 1996, p. 1). Among the technology to which students have access is a CD-ROM–equipped computer and access to FirstClass, an on-line bulletin board system through which they can interact with the mentor and other students. Participating schools are required to have direct access to the Internet with their own router and local area network. Most of the courses also make use of a public television network operated by the Open-Learning Agency. Each high school site must be able to view the broadcasts, aired in late evening or early morning, and tape them. In addition, the high schools must provide students with access to a teleconferencing unit with a line dedicated to that purpose, and a graphics tablet and media conferencing software for audiographic sessions (Hufty, 1996).

Virtual High School, a private school in Vancouver, BC, uses computers and on-line communication to allow students to set their own agendas. They pursue these agendas using technology to acquire and synthesize information. All students get a Powerbook and do much of their work from home by plugging into the school's own computer network. Working with learning assistants (they are not called teachers), students create their own curriculum. Teachers are viewed as mentors who know more than the students, but also as learners. The emphasis is on individually motivated learning programs. Some of the students design their own software working with commercial customers (O'Neil, 1996). The curriculum the students take is up to them. They decide what they are going to study and with whom. Courses do not exist. The teacher's role as authority who sets deadlines, decides what students are going to study, and determines how they are to demonstrate their understanding of the material becomes less significant (O'Neill, 1996). The teacher is more of a mentor in the true sense of the term. (In Homer's *Odyssey*, Mentor was Odysseus' friend, and undertook the education of Telemachus, Odysseus' son). It was first thought that there would be no need for a home base for the Virtual High School other than a space large enough for a computer server. The gregarious nature of the students, however, resulted in the purchase of an old house with places where students can plug into the information highway (O'Neil, 1996).

Installing a satellite dish on a high school campus allows schools to offer courses for as few as one student. Working with universities, such as Oklahoma State, high schools can add to their curriculum by purchasing courses. For example, the Columbus Alternative High School in Columbus, Ohio, offers satellite classes in the Japanese language.

Many high schools, such as the James Bowie High School in Austin, Texas, provide online bibliographic and encyclopedic services from Prodigy, CompuServe or America Online. In addition, each of the services offers a connection to the Internet and its infinite supply of information. School media centers can also connect to state and national libraries, thus expanding their print and nonprint collections.

At the MAST Academy in Miami, Florida, classroom instruction and student investigations are enhanced by several CD-ROMs including the CD/microfiche version of the Newsbank Electronic Index; a database of over 800 academic abstracts; a database containing thousands of articles from over 750 domestic and international magazines, newspapers and journals; and Masterplots II, a comprehensive reference source containing the texts from ten of the Salem Press Printed Reference Series in fiction, nonfiction, drama and bibliographies. Additionally, students and teachers have on-line access to 450 databases via DIALOG. The school also has a satellite dish that connects to 21 C-band satellites (Jenkins & Eads, 1996).

The Oracle Corporation, a leading supplier of database software for microcomputers and servers, has created the Oracle Channel. It combines satellite broadcasts with personal communication devices, allowing instantaneous interaction between the instructor and the student. The Oracle Channel integrates the most advanced viewer response systems, broadcast capabilities, and instructional techniques to provide a virtual classroom experience. This implementation of interactive distance learning for public training is the first of its kind in terms of scope and size. Services like the Oracle Channel are the first step in delivering state-of-the-art distance education to students (Reneke, 1995).

Remediation and English for Speakers of Other Languages (ESOL): Increasing the graduation rate is one of the seven goals included in Goals 2000. Almost every high school has students who get low grades, have lost interest, have failed a grade or two, and get low scores on standardized tests. They are the students at greatest risk for dropping out of school and for not succeeding in life. They are ill-prepared to be lifelong learners.

Using computer technology and software that emphasizes mastery of basic skills, application of concepts, positive work habits, and thinking skills, many high schools are developing programs to salvage at-risk students. For many such students, school work has little or no impact on the quality of their lives. These students begin their formal education with weak information-processing skills that are rarely augmented by specific instruction aimed at making them better learners. A combination of technology and personal attention has been found to be successful. At Haines City High School in Haines City, Florida, such a program has increased the graduation rate among at-risk students steadily. Computer-assisted instruction provides the means for students to work at their own level. The computer has infinite patience and doesn't move to the next level until the student is ready.

One of the major challenges in reaching the 90 percent graduation rate is finding ways to reach the growing number of non–English-speaking students who enroll in American high schools. Preparing these students to learn in an English-speaking world is a major problem. Typically, high schools establish special classes for the most needy of these students. Instruction is provided by teachers specially trained in ESOL and is often quite conventional.

Educators at Blair High School in Pasadena, California, have found a way to integrate technology to their efforts to meet the diverse learning needs of its limited English proficient (LEP) students. The 312 Hispanic, Vietnamese, Chinese, Japanese, Filipino, Indonesian, and Polish students all learn the same language—multimedia. According to their teacher, technology permits LEP students to participate in the learning immediately, regardless of their English or technological proficiency. A student entering the program is paired with another student of the same linguistic and cultural background. Together they search information databases using a personal computer. Students also work in groups based on their proficiency levels. A typical group might have the student proficient in reading and writing English as the leader, a non–English-speaking student responsible for graphics, and a student still struggling with written English creating hypercard stacks. One measure of the program's success is the fact that a cadre of LEP students is now responsible for publishing the school's newspaper electronically (Bruder, Buschbaum, Hill & Orlando, 1992).

The Horace Mann Academic Middle School in the mission district of San Francisco began a program to enable Chinese bilingual students to use Chinese on the computer. Using a Chinese translation software program, a subscription to America Online, and a digitized writing pad, students can use e-mail in Chinese to do research and to communicate with others who speak Chinese. The students initiated a pen pal request in three of the Chinese language newsgroups. They received over 300 e-mail responses from Hong Kong, Taiwan, Singapore, England, mainland China, and the United States. Because most of the Chinese pen pals expected the Chinese LEP students to be good English tutors, the LEP students became highly motivated to learn. They are now publishing the first online student newspaper in Chinese. They are also obtaining the first student Web site in both English and Chinese characters. The project has helped the students master English while furthering development of their primary language skills (Fang, 1996).

Technology as a Course

Historically, technology education has been conceived as a cluster of elective subjects in the curriculum. Courses like woods, metals, and drafting have existed in high schools for years, usually for the students not planning to attend college. In some cases, technology courses have been perceived as prevocational education, preparing students for further training in vocational education (Bell & Erickson, 1991). In other instances, technology courses became dumping grounds for students who were unable or unmotivated to succeed in more academically oriented subjects. With the advent of reports such as the one authored by the Secretary's Commission on achieving Necessary Skills (SCANS), however, technology as a course has taken on a new meaning.

Technology education is now viewed at one extreme as preparation for success in college, and to a lesser degree, as a graduation requirement for all students. In order for it to succeed in either capacity, the public perception of technology courses as shop classes for students of low ability must be altered. Educators in high schools in the United States and Canada are working to facilitate a change in the public's perception of technology education.

At Wheeling High School's Center for Applied Technology in Wheeling, Illinois, the technology seminar is an introductory course for all students, with instruction in the following areas: robotics, audio and video production, satellite communication, computer graphic design, laser fiber optics, holography, flight simulation, music synthesis, biotechnology, fluid and pneumatic power systems, and computer problem solving. At the Thomas Haney Secondary Center in Maple Ridge, British Columbia, all students earn a credit in technology. In the school's continuous progress educational system, students complete learning guides in robotics, sign-making, animation, video editing, silkscreening, scriptwriting, computer graphics, and toolmaking. The Governor's School in Northern Virginia has ten technology labs: life sciences and biotechnology, computer systems, energy systems, prototyping and engineering, TV production, microelectronics, industrial automation and robotics, optics and modern physics, aerospace, and geoscience.

The new technology education is broader in scope and more rigorous. It reflects the public's tacit recognition that basic education for the 21st century must prepare all students for contingencies which are at best vaguely forseeable.

TECHNOLOGY IN TRADITIONAL ACADEMIC PROGRAMS

In English/language arts, students use word processing as their primary writing tool. The development of student portfolios on CDs is a logical extension. Mathematics instruction is enhanced by the extensive use of graphing calculators. Animal dissections in science are accomplished without the use of specimens. Probes and sensors alter variables in laboratory settings to test different effects. Laser disk technology is used in foreign language classes to provide students with authentic situations for using a second language. French students lunch in a Paris cafe through programmed holographic manipulation and simulation. Television and satellite antennas access television programming in Spanish.

History comes alive through interactive simulations and historical re-creations. A picture atlas of the world on CD-ROM enhances teaching about other countries. Multimedia materials from the National Geographic Society combine visual images, video clips, music, voice, and text to engage student interest. Music theory is extended to more students by using piano and guitar laboratories. Students write orchestral arrangements and create their own music compositions using appropriate software. Satellites permit music teachers in one part of a state to listen to, critique, and advise students in another part of the state. Live theater uses computers to control the physical aspects of stage productions. Lighting schemes for musicals are programmed and stored on CDs. Schools subscribe to the collection of the National Gallery to Art for art criticism and the study of history. The works of Shakespeare, Bach, Frost, and Van Gogh are recorded on disk and retrieved.

High schools have fully networked business classrooms where students use word processing and spreadsheets and learn how to manage databases and present graphics. Computer-assisted drafting (CAD) systems train students for direct entry into the engineering world. Graphic arts classes use desktop publishing, publish the school newspaper, and generally operate professional printshops. Print and nonprint library collections are extended electronically. Student presentations of investigations are improved using Powerpoint and similar integrated software.

Where should computers be located to optimize student use? This is a question that is frequently asked and just as frequently debated. Many educators argue that the closer the computers are to students and teachers the more likely they are to be used. Citing the failure to integrate computers into daily instruction, others favor computer labs that can be shared by different classes. Ostensibly, it isn't an either/or situation. Computers in classrooms can be incorporated into daily instruction. Computer labs can lie dormant much of the school day if teachers do not choose to use them. A more important concern is how computers can be used to develop learning environments responsive to more students. Properly used, computers can replace the concept of the 900 square foot classroom with the concept of the world as classroom. They can change the role of the teacher from presenter of information to guide, facilitator, mentor, or research associate. They can change the role of the student from passive to active learner.

William Lynch, Director of the Educational Technology Leadership Program at George Washington University in Washington, D.C. (1990), cautions that there is a unique dimension to the interface that occurs between the individual student and the computer, because individuals bring with them different backgrounds, attitudes and beliefs. He writes, "a standard interface is not likely to meet the needs of all users" (p. 27). He sees the computer as the only reflective medium that is also interactive. "A computer with appropriate software can respond in innumerable ways to the varying responses of the user" (p. 27). The computer's novelty when compared to traditional instruction may offer an initial spark of interest to a reluctant learner. But learning is hard work, and initial interest may wane if the student has little desire to integrate new material into his or her cognitive structure.

ADMINISTRATIVE USES OF TECHNOLOGY

Technology can reduce the amount of paperwork for teachers, administrators and staff. It can improve schoolwide communication and can accelerate communication within and between school districts. It can refine attendance procedures and overall record keeping. It can provide more accurate records of student achievement for parents, other educators, and future schools or employers.

Technologically sophisticated high schools provide laptop computers for all teachers. One high school, Lake Region in Polk County, Florida, issues a Power Pack and a Style Writer to each teacher. They are taught how to use them by the full-time technical specialist. Using a local area network, teachers and administrators can communicate with one another regularly. Outlets are conveniently located throughout the school to facilitate network use. For example, general announcements can be broadcast over the electronic bulletin board or by closed circuit television. Since each teacher, administrator, and secretary has an electronic mailbox, specific messages are e-mailed from administrator to teacher or vice versa and from teacher to teacher. The network also allows the sending of copies of messages to one or more persons.

Teachers report attendance directly to an attendance office without need of conventional forms. Salient student information is downloaded onto the power packs of appropriate teachers. A software package enables teachers to eliminate grade books and plan books. Lesson plans are maintained on disks by the teachers and filed each week with the assistant principal. Teachers can also communicate directly with the school copy center. They simply create a handout, test, or worksheet, and transmit it to the copy center, where copies are run on the Risograph machine. Referrals to the dean are made electronically. Teachers log the student's name, the infraction and steps already taken. By checking the referral file, the dean knows in advance who will attend the lunch period detention on a given day. Rather than holding detention after school, the school does so during the lunch period. Students in detention eat a generic lunch and are unable to socialize with their friends.

The school calendar is maintained on the system. Any staff member can print out the weekly, monthly, or yearly calendar as needed. If a teacher wishes to add an event to the calendar, she or he clears it with one of the administrators and enters it in the appropriate file. Likewise, field trips (or field experiences, as they are called at Lake Region) are entered on the calendar with a list of the students who will attend. Similar lists are included for athletic teams, music groups, or other student groups who will be out of the school for a period of time.

When teachers have a problem entering grades, reporting attendance, or using the system, they request help from the technology specialist, who then helps the teacher and lists the problem and solution in the "help" file. Teachers with problems can then search the help file to see if the solution already exists before contacting the technology specialist directly. The technical assistant plans group inservice meetings based on common problems that teachers are experiencing. While the educators at Lake Region feel they are ahead of their colleagues in other district high schools, they believe they have only scratched the surface in realizing the potential of technology for improving the operation of the school.

CREATING LEARNING ENVIRONMENTS: TECHNOLOGY AND THE FUTURE

Winston Churchill wrote that "we shape our institutions and then they shape us." He was referring to the fact that a society's institutions exist to serve various functions. As they are organized to serve those functions, they in turn subtly influence society's members. Their hidden agenda is profound. The way in which high schools are structured may well contribute as much or more to a student's education than the written curriculum.

The conventional high school places students in classrooms, each of which is assigned a teacher and about 25–30 students, and occupies an area of 750–900 square feet. The furniture, desks or tables, all face in the direction of the chalkboard. Instruction is usually dominated by the teacher, with presentations and discussions the main fare. Students are exposed to the same material, in the same way, at the same rate. Homework is assigned by the teacher, and group tests are administered at the end of chapters or units to determine student learning. Everything is rather predictable. For students whose learning style requires structure, it is almost a perfect match.

Compare this setting with Disney's Epcot Center in Orlando, Florida. The dinosaur pavillion transports visitors back in time to experience a simulation of how things were when the dinosaurs roamed the planet. The Living Seas exhibit gives the illusion that you are actually under the sea observing the different life forms. A replica of the human body places the visitor inside looking out so that she or he experiences the body from inside the skin. These centers are not abstractions. They are meta-environments that teach by their very existence.

"Edutainment" programs, games that teach while entertaining, have become a force behind home computer buying. Many of today's high school students have CD-ROM–equipped personal computers capable of running interactive programs complete with sound, animation, and video clips of real events. Usually the personal computer comes equipped with various programs on the hard drive or a compact disk or two of reference material such as a thesaurus, a spell-checker, or a multimedia encyclopedia.

Software that mixes fun and learning has turned the personal computer into a lively, interactive tool. The number of programs featuring interactivity is growing rapidly. Soon, high school students may stay home from school so as not to interrupt their education. The old drill-and-practice software, typical of what once was considered effective educational programming, is no longer viable for students in the information age. These programs' linearity conflicts with the changed expectations that the students bring to school. John Kernan, CEO of Curriculum TV Corporation, predicts that "the ability to have a direct home-school connection, with interactive programming that's as attractive as MTV, will make a profound difference in American education (Armstrong & Jones, 1994).

The present is changing so rapidly that any prediction of what life or education might be in the 21st century is perilous at best. The trends, however, seem clear. Life in high schools will be different. Building on the creative present described in this chapter, some likely scenarios include the following:

- Virtual reality will be expanded. Students will be able to travel, recreate historical events, and build wind tunnels, all through programmed and packaged simulations under their control.
- Equipment to produce CDs will be a part of every high school media center. Students will be able to build portfolios of their accomplishments in all subject areas. When a student transfers or graduates, the CD will accompany him/her. The CD will become the report card of the future.
- Learning communities that transcend geographic boundaries will be established. Students will work with their peers from high schools throughout the country. They may also become members of multinational investigative teams.
- Monitors will range from large-screened, wall-mounted units to devices small enough to be carried in backpacks, on wrists, or as hand-held notebooks. Power packs will become standard issue for all students.
- Salient data about each student will be integrated into instructional programs to accommodate individual differences. Detailed learning histories, and current progress information on each student will be available for downloading by teachers, students, and parents via telecommunications.

- Teachers will instruct from their own homes and connect with students' homes through computer and telephone networks using audio-graphic technology that will allow live interaction between teacher and student (Frick, 1991).
- Artificial boundaries separating content will begin to disappear as the speed of information transmission broadens perspective and expands relationships.
- Classrooms will be replaced by learning spaces appropriate for specific learning tasks. Teachers will work collaboratively to help individual students learn. They will design technology interfaces to match the individual learning needs of each student.

In 1968, George Leonard, then the educational editor for *Look* Magazine, authored a book with the provocative title, *Education and Ecstasy*. In it he described a school for the year 2001. At the Kennedy school, students chose from an array of educational environments which were in operation from eight in the morning until six in the afternoon. The environments were really geodesic dome structures equipped with the latest technology. In one geodesic dome you found students seated at one of forty learning consoles facing outward toward a 10–square-foot learning display. Each student's learning display was reflected from a hologram–conversation screen that encircled the inner surface of the dome. Each display joined with the display on either side, creating a panoramic effect (Leonard, 1968).

When a student logged on the computer using an electronic identification device, his or her complete learning history was recalled from a central database. The student put on a combination earphone and brainwave sensor device that reiterated his or her last learning session. A dialogue between the student and the learning program then began. Five variables were present in all dialogues:

1. A data bank of basic, commonly agreed-upon knowledge, arranged in an interactive style

2. Basic material arranged in cross-matrix fashion so that random topics were included in learning sequences to add novelty and surprise

3. Analysis of the student's brain-wave pattern in terms of his or her general state of consciousness and short-term memory strength

4. The student's overt motor responses as typed on the keyboard or spoken into a directional microphone

5. Coordination and interaction between the material on different learning displays. (Leonard, 1968).

It is amazing to recount Leonard's insights about the use of technology in creating restructured environments conducive to student learning. In this book he argued that, ". . . if an environment fails to draw or educate, it is the environment's, not the learner's fault" (Leonard, 1968, p. 154). In the introduction to his chapter on "Visiting Day, 2001 A.D.," he wrote, "We don't really have to wait until the year 2001; it is only people, their habits, their organizations that take so long to move. The alternatives, the real alternatives, exist now" (Leonard, 1968, p. 140). With regard to the role of technology as a means for reforming high schools, his admonition is as true today as it was in 1968.

SUMMARY

The impact of modern technology, especially computers, on high schools is considerable and inescapable. Despite its availability, however, modern technology is seldom utilized for instruction in many high school classrooms. This underutilization obscures the virtually unlimited potential for improving teaching and learning through the effective use of technology. This does not mean that the use of technology should be an end in itself. It does mean that technology is a tool that should be used whenever it can maximize student learning.

Strategic planning is crucial to successful use of technology for instruction and other educational purposes. Decisions about what to purchase, where to place it, and how to use it for the improvement of teaching and learning are critical. One successful avenue for engaging in strategic planning for technology is the establishment of planning task forces that include representatives from stakeholders including teachers and other school- and district-level educators. This kind of planning helps ensure that final plans will be consistent with school and district goals and objectives, and acceptable to all parties who are implicated by the plan. The five major stages of implementation for this process approach are awareness, understanding, commitment, implementation, and assessment.

Instructional uses of technology discussed in the chapter included personalized learning, computer-assisted learning, distance learning, and technology courses. Technology is an effective teaching tool in traditional academic programs as well in the uses mentioned above. Word processing can be especially useful in English/language arts courses, graphing calculators can enhance mathematics instruction, and animal dissections in science can be accomplished without the use of specimens. Likewise, laser disk technology can be used in foreign language classes to provide students with authentic situations for practice with a second language, while history can come alive through interactions and historical re-creations.

The effective use of technology can help change the role of teachers from presenters of information to guides, facilitators, mentors, and research assistants. It can help change the role of students to that of active learners. The administrative use of technology also offers many opportunities to reduce the paperwork for teachers, administrators, and staff members, and can greatly improve communication both within and outside the school.

The rapid pace of change in the world of technology makes predictions of what the future holds risky at best. However, the likely scenario, as presented in this chapter, focuses on the possible future innovative use of technology such as virtual reality.

CONNECTIONS TO OTHER CHAPTERS

Some students who are turned off by traditional schooling can be turned on to learning when they have an opportunity to use technology. They see school as more likely to add to the quality of their lives. Teachers serving as advisers use technologically developed databases to help advisees make better decisions.

ACTION STEPS

1. Obtain and review several school technology plans. Investigate the process used to create them. Using these plans as guides, develop your own plan, incorporating the current best thinking in the instructional and administrative uses of technology. Once your plan is complete, develop a one-year calendar of events for implementing it.

2. Write a job description for a technology resource person for a high school staff.

3. Create independent study projects using the internet as a resource in two or more subject areas found in the high school curriculum.

4. Add to the list of future possibilities for technology and high school education.

5. Learn all you can about the use of virtual reality, and create a venue for learning in which students immerse themselves in a learning environment. You may focus on one subject or several.

6. Locate high schools using technology to improve administration and management and describe what they are doing. Compare your findings with the example provided in this chapter.

DISCUSSION QUESTIONS

1. Do you agree with McLuhan's assertion that all technology is an extension of the human organism? Explain your position using concrete examples.

2. Is Doyle's observation that the school's organization inhibits the proper use of technology (made in 1989) true today? Give reasons for why you think one way or the other.

3. How can technology be used to personalize the instructional process? Give specific examples.

4. How does technology as a course differ from technology integrated into various courses?

REFERENCES

Armstrong, L., & Jones, D. (1994). Revolution: Technology is reshaping education at home and at school. *Business Week, America ON-LINE.* McGraw Hill, Inc.

Bell, T. P., & Erekson, T. L. (1991). Technology education: Preparing students for success in college. *Journal of Industrial Education, 28*(4), 73–75.

Brandt, R., & Cortese, A. (1994). Bill Gates' vision: He's pushing microsoft past the PC and onto the information highway. *Business Week, America ON-LINE,* McGraw-Hill.

Breaking ranks: Changing an American institution. (1996). Reston, VA: National Association of Secondary School Principals.

Bruder, I., Buschbaum, H. M., Hill, M. & Orlando, L. (1992). School reform: Why you need technology to get there. *Electronic Learning, 11*(8), 22–28.

Carter, K. (1996). After the plan's approved: Keeping the technology planning process alive. *Technology and Learning, 16,* 28–37.

Doyle, D. P. (1989). *Endangered species: Children of promise.* New York: McGraw-Hill.

Fang, F. (1996). Traveling the internet in China. *Educational Leadership, 54*(3), 27–29.

Frick, T. W. (1991). *Restructuring Education Through Technology.* Bloomington, IN: Phi Delta Kappa Educational Foundation.

Hufty, H. (1996). Wired learning: Technology and distance education in the curriculum. *NASSP Curriculum Report, 26*(2), 1–6.

Jenkins, J. M., & Eads, L. J. (1996). MAST academy: Navigating toward tomorrow. *International Journal of Educational Reform, 5*(1), 101–106.

Lynch, W. (1990). Social aspects of human-computer interaction. *Educational Technology, 30*(4), 26–31.

Leonard, G. (1968). *Education and ecstasy.* New York: Delacorte Press.

McKenzie, J. (1996). Making web meaning. *Educational Leadership, 54*(3), 30–32.

McLuhan, M., & Fiore, Q. (1968). *War and peace in the global village.* New York: Bantam Books.

Monahan, B., & Tomko, S. (1996). How schools can create their own web pages. *Educational Leadership, 54*(3), 37–38.

O'Neill, D. K., Wagner, R., & Gomez, L. M. (1996). Online mentors: Experimenting in science class. *Educational Leadership, 54*(3), 39–42.

O'Neil, J. (1996). A conversation with Crawford Kilian. *Educational Leadership, 54*(3), 12–17.

Reneke, F. (1994). *Learning on ONLINE: The Future of Educational Technology.* Unpublished paper.

Thornburg, D. D. (1991). *Education, technology, and paradigms of change for the 21st century.* San Carlos, CA: Starsong Publications.

5

RESPONDING TO AFFECTIVE NEEDS THROUGH ADVISEMENT AND ADVOCACY

WHAT YOU WILL LEARN IN THIS CHAPTER

Providing for the affective needs of adolescents

High school guidance and counseling

Student assistance and peer counseling programs

The goals and objectives of teacher advisory programs

Characteristics of successful teacher advisory programs

Roles of teachers and other educators in high school teacher advisory programs

The advisory curriculum

Student anonymity must be banished (Breaking Ranks, *p. vi*).

Every high school student will have a personal advocate to help him or her personalize the educational experience (Breaking Ranks, *p. 29*).

Each student needs to know that at least one adult in the school is closely concerned with his or her fate (Breaking Ranks, *p. 31*).

Advocates can perform many of the advising tasks, referring students to guidance counselors when they see the need (Breaking Ranks, *p. 32*).

Providing for the Affective Needs of Adolescents

Educators in successful high schools plan and implement many programs and guidance activities that focus on meeting the affective needs of students. They realize that the affective aspects of teaching and learning are important and closely related to the academic success of their students. In spite of pressure to stress memorization and subject matter coverage, significant amounts of time and effort at successful schools are devoted to meeting the affective needs of their students.

Adolescents' need for guidance in today's rapidly changing and unsure world has been well documented in the literature and need not be reviewed here. However, examples of these changes include: (1) a loss of traditional family support systems; (2) the prevalence of violence; (3) the accessibility and increased use of drugs; (4) high divorce rates; (5) increasing numbers of youth with AIDS and other sexually transmitted diseases; and (6) changing social conditions. These and other major changes often result in a loss of self-worth, a loss of social place, and unclear values (Killin & Williams, 1995; Takanishi & Hamburg, 1997). For these and numerous other reasons guidance is, and must continue to be, a major focus in high schools.

High School Guidance and Counseling

Virtually all high schools now provide a variety of special guidance and counseling services and employ school counselors. The resulting traditional programs and services that are essential to the functions of high schools are not discussed here in detail because they are well described and documented in the literature and are much more widely understood than the major focus of this chapter—teacher-based guidance (teacher advisory) programs. However, the importance of the more traditional components of high school guidance should not be underestimated.

Comprehensive guidance and counseling programs, which frequently include teacher advisory components, are present in many effective high schools. For example, members of the guidance department at Farragut High School, in Knoxville, Tennessee, work with the school staff and various agencies to assist students in recognizing and solving educational, vocational, and personal problems. Counselors hold individual conferences with students and meet with groups to review and discuss courses of study, post-secondary plans, scholarship concerns, and other areas where they can be of assistance. Parents are encouraged to communicate with counselors whenever they have questions or concerns about any phase of their child's program. Specific services provided by the Farragut Guidance Department include:

- Personal and academic counseling (support groups, individual conferences, placement changes, referrals to outside agencies, homebound teachers, assistance in study and test-taking skills)

- Orientation and registration assistance (graduation requirements, school policies, registration, vocational orientation, schedule changes, post-secondary entrance requirements)
- A career lab that offers individual assistance (college reference books, career information, vocational school and college catalogs, college applications, scholarship applications)
- Group assistance (college representative visits, college night and career day, financial aid workshops)
- Testing programs (state proficiency, SAT/ACT registration materials, career interest surveys, advanced placement examinations, temperament tests)
- Records maintenance (academic records, report cards, pupil progress reports, health records)
- Processes (withdrawal requests, emergency progress reports, transcript requests)

Traditional counseling services and guidance programs have been refocused at many high schools because of the changing needs of students served. For example, counselors at Del Valley High School in El Paso, Texas, perform a multitude of services for students. They serve as mediators, advocates, career education consultants, interpreters (of both other languages and other school district transcripts), and cheerleaders. They strive to bring together the entire Del Valley Community—staff and administrative personnel, referral agencies, the students themselves, and their parents. The counselors understand that life in the last decade has presented students with circumstances that were not even envisioned a mere half century ago. Many times helping to solve these problems requires counselors to employ all the skills they possess. It is usual for them to deal with teen pregnancy and teen parenting, gang intervention, crisis intervention of all types, chemical abuse, child abuse, domestic violence, career placement, and enhancement of student self-esteem in the same day.

Advisory programs, (discussed in some detail later in this chapter) are also important components of comprehensive high school guidance and counseling programs. For example, educators at Central Park East Secondary School in New York place a high priority on the importance of guidance from teacher advisors. They have initiated a "Senior Institute" to describe the final 2 years of high school. During these 2 years, students pursue a common core curriculum that includes two interdisciplinary blocks and an additional 1 hour course. Advisory meets four times each week for 45 minutes with the ratio of advisees to advisor being approximately 12 to 1. Advisors frequently work individually with their advisees and know them well because they have served as their advisors throughout their high school years. All professionals, including the principal, are advisors.

According to principal Paul Schwarz, major goals of the Central Park East program include "making sure every student is known well, improving home/school communications, and ensuring that there are no 'cracks for students to fall through'." Parent conferences are well attended at Central Park East because they are scheduled at convenient times for parents (e.g., 6:00–6:45 PM, Thursdays) and advisors know their advisees and their families very well. Advisors, who serve as experts on their advisees, meet frequently with family members and other teachers to ensure effective communication about students' needs. One major focus of the advisory program is the provision of assistance to advisees in preparing their graduation portfolios (personal communication, April 10, 1997).

STUDENT ASSISTANCE AND PEER COUNSELING PROGRAMS

Formal student assistance programs have been added as part of the guidance program at some high schools. Dixie High School, St. George, Utah, has a successful student assistance program that offers a support system to students troubled by social, emotional, family, or substance abuse problems that may be affecting their educational performance. Students may refer themselves or be referred by concerned staff members, family friends, community agencies, or their peers. Once the students are referred, counselors talk with them about their concerns and suggest options and sources of assistance. Options may include in-school support groups or community agencies. In-school support groups, an integral program component, are held once a week during school hours, with each group being directed by two trained staff members.

Peer counseling programs, which offer students opportunities to talk with other students about personal and academic concerns, are part of the guidance and counseling programs at some high schools. These programs cover topics such as homework concerns, friendships and other relationships, problems, family or teacher difficulties, peer pressures, and decision making. Riverside High School in Greer, South Carolina, which seeks to meet the affective needs of a very diverse student population, has a peer counseling program. Students are not tracked at Riverside, but rather placed according to their academic and affective needs. They are supported throughout the year instead of being left on their own after initial assistance is provided. Special orientation sessions for new students are conducted, special parent orientation sessions are held, and each student is assigned a special friend. Guidance counselors also work closely with all students and follow groups from ninth through twelfth grade. Counselors maintain a very sophisticated behavior modification program that operates through the in-school suspension program. They provide follow-up assistance to students who have home, community, or emotional problems after they leave in-school suspension and help provide them with positive ways to approach the negative aspects of their lives.

The peer counseling program at Riverside offers students opportunities to talk about personal and academic concerns with other students. The program involves approximately 300 students through the Teen Institute and Students Against Driving Drunk. Teen Institute members are trained to listen to peer problems and to recommend sources of help. The success of this program has led to it being a model widely used in South Carolina and elsewhere, with Riverside students assisting in training students from other high schools. These and other aspects of the guidance and counseling program at Riverside are influenced by the widespread belief that every teacher should act as a counselor and a listener.

Peer assistant teams have also been implemented in some high schools. At Sturgis High School in Sturgis, Michigan, student teams help students deal with major issues in their lives. This program provides someone who listens non-judgementally to what students have to say. By sorting through their own problems in the presence of a peer, many students are able to find reasonable solutions. An additional important function of this group has been service as peer mediators. When two or more students find themselves in conflict, Peer Assistance Team members utilize training they have received in mediation techniques to help them resolve conflicts without violence. One result of this program has been an 80 percent reduction in the number of fights.

Sturgis High School also has a comprehensive student assistance program which is designed to support students who have problems dealing with the everyday rigors of school and adolescent life. Volunteer teachers and educational assistants serve as case managers for those who have been referred to the student assistance program. The program at Sturgis was originally established to help students work through substance abuse problems, but has evolved into a program that addresses all behaviors that are self-defeating and destructive. As parents, classmates, teachers, or other significant individuals recognize changes in a student or observe a consistent pattern of self-defeating behaviors, that student is referred to the student assistance team. The team then gathers data and makes decisions as to whether or not individual students would likely benefit from participation in the program.

Once a student is in the program at Sturgis, one of the team members serves as a mentor and listener. The team member contacts the student selected and works to establish a positive relationship. If the student is overly resistant to the approaches of the team member, some other approach is used. The vast majority of these students, however, are quite happy to have an adult who will listen to them and help them with their problems. These and other functions of peer assistance teams have improved the effectiveness of the guidance and counseling program at Sturgis.

The Peer Helper Program at Vestavia Hill High School in Vestavia, Alabama, is offered as an elective course for selected students in grades nine through twelve. It is a nationally recognized training course for "youth helping youth." Students are taught to help other students in grades from kindergarten through grade twelve by learning to be effective listeners, group leaders, and role models. During the initial course, students develop a sense of belonging in a trusting and accepting atmosphere in which they try new ideas, disclose information about themselves, and gain an understanding of the program's objectives, rationale, and philosophy. After learning about different peer facilitator roles, they are assigned to one of the system's schools 2 days per week. The remaining 3 days are spent with the instructor for the purpose of evaluation, additional training, and planning. Examples of activities conducted in this peer helper program include:

- New student program: A peer helper is assigned to each new student entering Vestavia High School.
- Elementary school program: Each peer helper assists in one or more elementary classrooms for the entire school year.
- Resource room tutors: Peer helpers assist students in the exceptional education program.

- Christmas family: Peer helpers deliver food and gifts to a family with children attending Vestavia.
- Special Olympics: Peer helpers help students in the severely handicapped class participate in the Special Olympics.
- Caring and support: Peer helpers give support to Vestavia students or families who experience a death or tragedy during the school year.
- Prom Promise: Peer helpers sponsor the Prom Promise Program which helps make students aware of the dangers of driving and drinking on prom night.

PEER MEDIATION PROGRAMS

Educators at many high schools are establishing peer mediation programs to strengthen guidance and counseling efforts. Peer mediation is used as a method of conflict resolution by helping students examine problems, identify issues, think through alternatives and consequences, and collaboratively reach a mutually satisfactory agreement to resolve problem situations. The peer mediation plan, which capitalizes on peer pressure, creates an atmosphere where problems can be solved in a mature and respectful manner. Students involved in the program as mediators are carefully trained to be non-biased, non-judgmental, and impartial.

The Cambridge Model of peer mediation, which has received national and international recognition as a quality program, is utilized at Cambridge Rindge and Latin School, Cambridge, Massachusetts. This plan was introduced in 1986 by the school's security director, John Silva. Cambridge schools are among the most diverse in the nation with students who are nationals from over 70 different countries speaking over 45 different primary languages. This peer mediation program offers students opportunities to "save face" in ways that avoid confrontation while retaining the respect of their classmates. Objectives of the Cambridge Rindge High School peer mediation program are presented in Figure 5.1.

Cambridge Rindge and Latin School faculty members, who are trained in conflict management and mediation skills, teach high school volunteers from the school's 2,500 students to become peer mediators. The peer mediation process is implemented when two classmates have a disagreement and emotions reach a breaking point. When disputing students opt for mediation over other discipline alternatives, they are brought to a discussion room where a student mediator, with an adult in attendance, attempts to negotiate a resolution that is acceptable to the disputing students. Over 90 percent of students at Cambridge Rindge and Latin School select the peer mediation process over other forms of disciplinary measures with agreement being reached in over 90 percent of all cases.

As important as the kinds of counseling programs and services just discussed are, they do not provide the personalized kind of daily guidance needed by all adolescents. Neither is this level of guidance typically available from guidance counselors. In addition to having many responsibilities, high school counselors typically have several hundred students assigned to them, which makes getting to know them and offering individual guidance virtually impossible.

Cambridge Rindge and Latin School   **FIGURE 5.1**

Objectives of Peer Mediation Program
- To reduce violence, disruption, vandalism, truancy, suspension, and discrimination
- To promote multiculturalism, racial harmony, positive school climate, and sensitivity to others
- To allow young adults opportunities to support peers through conflict assistance in problem solving
- To teach lifelong skills in dealing with conflict
- To resolve racial and ethnic disputes
- To take down defensive barriers and improve communication among students, administrators, teachers, parents, and school support staff
- To progress as society does—to add to the repertoire of traditional discipline which has been questioned on effectiveness: expulsion, suspension, detention
- To utilize positively the powers of peer pressure
- To teach and utilize listening, critical thinking, and problem-solving skills

---

Consequently, many adolescents needing help do not receive it unless guidance is viewed as everyone's responsibility and advisory programs are in place to provide the developmental guidance needed. The remainder of this chapter focuses on teacher advisory programs because they are generally viewed as a very effective way to improve the quality of guidance at high schools (*Breaking Ranks,* 1996; Jenkins, 1992; Myrick & Myrick, 1990; *One Student at a Time,* 1992).

TEACHER ADVISORY PROGRAMS

As noted by Sizer (1996), "For many American young people, school is the last, best sanctuary, the one place where a student can trust that an adult is concerned for him or her" (p. 86). In effective high schools, advisory programs help assure that all students have the opportunity to be known as "total persons" by at least one teacher. These programs help ensure that every high school student is known well, cared about, and assisted in many ways by at least one adult advocate/advisor (e.g., course selections, individual learning plans, referrals to specialists). Educators at these schools believe that the most effective way of providing developmental guidance to all adolescents is through advisory programs that directly involve teachers and other professionals. A basic premise of these programs is that each adolescent needs a friendly adult in school who knows and cares about him or her personally and who monitors his or her academic progress (Myrick & Myrick, 1990). The roles of these advisors vary, but all advisors work to eliminate the anonymity and isolation that often characterize high schools.

The recognition of the need for advisory programs is not new; some forms were implemented as long ago as the 1880s (Myrick, Highland, & Highland, 1986). One of the earliest references in the literature to formal high school advisory programs focuses on New Trier High School in Winnetka, Illinois. This advisory program, established in 1924, was called the advisory-personnel plan and was "designed to provide educational, vocational, social, moral, and ethical guidance and counsel to all the students in the school" (Clerk, 1928, p. 1). Advisors were assigned by grade level and remained with their advisors throughout their school careers. Advisors at New Trier High School were expected to be both teachers and friends to their advisees (Jenkins, 1997).

One of the authors was responsible for initiating a successful high school advisory program in 1971 at Wilde Lake High School in Columbia, Maryland. This program is based on the belief that guidance is everyone's responsibility, with each teacher working with approximately 20 students in multi-aged groups and being charged to become a "significant other" to their advisees. School counselors play key roles in working closely with the advisory program. The assistance of teachers in the developmental guidance program at Wilde Lake provides many benefits, including increased time for counselors to work individually with students with special needs. According to Principal Bonnie Daniel, the school is currently divided into clusters, each with an administrator, a counselor, and a group of advisees. The principal and teachers, with the exception of first-year teachers, serve as advisors. Teachers are employed at Wilde Lake with the understanding that the advisor role is required and is a very important responsibility (Jenkins, 1977, 1997; Myrick & Myrick, 1990; Wollman, 1998).

ADVISORY PROGRAMS AS INTEGRAL COMPONENTS OF GUIDANCE

Advisory programs are essential components of comprehensive developmental guidance programs. These programs should be based on the recognition that each individual is unique but progresses through common growth stages with related needs, rather than being based on a crisis approach focusing on situations and treatments (Myrick, 1993; Myrick & Myrick, 1993). The most effective way for teachers to involve themselves directly in developmental guidance is through an advisory program. This approach is designed to provide continuous adult guidance within the high school with the advisor becoming first and foremost a friend and advocate (Jenkins, 1977, 1997).

The importance of the teacher advisory component of high school guidance programs is not always fully recognized. In fact, school counselors who are professionally prepared to help students with personal problems are often not a student's first choice for help. Counselors lack the visibility of teacher and student peers, and their images are frequently associated with authority, discipline, and administrative procedures. On the other hand, teachers have a long history of helping students who have personal problems, with some teachers continuing to be a source of guidance to their students after they leave high school. A formal advisory program allows time and opportunities for teachers and students—advisors and advisees—to build relationships that are personal, meaningful, lasting, and satisfying.

Teachers are busy people with finite amounts of time. Their responsibilities often include teaching as many as 180 students per day, making it difficult or impossible to establish close relationships with all their students. Without an effective teacher-based guidance program, these teachers tend to take a greater interest in some students than in others, which usually means that only the favored students receive the personal support and guidance they need. However, some students who need guidance from their teachers may feel unworthy of their attention, be too shy to initiate relationships, or believe they are not liked well enough to establish close relationships with their teachers. Advisory programs help offset these kinds of situations by making it possible for all high school students to develop close relationships with at least one teacher. Advisory programs, when they are a high priority of guidance and counseling programs, help ensure that all students have the opportunity to benefit from the wise counsel of their teachers (Myrick, 1993).

An additional reason teacher advisory programs are an integral part of guidance and counseling programs is the high ratio of students to counselors in high schools. The typical counselor–student ratio is several hundred to one in virtually all high schools. There is simply no way counselors can establish close relationships, or even get to know, hundreds of adolescents well enough to provide them with continuing guidance and support. However, counselors can serve useful and essential purposes in many ways, both as a part of advisory programs and in other crucial guidance and counseling roles.

THE NATURE OF ADVISORY PROGRAMS

There are many definitions of advisory programs because they are typically designed to meet the needs of students at individual schools. However, Cole (1992) provides a general description that is typical of those found in the literature: "A teacher advisory program makes it possible for students to belong, meets their need to affiliate with a group, and makes caring manageable for a teacher, enabling the teacher to express concern in a personally satisfying way to a small number of individuals (p. 7)."

High school educators are implementing advisory programs for a variety of reasons. Chief among these reasons is a concern that many high schools have grown so large and impersonal that the school climate is unresponsive to many youth. For example, among the reasons for establishing an advisory program at Waukegan High School in Waukegan, Illinois, was recognition of the following problems that needed to be addressed:

- Excessive single-period and all-day unexcused absences
- Excessive single-class failure
- Inappropriate behavior patterns and poor interpersonal skills

- A sense of alienation resulting from school size
- An unacceptably high dropout rate
- Lack of student advocates
- Lack of access to guidance services
- Negative peer influence
- Lack of effective channels of communication
- Lack of effective orientation program for incoming students
- Lack of an effective home communications network

These reasons are typical of those provided by high school educators establishing teacher-based guidance programs. To overcome these problems, goals and objectives are written to guide advisory programs in directions that will serve students well.

GOALS AND OBJECTIVES OF ADVISORY PROGRAMS

Although goals and objectives vary from school to school, themes often emerge because of the common purpose and the developmental age served. These frequently include an emphasis on: (1) increasing the academic success of students (e.g., monitoring academic progress; developing individual learning plans; liaison with counselors, teachers, and other professional personnel); (2) assisting students in developing positive attitudes about themselves and others; (3) teaching students to behave responsibly and demonstrate increased capacities for self-reliance; (4) provision of small-group settings where each student can be known well and cared about; (5) encouraging feelings of belonging, security, and trust; (6) increasing communication; (7) improving school climate; (8) providing frequent contacts with advisors so that problem situations can be identified and timely interventions made; (9) allowing students who need special assistance from the counseling department to receive it in a timely manner; and (10) providing opportunities to develop strong positive relationships with family members. More specific goals and objectives identified by individual high school faculties are presented in the following pages.

High school educators have a great variety of goals and objectives for their advisory program. Catalina Foothills Alternative High School in Tucson, Arizona, reported the following objectives for their advisory program:

- Provide a structure for academic advisement
- Improve commitment on the part of advisors to academic advisory
- Contribute to the development of community on the campus
- Create a planned assembly schedule
- Allow for class-specific special programs
- Enhance opportunities for school and community service

Goals at Hodgson Vocational-Technical High School in Newark, Delaware, were divided into a number of categories to help ensure that the program has clear direction at all levels. These categories include:

Advisement Program Goals for School

- Improve school climate
- Reduce behavioral problems
- Enhance instructional environment
- Increase parental involvement and support
- Expand awareness of educational and career alternatives

Advisement Program Goals for Students

- Improve self-esteem
- Develop more positive relationships with peers, teachers, and parents
- Recognize teachers as supportive adults
- Improve academic performance and attitudes toward education
- Improve decision-making skills
- Improve problem-solving skills
- Improve listening and verbal skills

Advisement Program Goals for Teachers

- Improve coping skills
- Improve relationships with students
- Increase awareness of students' needs, problems, and desires

These examples are not intended to represent all valid goals and objectives, but rather to provide examples typical of those created in many high schools. Each school faculty, with assistance from other stakeholders, should create their own goals and objectives that will serve their purposes well, but they should review the salient literature (e.g., NASSP Model Schools Project; Learning Environment Consortium, University of Wisconsin).

CHARACTERISTICS OF SUCCESSFUL PROGRAMS

Although there is no magical list of components that guarantee success in advisory programs, some common practices emerge when successful programs are examined. The following represents some selected examples.

Successful advisory programs are those where (McEwin, 1981; O'Neil, 1997):

- It is clear to all involved that advisory time is not counseling time and does not substitute for therapy and other activities that require special expertise beyond the professional preparation of most teachers.
- Time is provided for caring and sharing, and adults demonstrate that they are interested in and care about their advisees.
- It is widely understood that it is not a "free time," but does include freedom from the regular classroom routines (e.g., textbooks, quizzes, tests, lectures, test reviews).

- Time for student involvement and communication, and the sharing of constructive, positive ideas is provided.
- Opportunities for teachers and other advisors to open new lines of communication outside the formal learning setting are provided (e.g., student to student, student to teacher).
- Care is taken to make sure family members and other members of the community are aware of the rationale for advisory programs and are knowledgeable about the activities associated with the program.
- Counselors coordinate the program and do not schedule other things during advisory time.
- Resource persons from the community are used, but not placed in charge of an advisory group.
- No teacher is assigned more than one advisory group.
- Virtually all certified personnel are assigned an advisory group, allowing a lower advisor-advisee ratio—15 to 1 is recommended—and ensuring wide involvement of professional personnel.
- Handbooks, resource guides, and other appropriate resources are readily available.
- The roles of principals, other administrators, and guidance personnel are clearly defined and understood by all stakeholders.
- Good discipline is maintained and everyone is aware that advisory time is a valued part of the school day.
- Students take an active role in the program.
- Clearly defined procedures exist and are followed.

There are also some pitfalls to avoid when establishing a new advisory program or revising an existing one. Some of the most treacherous ones are (Cole, 1992; Graham & Hawkins, 1994; Vars, 1997; Galassi, Gulledge & Cox, 1997):

- Insufficient planning time before beginning the program
- Inadequate preparation of advisors
- Incomplete development of topics and activities
- Lack of sufficient support for the program from administrators and/or counselors
- Staff members who are not willing to or capable of becoming effective advisors
- Scheduling decisions that place the program at risk (e.g., scheduling advisory for the last 30 minutes of school day)
- Depending on the advisory program to provide for all affective needs and not making guidance a continuing responsibility for all teachers to include in the total curriculum
- Not understanding and planning for the fact that coordinating the advisory program is a significant, time-consuming responsibility
- Lack of a consensus among major stakeholders regarding the primary needs to be addressed

- Having goals that are too broad to provide sufficient direction or too narrow to bring the advisor/advisee satisfaction needed to support the program
- Not guarding against "slippage" in the effectiveness of the program as it matures and becomes routine

These and related pitfalls should be acknowledged and planned for in all advisory programs. The good news is that they can all be overcome through thoughtful planning, implementation, and evaluation of programs.

SCHEDULING THE ADVISORY PROGRAM

High school educators report a variety of scheduling patterns for advisory programs. Following are some examples.

- Two times per week for 80 minutes (Catalina Foothills Alternative High School, Tucson, Arizona)
- Four times per week for 45 minutes (Central Park East, New York)
- One period per week on a rotating schedule (Alice High School, Alice, Texas)
- Alternating days for 30 minutes with about 20 advisees (Ashland High School, Ashland, Oregon)
- Daily for 15 minutes with 10 to 14 advisees (Champlain Valley Union High School, Hinesburg, Vermont)
- Daily for 1 hour during first 6 weeks, once per week for the remainder of the year (Colorado's Finest Alternative High School, Englewood, Colorado)
- Three times per week (Fenway Middle College Pilot School, Boston, Massachusetts)
- Two times per month with 15 or fewer students (Hodgson Vocational-Technical High School, Newark, Delaware)
- Daily for 23 minutes with approximately 10 students (Malta High School, Malta, Illinois)
- Monthly in group meetings, individually during the school day, and in their homes on Fridays (Metro High School, Cedar Rapids, Iowa)
- 90 minutes every other day with equal numbers of freshmen, sophomores, juniors, and seniors being assigned at random (Pueblo County High School, Pueblo, Colorado)
- Weekly for 1 hour (Urban Academy Inquiry High School, New York)
- Daily for 14 minutes with freshmen at the beginning of lunch (Waukegan High School, Waukegan, Illinois)

As can be concluded from this listing of schedule patterns, high schools do not select the same scheduling plans, but rather base their schedule on their programs' major goals and objectives. What was consistently evident, however, was recognition that the program was crucial to the success of the schools and the assignment of a special place in the schedule to advisory activities. It is not assumed in these schools that teacher-based guidance just happens because adolescents need it. The appearance of advisory programs in the master schedule confirms that they are assigned a high priority in the schools' curricula (Chapter 6).

Many high schools assign advisees to the same teacher advisor for their entire tenure at the high school. However, other high schools use plans in which advisees choose, or are assigned, new advisors each year. Many high school educators believe that assigning advisees to the same advisors for the length of their stay at high school provides continuity and allows advisees and advisors to establish long-term relationships. Others, however, feel that having new advisors each year allows advisees to establish multiple close relationships with teachers and peer groups. Whichever type of assignment plan is used, it is important to avoid putting special interest groups together which might result in discriminatory practices (e.g., exceptional education students, band members, students with the same career goal). It is widely believed that each advisee needs to be placed in a heterogeneous group of peers during advisory time (Myrick & Myrick, 1990).

Scheduling and other organizational components of advisory programs are important and should not be overlooked by those planning new programs or revising existing ones. However, as with other programs, success is measured by the actions of those responsible for implementation. The roles of some of the professionals most directly involved in advisory programs are now briefly discussed to provide a more comprehensive understanding of the total program.

ROLES OF THE ADVISOR

The roles of advisors vary somewhat from school to school, depending on the nature of the program and the needs of students at particular schools. Whatever the nature of specific roles played by teacher advisors, a major responsibility is to become a personal advocate (advisor) of advisees. As noted in *Breaking Ranks* (1996):

> Each student needs to know that at least one adult in the school is closely concerned with his or her fate. The personal adult advocate will be that person. The relationship between the student and the advocate should ensure that no youngster experiences the sense of isolation that frequently engulfs teenagers during this critical period of their lives. Having someone on his or her side can help a young person feel a part of the community. . . . The personal advocate will assume a function beyond that usually associated with a homeroom teacher or even a guidance counselor (p. 31).

Successful advisory programs have clearly articulated expectations regarding the role of the teacher-advisor. The following examples from selected high schools demonstrate some typical roles identified. It should be understood, however, that the primary role of teacher advisors is to work with individual advisees rather than to provide group guidance activities.

At Penn High School in Mishawaka, Indiana, the teacher-advisor is expected to:

- Encourage each student to access teachers and resources in the building in pursuit of academic excellence
- Be an empathetic advisor who serves as a first resource for students in matters of personal adjustment and academic counseling
- Serve as the primary contact between parents and teachers throughout his or her advisees' 4 years at the high school
- Encourage each student to select and participate in co-curricular activities best suited to their individual interests
- Assist students in the development of career plans and 4-year academic programs.

The advisory responsibilities at Catalina Foothills Alternative High School in Tucson, Arizona, are to:

- Monitor each advisee's academic and social progress
- Build a relationship of trust, confidentiality, support, and open communication
- Foster trust, friendship, and team building within the advisory group
- Serve as liaison and ombudsman for each advisee with the rest of the school staff
- Foster and facilitate formal and informal communication between parents and the school, including conducting parent-teacher conferences as needed
- Notify appropriate school personnel of problems that may be affecting advisees
- Assist students in solving school-related problems
- Follow the prescribed curriculum of Advisory
- Recognize each advisee's successes
- Maintain a portfolio on each advisee

Responsibilities of advisors at Waukegan High School in Waukegan, Illinois, include the following:

- Conduct a daily advisory
- Attend frequent, regular meetings with the advisory coordinator, advisory trainers, and other advisors during the non-student portion of the advisory period
- Initiate parent contacts by phone or letter in accordance with program guidelines
- Participate in periodic training sessions throughout the school year which will be held during the 30-minute non-student time
- Meet individually with advisees as the need arises
- Establish and maintain abbreviated files on all advisees (4-year planners, copies of progress reports and grade reports, log of parent contacts)
- Attend staff development sessions

These role descriptions, created in high schools with successful advisory programs, are typical of those found in the literature and reflect well the characteristics of successful advisors. For example, Bushnell and George (1993) identified several crucial characteristics of effective advisors which include: (1) caring about students; (2) relating to advisees as individuals; (3) being readily available to advisees; and (4) having positive attitudes. Obviously, these characteristics cannot be mandated or created by adopting particular organizational plans. However, the organization of advisory programs and the expectations of advisors are important factors that can greatly increase chances of success. Given sufficient support, most teachers can become dedicated, effective advisors.

The roles of advisors at Metro High School in Cedar Rapids, Iowa, are comprehensive and designed explicitly to assist students in their school performance and to help them in their personal lives. Educators at Metro report that the heart of their school is the advisor system with each teacher serving as an advisor for 15 to 20 students. Advisors meet with parents, guardians, and other concerned adults throughout each trimester. Students are assigned to the same advisor throughout their enrollment at Metro. Advisors meet with their advisees in monthly advisory group meetings and individually during the school day, and make home visits on Fridays. The advisor system is designed to provide maximum support to the student and appropriate assistance to the parents/guardians.

Each Friday, advisors at Metro receive information about their advisees' attendance and behavior. The advisor role encompasses behavior management as well as educational planning, career development, and guidance in work placement. Advisors inform parents/guardians and advisees of progress and work extensively with probation officers and social service agencies.

Advisors at Metro High School are advisees' strongest advocates and their most important link to school—a key to success. Parents and guardians are encouraged to call their child's advisor for information on attendance, behavior, and school progress, with advisors being available from 8:00 A.M. until 4:00 P.M., Monday through Friday. In addition to the advisory program, small class sizes at Metro provide the opportunity for teachers and students to know each other well. Students call staff members by their first names, helping break down the barriers established in less supportive environments. Administrators and teachers work hard to get to know students, to earn their trust, and to help them be a part of Metro's community.

The advisory role at some high schools also focuses on providing personal support to students and fostering communication skills, team-building, individual self-esteem, and trust. At Souhegan High School in Amherst, New Hampshire, advisors serve as the school's primary contact with parents and oversee all aspects of students' lives. Students develop an educational plan and post-graduation plan, learn about community service opportunities, and engage in many other activities that help them become successful students and productive citizens.

ROLES OF THE PRINCIPALS AND COUNSELORS

The degree of success of advisory programs depends significantly on the role played by principals and other school administrators. Principals are constantly observed by teachers and others who are attempting to determine the priorities of various school programs. Therefore, it is obvious rather quickly whether the advisory program is a high priority in the school curriculum. Most important, however, are the many decisions made by principals that influence the nature and effectiveness of advisory programs. Some examples of ways principals and other administrators can promote programs include: (1) giving the advisory period a workable time in the schedule; (2) providing continuing staff development activities; (3) demonstrating an openness to suggestions and modifications to the program; (4) holding all teachers accountable for being successful advisors; (5) providing for constant evaluation of the program; (6) providing sufficient time for teachers to be successful advisors; and (7) communicating the reality and possibilities of the program to the school board and central office personnel. (Cole, 1992; Jenkins, 1997; McEwin, 1981)

Counselors also play pivotal roles in advisory programs. Discussions of the implications of the recommendation for advisory programs in *Breaking Ranks* suggest that the personal advocate "will assume a function beyond that usually associated with a homeroom teacher or even a guidance counselor" (p. 31). This should not be understood to mean that the role of counselors is diminished in any manner. However, as noted earlier, counselors lack the visibility of teachers and are sometimes associated with images of authority, discipline, and administrative procedures. Counselors, with their typical assignment of hundreds of students, simply do not have the opportunity for daily contact with students and therefore may not be perceived by adolescents as "friendly advisors or helpers" (Myrick & Myrick, 1990). Working closely with teacher-advisors, however, can increase the positive influence of guidance counselors and of the guidance process itself by giving it a designated time in the schedule and place in the curriculum. With careful planning, strong advisory programs will enhance relationships between students and teachers, allowing guidance counselors the time they need to concentrate on the issues that confound students. Stated another way, quality advisory programs enrich the entire guidance program and enable counselors to be even more effective while influencing larger numbers of students.

Some examples of ways counselors work directly with advisory programs include: (1) conducting advisory activities that go beyond the preparation of teachers; (2) assisting new teachers with their advisory responsibilities; (3) communicating regularly with advisors about their advisees; (4) avoiding acting in ways that undercut the success of the program; (5) teaching advisors advisory skills and providing them with resources and ideas; (6) establishing external links for use when advisees need services beyond what the school can provide; and (7) consulting principals, parents, and others stakeholders (*Breaking Ranks*, 1996; Goldberg, 1998; Jenkins, 1996, 1997; McEwin, 1981). Clearly, without the capable assistance of counselors, the long-term health of any advisory program is at risk.

THE ADVISORY CURRICULUM

In addition to working with individual advisees, advisors sometimes focus on an advisory "curriculum" that provides themes and/or activities. This curriculum varies from school to school, depending on the needs of different student populations. Those responsible for the advisory program at many schools accumulate collections of activities (e.g., Teacher Advisement Handbooks) to serve as resources for advisors. Advisory calendars are also utilized at some high schools.

Suggested activities and related materials in handbooks and calendars are typically viewed as possibilities rather than a prescribed daily guide. Educators at some high schools also survey students and faculty to identify appropriate topics. Curricular frameworks are also used in some advisory programs. For example, the advisory curriculum framework at Souhegan High School in Amherst, New Hampshire, includes a focus on both content and process (Figure 5.2).

FIGURE 5.2   **Souhegan High School Advisory Framework**

Grade 9
Advisory groups (meets three times per week)
    Content focus
        Grade 9 transition
        Initial orientation to school culture and mission
        Effective habits of mind
        Portfolio development toward Division I final exhibition
    Process focus
        Personal relationship between advisor and student
        Interpersonal group communication
        Monitor academic progress of students
Non-advisory activities (meets two times per week)
    Focus
        Enrichment and/or academic support as determined by team
        Periodic advisor meetings and class meetings

Grade 10
Advisory groups (meets three times per week)
    Content focus
        Effective habits of mind
        Portfolio development
        Division I final exhibition
        Community service
    Process focus
        Personal relationship between advisor and student
        Interpersonal group communication
        Monitor academic progress of students
Non-advisory activities (meets two times per week):
    Focus
        Small group meetings to monitor portfolio/exhibition work
        Enrichment and/or academic support as determined by teacher
        Periodic advisor meetings and class meetings

Most high schools use the activities conducted through the advisory program to accomplish major guidance goals. For example, faculty members at Pueblo County High School in Pueblo, Colorado, state:

> The staff and students of Pueblo County High School believe that in order to meet the needs of the whole learner, educational experiences must extend beyond the academic classroom. The purpose of the advisor/advisee program is to establish a cohesive family unit by creating a multilevel, interactive environment between students and staff. This program is designed to personalize education, complement the curriculum, and assist students in developing skills and attitudes necessary to their success (*Pueblo County High School Handbook,* n.d.).

Souhegan High School Advisory Framework—*continued*

FIGURE 5.2

Grade 11
Advisory groups (meets three times per week)
    Content focus
    Graduation plan (including career and college plan)
        Effective habits of mind
        Portfolio development toward Division I final exhibition
    Process focus
        Personal relationship between advisor and student
        Interpersonal group communication
        Monitor academic progress of students
Non-advisory activities (meets two times per week)
    Focus
        Enrichment and/or academic support as determined by team
        Periodic advisor meetings and class meetings

Grade 12
Advisory groups (meets four times per week)
    Content focus
        Senior project: Oversee design of project, learning logs, presentation rehearsals
        College and career placement
    Process focus
        Personal relationship between advisor and student
        Interpersonal group communication: Emphasis on leading group
        Monitor academic progress of students
Non-advisory activities (meets one time per week)
    Focus
        Senior class meetings: Once every 2 weeks
        Senior advisors meeting: Once every 2 weeks

School-wide
    State of community/town meeting (meets three to five times per year)
    Crisis management (meets as needed)
    Survey administration or other school activities (meets as needed)

Faculty members, including counselors, then seek curricular activities that help meet goals. Therefore, in many ways, the preceding statement is "curriculum."

Despite the great variety of topics addressed in advisory programs, some common themes tend to emerge across advisory programs. Myrick (1993) gives examples of units of study used in many advisory programs:

- Understanding the school environment
- Understanding self and others
- Understanding attitudes and behaviors
- Decision making and problem solving
- Interpersonal and communication skills
- School success skills
- Career awareness and educational planning
- Community pride and involvement

Examples of topics/activities currently used in high schools include:

- Tutoring/mentoring, individual graduation plans, student-initiated instructional activities, continuing personal teacher–student relationships (Fairdale High School, Fairdale, Kentucky)
- Orientation to school, team building, goal setting, time management, study skills, current events, conferences, parties, group assemblies, self-esteem building, and social issues (Waukegan High School, Waukegan, Illinois)
- Health, sexuality, AIDS education, decision making, parenting, stress management, violence prevention, nutrition, SAT preparation, study skills, career planning and development, community service, civil rights and responsibilities, geography, community building, speaking, and writing and debating skills (Fenway Middle College Pilot School, Boston, Massachusetts)
- Career planning and citizenship, community appreciation, cultural appreciation, lifelong learning, cooperation, goal setting, and transition; teacher advisors receive examples of suggested activities that reflect these themes (e.g., understanding self and others, making decisions, understanding how feelings affect behavior) (Penn High School, Mishawaka, Indiana)

Advisors at many high schools receive suggested activities that reflect the kinds of topics and themes listed. At Penn High School in Mishawaka, Indiana, these activities, which reflect monthly themes, are accompanied with suggestions for use and information that tie the activities to grade level and/or school-wide events (e.g., follow-up on a video about setting goals viewed by all juniors) (Figures 5.3–5.7). Advisors are free to deviate from the suggested activities based on the needs of their advisees on a given day. Penn High School has an advisory coordinator who suggests activities to advisors and provides copies of the *Homeroom and Resource Period Handbook* for faculty members, parents, and other interested parties. This publication includes information on topics such as goals, philosophy and rationale, and guidelines (Figures 5.6 and 5.7). Advisees are assigned to the same advisors for the length of their stay at Penn with advisory meetings every other day throughout the school year.

Penn High School Sample Activity Sheet   **FIGURE 5.3**

AREA: KNOWLEDGE OF SELF AND OTHERS

CATEGORY: UNDERSTANDING AND ACCEPTING SELF

COMPETENCY: I HAVE CONFIDENCE IN MYSELF.
TIME: 1 CLASS PERIOD
GROUP SIZE: GROUP OR CLASS
GRADE LEVEL: 11–12
MATERIALS: PAPER AND PENCIL

"SHARING GROWTH EXPERIENCES"

INTRODUCTION:

This activity could be used as a closing exercise at the end of a school year for a group or class that had developed cohesiveness. Recalling and sharing "growth experiences" might help some high school students overcome the sense of "I am all alone" in facing problems and difficult situations. It will also contribute to hopefulness about positive outcomes.

PROCEDURE:

1. Define the idea of growth experience as difficulties overcome or some other kind of meaningful event. Discuss this briefly. Give personal examples.

2. Ask each person to recall and write a number of "growth experiences" from the past year or past few years.

3. Give each person the opportunity to share one experience.

4. Lead the group in a discussion of similarities and differences between people's experiences.

5. Summarize the purpose of the sharing experience and thank participants for their openness.

OBSERVATION NOTES:

You will need to direct the self-disclosure elicited from the group to a level appropriate for your purpose. Any self-disclosure requires some degree of group cohesiveness and this activity should not be attempted otherwise.

FIGURE 5.4   Penn High School Sample Activity Sheet

AREA: EDUCATIONAL AND VOCATIONAL DEVELOPMENT

CATEGORY: MAKING DECISIONS

COMPETENCY: I CAN IDENTIFY THE REAL PROBLEM
                        WHEN I HAVE DIFFICULTIES.
TIME: 40–60 MINUTES
GROUP SIZE: CLASS
GRADE LEVEL: 11–12
MATERIALS: NONE

"IDENTIFYING THE REAL PROBLEM"

INTRODUCTION:

Many times when a person experiences difficulties coping with a problem, his or her difficulties can be traced to denial, distortion, or misperception of the source of the problem. This activity introduces students to the means of more accurately defining problem situations.

PROCEDURE:

1. Introduce the need for problem identification as one of the most important steps in problem solving. Illustrate with the idea that in counseling, once a client has identified and "owned" a problem, the problem is almost solved. One of the most important functions of a counselor is to be a "mirror" to reflect back to a person what their situation is, so that the person can more accurately identify the problem.

2. Lead a brainstorming activity on what keeps people from being able to identify problems. Identify the following categories:

    a) Denial—People don't want to admit their problems and often blame others.

    b) Inaccurate self-perception—A person believes something about himself/herself that may not be true. Example: "People don't like me."

    c) Ignorance of options available—People don't consider a full range of options and feel unnecessarily trapped.

Penn High School Sample Activity Sheet—*continued*   **FIGURE 5.4**

3. Explain methods for overcoming these roadblocks to problem identification. Give examples to illustrate each.

   a) Denial—Often requires strong intervention from intimates or some major tragedy to "open up the eyes." Example: Alcoholism.

   b) Inaccurate self-perception—Communication and feed back is very important. People who talk through their problems rather than carry them around silently have a better chance of correcting misperceptions of self. Example: A person who thinks he or she is unattractive. It can often be helpful to put aside blame for others or blame on the situation and ask the question, "What can I do to make the situation better?" In exploring this question, the issue may be redefined more accurately. Remind students that talking to a friend or a counselor can also be helpful. You don't have to be crazy to benefit from talking to someone.

   c) Ignorance is often a road block to problem definition. Define a broad range of problems in which getting more information might be a first step. Examples: Occupational frustration, how to fix a car, how to raise children. Summarize that when problems are encountered, the first thing to do is get more information either by talking to people who know or by reading.

4. Give the class an opportunity to practice these skills. Present problem situations to small groups and invite members to work together to define processes for identifying the real problem.

5. Summarize by emphasizing the need for accurate problem definition in problem solving.

OBSERVATION NOTES:

Students who are referred for discipline reasons may benefit from this activity also.

FIGURE 5.5   Penn High School (Sample Memo)

Memo # 2

FROM: Jack Gardner
TO: Junior Homeroom Teachers
DATE: August 23, 1998

Today would be a good day to explore one or two getting acquainted activities, such as the activity enclosed or the activity on page 40 in your activity packet in the "Homeroom Box Office."

For policy review, please go over the handbook section of the student planner and the enclosed activity.

If you have any questions please call me at 2854.

FIGURE 5.6   Penn High School

Homeroom Philosophy & Rationale

Recommendations of our latest Program-Based Accreditation (P.B.A.), North Central Association (N.C.A.) studies, and more recently the recommendation of the National Report "Breaking Ranks: Restructuring the High School of the Future" indicated a need for a more personalized and individualized approach to teaching and learning at Penn High School. In part, we believe that we can accomplish this goal by establishing a Homeroom Program for our students. We believe a Homeroom would provide a consistent opportunity for our students to "touch base" with a significant adult at Penn. This relationship would continue throughout students' four-year experience. Homeroom teachers would act as advocates for their students as they get to know students' strengths and weaknesses.

Homeroom guidelines:
1. All students will be assigned and expected to participate (attendance will be taken)
2. All students will be assigned in manageable numbers to same grade-level homerooms
3. An assistant principal, two guidance counselors, and a group of homeroom teachers will be assigned to each grade

Planned activities for the Homeroom Period include:
1. Announcements—both written and video—PNN News
2. Activities such as goal setting, career planning, time management, study skills, etc.
3. Special programs and convocations

FIGURE 5.7   Penn High School Sample Expectations Sheet

The Penn High School Homeroom Period Expectations

■ At Penn High School homerooms will meet every other day.

The Homeroom Teachers Will:

- encourage each student to access teachers and resources in the building in pursuit of academic excellence

- be empathetic staff members who are the first resource for students in matters of personal adjustment and academic counseling

- be the primary contact between parents and teachers throughout a student's four high school years

- encourage each student to select and participate in co-curricular activities suited to their individual interests

- assist students in the development of career plans and four-year academic programs

The Homeroom Students Will:

- obtain important information from the Penn High School news network (PNN) and daily written announcements
- become aware of the rules and regulations at Penn High School
- distribute and receive school materials
- review study strategies
- discuss Penn High School issues and world concerns
- elect representatives to the many school organizations
- participate in one-on-one problem solving
- work together to develop positive self-worth
- work together to develop personal relationships and rapport
- participate in small group discussions centered around the Penn homeroom period
- develop career plans and four-year academic programs

Homeroom Teachers Will Not Be able To:

- assume responsibilities that belong to students
- control a student's social interactions
- get students to school on time
- contact other teachers for academic progress reports
- serve as a truant officer, a social worker, or a psychologist
- assume parents' responsibilities in their absence

■ Throughout their four years together, students and teachers will have the opportunity to form new and lasting relationships that last for years.

In addition to the kinds of curricular topics and units of study just provided as examples, time is also provided in most advisory programs for informal interactions between advisor and advisees, and among the advisees themselves. For example, advisees at Fenway Middle College Pilot High School in Boston, Massachusetts, are provided time to work with their advisor on homework, plan their schedules, and complete a general "check-in" to make sure that the student's work and emotional life are on track. Whatever the current topics, emphasis is placed on making sure that students get extra support, whether it is academic or personal, which can be critical to their success. At Fenway, advisory is also the place where advisees prepare for the final presentation of portfolios.

Some high schools provide a calendar of meeting dates and suggested advisement topics. For example, the advisement committee at Hodgson Vocational-Technical High School in Newark, Delaware, selected and recommended the plan shown in Figure 5.8.

The provision of themes and suggested activities is an important part of successful advisory programs. However, it should be understood that advisors should have the freedom to deviate from planned topics and activities when change can be justified by special circumstances. Advisors who ignore the curriculum and do not take their advisory responsibilities seriously, however, are never acceptable.

STAFF DEVELOPMENT

Many educators who become advisors will need staff development opportunities to help them acquire the knowledge and skills needed to be successful and confident in their developmental guidance roles. Topics that advisors may need to learn about, or review, include: (1) understanding the purpose and function of advisory programs (e.g., friend, advocate, sympathetic listener, sounding board); (2) building positive working relationships with advisees; (3) clarifying the roles of all participants; (4) identifying resources; (5) dealing with controversial topics; (6) building guidance units; and (7) basic guidance skills (e.g., responding to students' feelings, asking open-ended questions, complimenting, and confronting) (Cole, 1992; Myrick & Myrick, 1990).

EVALUATION OF ADVISORY PROGRAMS

High schools providing information for this project noted the importance of the continuing evaluation of their advisory programs. For example, the advisory program is evaluated throughout the year at Waukegan High School in Waukegan, Illinois. Advisors at Waukegan meet weekly to discuss problems and successes in an effort to improve and enhance the program. The advisory coordinator conducts student and teacher surveys, collects data, and compares it with data from previous years.

Surveys utilized by Waukegan and by Penn High School in Mishawaka, Indiana, address several areas including student attitudes toward school and "student-to-advisor" feedback (Figures 5.9–5.11). Positive results from these surveys and other

FIGURE 5.8   Hodgson Advisement Plan

Hodgson Vocational-Technical High School

Advisement was designed to provide a comfortable setting for conversation for small groups of students and an advisor. Students recommended topics in early October, and the Advisement Committee has included many of these topics in planning for advisement meetings.

September 16	Ice Breakers and Explanation of Advisement
September 29	Issues: What should we do about crowded halls? What do students think about incentives and rewards?
October 18	The Label game; examine ways in which people divide themselves and examine the positives and negatives
November 1	What kinds of pressure or stress do teens have to deal with? Ice breakers: Name Niks, Tic-Tac-Toe questions.
November 15	Topic: Pressure, stress and goals discussion: What positive ways do students have to deal with stress? Handouts: Health Habits Stress Test; What Everyone Should Know About Stress.
December 13	Magic Johnson's video on AIDS; tremendous feedback from staff; high student interest
January 27	Keeping out of trouble (17 minute video, 23 minute discussion) Students role play several situations such as: Your friend comes to your house and she has been drinking. She wants to go driving with you. What do you do?
February 28	You Deserve to be Happy (24 minute video, 16 minute discussion) Memorable discussion questions: What are five reasons you will not give up until you reach your goal? In what ways are you a positive person?
March 21	Stereotyping: How does stereotyping affect our lives? Do you believe stereotyping can be harmful? How can we improve the tone of decency here at Hodgson?
April 18	Driving and Drinking Are a Bad Mix: The Kevin Turnell Story video. Question: How do teenagers consider possible consequences in the decision-making process? How real are warnings not to drive and drink?
May 16	Teenage Relationships: Sex/Pregnancy. Video: Discussion of teenage relationships. List of myths and common questions parents and teenagers may ask.
Final Advisement:	*A Look Back at the Advisement Year* video: Students' suggestions for future advisements; discussion of the progress of advisement during the school year

ATTITUDE SURVEY
(SCHOOL)

A. Almost Always
B. Frequently
C. Occasionally
D. Almost Never

PART I

A. Environment - This school is a place where:

A B C D 1. Warm, friendly, open and humane relationships exist.
A B C D 2. Cooperation between people takes place.
A B C D 3. Good communication is important.
A B C D 4. Someone helps and supports students; they care about students as persons.
A B C D 5. There is sensitivity of individual differences and needs.
A B C D 6. Helping/caring relationships are important.
A B C D 7. People are encouraged to act responsibly.
A B C D 8. Everyone accepts students for themselves.
A B C D 9. Students are noticed, recognized, listened to—made to feel important.
A B C D 10. Students are not downgraded or put down.
A B C D 11. Parents, teachers, students set rules cooperatively.
A B C D 12. Students can make new friends of all ages and grades.
A B C D 13. Students can practice getting along with people.
A B C D 14. Parents are encouraged to be partners in the educational process.
A B C D 15. Students can trust most adults.
A B C D 16. Learning is important.
A B C D 17. It is important to talk freely with adults.
A B C D 18. Everyone wants to get the most out of almost everything.
A B C D 19. Students can explore their own interests.
A B C D 20. My goals are important.

B. Involvement in this school means:

A B C D 1. Parents, students, teachers are heard and listened to.
A B C D 2. Students do a lot of things that are important to them.
A B C D 3. Someone knows how students are doing in their classes.
A B C D 4. Students can talk to some people about their future.
A B C D 5. Students have a chance to decide things which affect them.
A B C D 6. People encourage students to solve their own problems.
A B C D 7. Most students participate in extra-curricular activities.
A B C D 8. Students are free to take risks.
A B C D 9. Students want to learn.
A B C D 10. People cooperate.
A B C D 11. People care about each other.
A B C D 12. Students are encouraged to think about what they believe and the way they behave.
A B C D 13. Students can be leaders.
A B C D 14. Students do most of the talking in the 3-way conference.
A B C D 15. Students learn to evaluate themselves.

C. Relationships mean:

A B C D 1. Teachers are concerned, caring, and helpful.
A B C D 2. Teachers guide students.
A B C D 3. Teachers can be trusted.
A B C D 4. Counselors, teachers, parents, and administrators work together for students.
A B C D 5. Students see advisors as "real people"—not phonies.
A B C D 6. Students and teachers care about people more than anything else.
A B C D 7. People don't downgrade (put down) each other.

FIGURE 5.10   **Sample Student/Advisor Attitude Survey: Waukegan High School**

ATTITUDE SURVEY

A. Almost Always
B. Frequently
C. Occasionally
D. Almost Never

STUDENT-TO-ADVISOR FEEDBACK

_____School Name
_____State
_____Date

Note to advisors: This feedback sheet may be used by you as an informative resource, or it may be implemented into your advisory group for feedback.

Please respond to the following statements anonymously to let your advisor know how you feel about advisor group. Only your advisor will receive the results of the responses.

A B C D   1. Your actions have caused me to respect you as an advisor.
A B C D   2. I respect you as a person.
A B C D   3. I feel you are warm, open, and honest.
A B C D   4. You are pleasant to be with.
A B C D   5. I feel you genuinely like me and care what happens to me.
A B C D   6. If I were in trouble, I think you would try to help me.
A B C D   7. You give me an opportunity to discuss things that are important to me.
A B C D   8. You allow me to make my own decisions about what I am to learn.
A B C D   9. You are careful to ensure that I have a clear understanding of what I am expected to accomplish.
A B C D   10. You encourage group discussion by not judging everything we say during advisory group.
A B C D   11. You talk with us, not at us.
A B C D   12. I feel free to disagree with your opinions.
A B C D   13. I do not feel pressured to give answers to conform to your opinions.
A B C D   14. I feel free to ask you questions.
A B C D   15. I feel that you listen to my questions.
A B C D   16. I think you would arrange to talk with me privately if I asked you to.
A B C D   17. I feel we practice the human skills in advisory group.
A B C D   18. You plan activities in advisory group that require my active participation.
A B C D   19. You encourage me to learn in a way that is best for me. Everyone does not have to do everything the same way.
A B C D   20. You encourage me to pursue my special talents, abilities, and interests.
A B C D   21. You challenge me to use my imagination.
A B C D   22. Your advisees are respected as individuals.
A B C D   23. You give special encouragement to those who need it.
A B C D   24. You give me good advice on my school choices.
A B C D   25. You provide enough guidance to ensure that students know where they are now and where they are going.
A B C D   26. We don't use put down statements in advisory group.
A B C D   27. You help students learn to measure their own progress.

ADVISOR QUESTIONNAIRE

Mark the response that typifies your feelings or situation.

1. How often have you met his year with your advisors individually or as a group?
   ___1–5 meetings ___6–12 meetings ___13–24 meetings ___25+ meetings

2. Have the materials that were prepared for the advisement program been helpful?
   ___Many were helpful.___ Some were helpful. ___I rarely use any of them.

3. Has the opportunity to have closer contacts with small groups of students actually produced some meaningful relationships for you?
   ___Definitely yes ___Probably yes ___Probably not ___Definitely not

4. Approximately how many parent contacts (letter, telephone, or face-to-face) have you made this year? (Count each contact, even if they involved the same people.)
   ___Less than 15 ___15–20 ___21–30 ___31–40 ___over 4 contacts

5. How would you describe your relationship to your advisement team?
   ___Very close ___Cordial ___A strained relationship ___No real relationship

6. Has the advisement program in any way affected the way in which you work with students in your classroom?
   ___Yes, definitely. ___There has been some effect. ___Probably no effect at all.

In the following items identify your level of satisfaction with the progress you are making:

7. I have skills to use when involved in directing a parent conference. ___Skilled ___Need practice

8. I am aware of resources where I can send my advisors for specific college and/or vocational information.
   ___Skilled ___Need practice

9. I can describe most courses in the course catalog and suggest alternatives that seem most appropriate to an advisee. ___Skilled ___Need practice

10. I can explain the district requirements for graduation to advisees and their parents.
    ___Skilled ___Need practice

11. I know how to maintain an advisement record folder for an advisee. ___Skilled ___Need practice

12. I know of techniques, activities, or standardized tests that I can suggest to my advisees to help them discover their interests. ___Skilled ___Need practice

13. I can initiate activities that are useful in helping a student set long-term goals.
    ___Skilled ___Need practice

14. I am able to explain standardized test results that appear in a student's folder.
    ___Skilled ___Need practice

15. I feel comfortable and I know how to approach other teachers in my building to work with them on problems relating to my advisees. ___Skilled ___Need practice.

16. I know when and how to refer advisees to other professionals in the school for appropriate help.
    ___Skilled ___Need practice

evaluation data have included: (1) substantially increased number of home contacts; (2) lower numbers of disciplinary referrals; (3) fewer failures; (4) increased student attendance; and (5) strong support (99 percent) among advisors for the program. Some representative comments from advisors and advisees from Waukegan High School are:

"The advisory offers a place where kids can talk about their problems."

"Students like the one-to-one contact."

"The individual performance reviews really help students understand the importance of grades."

"The students are becoming a family."

"This has been an enjoyable experience for me."

Student comments included:

"I like my advisor."

"Advisory is a place where I can get my questions answered."

"I like it when teachers take time to explain my grades (Personal Communication, 1997, E. Adler).

Semester and end-of-year reports are prepared and submitted to the Waukegan Committee for Research and Development and the administration.

The advisory at Souhegan High School in Amherst, New Hampshire, is also continually evaluated. Results from evaluations have led to a series of refinements and revisions since the program's inception. Annual survey data from students and parents are collected and bi-weekly meetings are attended by grade-level advisors, the advisory coordinator, and the advisory committee. Advisors also hold special meetings to reflect on the advisory program, share candid perceptions of its strengths and weaknesses, and plan ways to strengthen the program. After several years of evaluation, the faculty at Souhegan continues to espouse the values and importance of advisory.

CONCLUDING STATEMENTS

As with all school programs, the success of teacher advisory programs depends on the dedication, competence, and commitment of those responsible for teaching and serving adolescents. Guidance should permeate the entire high school. A meaningful curriculum, emphatic teachers, a strong formal guidance program, and a high-quality teacher advisory program promise to increase every high school student's chances to be successful in both academic and affective areas. For in highly successful high schools, guidance is considered everyone's responsibility, and this belief is reflected in the daily operations of the school.

As noted by John Lounsbury, the real restructuring of high schools is attitudinal as well as organizational (Lounsbury, 1996). This is an important thought to keep in mind as high schools include time for advisory programs in their schedules. Careful and continuing efforts are needed because of the major paradigm shift these programs require. Efforts expended, however, are well worthwhile when high schools become more personalized institutions and where all adolescents receive the guidance needed to become successful students and productive citizens.

SUMMARY

The important role of guidance activities and programs is widely recognized, accepted, and supported in successful high schools. Educators realize that the affective aspects of teaching and learning are important and closely related to the academic success of high school students. Virtually all high schools provide a variety of guidance and counseling services and employ school counselors. These services include those commonly associated with high school guidance programs (e.g., personal and academic counseling, testing programs) as well as newer programs such as student/peer counseling, peer mediation, and teacher advisory programs (e.g., teacher-based guidance, advisor-advisee).

Increasingly, advisory programs are being viewed as essential components of comprehensive high school guidance programs. These programs offer opportunities for teachers to be directly involved in developmental guidance. This approach is designed to provide continuous adult guidance within the high school, with advisors being friends and advocates of their advisees. Successful advisory programs provide time and opportunities for teachers and students to build the kinds of relationships that are personal, meaningful, lasting, and satisfying. The nature of advisory programs, goals and objectives, characteristics of successful programs, scheduling, staff development, curriculum, and evaluation are among key advisory program topics discussed in this chapter. Numerous examples from the successful high schools were also provided.

CONNECTIONS TO OTHER CHAPTERS

The importance of effective guidance for high school students links this chapter with all other chapters in this book. However, connections with Chapters 6, 7, 8 and 9 are especially important because these chapters specifically address scheduling, school organization, working with family and community members, and the high school teacher.

ACTION STEPS

1. Visit a high school guidance department and interview counselors and other personnel about the purposes and responsibilities of the guidance program. Include questions that will add to your understanding of topics discussed in this chapter (e.g., peer mediation, peer assistance, teacher advisory programs). Share what you learn with your classmates.

2. Interview at least two high school students about their perceptions of guidance at their school. If possible, select a school that has a teacher advisory program so that you may include questions about how they perceive the value of working with a teacher advisor. Prepare a paper that summarizes what you learn.

3. Commercially prepared resources for use in teacher advisory programs are becoming increasingly available. Using catalogs, the Internet, and other resources, explore what kinds of instructional materials are available for use by teacher advisors. Be prepared to report what you find in class.

4. Using what you have learned about the purposes of teacher advisory programs, prepare a series of three advisory activities that would be appropriate for an advisory group consisting of 15 tenth, eleventh, and twelfth grade students. You may decide what the topic will be, what has been done previous to the advisory activities, and so on. You may be called upon in class to demonstrate your activities with your classmates.

DISCUSSION QUESTIONS

1. After reading about and discussing the nature of guidance in today's high schools, compare these practices with the ways you experienced guidance at a high school you attended (e.g., peer assistance, peer counseling, and teacher advisory programs; individual interactions with school counselors).

2. As discussed in this chapter, teacher advisory programs are being established at increasing numbers of high schools. What do you believe are some of the major reasons this trend is growing? Are teacher advisory programs likely to be universally implemented in the nation's high schools? Why or why not?

3. Discuss the examples of teacher advisory goals from programs described in this chapter. Do these goals seem to mesh with the overall goals of the nation's public high schools? Would some goals cause controversy in local communities?

4. Implementation of successful teacher advisory programs creates a new set of expectations regarding the role of teachers in providing guidance for adolescents. Do you think some teachers are uncomfortable with this new responsibility? After reading the examples of teacher roles in advisory programs included in this chapter, how do you feel about becoming a teacher advisor?

5. After exploring examples of teacher advisory curriculum topics provided in this chapter, do you believe any of them are inappropriate for use in a public school by a teacher who is not a counselor? If yes, which topics, and why do you think so?

References

Adler, E. (October 8, 1997). Personal Communication.

Boyer, E. L. (1983). *High school: A report on secondary education in America*. New York: Harper & Row.

Breaking ranks: Changing an American institution. A report of the National Association of Secondary School Principals in partnership with the Carnegie Foundation for the Advancement of Teaching (1996). Reston, VA: National Association of Secondary School Principals.

Bushnell, D., & George, P. S. (1993). Five crucial characteristics: Middle school teachers as effective advisors. *Schools In the Middle: Theory into Practice, 3 (1),* 10–16.

Clerk, F. E. (1928). *Description and outline of the operation of the advisor-personnel plan at New Trier High School*. Winnetka, IL: New Trier High School.

Cole, C. G. (1992). *Nurturing a teacher advisory program*. Columbus, OH: National Middle School Association.

Cole, C. G. (1994). Teacher's attitudes before beginning a teacher advisory program. *Middle School Journal, 25 (5),* 3–7.

Galassi, J. P., Gulledge, S. A., & Cox, N. D. (1997). Planning and maintaining sound advisory programs. *Middle School Journal, 28 (5),* 35–41.

Goldberg, M. F. (1998). *How to design an advisory system for a secondary school*. Reston, VA: Association for Supervision and Curriculum Development.

Graham, D., & Hawkins, M. (1984). Advisement programs: Turning failure into success. *NASSP Bulletin, 68 (470),* 82–88.

Jenkins, J. M. (1997). Advisement and advocacy: Personalizing the educational experience. *NASSP Practitioner, 23 (4),* 1–6.

Jenkins, J. M. (1992). *Advisement programs: A new look at an old practice*. Reston, VA: National Association of Secondary School Principals.

Jenkins, J. M. (1996). *Transforming high schools: A constructivist agenda*. Lancaster, PA: Technomic Publishing.

Killin, T. E., & Williams, R. L. (1995). Making a difference in school climate, counseling services, and student success. *NASSP Bulletin, 79 (570),* 44–50.

Lounsbury, J. H. (1996). Personalizing the high school: Lessons learned in the middle. *NASSP Bulletin, 80 (584),* 17–24.

McEwin, C. K. (1981). Establishing teacher-advisory programs and practices in middle level schools. *Journal of Early Adolescence, 1 (4),* 337–348.

Myrick, R. D., Myrick, L. S. (1990). *The teacher advisor program: An innovative approach to school guidance*. Ann Arbor, MI: ERIC Counseling and Personnel Services Clearinghouse, University of Michigan.

Myrick, R. D. (1993). The teacher as advisor. In R. D. Myrick, *Developmental guidance and counseling: A practical approach* (second edition). Minneapolis: Educational Media Corporation.

Myrick, R. D., Highland, M., & Highland, W. (1986). Preparing teachers to be advisors. *Middle School Journal, 17 (3),* 15–16.

One student at a time: Report of the Task Force on High School Education (1992). Austin, TX: Texas Education Agency.

O'Neil, M. (1997). Making time for caring. *Schools in the Middle: Theory into Practice, 6(4),* 23–26.

Pueblo County High School Handbook (n.d.). Pueblo County Schools, Pueblo, CO.

Sizer, T. R. (1996). *Horaces's hope: What works for the American high school*. Boston: Houghton Mifflin.

Takanishi, R., & Hamburg, D. A. (1997). *Preparing adolescents for the Twenty-first Century: Challenges facing Europe and the Untied States.* New York: Cambridge University Press.

Vars, G. F. (1997). Creating options: Getting closer to middle level students: Options for teacher-advisor guidance programs. *Schools in the Middle: Theory into Practice, 6 (4),* 16–22.

Wollman. R. (1998). Advisement and advocacy: Personalizing the learning process. *The High School Magazine, 5 (4),* 4–12.

6

ALTERNATIVE SCHEDULING FOR TEACHING AND LEARNING

WHAT YOU WILL LEARN IN THIS CHAPTER

The traditional schedule and its limitations

The varieties of block schedule: Copernican-style schedule, A/B, 4 × 4, and hybrid models

Issues associated with new block schedules

Each high school teacher involved in the instructional program on a full-time basis will be responsible for contact time with no more than 90 students during a given term so that the teacher can give greater attention to the needs of every student.

High schools will develop flexible scheduling that allows for more varied used of time in order to meet the requirements of the core curriculum.

The Carnegie unit will be redefined or replaced so that high schools no longer equate seat time with learning.

—*Breaking Ranks, p. 45*

SCHEDULING THE HIGH SCHOOL

Organizational Principles from The Coalition of Essential Schools

The Coalition of Essential Schools, as discussed earlier, was founded by Theodore Sizer in 1984 following the publication of his book *Horace's Compromise* (1984). Sizer developed a set of nine principles to which schools that were members of the coalition subscribed (Sizer, 1992). One of those principles is the "student as worker." Visualizing a different sort of teaching and learning process for the high school classroom, Sizer argued that students must assume more and more responsibility in the learning process. High school students must be helped to move from their roles as passive recipients of teacher-talk to more active learning characterized by students teaching themselves and each other, with the primary roles of the teacher being coach and facilitator. In 1992 Sizer asserted that the concept of student as worker had direct implications for the school schedule. "Teachers," he wrote, "find that they need larger blocks of time; the daily schedules have changed at many Essential Schools" (p. 211). In this chapter the reader will discover that the long block schedule may soon become the norm in the American high school.

THE EMERGING HIGH SCHOOL SCHEDULE

> Right now, in most high schools, the schedule is frozen, glacier-like, into 50-minute segments that dictate the amount of instructional time devoted to each course, regardless of what would be most appropriate on a particular day (*Breaking Ranks*, 1996, p. 47).

The Traditional High School Schedule

The traditional high school schedule is familiar to virtually every educator and to generations of American citizens. In 1982 the Committee of Ten recommended that every high school center the work of each student upon five or six academic areas in each of the 4 years of high school. The Carnegie Unit came next and formalized it, requiring 120 hours of instruction per credit unit.

Since that time, the high school day has usually been divided into six or seven periods of equal length, with additional time for lunch and home room. Class periods for every subject have usually been 50 or 55 minutes in length, with 5 to 6 minutes between classes to allow students to get from one side of the building to the other. Course credits were in Carnegie Units, according to the number of hours the student spent in a particular class. The typical class probably consisted of a review of the previous day's homework, a presentation by the teacher, questions and answers/discussion about the presentation, and assignment of homework for that evening. This model has been the standard in the majority of American high schools for most of the last century, except for a short-lived attempt at what came to be called modular scheduling in the 1960s and 1970s (Carroll, 1990).

Numerous attempts to redesign the high school schedule were made in the early 1980s following the publication of the *Nation at Risk* report (National Commission on Excellence, 1983). Although the report addressed all levels of education, it concentrated on high school education. Since that time, declining resources, pressures for increased accountability from a variety of sources, state legislation, a push to graduate ever greater percentages of high school students with little or no increase in funding, and a general dissatisfaction with the high school experience among students and parents has caused a dramatic change in the shape of the high school schedule. The traditional high school schedule may soon be the norm in dramatically fewer American high schools.

Problems with the Traditional Schedule

Canady and Rettig (1995) have written at length about the problems with the traditional, relatively brief, single-period high school schedule. They asserted that the traditional schedule has contributed in various ways to a serious decline in the social climate in the high school. They maintained, for example, that the traditional schedule helps foster the increasingly impersonal nature of high school by creating learning environments in which it is difficult for teachers and students to come to know each other well. Teachers who must interact with up to 150 or more students per day are usually able to develop meaningful relationships with only a few students. Students who have few positive relationships with teachers, and who have limited opportunities to remain with student cohort groups for any meaningful length of time during the day, are likely to feel less social pressure to behave responsibly, exacerbating the discipline problems that occur in the classroom and hallways. The traditional schedule requires students to move through the hallways rapidly five or six times each day, and these class changes are particularly conducive to discipline problems, especially at lockers and in dressing rooms. Valuable learning time is also lost as a consequence of frequent class changes. Such circumstances hinder the efforts of both teachers and students.

Canady and Rettig (1995) also reasoned that the traditional high school schedule has erected barriers to effective teaching and learning. Some students, for example, have to spend an entire semester or even a year in courses they are destined to fail; such students, realizing they have no chance to pass the course, are unlikely to use the time wisely and may prevent other students from learning as much as they could. The traditional schedule is not sufficiently flexible for teaching and learning; only instructional activities that fit easily into a 50-minute period have been regularly selected for use. Such restrictions have contributed to an overreliance on the lecture method that has continued in a time when teaching as telling has lost much of its effectiveness with American students raised in a video culture. Short classes, Canady and Rettig maintained, have provided too little time for follow-up, reinforcement, independent practice, reteaching, research, or other learning activities that might lead to greater academic achievement.

There are other instructional problems with the traditional schedule. The addition of increased graduation requirements in the wake of the *Nation at Risk* report

(National Commission on Excellence, 1983) has cut the average amount of time available to be devoted to each requirement. Start-up and clean-up times, occurring six or seven times each day, consume large portions of class time that could to be devoted to instruction. Teachers have difficulty planning and delivering integrated curriculum within the short time frame. Fewer opportunities for acceleration to new levels of coursework or remediation of failed coursework are possible in a school year if the schedule only offers six or seven daily options instead of the eight possibilities in a block schedule. Students must deal with varying requirements of six or seven teachers per day—homework, tests, varying academic and behavior requirements; no other workers face such a blistering array of requirements from so many different but equally powerful supervisors. In the same way, however, record-keeping concerns for teachers are multiplied when arranging for homework, tests, and other items for 150 or more students in six or more daily classes. Dissatisfaction with these difficulties has led many American high schools to enthusiastically embrace new models of scheduling (Canady & Rettig, 1995).

COPERNICAN-STYLE SCHEDULES

One of the first viable alternatives to the traditional schedule has come to be identified by the name *Copernican,* because its developer saw the plan as a revolutionary development in the use of time in American high schools (Carroll, 1990). In place of the traditional schedule J. M. Carroll designed a time frame that involved students in only one or two classes per day. He called these classes "macroclasses" because they last from 2 to 4 hours daily. One option would be for the class to last for 4 hours daily; the course would then be completed in 30 school days (a 6-week course). Students would enroll in six of these for a total of 36 weeks, completing virtually the same number of credits in a year as would students who took six classes a day for an hour each. A second option would offer students two macroclasses per day, 2 hours each for 60 days, the equivalent of a trimester. At the end of the year, students in such a program would also complete the same six courses as students in the traditional schedule (Carroll, 1990).

Carroll maintained that the chief advantage of the Copernican style schedule is that the longer class period virtually mandates change in the instructional strategies employed by teachers. He contended that "the schedule change is not an end in itself but a means to create a classroom environment that fosters vastly improved relationships between teachers and students and that provides much more manageable workloads for both teachers and students" (Carroll, 1994, p. 106). The primary benefit of the Copernican schedule, according to Carroll (1990), is that it radically reduces the number of students a teacher must contact daily, and the number of class preparations the teacher must make. This permits teachers to get to know their students and to plan instruction in a much more personal, and hence effective, manner.

Such a structure would also "dejuvenilize" American high schools, Carroll adds, by moving high school students beyond the "impersonalized, unproductive, frenetic" environment produced when students must change locations, focus, and relationship constellations as many as nine times a day. Such a schedule probably exacerbates the most undesirable juvenile habits of teenagers rather than facilitating more relaxed, reflective, stable, and adult-like behaviors. (Carroll, 1990).

Parry McCluer High School (PMHS) in Buena Vista, Virginia, with 350 students in grades nine through twelve, offers an example of how a small high school can effectively adapt the Copernican scheduling process. At PMHS the schedule produces what educators there have named EXCEL, "Extended Classes for Enhanced Learning." The school year there is divided into 12-week trimesters, each of which contains a 60-day term. This arrangement allows for in-depth coverage of the material, giving students more time to seek extra help from their teacher. Each day has one 120-minute block class, one 110-minute class, with an additional 45-minute period added to one class (or used for independent study) during the afternoon. The school day at PMHS also contains 36 minutes for lunch, 15 minutes for class changes, and additional time for electives, for a total of 376 minutes. Students take 2-hour block classes, and in the afternoon they have the option of an extra 45 minutes in either class or an independent study; the staff believes that this afternoon option offers some flexibility regarding student learning rates. The state of Virginia requires 150 clock hours per course, and the PMHS schedule allows 160 hours for the first block and 155 for the second.

During each of the three terms a PMHS student enrolls in two major subjects, completing a total of six courses per year. One day in a block class is the equivalent of three days in a traditionally scheduled class, and educators at PMHS point out that regular class attendance is of the utmost importance to a student's success. To miss one calendar day means missing three course/class days.

The staff at PMHS believes that their Copernican-style schedule produces a host of important benefits for their students. Students focus on only two subjects per term, which yields more time for each student to spend with one teacher; thus producing more completed work and more immediate feedback and help from the teacher. Less time is wasted with interruptions, class changes, and class start-ups; students have more time to devote to the tasks of each class. Students at PMHS can schedule more classes in their 4 years of high school, so they take classes they might otherwise have been unable to. Graduates are therefore well-rounded individuals with more future options. Juniors and seniors have more time and opportunity to take advantage of post-secondary enrollment possibilities.

Students who need extra time and assistance can easily receive it as a result of the availability of the extra 45 minutes per afternoon in either major course. The student failure rate at PMHS has been reduced and students have also been able to accelerate their progress by taking two additional courses per term on independent study; students can take three consecutive mathematics or foreign language courses in 1 year. Additionally, PMHS educators maintain that more blocked class time allows students to participate in a variety of instructional activities that deepen understanding and make course content more meaningful.

Benefits for students lead to benefits for teachers. Teachers at PMHS teach six classes during the year (two each trimester) rather than five, so the teacher–student ratio is substantially lower with 15 to 17 students in the average class rather than 25 to 30 previously. The lower daily student load permits teachers more time to plan for individual students; yields quality instructional time for demonstrations and hands-on activities; and encourages the infusion of technology into the teaching process. Teachers have fewer, more concentrated class preparations, and are able to give more attention to instruction. Smaller class sizes and fewer classes per day also permit teachers to engage in more monitoring of student progress and yields more time for remedial instruction and enrichment, all of which create a better day for both teachers and students.

Jenny Sue Floyd, PMHS mathematics teacher, was worried that students would be bored during the long periods, "but it hasn't worked out that way at all. We have so many activities that students stay interested. I have lots of different activities to illustrate what I'm trying to teach. . . . We have students who actually want to come back for the third hour in the afternoon to do more work." In the smaller classes, "I've found that quiet students tend to open up more. Of course, it's harder for them to hide what they don't know." Floyd's biggest worry was the length of time that might exist between consecutive mathematics or foreign language courses. "One thing is certain," said Floyd. "The traditional schedule was not working. I don't know if what we're doing now is the right one, but it's definitely an improvement. In the shorter periods you couldn't teach with technology. You can't learn software in 50 minutes. And if you're not putting technology in the classroom, you're not doing it right" (*Buena Vista News Gazette,* March 22, 1995).

Student comments are equally positive. Comments from PMHS students about the Copernican-style schedule at their high school include the following:

> "The smaller classes are better. There's more one-on-one. It's helped build my self-confidence."

> "I like the new system because we are able to relate the stories to real-life experiences in our discussions."

> "The classes are easier this year. You only have to study for two exams at a time."

> "My fingers got really tired after a while." [Typing class]

> "You get more help from the teacher and other students during the school day, so there is less homework at night. That makes it easier for students who play sports or who have a job." (*Buena Vista News Gazette,* March 22, 1995)

School leaders at PMHS add that benefits of the Copernican-style schedule also accrue to business and commercial interests in the community. Students graduate with more functional and technological experience, which makes them better employees. Better high schools attract new businesses, which will improve the overall business climate. Excellent schools attract businesses and home-buyers to a community, thus improving the tax base and providing new jobs. Although the authors are uncertain if the benefits of the block schedule can be directly correlated with improved business conditions, educators at PMHS are convinced that it is so.

One potential problem existed for students who played sports—athletic eligibility. Students who failed either block course in one semester would be ineligible to play sports during the next term because one failure usually made it impossible to earn the mandatory 2.5 course credits through the end of the first semester, as required in Virginia. Another problem arose in activities like band, yearbook, and the school newspaper. Because students took these classes for only one term, participation in these courses during the rest of the year was considered extracurricular and had to occur after the end of the formal school day. But educators at PMHS and elsewhere declare that these are logistical problems that can and have been worked out.

The program at PMHS has combined the trimester Copernican-style schedule with a fourth quarter or trimester option—an extended school-year summer program that yields tuition-free, year-round education opportunities, and has done so since 1973. PMHS offers a fourth quarter summer session during which students take classes for remediation, enrichment, or acceleration. According to school leaders, over 60 percent of PMHS students, and many students from other districts, take advantage of the fourth quarter each year.

Principal Bill Reid at L.V. Rogers Secondary School (RSS) in Nelson, British Columbia, wrote that he will never forget the day a high school student cried in his office:

> The tears were caused by the stress of studying for five government exams, preparing a science report, completing a history essay, finishing an English novel, and balancing all this with her part-time job. This experience was one of a series of events which started me thinking about the way secondary schools are organized in British Columbia. Why do we create a frenetic atmosphere of constant movement driven by a bell system? Why do we create systems in which learning is piecemealed into 55 minute packages which encourage lecturing? Teachers deal with 150 or more students at a time and many students fall through the cracks that develop in an organizational structure which encourages abuse and procrastination (Reid, 1995).

This incident became the stimulus for a new Copernican-style schedule at RSS, a school of 660 students, a long way from Parry McCluer High School in Virginia. The new schedule at RSS, which educators there call the "Horizontal Timetable," was implemented in September, 1992. (Figure 6.1 is an illustration of the Copernican schedule at RSS.) Similar to the modified Copernican schedule at Parry McCluer High, students at RSS take two courses at a time instead of the traditional six, seven, or eight; classes last for 150 minutes. In addition to the "macroclasses" A and B, the schedule features an alternating week so that the two macroclasses are offered at different times during the day. Tutorial and seminar times are also built into the schedule. The change in schedule resulted, says Reid, in dramatic changes in teaching strategies.

Five years later, a number of indicators revealed the positive results of changing the schedule. A school board survey showed that 97 percent of the parents supported the new schedule. Examination results, scholarship awards, and surveys all supported the new schedule. Since the implementation of the new schedule a variety of school academic records have been set: highest number of Ministry Scholarships in a single year, highest number of scholarship-qualifying scores on government exams, highest number of students achieving honor roll status, highest passing rate in most individual courses, and highest graduation rate. Failure rates in a number of courses requiring provincial exams dropped dramatically, while the number of students taking these difficult courses increased.

Declining failure rates (e.g., failure in tenth grade science dropped from 20 percent to 3 percent) led more students to select an academic science class in eleventh grade. Students who did fail a course at RSS often took advantage of the opportunity

FIGURE 6.1   L. V. Rogers Timetable

Week 1					
	Monday	Tuesday	Wednesday	Thursday	Friday
Seminar 1 7:30–8:30	Choir		Choir		Choir
First Period 8:45–11:15	A	A	A	A	A
Tutorial 11:15–11:45	Time available for student homework, extra help, clubs				
11:45–12:45	lunch				
Second Period 12:45–3:15	B	B	B	B	B

Week 2					
	Monday	Tuesday	Wednesday	Thursday	Friday
Seminar 1 7:30–8:30	Choir		Choir		Choir
First Period 8:45–11:15	B	B	B	B	B
Tutorial 11:15–11:45					
11:45–12:45	lunch				
Second Period 12:45–3:15	A	A	A	A	A

to repeat a critical course, such as a graduation requirement. The school also experienced an increase in enrollment in self-directed learning courses. School leaders exulted, "We expected some improvement in school climate but were very pleasantly surprised by the extent of the change. Although we anticipated a similar or slightly reduced number of discipline problems, we found discipline problems were virtually eliminated" (Reid, 1995). Perhaps the highest praise for this Copernican-style schedule is that by 1995, 19 additional British Columbia secondary schools had adopted a similar schedule. Educators at RSS offered several recommendations for those who seek to implement a Copernican-style schedule. They emphasized the importance of inservice for teachers because an immense effort is required to enable teachers to move away from lecturing. Reconfiguring the curriculum is essential because a course that would be offered over 36 weeks might now be offered in 6. More practically, educators at RSS point out that it is important to keep equipment in specialty areas operational. If, for example, a sewing machine or computer breaks down for several days, the equivalent of 2 weeks of instructional time may be lost in classes where these machines were in use.

In building the master schedule, schedulers at RSS

> . . . start from scratch every year, using a conflict matrix to create the best possible situation for the greatest number of students. We pay close attention to the placement of courses so that students can get the full benefit from the flexibility of the timetable. For example, French 11 is programmed before French 12, Introductory to Mathematics 11 is before Mathematics 11. Although these are common sense planning strategies, it is surprising how easy it is to miss one of them in the middle of timetable construction (Reid, 1995).

Principal Reid has thought long and hard about the benefits of the Horizontal Timetable. In developing the schedule at RSS, he and other educators there were pursuing a vision of a schedule that would create the right answers to the following "what if" questions. The answers to the questions Reid asked rhetorically offer a list of potential benefits for the Copernican schedule.

What would it be like if . . .

- Instruction was not interrupted for Career Preparation, as the work experience could be scheduled for a quarter or for afternoons or mornings only.
- Senior team players could arrange to have only one course during their season of play.
- Team members had a minimum of contacts to make in order to find out what was missed as a result of tournament play.
- A student who wished could graduate as much as a half year earlier by completing course requirements.
- A student who failed a course could repeat it, repeat the final exam, or complete makeup work, and still get credit in the year the course was started.
- Students in the school's rehabilitation program could be mainstreamed at any time to pick up a course if their educational program required it.
- Fewer textbooks were needed to service classes and fewer books were floating around the building or laying in students' lockers. A wider range of books would be affordable.
- Students who failed to graduate in June could pick up a course in September without committing themselves to a full year of school.
- The curriculum could be learner-focused, encourage a range of teaching activities in the classroom, and discourage traditional teacher lecture situations.
- Intensity of courses was increased with immediate success achievable.
- Students who had a difficult time and came back in September could have tangible rewards more quickly for their efforts instead of having to wait until the end of the year.
- Students who had trouble adjusting to eight different teaching styles could have a less stressful time in school.

- Report time was easier because each teacher had only two classes to grade, and report cards were more meaningful, with written teacher comments.
- Students could immerse in a subject prior to a government exam and concentrate on that subject and one other instead of six, seven, or eight.
- There was little impact from assemblies, etc.: no more "we've hit F Block four times already."
- It was easier for counselors to contact a student's teachers in confidential situations and the teacher would be better able to remember the student.
- Teachers could give more individualized attention because they would not be dealing with almost 200 students.
- We eliminated the constant movement from one teaching area to another by specialty teachers and allowed the set-up of materials just once.
- Chronic tardiness and absence was noticed quickly, and the parents could be involved immediately. Problems could be dealt with by the teacher, with major problems handled at the office.
- It was easier to maintain cleanliness in the classroom (students writing on desks, etc.).
- All the set-up and clean-up time currently used in practical arts courses was replaced by time on task.
- Anecdotal report cards and student portfolios could be developed.
- Laboratory practical exams could be set up and left in place.
- Teachers had flexibility to organize their day to cater to student needs or desires.
- The constant student movement to and from lockers and classes was gone and students were able to organize themselves easily, needing only two binders and two textbooks.
- Home room periods and block changes were virtually eliminated.
- The learning assistants in the Special Services Room had more time for actual student academic help.
- The problem of students having "a whole bunch of tests or essays piled on all at once" was eliminated, homework was more controlled, and makeup tests were easier to arrange.
- Field trips could be organized during the week for a full morning or afternoon with no impact on other classes.
- Time was available each day for student help with coursework and doing homework.
- Guest speakers and community involvement were easier to arrange.
- No bells were needed.
- Breaks in class could be taken at natural points (after a test, at the end of a presentation) instead of whenever the bell rang.
- Parent contact was easier when student effort was a problem (Reid, 1995).

Atlantic High School (AHS) in South Daytona Beach, Florida, where 1550 students were enrolled in 1997, illustrates that the Copernican-style schedule also works well in larger high schools. In the mid-1990s principal Chris Colwell led the implementation of a dramatically new high school program in Volusia County, Florida, culminating in the opening of AHS. As a part of that new high school model (but only a *part,* Dr. Colwell insists), the school schedule was organized into a

FIGURE 6.2   Block Scheduling Sample Copernican Schedule

Block Scheduling—
Sample Copernican Schedule

Time:	1st Tri	2nd Tri	3rd Tri
7:25-9:30	Eng I	Alg II	Electronics
9:30-9:45	SHARK BREAK		
9:45-11:50	Comp Keybd	2-D Art	Biology I-Hon
11:50-12:35	LUNCH		
12:35-2:40	Life Man/Per Fit	Spanish I	Creat Writing
9 CREDITS			

trimester design in which each of the three daily block classes meets for approximately 2 hours and 5 minutes. Students earn a total of nine credits per year, three in each 12-week trimester. Figure 6.2 illustrates a sample schedule at AHS, with one 15-minute break in the morning and a 45-minute whole-school lunch time. Perhaps because of Florida's weather and a large enclosed courtyard, Colwell reports that having all 1,550 students off for that long lunch has presented no serious problems in the 4 years the schedule has been in operation.

Teachers at AHS teach two blocks and have one for planning, which allows a generous amount of planning time. In exchange, teachers have a slightly larger average class size and they commit to 25 hours of tutoring time and 60 hours of staff development each year. Principal Colwell emphasizes the importance of assembling the schedule carefully, beginning with a mandatory family registration process and culminating in hand-scheduling every student during the summer. He also points out that the Copernican-style 2-hour–plus schedule virtually forces teachers to make substantial changes in the way they teach, which is another reason to provide generous planning time each day.

It certainly would be wonderful if all of the hopes for the Copernican schedule were actually realized in all schools with Copernican schedules. Carroll (1994) reported on the results of eight high schools using various versions of the Copernican plan. According to that evaluation, six of eight schools reported improved attendance, four of six reported a decrease in suspensions, and seven of eight had a substantial reduction in dropout rates. All eight schools reported greater mastery of content as measured by the number of credits earned per student. Finally, in the 33 comparisons made between traditional schedules and the Copernican programs, 27 favored the Copernican, 5 favored traditional schedules, and 1 showed no change. If results like these accompanied every transition in school scheduling, it might lead to a Copernican "evolution" after all.

ALTERNATING DAY (A/B) SCHEDULES

Far more common than the Copernican schedule is a variation of the block schedule known as the Alternating Day or A Day/B Day schedule. A school with such a schedule arranges for most classes to meet every other day, but for twice the length of the traditional period. When a school offers students the possibility of enrolling in six basic courses over the school year, three classes usually meet for two periods each—every other day throughout the school year. If a school offers seven courses, one class would be added each day for only one single period, meeting much like a regular period would—once a day, every day, all year long. If the school has an eight-period day, the new alternating-day schedule would have odd-number–period classes meet for two periods on one day (A day) and even-numbered classes meet for two periods on alternate (B) days. Students would then have the possibility of a four-period block of classes that meet every other day for two periods each all year long (Canady & Rettig, 1995).

In gathering data for this book, the authors found many high schools using an alternating-day schedule. For example, since 1984, Granger High School in West

Valley City, Utah, has used an eight-period block in which each period meets for 86 minutes on alternate days. Many others are similar. For example, John Stark Regional High School in Weare, New Hampshire, utilizes an alternating-day block schedule, with 100 minute classes 4 days a week. Lebanon High School in Lebanon, Indiana uses an "8 block," in which all classes meet on Monday for 40 to 45 minutes; during the rest of the week, classes are 85 minutes long—periods 1, 2, 5, and 6 meet on Tuesdays and Thursdays, and periods 3, 4, 7, and 8 meet on Wednesdays and Fridays.

Champlain Valley High School (CVU) in Hinesburg, Vermont, has used an eight-period alternating day schedule for a number of years. CVU is a grade nine through twelve union high school serving four towns, with an enrollment of 912 students. The first year block scheduling was tried at CVU, the schedule contained eight periods. On Mondays and Wednesdays students and teachers worked through periods 1, 3, 5, and 7; on Tuesdays and Thursdays the schedule offered periods 2, 4, 6, and 8. Every period lasted for 90 minutes. On Fridays during the first year all eight classes met for 45 minutes each. So, students and teachers had 4 days of block schedule, moving through eight double periods; on Fridays the schedule reverted to the traditional day of eight 45-minute periods.

In some cases, the implementation of a modified schedule such as the one at CVU is met with a degree of trepidation among staff members. Retaining at least one day of short, "regular" periods gave the staff a sense that not everything had been abandoned in favor of an untried innovation. By the end of the first year at CVU, the faculty believed that the Friday schedule was a "waste of time." In 1995 the schedule at CVU was one of strictly alternate blocks, with Fridays alternating as either an A day or a B day each week.

Copperas Cove High School (CCHS) in Copperas Cove, Texas, has implemented the alternating-day eight-period schedule. On "Blue" days periods 1 to 4 meet for 90 minutes each; on "Gold" days periods 5 to 8 meet for the same length of time. The time frame looks like this:

Period 1/5   8:00–9:30 A.M.

Period 2/6   9:38–11:18 A.M.

Period 3/7   11:26 A.M.–1:22 P.M., including lunch

Period 4/8   1:30–3:00 P.M.

The move to the block schedule at CCHS required some modifications. Special arrangements were made for athletics, band, and choir to meet every day, as well as some special classes in mathematics. Graduation requirements were modified, as they are in many schools that move to a block schedule; graduation requirements have increased from 22 credits in 1994 to 28 credits in 1997.

An evaluation of the CCHS block schedule conducted at the end of the first year yielded favorable results. Among the more desirable outcomes were these:

- Increase of 33 percent in foreign language enrollment
- 50 percent increase in fine arts enrollment
- 15 to 20 percent increase in electives (journalism, yearbook, creative writing, achievement test preparation)

- 100 percent increase in advanced placement (AP) mathematics enrollment
- 100 percent increase in enrollment in business and vocational courses
- Discipline referrals were down by 37 percent (tardies down by 31 percent; fights by 20 percent; defiance by 45 percent; tobacco by 43 percent)
- The incidence of severe discipline problems was down by 35 percent
- Students spent less time in the hallways, remaining settled during the class periods
- Students took two additional courses
- The percentage of As on report cards increased (from 30 percent to 36.7 percent) and the percentage of Fs decreased (from 8.9 percent to 7.6 percent)

When CCHS students were surveyed in the first year of the block schedule, 113 favored the block, 21 favored the regular schedule, and 11 were undecided. Eighty percent said teachers were using the time wisely, but some students said too many teachers were still giving long lectures and worksheets. Some teachers were using only 45 minutes and then doing nothing, some students complained. Ninety-two percent of the students believed that the block schedule had a positive effect on the school environment.

A memo to the school principal from the athletic director at the end of the first year illustrated the enthusiasm of some members of the school community:

> Please know that the block scheduling system that we currently have in place is a big help to the athletic department and what we try to accomplish with athletic teams and programs. Having an hour and a half time schedule allows us to practice, shower, and have a study period. I enthusiastically support block scheduling and hope you will plan to do this schedule in the future.

As a result of their experience thus far with the alternating-day, 90-minute period, educators at CCHS offer the following recommendations to those who seek to implement a similar schedule:

- Do less—better! Make departmental plans that highlight what the members of a department want to do well. Focus—spend more time on specific objectives.
- Teachers should investigate the individual learning styles of students and ask themselves how they can package the material to be congruent with those specific learning styles.
- Examine how cooperative learning can be used to maximize peer assistance. Some students learn better from peers than from teachers.
- Learn how the communication skills (writing–speaking–listening–reading) can be used in instruction. How will the longer classes allow the teacher time to foster student use of these skills?
- Ask how classes can be more interactive.
- Determine whether a portion of the class time can be used for seniors to assist freshmen with their academic work. Could seniors be matched up with freshmen through the English classes and be allowed time each week to work with these students?
- Ask whether different types of performance-based assessments could be used to add relevance to class.

- Be tenacious about eliminating passive learning experiences. Can we make assessment active, not passive?
- Discover what material in mathematics and science can be presented at the same time. What about English and social studies? Can materials be presented to take advantage of "teachable moments" or themes? What can we tie together?
- Can outside speakers or supplemental materials be used to enrich classroom activities?
- Can TAAS (Texas state test) materials be used during each class? Can TAAS objectives be taught in vocational and special education?
- What can students do differently? Ask them. Plan an environment that allows security, freedom, fun, hope, and power.
- The key to making block schedules work lies in all of these considerations. The key is not more worksheets, more passive seatwork, more individual work, more homework, and so on. It cannot be more of the same.

At Coloma High School (CHS), in Coloma, Michigan, an eight-period block/seven-credit schedule utilizes an A/B day format (Figure 6.3). Students enroll for four classes meeting for 85-minute periods on Mondays and Wednesdays, completing the rotation on Fridays with classes lasting 45 minutes. Three other courses and what they call a seminar are taken on Tuesdays, continued on Thursdays, and completed on Fridays.

On Tuesday and Thursday at CHS, the second block of the day is a non-credit seminar period in which enrichment and remediation activities are offered to all students. All non-instructional activities—assemblies, class meetings, blood drives, pep sessions, group testing, college representatives' presentations, and so on—are confined to the seminar period. The seminar period at CHS can also be used for completion of assignments, securing extra help from teachers, using the library, attending meetings, making up tests, and a variety of other activities. At CHS, educators insist that the seminar period is distinctly not to be used for sleeping, card playing, or socializing.

For the first 10 minutes of the seminar period, all students at CHS remain in their seminar classroom. This is a convenient time for taking attendance and communicating important information to students. The first half of the seminar period is a "restricted movement" time, meaning that students who already have a pass may leave, but others cannot have a pass written by the seminar teacher during this time. The second half of the period is a "free movement" time. During the last 5 minutes, all students must return to the seminar room. On Fridays, the seminar block becomes an advisory block; students and teachers meet in a teacher-based advisory program. At CHS, teachers teach four periods daily, have responsibility for a seminar/advisory group, and have a daily planning period. Figure 6.4 illustrates a typical teacher's schedule at CHS, in this case a Spanish teacher.

Hillcrest High School (HHS) in Springfield, Missouri, has fully implemented the alternating-day schedule, in a way similar to Coloma High School—eight periods, seven credits. Each class meets for 85 minutes on alternate days, and the Channel One television program is viewed daily. Teachers teach five periods plus an advisory seminar (see Figure 6.4). On Mondays and Wednesdays teachers have periods 1, 3,

FIGURE 6.3   **Coloma High School Student Schedule**

STUDENT SCHEDULE:

It will be noted in the illustration below that a student takes four 85-minute courses on Monday, repeating those courses on Wednesday for 85 minutes and completing the rotation on Friday for 45 minutes. Three other courses and a seminar are taken on Tuesday, repeated on Thursday, and completed on Friday. This plan allows a student to take seven, rather than the present six, courses each semester. It also allows for uninterrupted block time and provides for tutorial and mastery learning opportunities through the seminar period.

8-BLOCK, 7-CREDIT SCHEDULE
Student Schedule

MONDAY	TUESDAY	WEDNESDAY	THURSDAY	FRIDAY
1 Spanish II	2 Algebra II	1 Spanish II	2 Algebra II	1 2
3 English II	4 Seminar	3 English II	4 Seminar	3 Advisor Base
5 Chemistry	6 Phys. Ed.	5 Chemistry	6 Phys. Ed.	5 6
7 Am. Hist.	8 Auto Shop	7 Am. Hist.	8 Auto Shop	7 8

5, and 7; on Tuesdays and Thursdays periods 2, 4, 6, and 8 meet. Fridays at HHS, like Coloma, have all eight periods, 43 minutes each, plus advisory seminar.

HHS principal John Laurie is so committed to the block schedule that he edits a regular problem-solving newsletter on the topic. Dr. Laurie argues that it is much easier for students to transfer into an alternating-day, year-long block schedule than into a school using a 4×4 block schedule with classes that meet daily for the length of a traditional semester, because the courses in the alternating-day block move at about the same pace as the traditional schedule. It has been Laurie's experience that retention of course material by students, except perhaps in mathematics, is enhanced because of the opportunity to present, practice, and confirm in the same period, before students leave the classroom. There is time for daily reteaching and review at the beginning of each class instead of the traditional and ineffective "Are

Typical Teacher's Schedule at Coloma High School: Teachers continue to teach five periods/blocks and are responsible for a seminar/advisor group and have a planning period each day.

FIGURE 6.4

8-BLOCK, 7-CREDIT SCHEDULE
Full-time Teacher Schedule

MONDAY	TUESDAY	WEDNESDAY	THURSDAY	FRIDAY
1	2	1	2	1
Spanish II	Spanish I	Spanish II	Spanish I	2
3	4	3	4	3
Spanish III	Seminar	Spanish III	Seminar	Advisor Base
5	6	5	6	5
Spanish I	Conference	Spanish I	Conference	6
7	8	7	8	7
Conference	Spanish II	Conference	Spanish II	8

there any questions about homework?" to which teachers in the traditional schedule are forced to resort.

In one issue of the newsletter, *Networking News,* Laurie estimated that in 1994 one-third of American high schools had moved to a block schedule (J. Laurie, personal communication, March 1995). This estimate is affirmed by Gordon Cawelti's national survey (Cawelti, 1994).

Rutherford High School (RHS) in Panama City, Florida, uses an alternating-day, eight-period schedule. With 1865 students, RHS is the most culturally diverse and economically disadvantaged high school in Bay County, Florida. On "even" days periods 2, 4, 6, and 8 meet; on "odd" days periods 1, 3, 5, and 7 are offered. Students are dismissed every Wednesday at 12:30, and the remaining time is used for staff development.

The combination of the new schedule and staff development has led to a number of curriculum innovations at RHS. In AP English Literature, for example, the teacher assigned *Madame Bovary* over the summer, then used the extended time in the school year to dramatize the novel. In American History, simulations are more common, including a World War I simulation in which students were divided into countries and alliances. In World History, after studying feudalism, students actually built medieval castles. The debate teacher is pleased that the class can hear a complete debate, from beginning to judgments, within the context of a single period. The painting class now does large-scale murals, and can integrate the murals with art history and culture because there is time to do the required research. In typing class, students have time to type a document, have it evaluated, and retype it in the same class; the teacher can make corrections on a computer screen immediately, saving paper and time between feedback. In driver education, students can have classroom and range experiences in the same day.

Many other high schools use a variation of the A/B block schedule. Oak Ridge High School, for example, in the center of the city of Orlando, Florida, has 2,100 students, 70 percent of whom are minorities. Oak Ridge is in the third year of what they describe as an A/B Rolling Block. Each day has three periods, each lasting from 100 to 110 minutes; teachers have one planning period every other day. The periods are organized like this:

Day One	Day Two
1	2
3	4
5	6

At Oak Ridge the process began when the long-time principal insisted on a change over teacher and parent objections. Eventually, faculty, parents, and students have come to a position of strong support for the alternating day schedule. Comments from staff include these:

"Every teacher had to change the way they taught. Love it now."

"Twenty-year-old yellow lesson plans couldn't work anymore."

"It was like the first year of teaching all over again, for everyone."

"AP scores are improving or maintaining."

Many high schools have variations of the A/B rotating schedule. Palm Beach Gardens High School in Palm Beach Gardens, Florida, uses a seven-period A/B schedule in which six of the periods rotate on alternating days. The 5th period is a traditional daily event. At Lyman High School (LHS), in Seminole County, Florida, a year-long alternating-day schedule has been in operation since 1990. Each class has 122-minute periods, with 6 minutes of passing time between periods. Teachers have planning every other day at LHS. Wednesday is the traditional schedule, and Wednesday is a communications day because all students take English on that day. The schedule for the week looks like this at Lyman:

M	T	W	TH	F
1	2	1–6	1	2
3	4	1–6	3	4
5	6	1–6	5	6

At LHS, teachers have also come to support the block schedule vigorously, although teachers have mixed feelings about some aspects of it, especially the traditional schedule on Wednesdays. The majority of the staff seems to agree that the once-weekly single period on Wednesday is most useful for review and introductions of new units. The brevity of the Wednesday period at Lyman usually means that students will not be actively involved in the lesson or have much opportunity for student–student interaction. Basically, teachers at LHS dislike Wednesday—"too much of everything," they say. Wednesday is too busy, too hectic.

At LHS, teachers assert that traditional teaching happens in the traditional period. During the block periods, however, they change their teaching strategy as often as possible, and even traditional teachers alternate lecture and seatwork.

The teachers at LHS admit that having a planning period every other day is very difficult for them. One teacher said that "by Friday teachers are whipped." This same teacher, however, asserted that neither she nor the great majority of her colleagues would want to go back to a totally traditional schedule. The block is easy for science teachers, says the staff at LHS; they are already prepared to do extended classes. At LHS, the mathematics teachers love it—they are able to use more technology and get students involved in far more projects and laboratory activities. As one mathematics teacher reported, "I thought it was stupid. I love it. I would never want to go back."

There are other concerns related to the block schedule at LHS. One teacher commented that the 2-hour block "can be boring for the teacher who has a class that doesn't respond." Courses that require new preparations are very tough, teachers say, with an alternate-day planning time. But others point out that having a class every other day gives the teacher time to prepare, grade papers, and think about what to do next. Some teachers at LHS find that the block schedule makes it harder to orient ninth graders into the system—2-hour classes are very long for them. Teachers in the lower level math classes at LHS (pre-algebra) enjoy the double periods less because "many students don't want to be there."

Other comments from teachers at LHS include:

"Varying the activity is the key."

"Two hours is too long for the typical physical education period."

"We review regularly."

"You have to change—no choice. Staff development is key."

"It's a good shift. It makes us grow professionally."

"Allows time for showing complete films, even with follow-up discussion and closure."

Lyman students also offered comments on their experience with the block schedule. They generally agreed with their teachers, especially about Wednesdays. One student said, "I hate Wednesdays; I don't know how we learn anything." Another pointed out that teachers often used Wednesdays for short quizzes, an event for which the students cared little. Other student comments included these:

"If the teacher isn't prepared for the day (122 minutes), it's really bad."

"Teachers have more time for explaining. They can teach for understanding."

"Teachers have more time to relate the class to real life."

"More time for doing homework."

"It saves energy—eliminates the need for carrying so many books."

"The block schedule works as well for honors and regular students."

"It all depends on the teacher and the pace of the activities in the class."

"We still have to do some homework (e.g., write up the physics labs) but we understand it all."

Canady and Rettig (1995) identify numerous potential advantages for the alternating-day and other versions of the block schedule, much like those articulated previously by practitioners like William Reid:

- All teachers get more high-quality instructional time because the alternating day eliminates a great deal of time otherwise lost to procedures, routines, and interruptions from class openings, closings, and so on.
- Teachers are able to plan extended lessons like those identified earlier at Rutherford High School. This is especially valuable in subjects like science and art that require extensive set-up and clean-up time; the set-up time is cut in half. Consequently teachers are more likely to schedule hands-on activities. English classes experience a more complete writing process: Prewrite, first draft, edit, revision, computer lab for polished copy—can all be done in one period. For this reason, English teachers attempt more integration of their areas, and more workshop approaches combining literature and composition. Band and orchestra teachers spend a smaller percentage of class time on packing, unpacking, and tune-up, and more time on actual rehearsal.
- Because the number of class changes is reduced, some passing time becomes instructional time. Fewer transitions mean fewer tardies and reduced discipline referrals. Even when discipline problems do occur, Canady and Rettig claim, every-other-day periods mean an extended "cooling off" time.
- Custodial staffs report that schools are cleaner and experience less vandalism (Canady & Rettig, 1995, p. 40).
- Teaching with a variety of instructional models is encouraged. Before experience with the long block schedule, teachers often worry that their students will not be able to pay attention for 90 to 100 minutes. Canady and Rettig contend that it is not the length of time but the activity within it that determines the quality of any classroom experience, whether in short or long classes. A 90-minute lecture is nearly as impossible for the teacher to offer as it is for the student to endure. Over and over again, the refrain is the same—altering instructional strategies is essential to the success of altering the bell schedule.

- Canady and Rettig contend that longer periods permit concentrated work in specialized programs, such as vocational programs held at other centers. It is possible that such arrangements could also cut transportation costs to these centers if the number of trips to and from such centers is cut back to accommodate the alternating-day schedule.
- Canady and Rettig, and many practitioners involved in a block schedule, agree that in the block schedule, students have fewer classes, quizzes, tests, or homework assignments on any one day.
- Work missed because of absences is easier to gather and easier to monitor, although absences are more serious because one absence is the equivalent of two in a regular schedule.

Canady and Rettig point out that the A/B schedule can be modified in any number of ways when it is important to do so. Many of these modifications have been illustrated in the descriptions of real schedules offered previously. We recommend the book, *Block scheduling: A catalyst for change in high schools* (Canady & Rettig, 1995) to readers who require even greater detail than can be offered here. Among the modifications they discuss are:

- A special seminar or activity period can be used for clubs, intramurals, advisory time, detention, schoolwide assemblies, discussions, mini-courses, or other purposes.
- A six-course schedule can also leave two classes as singletons meeting every day. Periods 1 and 2 could alternate every other day, 5 and 6 could also alternate, and singleton periods 3 and 4 could be combined with lunch daily to make a third block.
- Seven-course models usually have one standard course (e.g., period 5) with odd courses blocked on A day, and even courses blocked on B day.
- With seven-period schedules, period 7 can be standard at the end of the day for athletic practice, band, and other similar uses.
- A school could double-block only 2 days a week, 4 days a week, 2 of every 4 days, and so on. One could double-block on Wednesday and Thursday, keeping singles for Monday, Tuesday, and Friday.
- Schedules can alternate so that courses 1 and 2 alternate, courses 6 and 7 alternate, and courses 3, 4, and 5 stay as singletons.
- Schedules can hold the first period standard, combined with a home room/activity period, and then alternate 2–4–6 and 3–5–7

THE 4 × 4 SEMESTER PLAN

In the fall of 1996 at Newberry High School in Newberry, Florida, principal Wiley Dixon led the move to a new eight-period block schedule. Newberry is a small rural high school of 540 students in a conservative, less-than-affluent community where 40 percent of the students receive free or reduced lunches. Teachers went from teaching five out of seven periods to teaching three out of four daily, with each formerly year-long course now lasting one semester. Approaching such a change in these circumstances might have led to serious criticism and opposition from both the community and the teaching staff.

Dixon approached the transition very carefully. Candor was important in working with both teachers and parents, says Dixon; he made sure, for example, that he did not promise more than a new schedule could deliver. The small size of the school helped make it possible for the principal to develop support for the new schedule in a very personal way. He met, for example, with every class-year group on consecutive days, carefully explaining what he believed would be the benefits of a different schedule to each group. Eventually a survey of students found 85 percent in favor of a different schedule. Dixon believed that among both students and parents a certain "pride in being first to do something innovative, in the district, for a change" also led to support for the new block schedule.

An initial survey of the faculty was favorable to the change, but teachers were apprehensive; they "were willing but not committed," said Dixon. Teachers also did not want to give up the beginning of the year's pre-school planning time for the staff development that Dixon believed to be essential to the success of the transition. So the change was postponed. After more work by Dixon to develop staff support for a new schedule, a second survey eventually indicated that 95 percent of the faculty endorsed a new schedule, answering "Yes, without reservations."

Because it was a small school, several modifications of the 4 × 4 semester block schedule were still necessary to make the transition effective, but the small size also permitted the principal to deal with those modifications individually, much in the same way he developed the initial support for the transition. The perennially popular and politically powerful band, for example, was allowed to meet daily all year long for 90 minutes. Foreign language may have been a problem in a large high school but at NHS, with only two teachers in this area, individual negotiations smoothed the way for the transition. Communicating with students through English classes is no longer possible, for example, because not all students are taking English every day in the 4 × 4 environment. The school received permission from the district office to add 10 minutes to the length of the school day so that the schedule would accommodate four 90-minute periods per day rather than seven 50-minute periods.

Parents at NHS were not quite as apprehensive about the change as has been the case in some more affluent, suburban neighborhoods. At NHS, for example, the concern about AP courses was muted. The 4 × 4 block schedule that was eventually implemented, however, actually allowed students to take more AP courses because students could take more academic classes in 4 years. At NHS more students are now taking AP calculus in their senior year. AP calculus is combined with a "research" class and the twin courses meet for 90 minutes daily all year. Dixon maintains that "more students are building toward enrollment in AP courses, because students can catch up, by increasing the mathematics courses in which they are enrolled at any particular time."

Club day occurs twice a month (Figure 6.5). Each period is shortened by 5 minutes and passing times are also shortened by 5 minutes. Students have 60 minutes

Newberry High School Club Day Bell Schedule 1996-97   FIGURE 6.5

On Club Days, all students will attend the same lunch period

Period 1	8:05	9:30
Period 2	9:35	11:00
LUNCH	11:00	12:00
Period 3	12:00	1:25
Period 4	1:30	2:55

Day 1	**Day 2**
Student Gov't	Environmental Club
Pep Club	National Honor Society
Excel	FBLA
Mu Alpha Theta	Chess Club
Band Officers	SADD
SECME	Pre Collegiate
FFA	DCT
Basketball Committee	Criminal Justice Explorers
Drama	Spanish
FEA	Youth in Government

for lunch and a club meeting. The club day schedule operates for 2 days in a row—half the clubs meet one day, half the next—so that students can be actively involved in more than one club.

Staff development was an important part of the transition at NHS. Much of the limited time available was focused on using technology in learning and in cooperative learning as a classroom strategy. Ultimately, the whole faculty made a commitment to use the same basic rules when using cooperative learning in their classes. Those common rules include:

- Get ready to work quickly
- Sit face to face
- Stay with your group
- Stay on task
- Use voice control

The combination of the new schedule and staff development has led teachers to use many more labs in appropriate classes, more cross-disciplinary teaching, and substantially more strategies like cooperative learning. The proper pacing of the curriculum in the new schedule remained a faculty concern throughout the year, even though it had been addressed by staff development prior to implementation. Although staff development helped with the process of repackaging the curriculum for the new schedule, faculty anxiety about the difficulty of compressing a year's content into a semester remained.

To forestall potential problems with standardized tests that might have resulted from extended time between course completion and test taking, the staff at NHS has focused on improving the test-taking environment. Quick reviews for standardized tests are offered just prior to the assessment. Before the latest round of state testing, the faculty at NHS held a 20-minute period for daily review with students, the first thing every morning. Students were grouped for these reviews by "test-taking speed" so that students would not quit too soon in response to seeing other students leave. The principal canceled morning announcements and the TV news program and everyone reviewed. The staff is confident that this procedure, combined with the new schedule, will ultimately work to the benefit of both students and teachers.

Results during the first year of the 4 × 4 block schedule have been very positive. Tardies are virtually nonexistent now that students have a 10-minute passing time between classes instead of the 4 minutes they had in the old schedule, and the 10-minute passing time appears to present no special new problem because of its length. Students are not resisting "double homework" in each subject. Good teachers, says the principal, are even better in the new arrangement. Science, physical education, and art teachers love it because of the increased flexibility the block schedule offers. The Spanish teacher "much prefer(s) the block—for competitions in foreign language particularly." The home economics teacher agrees that the block schedule works much better in her area, providing time for guest speakers, the use of more complex recipes, and extended role-playing exercises. Some teachers are worried about the amount of content they can cover, and are concerned about identifying the essentials of the curriculum in their area. Many of the staff are anxious to determine whether future test scores will support their decision to alter the schedule.

Thomasville High School (THS) in Thomasville, North Carolina, uses a similar 4 × 4 semester schedule, with four 90-minute classes meeting daily for 90 days. Here as elsewhere, the implementation of a block schedule has required many modifications. Final exams at THS are given at the end of each term, including North Carolina End-of-Course tests at both mid-year and year-end. The school received a number of waivers to facilitate block scheduling; end-of-course state testing was only one. Athletic eligibility requirements had to be changed from passing five of six courses to passing three of four. Time requirements for the Carnegie unit were reduced from 150 hours of seat times to 135 hours.

A particularly thorny and complex problem for new block schedule programs, graduation requirements for transfer students, has received a great deal of insightful attention at THS. Such requirements are individually determined, with a formula that adds the potential number of credits the student could have earned at the previous school to the number of units they are eligible to earn while at THS, and then subtracting four units. For example, a senior transferring at the beginning of the first semester may have earned only six units in each of ninth, tenth, and eleventh grades in the school from which he or she transferred, plus eight units in twelfth grade at THS; that student must have 22 units to graduate (26 units minus 4).

Using the same formula, educators at THS determine that a senior transferring mid-term during the first semester could have earned six units each in grades nine, ten, and eleven, plus two units during the remaining of the semester at THS. That student can earn four more units in the second semester and therefore needs 20 units to graduate (24 potential, minus 4). A junior who transfers could have earned six units in ninth and tenth grades, plus 16 units in eleventh and twelfth grades, needing 24 units to graduate (28 potential, minus 4). A sophomore who transfers could earn six units in grade nine, and 24 units in grades ten through twelve; that student would be required to have 26 units to graduate (30 minus 4). Regular, nontransferring students are required to have 27 units of credit for graduation beginning in 1997, increased from 21 in 1994.

In addition, at THS, a Student Services Management Team regularly meets to deal with students experiencing transfer problems. Each case is addressed individually. Students may receive partial credits for work already completed. In a decision aimed at ensuring cohesiveness and consistency in classes, no new students transferring from a traditional school are added to regular courses after the first 6-week grading period during the first term.

The Advancement Center at THS was proposed primarily to assist students transferring in from traditional high school schedules in completing credits for the term in which they enroll at THS, and to help prepare these students to integrate into classes under the block schedule. The uses of the Advancement Center have been expanded to include individualized coursework for special-needs students and provision of a study period for students removed from courses because of irreversible failing status. Staffed by a certified teacher, the Center is equipped with computers networked with mathematics and English courseware. This courseware enables students to receive diagnostic–prescriptive, individually-paced instruction in these areas. Students are placed in and out of the Advancement Center on widely varying schedules; a student having extreme difficulty with one objective in an academic subject might be scheduled to receive help on a very short-term basis, whereas a late-enrolling student from a traditionally scheduled high school might be there for all four classes for the remainder of a term.

At Mayfield High School (MHS) in Las Cruces, New Mexico, principal Robert Orgas (Personal communication, June 9, 1995) described a fairly standard format for the 4 × 4 semester. At MHS, periods are 85 minutes long, with a 10-minute passing time between periods and a single 50-minute lunch. The 1,550 students in grades eight through twelve take eight classes per year; faculty teach six classes over a year, with one 85-minute planning period daily. MHS has no half-credit classes; a prolonged curriculum-development project helped the faculty eliminate those courses. All AP courses are offered in the spring, and are matched with a prerequisite to provide the necessary exam preparation. AP courses are carefully divided between eleventh and twelfth grades, so a student can take them all. Students cannot take required classes out of sequence (e.g., students must take American history in their junior year).

At MHS, students need 29 credits to graduate. A student with 6 credits is a sophomore, 13 credits identifies a junior, and 20, a senior. Transfer students:

- Must have their transcript evaluated on an individual basis
- Must take a full-credit course to make up any half-credit courses they bring in
- Must meet a sliding scale of graduation credits, depending upon the year they enter

Educators at Flagler/Palm Coast High School (FPCHS) in Bunnel, Florida, moved to a 4 × 4 semester schedule basically because declining state revenues were forcing cutbacks in staffing that gave the district a choice between moving to a block schedule or changing from a seven- to a six-period traditional schedule. Principal Larry Hunsinger stated that "Going to a six-period day would have killed the elective program." Students at FPCHS now take four courses during the first semester and four during the second; each class meets for 85 minutes daily for 18 weeks.

Hunsinger says that the staff at FPCHS has experienced a number of advantages as a result of the change to the 4 × 4 schedule. Among those advantages are:

- Fifty percent of the school's students now make the honor roll, compared with 27 percent in the 7-period day.
- All students have increased their grade point average.
- Daily attendance went from an average of 88 percent to 95 percent, probably because of a new policy that exempts students who have perfect attendance from the final examination requirement.
- Discipline referrals to the dean's office have been cut in half.
- The dropout rate is 1.1 percent—among the lowest in the state.
- The 13-minute break time gives students the feeling that they have more social time.
- The new schedule changes the principal's role to instructional leadership.
- Because they spend twice as much time at a stretch with teachers, the students feel the teachers care about them.
- They have experienced a large increase in dual enrollment with the local community college.
- Student grades no longer drop from middle school to high school.
- Students can take more higher-level mathematics classes than before.
- They have added more English and mathematics courses so students can be continuously enrolled in these areas.

These advantages, of course, did not come without constraints. The school needed a waiver from the Florida High School Activities Association, which mandated that students have to be passing five subjects to participate in extracurricular activities; students at FPCHS were only taking four. Students have to be carefully counseled to take two academic courses and two electives each semester. Teachers must make hard choices about essential content. The district spent $40,000 on staff development before implementing the new schedule. School leaders monitor classes to encourage teachers to have at least three activities each period. Exceptions common to other schools were made for band and chorus—they are offered every other day for the entire year; AP courses meet every day, all year, in a double block with a class called "Research." All of these constraints notwithstanding, 96 percent of teachers affirmed the new schedule; 98 percent do not want to go back to the seven-period day. A student survey indicated that 96 percent preferred the new schedule.

Wasson High School (WHS), Colorado Springs, Colorado, went on the 4 × 4 semester block schedule in 1989, according to principal Jackie Provenzano (J. Provenzano, personal communication, March 17, 1995). At WHS, some of the standard components of the 4 × 4 semester were used, such as four 90-minute classes 5 days a week; there are important differences at WHS as well. Most importantly, the school schedule revolves around four "terms" instead of two semesters.

At WHS, for example, a course that formerly met for 180 classes of 50 minutes now meets for 90 classes of 90 minutes. Courses that previously ran for an 18-week semester last for 9 weeks at Wasson, making it possible for students to enroll in two such courses in one half of the school year. A 15-minute passing time is inserted between the two morning block classes, with a 10-minute passing time in the afternoon. A 50-minute lunch time is shared by students and teachers. Tenth- and eleventh-grade students must take four block classes daily; seniors must take three.

According to principal Provenzano, the results of this variant of the block schedule at WHS include the following:

- More individualized and less fragmented instruction because teachers are dealing with only half their annual student load at a time
- Increases in AP scores
- More interdisciplinary courses
- An increase in the number of community-school connections
- More elective choices for students
- An increase in the number of credits earned by students.

Additionally, there has been a 6.7 percent increase in the honor roll, a 9.2 percent decrease in the failure rate, a 22 percent increase in students continuing to postsecondary education, a 4.4 percent increase in the attendance rate, and a 45 percent increase in students scoring a 3 or higher on the 4 point scale for AP examinations. New interdisciplinary courses have emerged as a result of the block schedule: Earth Watch is a combination of social studies, science, and English departments; American Studies unites Junior English and American history; Colorado Past, Present, and Future represents social studies and English; and a course called Geo Geo combines geology and geography into one.

Clearly, an atmosphere conducive to successful innovation prevails at Wasson. In fact, the staff at WHS has shared information on their version of the block schedule with nearly 1,000 schools and they have had visits from nearly 100 schools representing more than 40 states. The staff at WHS has even supplied information to the President's staff.

Provenzano asserted that instruction has changed dramatically as a result of their new 4 × 4 schedule:

> Our teachers are relying less on lecture than in the past, focusing instead on cooperative learning, critical thinking, and problem solving. Interdisciplinary and team-taught classes have been added to the curriculum, stressing the connection between separate subjects. When students see the relationships between subjects, rather than view them as separate categories, learning makes more sense.
>
> Our teachers are also moving away from the "sage on the stage" role, with more student involvement and more student-directed learning situations. The notion of "student as worker" and teacher as coach accurately describes the basic shift in classroom interaction between student and teacher. The resultant buy-in and involvement on the part of our students has been very positive.
>
> The move to longer blocks of instructional time made it quite clear to teachers that the lecture would not suffice as the only mode of instruction. Strategies of cooperative learning, problem solving, critical thinking, 4MAT, TESA, and a variety of educational methodologies now play more of an integral role in the classrooms than on our traditional schedule (Provenzano, Personal communication, March 17, 1995).

At University High School (UHS) in Orlando, Florida, principal Judith Cunningham and assistant principal Penny Sell have led the effort into 4 × 4 semester block scheduling in Orange County Schools, and they have done so with an exceptionally large student body of 3,500 students. Cunningham provides this rationale for visitors inquiring about the new schedule:

> The 4 × 4 schedule is a nontraditional method of blocking time designed to enhance student learning. If our graduates are to be successful in today's competitive and global economy, they must receive a significantly better education than achieved by any previous generation. To meet these higher standards, students need the opportunity to take more classes and teachers need more time to plan, evaluate lessons, and interact with students and parents.
>
> With the 4 × 4 schedule, classes are expanded to 90 minutes and students are given the opportunity to choose more courses. The 90-minute block will provide students with more intensified practice to develop critical thinking skills and gain concepts in a given content area. Students also need to know how to find information, think, solve problems, apply, and interpret information. This type of learning is facilitated by a 4 × 4 schedule.

Key components of a 4 × 4 semester block schedule at UHS are:

- Students take four courses per term.
- Term 1 meets from August through December.
- Term 2 meets from January through May.
- Classes meet for 90 minutes every day.

- A one-credit course is completed in one term.
- A half-credit course is completed in 9 weeks.
- Students can earn up to eight credits per year.

Preparation for schedule change at UHS was similar to the process followed by Wiley Dixon at Newberry High School, but size made everything more complex. The transition at UHS began, says Cunningham, with a change in philosophy stimulated by the publication of *A Nation At Risk* (National Commission on Excellence, 1983) and the many studies and documents that followed. Cunningham contended that it no longer made sense to have factory-style schools when the world had moved away from the factory model. Cunningham calls their school process "under construction" because the school is changing from the ground up. "We took a long look at the students we served, especially at the dramatic 40 percent attrition rate; 40 percent of our students would be different from the group that started the year. We looked at test scores, dropout rates, and other factors, and we concluded that we need to be more than staying even." Cunningham and the UHS staff began the restructuring process with the block schedule, as have so many other high school educators, because she believed that "You cannot do other things without an alternative schedule first."

Building teacher readiness began with the driving question: "What do our students need?" Discussions around this question were combined with visits to schools that had different schedules. A committee made up primarily of teachers spent some of their planning time as a schedule committee. Eventually teachers were asked, "What schedule do you think you want?" Out of 140 teachers, only five did not want to adopt the 4 × 4 schedule.

The new schedule was implemented in a large high school in a large, politically and socially conservative county. Members of the school district office gave their approval to the project, in spite of the logistic difficulties that such a transformation would encounter. UHS was just one of a dozen high schools within the district to which students might transfer; it was a high profile school and changes would be broadcast across the district. The central office staff, however, had confidence in UHS as a good site for a pilot program. "It was difficult to be first. Difficult because of the student mobility rate. It took a lot of public relations," said Cunningham, "and parents and students came to like the idea that students could earn eight credits instead of six."

Principal Cunningham had at least three challenging groups to deal with to make the transition to the 4 × 4 schedule work well: the district office, the community, and teachers. To do what they wanted, the school staff needed to increase the length of the school day by 1 hour, dismissing at 2:45 instead of 1:45; this alone was a dramatic departure from county policy. All of the high schools in the school system had been on a six-period day prior to the pilot, so UHS had to add time and make up for what came to be called a "condensed curriculum," different lunch shifts, and other many other problems.

The principal believed in, and insisted on, a minimum of 90 minutes per period as optimum for the new schedule. Two years later she said that this seemed about right; less time requires too much curriculum sacrifice. The pilot at UHS "blew the district bus schedules and the transportation plan," and, "buses 'drive' everything"; UHS had 60 buses. Consequently, administrators at all of the feeder elementary and middle schools had to agree to swap student pick-up times with the high school. So a successful pilot required not just tremendous adjustments philosophically and logistically, it required UHS leaders to have the cooperation of all the elementary school and middle school principals in their part of the school district.

The length of the teachers' day was the same, but problems in this area remained. Teachers formerly had 40 minutes after school for personal planning. Under the new schedule, teachers got a total of 90 minutes planning daily. For this to work, staff members at the district office agreed to increase the teacher allocation at UHS, because teachers had been teaching five out of six periods and now had to teach six out of eight periods. The school needed about 10% more teacher units to make the new schedule work without severely penalizing the teachers who would be expected to implement the scheduling plan.

Other problems had to be worked out. The district management information systems office (MIS) had to agree to change all recording procedures for grades and attendance, a prodigious task. The new schedule also required policy changes regarding attendance, early graduation, progress reports (now eight times a year), discipline (e.g., suspensions for 10 days would doom the student to failure), teacher duties (duty can no longer take the teacher's whole planning period). Now teachers who volunteer to assume duties (e.g., hallway supervision) get a salary supplement. Teachers who supervise lunch get their own lunch free. Every problem was attacked until a solution, some of them obviously novel, was worked out.

With regard to preparing the community, they knew what the problems were going to be. The principal began with an approach similar to the one that was used with teachers: What do parents want for their students? School leaders sent a newsletter to all parents and held numerous small group meetings by grade levels, because freshmen parents have different concerns than junior and senior parents. At these and other sessions, school leaders used a PowerPoint presentation on why the schedule change was being considered (e.g., highlighting the failure rate of so many students), and how the new schedule would be implemented. A follow-up survey was sent to parents.

School leaders at UHS had an evaluation plan from the beginning. Similar to Newberry High School, they approached the project with candor and openness with parents without over-promising. Parents received sample schedules, and communications illustrated anticipated benefits. School leaders worked hard to make the case to parents that the current schedule was not working; they "sold" the students first (e.g., on the benefits of the new schedule for acceleration and remediation), and the students sold the parents. Whereas Wiley Dixon at the small Newberry High School could talk with every grade level class, at UHS the size of the school made this difficult or likely to prove unproductive. Cunningham then made closed-circuit TV presentations to groups of students until virtually all 3500 students had been involved.

Educators at UHS (big school) agree with their colleagues at NHS (small school) that schedule changes of any kind require that leaders have a positive working relationship with band directors. At UHS 10% of the student body (350 students) was in band. Eventually, discussions led to an agreement that students could take band for two credits, all year long, which meant that band students could only add one additional elective over 1 year rather than 2. This gave the director much more time with band students, especially the ninth- and tenth-grade students, and senior band students were placed in two band groups on alternating days, matched with an English teacher who agreed to an A/B schedule opposite the band classes. Juniors and seniors were given the option of the one half credit for band. Most seniors at UHS did not need the second credit.

Foreign language presented another challenge for UHS. At levels one and two, students could take one or two courses in 1 year. If they take two courses in 1 year, they take level 1 in the fall and level 2 in the spring. If they take one foreign language course during the year, it would be taken in the spring, and then level 2 would be taken that following fall. These arrangements have resulted in the numbers of students in advanced sections rising, with Latin 5 and Spanish 5 offered in 1996 for the first time.

Advanced Placement (AP) courses at UHS, as well as at many other high schools, required special attention when the new schedule was considered. AP courses at UHS are offered for 1.5 credits, from October to May. Students take a one-semester elective (e.g., driver's education) from August to October and then take the AP course for the rest of the year. Scores are reportedly higher than ever; 73% of the students taking the exams in 1995 scored a 3 or better. A few courses remain scheduled for the January to May term, as they always have been (e.g., European History). Parents of AP students at large urban UHS were no more of a problem than they had been at small rural Newberry High School—the principal had prepared the case well, and the demographics of the school, said Cunningham, are "more focused on the average students."

As a result of the change in schedule at UHS, said Cunningham, "poor teachers don't get better, but students like the fact that they have them only half the calendar period. It is much more like a college schedule that the students will have later. Complaints about poor teachers have been cut in half. Beginning teachers learn from their mistakes and can make corrections much earlier than waiting for the next academic year."

Another part of the strategy for moving to the new schedule at UHS was to handle problems when they arose instead of trying to guarantee no problems would emerge. "The more curriculum exceptions you make the more you water down the program" was the perspective taken by school leaders. Principal Cunningham sent a letter to the faculty emphasizing her honesty, expressing sympathy, and promising to respond to unanticipated difficulties. And unanticipated rough spots did appear:

- Some unanticipated problems came up about accelerated graduation.
- They did not expect so much difficulty in communicating information (e.g., about school pictures) to students, when not all students have English every day.
- The need for balancing student schedules between academics and electives came as a surprise; after the first year, however, counselors have had the time to plan student schedules more effectively.
- MIS (computer programs) did not transfer data to the district records correctly.

■ The school had to add more courses to the curriculum, and the approved state course code directory was thin. Educators at UHS have now added new and refreshing courses to the curriculum (e.g., African-American History).

Canady and Rettig (1995) address special concerns for developing the 4 × 4 schedule. Make sure that important curriculum components have sections offered in both terms, and that each semester is balanced between core and elective courses. They emphasize that the 4 × 4 schedule really requires two annual schedules; making sure the two semesters balance is absolutely essential.

Successful efforts in changing from a traditional schedule to an alternative version seem to follow similar pathways. Principals Dixon, Cunningham, and others took fairly similar steps to secure support and approval for the move to a new schedule, in spite of substantial differences in the size and demographic makeup of the student body. Canady and Rettig (1995) support the strategies employed by these and other successful principals when they recommend these steps:

■ General presentations on the pros and cons of various models of block scheduling
■ School visits by staff, students, and parents to examine successful models
■ Panel presentations in the local school setting by teachers from schools operating block schedules
■ Plenty of time for faculty discussion
■ Working for a consensus approval or a super-majority vote in favor of a new schedule
■ Parent and community meetings
■ Assemblies for students conducted by students from other schools or by their peers who have visited other schools
■ Distribution of relevant research data and implementation procedures
■ School board presentations and approval
■ Staff development that helps the faculty move to implement appropriate curriculum designs and effective instructional strategies.

VARIOUS COMBINATION SCHEDULES

Mount Everett Regional School (MERS), Sheffield, Massachusetts, is a member of the Coalition of Essential Schools, along with many high schools implementing a version of a block schedule. MERS contains grades 7 through 12, as do many regional high schools in New England. At MERS the staff has been offering what they call an "Odyssey Schedule," a two-semester plan of three 90-minute periods and one 45-minute period daily. The schedule has been in place for a number of years. Teachers teach three 90-minute classes and have a daily 45-minute planning period for one semester; the second semester the teacher teaches two 90-minute classes, a 45-minute course, and has a 90-minute daily preparation period. Figure 6.6 illustrates a sample four year schedule for a typical student at MERS.

Mount Everett Regional School Sample Four-Year Student Plan FIGURE 6.6

STUDENT #1

FRESHMAN YEAR		SOPHOMORE YEAR	
SEMESTER I	**SEMESTER II**	**SEMESTER I**	**SEMESTER II**
PE/I-COURSE	PE/I-COURSE	I-COURSE/PE	I-COURSE/PE
AMERICAN GOVERNMENT	CONSTR. TECH.	ENGLISH II	COMP. PLANT & ANIMAL PHYS.
ENGLISH I	PRE-ALGEBRA	FOOD & NUTRITION	WORLD HISTORY
LUNCH	LUNCH	LUNCH	LUNCH
BASIC ART	SCIENCE OF THE UNIVERSE	ALGEBRA I	CRAFTS

JUNIOR YEAR		SENIOR YEAR	
SEMESTER I	**SEMESTER II**	**SEMESTER I**	**SEMESTER II**
OFF CAMPUS PROGRAM	OFF CAMPUS PROGRAM	I-COURSES	I-COURSES
		ENGLISH IV	POTTERY
MEDIA	COMMUNIC. TECHNOLOGY	ACCOUNTING I	CHILD DEVELOPMENT
LUNCH	LUNCH	OFF CAMPUS PROGRAM	OFF CAMPUS PROGRAM
U. S. HISTORY	ENGLISH III		

At Cambridge Rindge and Latin School (CRLS) teachers and students began using a new schedule in the fall of 1994. The schedule (Figure 6.7) was intended to provide a platform for even further change in a school where change has been the norm. Students have eight course choices, with six classes a day on a 4-day rotation, repeated over 8 days. Time blocks are 50 and 65 minutes, compared with the 43 minutes offered in the old schedule. To accomplish this, 11 minutes were added to the length of the school day and total instructional time was increased by 30 minutes.

FIGURE 6.7   Cambridge Rindge and Latin School Student Schedule

Student Id 0007961	Student Name		Grade 12	Hrm R310	Sex M	Hse A	Counselor 002 AXTMAN G

Semester 1

Time	Day "1"	Day "2"	Day "3"	Day "4"	Day "5"	Day "6"	Day "7"	Day "8"
07:15 08:05	(AM)	(AM)	(AM)	(AM)	(AM)	(AM)	(AM)	(AM)
08:15 09:05 (A)	(1)	(2)	(3)	(4)	(1)	(2)	(3)	(4)
09:08 10:13 (B)	(2)	(3)	(4)	(1)	(2)	(3)	(4)	(1)
10:16 11:06 (C)	(3)	(4)	(1)	(2)	(3)	(4)	(1)	(2)
11:06 12:25 (D)	(5)	(6)	(7)	(8)	(5)	(6)	(7)	(8)
12:28 01:33 (E)	(6)	(7)	(8)	(5)	(6)	(7)	(8)	(5)
01:36 02:26 (F)	(7)	(8)	(5)	(6)	(7)	(8)	(5)	(6)
02:30 03:15	(AFT)	(AFT)	(AFT)	(AFT)	(AFT)	(AFT)	(AFT)	(AFT)

At CRLS, most courses meet 3 days out of a 4-day cycle. Some courses meet three times in the 8-day rotation. Class periods 1 to 4 rotate in the morning, during time blocks A to C. (Figure 6.7). Class periods 5 to 8 rotate in the afternoon, through time blocks D to F. This enables the staff to avoid having the same class periods meeting just before lunch or late in the day, class times equally unpopular with both teachers and students. The new schedule permits students to register for eight courses in a year instead of seven. The aim of the new schedule, said educators there, was to permit students more flexibility in choosing electives, enrichment courses, tutorials, and internships. Designers of the schedule hoped that students would use the time to explore the arts and elective areas, and that teachers would have more time to explore some subjects in greater depth. The schedule also allowed for increased numbers of seminars and tutorials that would "support students' academic work and special interests."

Lake Brantley High School (LBHS) in Seminole County, Florida, uses a combination of an A/B alternating-day schedule and the 4 × 4 schedule in a large, suburban, affluent community. Most classes are offered every day for a semester, but many are offered on alternating days all year long. Here, AP and honors courses have a high priority; AP classes are consequently offered every other day for the entire year. At LBHS, the following courses are offered on an A/B schedule: English, biology, chemistry, physics, AP art, AP psychology, American history, government/economics, European history, foreign language, and AP computer science. Other courses are offered on a daily double block of time, including mathematics courses; except for calculus, which is offered for 260 clock hours, and 2 academic credits; AP statistics is offered daily for 1 credit.

Teachers report that this mixed type of schedule can be confusing to teachers who have to teach the same course in a different scheduling format. One group of AP students contended that "the more difficult the class, the more difficult it is to have it every other day." Students in the same department, but not in AP courses, enjoyed the block schedule more, asserting that the "day goes by faster and we get more credit toward graduation," and "More electives are possible."

An interview with a class of first-year students at LBHS yielded the following comments about coming from the middle school into a block scheduled high school:

"Note-taking classes are harder for 2 hours."

"I feel like I have a second chance if I really mess up in a course."

"It makes me mad that the school raised the required number of credits for graduation."

"The day goes faster."

"Overall, I have less time to learn."

"It means I have fewer big exams on the same day."

These students reported that they did have problems balancing required and elective courses across the semesters. They agreed that the block schedule saves instructional time in physical education and band. The block schedule, however, requires more self-discipline in band students because the student has to practice between days of class. After a day of conversations with a variety of students at LBHS, it seemed to the authors that AP students were split in their opinion of the block schedule, average students seemed to like it, and students who might be classified as less successful seemed to love it.

Because much of the burden of scheduling individual students falls on school counselors, at LBHS and elsewhere, many counselors feel overworked by the demand for scheduling new students into the correct classes. One counselor at LBHS reported that the time she spent on the computer has tripled after the move to the block schedule. On a brighter side, counselors report that they do see more students for counseling and can spend longer units of time with the students they do see. They recommend that other counselors involved in the 4 × 4 schedule focus on the semester courses:

- Make sure the schedule has an adequate number of semester courses in which to schedule transfer students.
- Have ample numbers of semester courses with which to back AP courses (e.g., matching AP biology with Life Management and Personal Fitness).
- Be aware of the need for more semester-length physical education classes.
- Late summer transfers (students who come in 2 weeks to a month behind) should be given a light load or started in October on a semester course.

The registrar at LBHS is intimately involved in the scheduling process. Her experience has led her to the following conclusions. An effective schedule at an affluent, complex, college-oriented high school has to be built around the courses that will be A/B courses. Singletons are, as most registrars know, "schedule-killers." She recommends thinking more of scheduling packages of classes so A/B courses fit well—academic courses paired with electives. She suggests giving flexible credits for serving as aides and for students who assume other school-related responsibilities. She says to keep in mind the need for more general electives throughout the school year.

At Juneau Douglas High School in Juneau, Alaska, a compromise schedule is firmly in place. The school utilizes a six-period rotating block, with six periods of 50 minutes on Monday and Friday and four 75-minute periods on Tuesday, Wednesday, and Thursday. The week looks like this:

M	T	W	TH	F
1	3	1	1	1
2				2
3	4	2	2	3
4				4
5	5	5	3	5
6	6	6	4	6

La Grande High School in La Grande, Oregon, uses a basic 4 × 4 schedule of four 88-minute periods, with 58 minutes for lunch, and 8 minutes of passing time between periods. Every Wednesday at La Grande is "flex day." The first, third, and fifth Wednesdays of the month are Teacher Access Days, when students come to school voluntarily from 7:30–9:00 A.M. to receive assistance, take tests, do labs, and for sundry other reasons. This flex day model serves a little more than 50% of the student body in a year's time. It is especially valuable to students who are absent or involved in athletics or other activities that cause them to miss classes. The second and fourth Wednesdays are devoted to what they call the Faculty Forum—a staff development time from 7:30–9:30 A.M.; classes start at 10:04 A.M. on these days.

School leaders say that they have made tremendous gains as a staff because of this released time. They are divided into five subgroups and make decisions on an 80% consensus model.

In 1984, Lubbock High School in Lubbock, Texas, moved to a "four-day academic week" of six 70-minute classes and one half day of activity classes on Friday; Friday offers three classes plus an "Administrative Cluster" period for assemblies and innovative special interest courses, an organized club program, interscholastic athletics, band, choir, orchestra, ROTC, and service learning experiences. Students must be scheduled for 4 hours on Fridays.

In the fall of 1997, all high schools in the school district of Marion County, Florida, moved to a combination schedule that featured what they described as a "4 $\times$ 3 $\times$ 1" schedule. The fall semester would be a four-course, double period schedule typical of the 4 $\times$ 4. The spring would offer only three double courses, with students leaving the campus immediately after an early lunch. The exception to this would be students who remained for the afternoon course, one double period; these would be students who may have failed a course during the first semester or who, for some other reason, might need or want to enroll for more coursework.

Issues Associated with the Transition to a New Block Schedule

Canady and Rettig (1995) provide a catalogue of concerns to be considered during the transition to a new schedule. Many of the schools previously described encountered and resolved the problems associated with these concerns. They describe the issues in detail in the following sections.

Retention of Learning   Teachers, parents, and students all express concern about the possibility that as much as a year could pass between mathematics courses if a student took one in the fall semester and waited until spring of the next year to take another. What about the loss of learning that might occur during this extended period? Experience indicates that brief reviews bring students to a point of readiness. Canady and Rettig point out that loss of learning is related to how well the subject was learned in the first place, and argue that the block schedule lends itself more to the kind of teaching that leads to learning to a level of automaticity. In summary, Canady and Rettig assert that loss of learning is not a substantial problem for the transition to a block schedule.

Minutes per Course   The switch to a 4 $\times$ 4 schedule may result in fewer minutes per class over the semester unless the school day is lengthened. A typical traditional course offers 9000 minutes a year, and a block course yields 8100. In some states this may cause a problem with accreditation. Also, many teachers have found it necessary to reduce the curriculum, eliminating objectives thought to have lower priority. Therefore, concern about "curriculum integrity" moves to the center of the discussion.

Course pacing   Teachers in a school that changes to 4 × 4 may forget how fast the year goes and panic when Thanksgiving arrives and it is half over. Careful attention must be given to the development of course-pacing guidelines. Many of the schools described have engaged in staff development aimed at improving teachers' ability to adjust the pacing of their courses.

Course Sequencing and Foreign Language   As can be seen in the previous descriptions, foreign language teachers may object to 4 × 4 because they are concerned that studying a foreign language every other semester will lead to great loss of learning and retention. They fear the students will need too much time for review. Canady and Rettig (1995, pp. 91) suggest:

- Altering the sequence of foreign language so that students take two courses in 1 year, and complete their 2 years in one. Students could finish Spanish IV by the end of their sophomore year. If they did this, students who desired could take a second sequence of languages their junior and senior years; this should especially appeal to college-focused parents and students.
- Students could begin their foreign language sequence in their junior year.
- Schools could add additional levels of high school foreign language to the curriculum; the equivalent of 8 years would be possible.
- Students desiring additional foreign language instruction could participate in dual-enrollment college courses.

Music programs   Canady and Rettig echo what school leaders described previously have discovered—music programs are very complex at the high school level, often with three different levels of band (concert, symphonic, wind ensemble, jazz, etc.), each of which becomes a multi-grade-level singleton. School schedules are traditionally worked around the music program; this will continue to be the case with a new block schedule. Performances are often correlated with holidays and sports which are only at certain times of the year. Music supporters reject the idea of being in band for only one semester. Canady and Rettig (1995, p. 93–94) offer these solutions:

- Require students to enroll in music both semesters, earning two credits of music yearly. They would take three courses and music, for a total of six other credits, annually; many students in the example schools do just that. They would still have the same number of other classes as in a traditional schedule. But the central question for Canady and Rettig is: Should 25 percent of a high school student's program be in music?
- Require enrollment for one semester, with a second semester elective. Where this has been done, virtually 90 percent of the students continue to enroll for the second semester; others agree to practice with the band that semester without credit.
- Offer music programs as year-long singletons paired with another singleton class. The second singleton can be musically oriented or it can be AP, art,

yearbook, school newspaper, athletics, or foreign language. This could be done every day as two single periods or for 90 minutes every other day.

- Offer a schedule with six semester-length block courses and 2 year-long singleton courses for *all* students.

Special Education   Canady and Rettig declare that the block schedule is better for exceptional students. Fewer courses may lead to greater success. Students can take just three courses and reserve the fourth for resource assistance. They say that inclusion can often work better because scarce exceptional education teachers can travel to several classes during the same block, reducing the need to cluster students in one class.

Cooperative Work Programs   The main concern of educators in this area is how to parallel required hours of work experience that earn additional credits with the concentrated course. Possibilities include:

- Compressing the work experience into one semester.
- Offer these courses as singletons at the end of the students' day. Students could attend class until noon, as they typically do now, and go to their work experience in the afternoon as usual.
- Offer the class as a double period every other day, alternating with the student going directly to the work experience. The vocational class could be "married" to an academic class so that the two together make up one block for the year. Students could take each class every day or they could be alternated for a full block of time. The teachers could team as desired in tech prep; the course could be English focusing on technical writing and reading or presentation skills related directly to the vocational course in marketing, for example. Drafting could be paired with geometry or horticulture with biology.

Advanced Placement   Many people are concerned about the effects of the block schedule on AP examinations. These examinations are traditionally given in May, so if a course is completed in January, will this negatively affect the test in May? Also, if a course starts in January, will they have covered enough to do well on the test in May? Accommodations that Canady and Rettig suggest have been adopted by many of the schools described earlier in this section:

- Some schools schedule an AP course for two semesters, giving it a different title the second semester.
- Others provide review sessions in the spring in preparation for the examination.
- The course can be offered as a year-long singleton or on alternate days as a block for the whole year.
- The singleton course might be paired with a credit for independent study or research as the second half of a block.
- Because many students take more than one AP course, the classes can be matched or married in single periods all year long as a block, similar to music.

- A school can offer a 9-week elective followed by 27-weeks of instruction in an AP course.
- Another might offer a 27-week AP course followed by an elective or an AP review class.

Canady and Rettig suggest that the College Board should adjust its testing schedule to accommodate the large number of schools doing the block schedule, with tests at least twice annually, and that schools should lobby for this accommodation on the part of the College Board.

College Dual-Enrollment   Canady and Rettig note that the block schedule should be a boon to dual enrollment because it is more like a college program. Starting high school earlier in August should allow the spring semesters to be congruent in high school and college.

Student Transfers   Students arriving mid-year into a 4 × 4 school from a traditional calendar must be placed somehow. This is a big problem because students coming in have to enroll in courses in which the students have covered twice as much content, and the new student will likely be behind. Also, they may have taken other courses that will have to be dropped because they are moving from taking six or seven courses to four per day. The same problem exists for students transferring out. Canady and Rettig observe that:

- Transfer is already a problem, with courses not offered or requirements that are different, so this should not stop the move to the block schedule.
- This may actually discourage parents from moving in the middle of the year, which would be a good thing for students and the school.
- Transfers during the second semester are not as much of a problem because they will be ahead of the class that has just begun the course. Students can easily fit into any class.
- Students may get complete credit for some courses, depending on the time of enrollment or transfer (based on end-of-course tests) and be placed in classes to complete others.
- Larger schools may be able to operate a single-period daily schedule inside the regular program parallel to the 4 × 4. Transfer students can be placed here easily.
- "For whom do we plan the program, the 90 percent who remain all year or the 10 percent who come and go?" (Canady & Rettig, 1995, p. 103)

Credits Required for Graduation   It is possible for some students to graduate in 3 years instead of 4. Districts can also increase graduation requirements, adding service, arts, language, and others. They could also require that certain courses be taken certain years (e.g., mandating that Government and Economics be taken in the senior year, or guidance counselors can schedule students so that it takes 4 years to graduate). Or many more students can take AP courses and dual-enrollment.

Early graduation will be good both for advanced students and for students who have been retained.

Schedule Balance   Make certain that student schedules are not unbalanced, with core classes requiring a great deal of work one semester and electives the next.

Adaptation of Policies   Adapt attendance policies (say, from 20 days to 10 days absence) so that students who miss a certain amount do not get credit. Criteria for athletic eligibility must also be adapted so that they are passing three out of four courses, for example. Also, suspension and expulsion policies need to be examined; students can be expelled for a semester instead of a year.

Teacher Issues   Planning time and other contractual issues will need to be worked out. Bringing the teacher union into the discussion early will help to resolve potential conflicts before they disrupt the planning process.

Costs   Whether a block schedule costs more depends on the current schedule. Schools using an eight-period day will likely have the same cost when they change to a block schedule. Schools currently using either a schedule in which teachers teach five out of six periods or six out of seven periods will experience an increase in class size or a need for more staff. This is because an increase in teacher planning time is implied in the transition to a schedule with teachers teaching only six out of eight periods. Schools where teachers currently teach five out of seven periods could experience a decline in class size, or staff size may be reduced.

RESEARCH ON THE BLOCK SCHEDULE

Innovations that take an institution like the American high school by storm, as has the block schedule, generally do so without benefit of a great deal of prior research. Without true laboratories in which to conduct controlled experiments, practitioners often implement new programs or curriculum because they appeal for reasons other than research support. At the time of this book's publication, such research was only beginning to be conducted and reported, yet 137 doctoral dissertations had already been completed on the subject! We identify a few research references here for those who seek such information:

Eineder, D., & Bishop, H. (1997). Block scheduling the high school: The effects on achievement, behavior, and student-teacher relationships. *NASSP Bulletin, 81,* 45–54.

Hamdy, M. (1996). *Block scheduling: Its impact on academic achievement, and the perceptions of students, teachers, and administrators.* Doctoral dissertation, Florida Atlantic University. Dissertation Abstracts, Volume 57–09, Section A, p. 3796.

Irmsher, K. (July, 1996). Block scheduling in high school. *Oregon School Study Council Bulletin, 39,* p. 69.

King, B. (1996). *The effects of block scheduling on learning environment, instructional strategies, and academic achievement.* Doctoral thesis, University of Central Florida. Dissertation Abstracts, Volume 57-07, Section A, p. 2771.

Kramer, S. (1997). What we know about block scheduling and its effects on math instruction, Part II. *NASSP Bulletin, 81,* 69–82.

Schroth, G. (1996). The effects of block scheduling on student performance. *International Journal of Educational Reform, 5,* 472–76.

THE FUTURE OF THE HIGH SCHOOL SCHEDULE

Certainly no one could have predicted the speed with which the block schedule has been adopted by American high schools. At the beginning of the 1990s only a handful of high schools had made the switch from a traditional schedule to one or another version of the block schedule. At the beginning of 1997 a survey of Florida high schools (George, 1997) indicated that approximately 175 high schools had made the transition to a block schedule in that state alone. If other states experience a similar rate of transition, and if the schools that have made the transition continue to use the block schedule, a quiet but substantial transformation in the use of time in the high school will have occurred.

SUMMARY

The traditional high school schedule usually divides the school day into six or seven periods of equal length, with time allotted for lunch and home room. Class periods for each subject are typically 50 or 55 minutes with a few minutes passing time provided. Courses are credited in Carnegie units, tied directly to the number of hours students spend in class. Often, classes in these schedules follow the pattern of review of previous day's homework, presentation by the teacher followed by questions and answers, and assignment of homework. However, the traditional high school and the nature of teaching conducted in that schedule are undergoing significant changes in many successful contemporary high schools across the nation.

Some of the reasons increasing numbers of high schools discussed in this chapter are moving away from the traditional schedule to more flexible scheduling models included: (1) the impersonal nature of high schools; (2) lost learning time and discipline problems caused by the frequent changing of classes; (3) time limits that provide barriers to effective teaching and learning such as follow-up, reinforcement, reteaching, and research; (4) difficulties associated with teachers planning and delivering integrated curriculum in the short time spans available; and (5) few opportunities provided for acceleration to new levels of coursework or for remediation. Moving to more flexible models of scheduling helps reverse these problems and provides many opportunities for innovation and positive change.

Several major flexible scheduling models were presented including the Copernican plan, alternating day schedules, the 4 × 4 semester plan, and various combination schedules. Extensive examples from a variety of successful high schools using each of these major scheduling models were presented.

CONNECTIONS TO OTHER CHAPTERS

The effectiveness of high schools for the new century will be heavily influenced by the manner in which time, space, and people are organized to promote teaching and learning. How learning time is organized in the schedule influences how teachers and students work and learn together. The organization of teachers and learners (chapter seven) influences how they use the time the block schedule makes available to them.

ACTION STEPS

1. This could be a good time to find out what practicing teachers think about the issues associated with the block schedule. A small group comprised of you and your peers could conduct a survey about these concerns. First, translate the issues into interview questions. Then find a group of teachers to survey. You might want to identify a group of at least 10 to 15 teachers from one or more schools with the same type of schedule and summarize their responses to questions about the issues. Or you may want to identify four to five teachers from each of the different major block scheduling varieties and compare how teachers from each setting feel about the issues. Another way to do the survey would be to identify groups of teachers from several subject areas like mathematics, foreign languages, and music, who seem less enthusiastic about the block schedule; see how their responses differ from one another, or how they compare with teachers from other departments. If you are learning in a class or workshop, having a number of small groups approach it differently will give you valuable insights into the schedule that will be in place in high schools for the first years of the new century.

DISCUSSION QUESTIONS

1. How persuasive are the arguments about the deficiencies of the traditional schedule?

2. Might some of these limitations be corrected without changing to a block schedule?

3. Which of the block schedules appeals most to you? Why?

4. How do you account for the tremendously rapid spread of the block schedule in high school programs?

REFERENCES

Breaking ranks: Changing an American institution. (1996). Reston, VA: National Association of Secondary School Principals.

Canady, R. L., & Rettig, M. D. (1996). *Block scheduling: A catalyst for change in high schools.* Princeton, NJ: Eye on Education.

Carroll, J. M. (1994). The Copernican plan evaluated: The evolution of a revolution. *Phi Delta Kappan, 76 (2),* 105–113.

Carroll, J. M. (1990). The Copernican plan: Restructuring the American high school. *Phi Delta Kappan, 71 (5),* 358–365.

Cawelti, G. (1994). *High school restructuring: A national study.* Arlington, VA: Educational Research Service.

George, P. & Dow, J. (Winter 1997). *The building blocks of school reform: An investigation of the use of block scheduling in Florida.* Research Bulletin, vol 24, Nos 1 and 2. Sanibel, FL. Florida Educational Research Council, Inc.

National Commission on Excellence in Education. (1983). *A nation at risk: The imperative for educational reform.* Washington, DC: United States Government Printing Office.

Reid, W. (1995). *Restructuring a secondary school with extended time blocks and intensive learning.* Unpublished manuscript.

Sizer, T. R. (1992). *Horace's school: Redesigning the American high school.* Boston: Houghton Mifflin.

Sizer, T. R. (1984). *Horace's compromise: The dilemma of the American high school.* Boston: Houghton Mifflin.

CHAPTER 7

THE ORGANIZATION OF TEACHERS AND LEARNERS

WHAT YOU WILL LEARN IN THIS CHAPTER

The importance of creating a sense of smallness in big high schools

Academic teaming as an alternative to academic discipline-oriented departments

The areas in which teachers work together on academic teams

The dramatically new organizational strategy, career academies

The "house" concept and how it applies to high school

Ways in which heterogeneous grouping can be implemented in high school

High schools will create small units in which anonymity will be banished.

The high school will reorganize the traditional departmental structure to meet the needs of a more integrated curriculum.

Each high school will present alternatives to tracking and ability grouping without restricting the range of courses and learning experiences it offers .

—*Breaking Ranks, p. 45*

INTERDISCIPLINARY ORGANIZATION IN HIGH SCHOOLS FOR THE NEW CENTURY

In *Breaking Ranks* (Commission, 1996), the members of NASSP committed themselves to a restructuring of high schools that would create smaller learning units in which personal anonymity would be banished. The restructuring would move dramatically away from traditional departmentalized organization toward a more integrated and interdisciplinary approach to curriculum and instruction. The Coalition of Essential Schools urged American high school educators to engage in a reorganization that would lead to more personalized teaching and learning.

In December 1996, Timothy Dyer, then Executive Director of NASSP, reiterated his organization's commitment to the reorganization of high schools in a way that would create schools no larger than 600 students. He described it this way:

> This will be extremely difficult for some schools. But, it is critical if you're serious about personalizing schools. We are not talking about tearing down buildings and building smaller schools, smaller facades. We are talking about organizing schools into learning communities that are no larger than 600, in which faculty members and students stay together for the entire high school experience (with rare exceptions) and become very well acquainted with each other both in terms of their intellectual pursuit and of other issues that must be addressed as the high school years unfold (Dyer, 1996, p. 5).

Educators in the new American high school are searching for ways to make big schools feel smaller. If it is impossible to tear down high schools of 3,500 to 5,000 students, as Dyer states, high school educators are discovering that it may be possible to restructure the school to create smallness inside the bigness. Using new scheduling strategies, organizing teams, houses, schools-within-schools, and more flexible forms of instructional grouping, high school educators are hoping to transform the way the school *feels* to those who learn there.

In a very real sense, the history of the American high school has been one of attempting to balance the twin goals of curriculum richness and a sense of community. Educators in the 20th century have attempted to organize and operate American high schools so that the curriculum exhibited rigor, breadth, diversity, and complexity. Teacher subject specialization and departmentalization have made high standards inescapable. Some observers contend that high school educators, in their zeal to produce a world-class curriculum, overlooked the need to balance that curriculum with a sense of community that gives learners and teachers a sense of caring and concern for one another.

Contemporary attempts to restructure the American high school have been aimed at restoring the balance between curriculum and community; high schools must have both a rich and rigorous curriculum and a strong sense of community where faculty and students feel connected to one another in appropriately personal ways. It is possible to balance curriculum and community by using proven organizational strategies.

It is likely that many American high schools of the 21st century will begin to resemble a set of Russian nesting dolls. Remove the first doll in the set and another one appears underneath. Remove that one, and a third one appears; remove that one, and discover an even smaller one inside it. Often a fifth doll, smallest of all, hides at the core of the group. The emerging American high school has begun to resemble the set of Russian dolls—organized so that overall size has smaller units within it, and each smaller unit increases the opportunity to focus on the individual student.

Educators have begun to search for alternatives to punitive, coercive, and negative ways of motivating their charges to fulfill their responsibilities. Educators hope that organizing high schools that feel smaller, so that students and teachers feel part of the same team, will help to motivate everyone to do a world-class job of learning. Academic teams, houses, academies, integrated curriculum, and alternatives to traditional forms of instructional grouping are at the heart of these efforts to create that feeling of smallness inside the big school.

ACADEMIC TEAMING

What is an Academic Team?

A high school academic team is a group of teachers who share the same students, usually at the same grade level, and who combine their talents to offer all or most of the core academic subjects. Often this team also shares a common planning time and sometimes the team members have classrooms in close proximity to one another. At Oak Ridge High School (ORHS) in Orlando, Florida, the teams are primarily for teachers who work with the ninth grade class; this is often the case in other high schools. A typical team of 120 students and four teachers at ORHS would have this sort of teacher composition:

Mathematics teacher: three sections of pre-algebra, two sections of Algebra 1, one section of geometry

English teacher: five sections of English 1; one section of leadership

Social studies teacher: five sections of global studies; one of American history

Science teacher: four sections of biology; one section of zoology

Dramatically new and productive ventures can emanate from groups of high school teachers and students organized in this way.

There are also a number of things that an academic team is *not*. Academic teaming is not synonymous with the term "team teaching." On a high school academic team, teachers may or may not work together to develop and deliver instructional units or common curriculum projects. Most often, teachers firmly retain their subject specialization identities and teach within those boundaries almost all of the time they are with students. Academic teaming does *not* mean that departments disappear and that curriculum is always integrated. Academic teaming at the high school level also does *not* mean that teachers must coddle their students and treat them as if they were still in elementary or middle school. Academic teaming in the high school *is* a way of keeping the curriculum rigorous while attempting to use an organizational strategy to build more of a sense of community into the school so that the students will learn more than they otherwise might. When high school teachers work together on teams, they usually do so in four specific areas, each of which increases opportunities for personalizing education for the students on the team.

The Four Areas of Academic Team Life

Organization

First, teachers on teams discover that they are involved with a totally new set of colleagues discussing a totally new set of questions. The discussions more often relate to the students they share rather than the subject areas they teach. Establishing an effective way of meeting and conducting team business usually becomes the first item on the new team's agenda. At McNeil High School in Austin, Texas, teams are asked to develop effective answers to these initial organizational questions:

- Who will make the agenda for our meetings?
- How will items get on the agenda?
- Who will do recording?
- How will we reach decisions?
- How will we manage communication?
- How will we manage the team calendar?
- How will we manage progress reports after 3 weeks?
- How will we manage failing students?

After a few sessions together, teams of high school teachers often discover that the team is not just one more task foisted upon them for the supposed benefit of their students; they soon realize that academic teaming can be a great benefit to teachers. The teachers begin to take advantage of the new organization to design and implement common rules and procedures to govern student behavior more effectively. In a sense, the team of teachers "gangs up" on the students, but in a much more positive, consistent way than may have happened in the past. Figure 7.1 serves as an illustration of a letter to parents that incorporates the spirit of high school team organization.

Teachers on teams identify a set of rules and procedures that they are willing to insist upon collaboratively with the students on the team; these become the team rules. Figure 7.2 includes an example of such team rules at McNeil High School. School rules and individual classroom rules for every teacher still apply; team rules and procedures are those things that this group of teachers believes are the most important items for *their* team. Team rules may be posted in the classrooms of all of the teachers on the team, discussed with the team's students, and enforced jointly by all of the members of the team. The team usually develops a set of consequences for managing student behavior and enforcing the rules the team establishes. Figure 7.3

Sample Letter to Parents   **FIGURE 7.1**

McNeil High School
5720 McNeil Drive • Austin, Texas 78729
512/258-3199 • FAX 512/331-9554

MAVERICKS

Dear Students and Parents of Team 3:

Welcome to McNeil High School! Once again, to continue offering our students excellence in education, academic teaming will be a vital part of your child's school year at McNeil. As an academic team, it is our desire to provide ninth grade students with a consistent learning environment.

On "A" Days at 1:45, teachers of team 3 will be meeting to exchange information and form strategies to better facilitate learning and environments for the students on our team. If necessary, please contact the team leader, Gloria Wilie, to arrange for a parent or student conference.

On "B" days at 8th period, most of our students will have an EXCEL class. The first half of this time will be used for study skills, group activities, discussions, counseling, and whatever else we as a team of students and teachers deem appropriate. In the second half of the class, students having difficulty in a specific class will be directed to that teacher for tutoring, or the student will use the time for study. Other tutoring times outside of the school day must be scheduled with the individual teacher.

Our team has developed a set of rules and consequences we feel necessary to maintain a positive learning environment for all students. Please read this attached notice. We welcome your comments. We look forward to meeting you at open house coming up very soon.

We, as a team, want to make this transition into high school a positive and productive one. Our expectations are high. The learning environment is a combination of both home and school. We look forward to this joint venture. Together we can make a difference!

Sincerely,

Gloria Wilie, *English*

                              Malcolm Scott, *Geography*

Scott Semmens, *Biology*   Kathryn Helm, *Mathematics*

Terri King, *Biology*   Nancy McDonald, *Mathematics*

"Vision Into Reality"

FIGURE 7.2   Sample Statement of Team Rules

FRESHMAN TEAM BEHAVIOR POLICY

EXPECTED BEHAVIORS

1 Be on time.
2 Bring all necessary materials.
3 Dress appropriately.
4 Respect others.
5 Follow teacher/group instructions.
6 Be in compliance with substitute teachers.

CONSEQUENCES

2 Violations ➔ ➔   1 Hour Detention
3 Violations ➔ ➔   2 Hours Detention
4 Violations ➔ ➔   Parent Contact; Referred to Principal for Detention

NO SHOWS TO DETENTION ➔ ➔ ➔ REFERRED TO PRINCIPAL

⌘Infractions evaluated weekly

DISCIPLINE MANAGEMENT PLAN

Academic Team: Helm _____ Scott _____ Semmens _____ Wilie _____
Student's Name: _____ Advisor _____

- ● Student counseled by teacher and plan for improvement made by teacher and student.
  Date: _____

- ● Student behavior discussed in team meeting. (File started)
  Date: _____

- ● Student meets with team.
  Date: _____

- ● Telephone Contact with Parent
  Date: _____

- ● Team meeting with parents.
  Date: _____

- ● Student assigned Detention Hall—
  Date: _____

- ● Team referral to Assistant Principal
  Recommendation: _____
  Date: _____

illustrates one set of hierarchical consequences that match a set of team rules and expectations.

Team procedures (e.g., policies for accepting late work, regulations for using the phone, student use of the bathroom, and so on) can also be established and taught to the students in a way that makes the whole group, perhaps even the entire grade level, work more smoothly and efficiently.

If a team of teachers has developed and implemented common rules and procedures, this is often sufficient to persuade the individual teachers of the value of working together in at least limited ways. When teams of teachers have a common planning time, teacher collaboration on teams does not usually stop with common rules. High school teachers, like teachers at every level, enjoy talking about their students, especially the most rewarding and the most challenging or difficult; one of the primary benefits of academic teaming is that, because teachers work with the same students, sharing information about those students is often both intensely interesting and beneficial to each of the teachers involved. When school administrators are assigned to teams as ex officio members and meet regularly with teams, the discussions can be even more fruitful.

Teachers on teams discover that they can do many things better as a team than as isolated individuals, and that many aspects of team business must be attended to early in the year in order for the team to get off to the best start. At McNeil High School the "Things-To-Do Checklist" (Figure 7.4) helps teachers new to teaming and helps remind veterans of important tasks to be attended to. The tasks deal with virtually every aspect of teaming, not just simple organizational activities.

Teachers on teams often spend their common planning time discussing what they have in common—their students. Furthermore, teachers discover that as they exchange information about their students, their collective stock of knowledge about their students grows and grows. Each teacher ends up knowing much more about the students than they could have discovered alone. Fortunately, the experience of many educators involved in teams is that individual teachers become more positive and more empathetic toward the students on the team. The more the teachers talk about the students they have in common, the more willing they become to take supportive action on behalf of the students.

Consequently, the number of conferences teams of teachers hold with students, parents, counselors, and other educational specialists tends to rise dramatically. With teams in place, conferences with students can be more productive and pleasant. An example of a form letter from a team to a student who is being called in for a team–student conference is presented in Figure 7.5. Conferences with exceptional education teachers about students they share with the team may occur more frequently than when teams do not exist. Team–parent conferences, as well as those with students, tend to be much more positive and productive events than when individual teachers attempted to meet and reason with parents and students. Such conferences tend to aim more often at collaboration on behalf of the student, rather than dissolving into occasions for mutual recrimination and finger-pointing. Action plans that all parties agree to participate in are far more likely results of such interaction. Little wonder that more and more high school teachers are willing to devote the time and energy necessary to be productive parts of such team conferences. In

Things-To-Do Checklist   FIGURE 7.4

Prior to the beginning of school

A. Decisions
   Team goals
   Rules and expectations for students
   Team discipline plan (work with administrator)
   Late work policy
   Team packet for students
   Team schedule (days to meet, location, files, etc.)
   Advisory scripts and schedule
   At-risk plan
   Student reward/motivation plan
   Week one agenda

B. Tasks
   Prepare student packet
   Prepare team folder for each student
   Prepare team forms, conference calendars, etc.
   Prepare rules to post
   Prepare copies of yearly plan of each subject for each team member
   Prepare "team plan" for first six weeks

C. Initial planning for Interdisciplinary Team Teaching
   Share content scope/sequence and yearly plans (copy to each team member)
   Brainstorm
       Transfer of learning from content to content
       Two-content teaching activities
       Team projects (campus, community, etc.)
       Thematic units

First week of school

A. Compile cross-team list (student on two teams)
B. Discuss class sizes, intra-team transfers, etc.
C. Plan Week Two agenda
D. Compile student folders as material is available

Second week of school

A. Share test scores from week one content assessment (reading comprehension and
   vocabulary; pretests, etc.)
B. Schedule counselors to meet with team for assessment
C. Schedule nurse to share health concerns
D. Assess advisory composition; consider schedule changes
E. Discuss plan for Open House
F. Consider parent conference priorities
G. Plan next week's agenda

FIGURE 7.5   Sample Summons to a Team–Student Conference

McNeil High School
Student/TEAM Meeting

Dear _____ ,

Your team of teachers decided it would be beneficial to you and to us in helping you to be more successful in the 9th grade to meet with us a few minutes on this date:

Day _____ **Time** _____ **Place** _____

Please check areas you think you need help on improving. Our job as teachers is to help you learn and achieve as much as is possible. Add any comments you think are appropriate and helpful to us as your team of teachers.

_____ **Be on time to class**   _____ **Be prepared for class**
_____ **Participate in class**   _____ **Be respectful to others**
_____ **Be more responsible**   _____ **Get organized**
_____ **Follow instructions**   _____ **In compliance with teachers**
Other comments: _____
_____

Sincerely,

Team 3 Teachers:
   Ms. Wilie, Ms. Helm, Mr. Scott, Mr. Semmens

USE THIS AS YOUR PASS TO ATTEND!!

many schools, the rule agreed to by the team is "If you have a conference, I have a conference."

A final part of the organization of academic teaming is the control that teams begin to exercise over issues like scheduling students on the team. In many high schools, school leaders empower teachers to analyze the appropriateness of student placements and make changes when a different placement benefits the student and the teachers involved. This means that in the first few weeks of a new semester, teams of teachers examine the classroom configurations they have been provided, and discuss and implement adjustments to the schedules of students that will result in more productive experiences. Teachers change the schedule and inform the registrar, rather than the reverse; this is often an important role of each student's advisor. For teachers, the sense of community that results from all of these activities can be an important reward of academic teaming.

Community-building

Once teachers realize that the team can work to their benefit, they are often more willing to engage in activities that will further enhance the students' sense of community on the team and in the school. However, high school teachers are quick to point out that "This is not middle school," meaning that they believe students at the high school level should be beyond the "cute" team activities more characteristic of teams in the sixth, seventh, and eighth grades. High school teachers correctly assert that their students should be able to identify with more than a hundred or so students. Consequently, teams of teachers at the high school level are more likely to work to build, for first year students in particular, a sense of belonging (e.g., to the "Class of 2001"). This class/year identity is a logical progression from elementary, through middle school, to high school. The high school does not ignore the need for a personalized learning environment; educators seek to create the most appropriate one for that level. One school's suggestions for team activities can be seen in Figure 7.6.

The Ninth Grade

Often the teaming effort focuses most sharply on the ninth grade (Peterson, 1996). Educators in many school districts around the nation identify the ninth grade year as the source of their greatest concerns. In many districts first-year students are failing in huge numbers, losing credits in a way that places them at risk for dropping out when they grow another year older. Low grade point averages lead in the same direction. The great majority of students referred to the office for discipline problems come from the ninth grade. Parents angrily and anxiously complain about the difficult transition for their children, and for themselves, between the middle school and the high school. Little wonder that much of the effort at creating smallness inside the bigness of the average high school focuses on the ninth grade.

"We are better able to control the influences that shape them in the ninth grade house," says Bonnie Daniel, principal of Wilde Lake High School in Columbia, Maryland. "We can better control the people they hang with, the upperclassmen they will emulate. It is very hard to change those patterns once they are set." Keeping the ninth graders together is a factor in raising academic achievement and reducing discipline problems, according to Wilde Lake assistant principal Richard

FIGURE 7.6   **Sample Posting of Team Activities**

IDEAS FOR TEAM ACTIVITIES

Honor Roll Pizza Party
Honor Roll Ice Cream Party
Honor Roll Movie/Popcorn Party
Attendance Award Day
Donut Get Together
Team Building Day
Field Trip to Sea World

Wilson (Peterson, 1996, 2D). In some high schools, hazing of freshmen by older students is so severe that freshmen are afraid to walk the halls between classes. "The seniors scare you," said one member of a ninth grade class. "They say they are going to give you a pink belly, hit you. And if they don't like you, they might." Organizing ninth graders into teams or houses helps provide them with a greater degree of personal safety, an aspect of school about which parents are particularly concerned (Peterson, 1996, 2D).

At Newberry High School in Newberry, Florida, for example, the "Ninth Grade Team" was created by the School Improvement Committee because of the same kinds of concern for problems with students at that level. Because it is a small school, one team comprises the whole group of ninth grade students and their teachers. At an orientation to the high school in the fall, ninth grade students are introduced to the team and to the specialists who serve the team. On the first day of school the students meet their academic teachers as well as the physical education teachers, the dean, the ninth grade counselor, occupational specialists, and the school administrators. They tour the school, find and practice opening their lockers, get their schedules, and get most of their questions answered early in an anxiety-reducing environment. At the end of that first day the ninth grade class has an ice cream social to get the year started in a positive way.

A day or two after that, the ninth grade team at NHS has its first class assembly, where students are provided with an overview of the plans for the year and get a start on the class officer election process. Eventually, team field trips, career tours, homecoming, athletics, class government, school government, and other affairs revolve around the ninth grade class, developing a sense of unity within the group. A first-semester ninth grade retreat focuses on building a feeling of belonging and commitment to the class, and creating a willingness among its members to persist together until graduation. An end-of-the-year class trip will wrap up the freshman year. Teachers hope that the class will carry this sense of community with it through the remainder of its years at NHS.

Teamed Instruction

When many high school teachers first hear about academic teaming they think of team teaching, and the prospect of attempting to work so closely with another teacher is often daunting. Veteran teachers know how much planning time is required for quality instruction in their own classrooms, and may be reluctant to use their limited planning time for what may seem to be experimental purposes. Teamed instruction is only one part of academic teaming and, although it can be a very important and exciting part, it can consume a great deal of time and energy. Good planning and communication skills are also essential parts of academic teaming. When teachers have received the organizational benefits of academic teaming, and when a sense of community begins to create an ethos of good feeling between teachers and students, more teachers are willing to consider teamed instruction. This is especially so if teaming in this way can inject into their professional lives fresh curriculum, new instructional strategies, and the excitement of working with peers whom they respect.

Often, teamed instruction is much less complex and demanding than teachers imagine. Typically, teachers on teams who seek to combine their instructional efforts may even do so at first as if by accident. For example, they may discover as a part of their discussions during common planning time that the students they share are having difficulty with note-taking skills. At NHS, for example, teachers on the ninth grade team work hard at the beginning of the year, now that they can anticipate this problem, to teach their students a common, effective note-taking system to be used in all their classes. The team of teachers at NHS takes instructional time at the beginning of each new year to teach the students specific study skills that can be reinforced in every class. Time management, safety, goal-setting, motivation, textbook skills, and other topics are a part of the beginning of the year in the ninth grade at NHS.

In the same way, teachers on a team may discover that their plans for giving tests and other major assignments have been uncoordinated, prior to academic teaming, with the result that on too many occasions their students have more than one such assignment or test due at the same time. Developing a schedule of subject test days and due dates may relieve the pressure on students and result in higher quality work turned in. Sometimes this common effort, relatively unplanned, expands to what might be called parallel planning.

Teachers may discover that some places in their curriculum have considerable connections of which they had been unaware. Consequently, the teachers may decide to rearrange their curriculum schedules in a way that permits them to work in parallel ways with the students in both of their classes. Teachers on the team, or across a grade level, may carry this a step further by the use of a curriculum matrix (Figure 7.7) to investigate their common curriculum plans. Teachers can each list the major curriculum topics they will be addressing during the first semester, then combine their plans on the matrix to discover a "curriculum map" of the whole period. The history teacher on the team may discover that a number of areas of her curriculum are correlated to what is being taught some other time of the year in American literature. The science and mathematics teachers on the team may learn that they are dealing with similar skills or concepts, also at different times. It sometimes takes very little effort to rearrange the schedule so that topics can be more closely connected and students can study them simultaneously. Such parallel planning can lead to common assignments, field trips, films, guest speakers, and many other activities that enhance learning experiences in positive, enjoyable ways.

Teachers may also integrate their curricula to produce what are known as interdisciplinary units, and although much has been written in recent years about such efforts in curriculum integration, most of that literature describes activity at the elementary and middle school levels (Beane, 1995). At the high school level, this sort of interdisciplinary activity remains rare and controversial. High school teachers frequently ask questions like "What is interdisciplinary teaching?" "When is it appropriate?" "How does it fit into the required curriculum?" "Will I lose my autonomy?" and "Will my subject lose its definition if I participate in interdisciplinary work?"

Educators at Parkway South High School in Manchester, Missouri, moved to teams in English/American history as a consequence of the Coalition of Essential Schools emphasis on increased personalization of the high school, says Patrick Conley, principal. (Personal communication, March 30, 1995). All ninth grade students are teamed in English and American history. One additional team includes the science teacher. Teachers have the same 50 students in a 2-hour block; they have common planning time, when they work on integrated curriculum when appropriate and cooperate to devise pedagogical strategies to motivate individual students. Teachers can also group and regroup students as appropriate within the two-subject team to

FIGURE 7.7   A Curriculum Matrix

Month

Subject	August	September	October	November	December
English					
Social Studies					
Mathematics					
Science					
Elective					

improve learning. In addition, teachers can adjust the use of time within the block to accommodate speakers, field trips, and in-depth project work.

There have been many successful attempts to unify the curriculum by combining American history and American literature into American Studies or Humanities courses, but far fewer attempts to bring together two or more subjects into shorter team-taught units. At McNeil High School (MHS) in Austin, Texas, and a few other high schools, atypically strenuous efforts have been made to move in the direction of interdisciplinary work within the teams. In an attempt to encourage such planning, for example, school leaders offer step-by-step planning guidelines to teams at MHS that might be willing to develop an interdisciplinary, team-taught unit (Figure 7.8). We believe that the near future is likely to bring a substantial expansion of such efforts, as teachers on teams discover that they can work together successfully and that such interdisciplinary curriculum plans produce learning experiences that both teachers and students value.

Governance

Research (e.g., Plodzik & George, 1989) and experience indicate that teaming sometimes continues in one additional area, where decision making, problem solving, and policy development become an important part of the life of the team. Quality high school programs, especially those incorporating the innovations described in this book, are far too complex to be managed unilaterally by one or two people in the front office or even by those people in combination with department chairpersons. Even if it were possible to organize and operate a high school unilaterally, it would not be desirable to do so. Modern high school programs featuring academic teaming discover that the team becomes an additional important locus for decision making, problem solving, and the development of school guidelines.

Teachers on teams that successfully work through the other three areas of academic teaming often find themselves motivated to assume more responsibility for the decisions that affect their school lives and the school experiences of their students. Teamwork in such situations usually involves some form of representative government system. Often each team has a leader who represents the other members at regular meetings of a governing schoolwide group. The team leader acts as a liaison between the team he or she leads, the administration, various departments, and other teams in the school. Leaders may work with others outside the team to make decisions about space allocation in the building, new curriculum, disbursements from the school budget, selection of new staff members, teacher assignments, schedule modifications, special events, testing, and many other issues.

Within and between teams at the same grade level, usually ninth grade, different sorts of tasks are addressed in team meetings. Teams of teachers may find themselves involved in a great number of topics that have not been the usual fare at teacher meetings. For example, at a team meeting of teachers on ninth grade teams at Oak Ridge High School in Orlando, Florida, the following agenda became the focus of the "Freshman Learning Center" meeting:

1.   Strategies for the High School Competency Test
2.   Literacy project

TEAM PLANNING TO DEVELOP INTERDISCIPLINARY UNITS

1. Discuss curriculum taught in the basic skills areas to generate possible topics for interdisciplinary units.

2. Select a topic.

3. Each teacher must determine what objective(s) they want to achieve for their area.

4. Each teacher must determine the amount of required work for their area.

5. Teachers develop an assortment of optional activities that correlate with the required work.

6. Teachers must decide the amount of time needed to complete required work and optional activities. Team needs to develop timeline to keep students on target.

7. Develop system of grading.

8. Develop a copy of learning contract.

9. Check with librarian for appropriate library visits.

10. Distribute to each student his/her copy of the learning contract.

11. All team teachers involved meet to evaluate required work.

3. Discipline statistics

4. Working with exceptional education students

5. Teachers' visit from Port St. Lucie County

6. 4MAT workshop

7. Concerns/comments

As is evident from the list, the meeting dealt primarily with matters of instruction, assessment, and student management, but also included a staff development session with teachers from another district who were interested in academic teaming. The content of such meetings is distinctly different from that of meetings within academic departments. Both groups are important and each contributes to the quality of the high school experience. At McNeil High School, school leaders offered these essentials for teams to work together effectively:

- No absenteeism (from team meetings) except for emergencies
- Work toward consensus
- Cooperation and support
- Honesty and trust
- Flexibility
- A clear agenda and careful record keeping
- A specified meeting place
- Stay on task in meetings
- Be on time to meetings
- If team members are upset, they should air their feelings with the team or team leader

ACADEMIC TEAMING IN VARIOUS SETTINGS

Although academic teaming has not spread across the high school landscape with the same speed as have alternatives to the traditional schedule, new examples of successful teaming come on line almost daily. In many schools, teaming is restricted to the ninth grade, and in others it includes the tenth. In a very few, all teachers are teamed in some significant way. We predict that the speed with which high schools adopt academic teaming may, in the next decade, approach that now associated with the block schedule.

Penn High School in Mishawaka, Indiana, with 2300 student in grades nine through twelve, has been using what they call "Integrated Studies" (IS) for a number of years. Teachers on teams work with the same group of students who *choose* to be in the program. Students register for a block of five classes in the ninth grade and four in the tenth, eleventh, and twelfth grades. Sample student courses include (for freshmen) English 9, Algebra 1, Biology 1, World Geography, and keyboarding. Seniors might take Advanced Computers, Advanced Mathematics Concepts, Government and Economics, and Communications Technology. Students must enroll for the whole block.

Principal Sweeney describes the program:

> The major difference between IS and the more traditional academic curriculum is that instructors in each course work as a team to tie the material being covered together. This interdisciplinary approach, which is similar to the teaming program at both Grissom and Schmucker Middle Schools in our district, makes the learning more meaningful and immediate for students. The 'real world' is integrated, not fragmented. Integration provides a realistic system for learning. The program builds basic skills first, then integrates to achieve higher skills.
>
> Students are the big winners! They develop sound skills and knowledge in a first-rate educational program. They see relationships between the subject areas and increased meaning in what they study. As a result, they are more motivated. Parents and families benefit because parental involvement is part of the program. Class projects and themes include individual, family and community topics. Parents are also kept more informed throughout the program about activities, student performance, and expectations.
>
> Employers benefit from a better educated workforce. High school graduates can demonstrate such competencies in areas such as mathematics and science, interpersonal skills and applying technology. Post-secondary schools benefit by receiving students who understand the relationships between the real world and their academic studies. These students come prepared to learn with the ability to access information, communicate with others, and work within the adult world (Personal communication, April 4, 1995).

Selected student comments about the IS program at Penn include these:

> "I have never worked so hard, explored ideas so much, and felt so good about the education that I am receiving."
>
> "I enjoy how the teachers adapt the material into real world experiences that we can use."
>
> "I often questioned what 'this' had to do with real life. Now with Integrated Studies that question has been answered."
>
> "I don't really look at the program as school anymore, I look at it as an experience.
> (Eugene Sweeney, Personal communication, April 4, 1995).

Most courses in the curriculum at Penn are non-leveled. The movement against tracking has evolved slowly at Penn and is characterized by the absence of so-called basic-level courses. According to Sweeney, teachers at Penn are committed to providing experiences that are common for all students, challenging and stretching them, while at the same time making accommodations for their different abilities and time. Perhaps the best examples of these are the special education students who are included in the regular education program. Teachers, working side by side with a special education teacher, are learning to make adaptations in their classrooms to meet the needs of special education students.

At Robert E. Lee High School in San Antonio, Texas, principal Bill Fish reports that for 10 years the school has been using academic teaming as an approach to working with at-risk students. An academic team exists for this purpose at each grade level. In the ninth grade, students in the team enroll for a four-class block; tenth and eleventh grade students participate in a three-class block. As Fish says, "We want to shift from a content focus to a client focus." The faculty has phased out the basic track and has attempted to emphasize moving students into more advanced classes.

At Saint Augustine High School in Saint Augustine, Florida, principal Paula Steele reports that the school has organized all 650 ninth grade students into five academic teams of five teachers each (English, mathematics, science, social studies, and a course called Team Transitions that includes technology laboratory, critical thinking training, and keyboarding skills). Students take two electives outside the team. All ninth grade teams are housed in one wing, with the exception of the science and technology labs. Teachers on teams have a two-period block of common planning time. Staff development has substantially improved the willingness and ability of the teachers to work together for the benefit of their common students. After one year of teaming, attendance was up, the number of ninth grade students making the honor roll had grown, and the number of ninth grade students failing a course had dropped substantially (Personal communication, December 13, 1996).

At Salem High School in Conyers, Georgia, principal Bob Cresswell spearheaded a successful reorganization into comprehensive academic teaming that began in the fall of 1991; all 1,200 students in grades nine through twelve are members of academic teams. As described by Cresswell (1996, p. 28):

> The initial goal was to break the isolation of the teaching staff so as to enhance opportunities to model communication, collaboration, and collegiality for the students. Academic teaching teams were formed for ninth and tenth grades that consisted of four teachers (English, math, social studies, and science) with common planning periods (110 minutes per day) and a four-hour academic block. Teams were encouraged to meet at least two to three times per week to plan. Students were assigned to academic teams for the length of the school year. This structure provided consistent opportunities for teachers and students to get to know one another.

Approved by the Georgia State Board of Education in July 1991 as a Demonstration School Site for High School Restructuring, Salem High has been organized into heterogeneously grouped teams, each responsible for setting up its own schedule within a 4.5-hour block of academic time. Teachers were also given a voice in important decisions about the school, including budget, hiring new personnel, and the establishment of programs to meet the needs of the students. The school has become a place where the staff and students have a sincere sense of ownership. In 1993 the staff at Salem added teaming at the eleventh and twelfth grades, "allowing for the understandable need for more choices in these upper grades."

Principal Cresswell is convinced that teaming high school students with teachers for an entire year has a "tremendous impact on student learning." These students develop a unique ownership in their team which allows for incredible trust among students and teachers and among students and their peers. (Personal communication, December 15, 1996).

> The benefits are very obvious. Students can become risk-takers with the assurance that they will be understood by their peers because of the bond they share. Teachers also find a much greater ability to deal with the whole child as they monitor a student's progress from class to class and can discuss circumstances which may influence learning. Also, high school teachers no longer feel the isolation of closing the doors of their classrooms and being on their own. Parents are delighted with the team concept. Where once the doors to information about the student seemed to close when students entered high school and having a parent conference where all teachers were present was almost impossible, at Salem this is commonplace. Teachers meet with parents regularly to discuss instructional concerns. The information that parents are able to obtain is much more detailed and thorough, and a clearer picture of the student is seen by all (Personal communication, March 6, 1995).

Cresswell asserts that "the cooperation, collaboration, and collegiality that are integral parts of teaching teams provide support, inspiration, and a wealth of ideas for the teachers." As in other high schools, the teachers use common planning time to discuss concerns, to plan instruction and interdisciplinary units of study, and to meet with parents and other teams at the same grade level to collaborate on curriculum issues. "The teaming concept in high school sets a solid foundation for classroom innovation which is the focus of Salem High School." "Teaming, to me, is the key," says tenth grade language arts teacher Betsy Cameron. "We share ideas. We're supporting the students better. Kids are less likely to fall through the cracks. It is very successful, very rewarding, and very fulfilling." (Personal communication, March 6, 1995).

At McNeil High School, Alan Veach, previously a middle school principal and currently director of the new high school, says:

> We have carried many of the 'middle school' philosophies to our new high school, and they are working just fine. Academic teams are fully in place at the freshmen and sophomore level and each team has a common planning period to discuss students' needs and to plan interdisciplinary units. The eight team leaders meet with me every 2 weeks to discuss any problems and help plan for team activities. Academic teams meet weekly to share ideas on instruction and curriculum. Such meetings provide the planning time for teachers to collaborate on lesson plans, semester outlines, and 6-week syllabi, as well as providing a forum for sharing effective teaching strategies (Personal communication, April 25, 1995).

Few educators appear to have planned for the incorporation of academic teaming more thoroughly than those at MHS. They have carefully identified the goals and objectives of teaming at MHS, focusing on the improvement of instruction and student services (Figure 7.9). They have clarified what academic teaming is for them, and what it is not (Figure 7.10). They have also spelled out the essential ingredients for effective academic teams (Figure 7.11), identifying the responsibilities that should be assumed by each member.

FIGURE 7.9   Sample Goal/Objective Statement for Academic Teaming

---

Academic Teaming at McNeil High School

Instructional Goal: *To Improve Instruction and Student Services Through Academic Teaming*

Objective I: To ensure the success of academic teaming

    A. Regular team meetings
    B. Problem-solving is more successful with four teachers
    C. Professionalism enhances teacher self-esteem and morale
    D. Team members contribute positively to the total learning experience

Objective II: To establish consistency in norms and expectations

    A. Consistency in policies on late work, discipline, expectations, mastery learning, study skills
    B. Students have a sense of belonging to a small group. Teachers refer to what students are doing in other classes and relate it to their own discipline

Objective III: To increase the success rate of students

    A. Communication between teachers increases the success rate of students
    B. Teach the whole child—academics, social, and emotional skills
    C. Team effort expedites the identification of students in need of special services
    D. Parent-teacher team conferences

Objective IV: To incorporate interdisciplinary teaching

    A. Coordination
    B. Informal transfer
    C. Team teaching
    D. Thematic units

Academic Teaming is a Professional Approach to Teaching   FIGURE 7.10

Academic teaming is . . .
an instructional organization in which a group of teachers pool their resources, interests, expertise, and knowledge of students to jointly assume the responsibility for meeting the needs of a common group of students.

support and assistance to provide sound classroom management

the sense of belonging to a small group which has common goals and whose members are supportive of one another.

a common group of students who are assigned a common group of teachers who share a common planning period.

improved student discipline and behavior.

a productive classroom/school environment which effectively deals with affective behavior (human relations, responsibility, citizenship, etc.).

the correlation of subject matter, content, and concepts through planned repetition and reinforcement.

a strategy for identifying problems and working together for improvement in a combined supportive setting rather than one of isolation.

the opportunity to share ideas, plans, student information, and classroom observations.

worth the effort.

Academic teaming is not . . .
the elimination of departments or content area teachers working together.

teachers taking turns conducting classes.

a large group instructional area.

homogenization of teaching styles.

a daily coordination of interdisciplinary subject matter.

dependent upon a particular building structure.

a panacea for all problems.

easy at the outset.

FIGURE 7.11   Essential Ingredients for Effective Teams

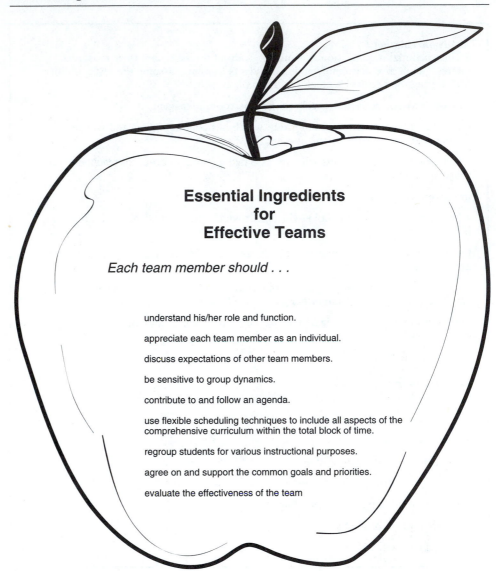

**Essential Ingredients
for
Effective Teams**

Each team member should . . .

understand his/her role and function.

appreciate each team member as an individual.

discuss expectations of other team members.

be sensitive to group dynamics.

contribute to and follow an agenda.

use flexible scheduling techniques to include all aspects of the
comprehensive curriculum within the total block of time.

regroup students for various instructional purposes.

agree on and support the common goals and priorities.

evaluate the effectiveness of the team

A careful examination of Figures 7.9, 7.10, and 7.11 will identify the sort of organization and the nature of assignments that emerge from a sizable high school fully involved in teaming at both the ninth and tenth grade levels. At MHS, there are four teams at the ninth grade level and four teams at the tenth grade level; each team has the equivalent of approximately four full-time teachers. It may not be immediately obvious, but it can be understood by examining the schedule that MHS (Figure 7.12) is operating on an eight-period, alternating block, A/B schedule, in which teachers teach three classes and have a 90-minute planning time daily. For example,

McNeil Clock Schedule   **FIGURE 7.12**

Period		Begin	End	
1/5..................................		9:05	10:35	
2/6.................................		10:40	12:15	ANNOUNCEMENTS
3/7..................................		12:20	2:30	
A:	**Lunch.....12:15**		**12:55**	
	Class........1:00		**2:30**	
B:	**Class......12:20**		**12:50**	
	Lunch.....12:50		**1:25**	
	Class........1:30		**2:30**	
C:	**Class......12:20**		**1:20**	
	Lunch.......1:20		**1:55**	
	Class........2:00		**2:30**	
D:	**Class......12:20**		**1:50**	
	Lunch.......1:50		**2:30**	
4/8................................		2:35	4:05	

the ninth grade Team 1 has a common planning time the second period every other day (Figure 7.13). The eighth period is devoted to a tutorial where team members will be available for support services, and the period is also used for various other team activities. A similar schedule is followed by the teams in the tenth grade

FIGURE 7.13   Team Schedule Grid—Ninth Grade

NINTH GRADE TEAMS WITH ASSIGNMENTS

TEACHER	TEAM 1	1	2	3	4	5	6	7	8
McGuire	ENGL	Engl 1	CONF.	Engl 1	Engl 1	CONF.	Engl H/T	Engl 1	EXCEL
Gordon	SCI	Biol T	CONF.	AP Biol.	Dept. Ch.	CONF.	Biology	AP Biol.	EXCEL
Dixon	SCI	AP Chem	CONF.	AP Chem	Lab Mgmt.	Biology	Biology	Biology	CONF.
@ Deason	MATH	Alg. 1	CONF.	Alg. 1	Alg. 1	Geom.	Math Lab	CONF.	EXCEL
McDonald	MATH		Alg. 1						CONF.
Cassity	S.S.	W. Geog	CONF.	W. Geog	W. Geo. H	W. Geog	CONF.	W. Geog	EXCEL
	TEAM 2								
@ Brown	ENGL	CONF.	Eng. H/T	Engl 1	Engl 1	Eng. 1	CONF	Engl 1	EXCEL
Mertink	SCI	CONF.	Biology	Biology	EXCEL(10th)	Biology	Biology	Biology	CONF.
Morgan	MATH	CONF.	Math Lab.	Geom.	Alg. 1	Alg. 1	Alg. 1	CONF.	EXCEL
McDonald	MATH	Alg. 1						Math Lab.	CONF.
George	S.S.	CONF.	W. Geog	W. Geog	W. Geog	CONF.	W. Geo H	W. Geog	EXCEL
	TEAM 3								
@ Wilie	ENGL	Engl 1	Engl 1	CONF.	Engl 1	CONF.	Engl 1	Eng H/T	EXCEL
Semmens	SCI	Biology	Enviro Sci	CONF.	Biology	Biol T	CONF.	Biology	EXCEL
King, Terry	SCI	Coach/Conf	Anat.	Coach/Conf	Coach/Conf	Coach/Conf	Biology	Anat.	Coach/Conf
Helm	MATH	Math Lab	Alg. 1	CONF.	Dept. Ch.	Alg. 1	Geom.	CONF.	EXCEL
McDonald	MATH			Alg. 1		Alg. 1		CONF.	CONF.
Bixler	MATH				Math Lab				
Scott	S.S.	W. Geog	W. Geo. H	CONF.	W. Geog	W. Geog	CONF.	W. Geog	EXCEL
	TEAM 4								
Dawson	ENGL	Engl 1	Engl 1	Coach/Conf	Coach/Conf	Engl 1	Engl 1	Coach/Conf	Coach/Conf
King, Erin	ENGL							Eng H/T	Coach/Conf
Reeb	SCI	Biology	Biology	Coach/Conf	Coach/Conf	Biology	Biology	Coach/Conf	Coach/Conf
King, Terry	SCI	Coach/Conf	Anat.	Biology	Coach/Conf	Coach/Conf		Anat.	Coach/Conf
@ Marling	MATH	Geom.	Alg. 1	Alg. 1	CONF.	Math Lab	CONF.	Alg. 1	EXCEL
McDonald	MATH				CONF.		Alg. 1		CONF.
Grant	S.S.	W. Geog	W. Geog	W. Geog	CONF. *	W. Geog	CONF.	W. Geog	EXCEL

(Figure 7.14), but the EXCEL period for tutorial and other team activities is scheduled at different times of the day for different teachers.

Round Rock Independent School District in Austin, Texas, where MHS is located, has taken teaming so seriously that they have extended their emphasis on teamwork to include vertical teaming on a K–12 basis. What the district calls "Linking for Learning" involves organizing the district into three vertical teams of the three high schools, each with its own middle and elementary feeder schools. In addition to other activities, the district devotes 2 to 3 days of training annually to vertical staff development. During this training, teachers from all grade levels deal with common curriculum and instructional strategies. Out of this vertical teaming comes a surprising number of activities that involve high school, middle school, and elementary students and teachers in mutually beneficial educational interactions.

At Oak Ridge High School (ORHS) in Orlando, Florida (Orange County), teaming has improved the ninth grade educational experience for virtually everyone involved—teachers, students, parents, and administrators. At ORHS six teams of four teachers each (English, mathematics, biology, and global studies as a mandated elective) work with 125–140 students. Educators in Orange County schools have discovered that placing ninth grades in separate buildings leads to many positive outcomes, so that in virtually every school in Orange County, ninth graders are either housed in a separate building (Ninth Grade Center) adjoining the main high school campus or in a separate part of the main building itself.

Teaming is in its fourth year at ORHS, and in order to make it work well educators have implemented several important policies. Believing that small classes are essential to the success of students at the ninth grade level, the faculty committed itself to ninth grade class sizes under 30 students, meaning that without additional funds to support that decision, senior classes are much larger than those for freshmen. Ninth grade teams each have a common planning time, shared school space so that their classrooms are in close proximity, and the same students; all ninth grade students take Global Studies as a "forced elective" so that the teaming arrangements are complete. Teachers have one off-team class at an upper level, to round out their loads and to give them some variety in their assignment.

Scheduling the ninth grade teams first also helps to make teaming work well at ORHS. Academic departments are asked to keep ninth grade teams in mind when they propose their schedules. Schedule developers tell the department chair when the team teacher in that department needs to have planning time and free periods scheduled. An effort is made to balance ninth grade electives to be sure students have plenty to choose from when their teacher teams are planning. As many know from experience, singletons like band offer real challenges to making the schedule work. At ORHS, all band students must be on one team because band classes are singletons.

Teachers on teams at ORHS have implemented activities reflecting the four areas discussed earlier. Teams meet twice a week and team discipline plans are in place on each team, fitting with the OCPS overall discipline plan. A substantial number of team–student conferences, especially during the first semester, focus on the discipline plan plus behavior contracts implemented between the team members and individual students. The second step of the team discipline plan is to bring in the parent, but

FIGURE 7.14 Team Schedule Grid—Tenth Grade

TENTH GRADE TEAMS WITH ASSIGNMENTS

TEACHER		1	2	3	4	5	6	7	8
TEAM 5									
Woodyard	ENGL	Eng. 2	CONF	Eng. 2 H/T	Eng. 2	EXCEL	CONF	Eng. 2 H/T	Eng. 2
Hailes	SCI	x	CONF	x	Chem	EXCEL	Chem	CONF	Chem H/T
Donald	SCI	Coach/S.H.	CONF	Phy Sci	Coach/S.H.	Coach/S.H.	CONF	Phy Sci	Coach/S.H.
@ Munoz	MATH	Alg 4B	CONF	Alg 4B	Alg 2H	EXCEL	Geom	CONF	Geom
Parker	SOC. ST.	Wor Hist	CONF	Wor Hist	Wor Hist	x	W. Hist H	Wor Hist	CONF
TEAM 6									
Jenkins	ENGL	Eng. 2	Eng. 2	Coach/Conf	Coach/Conf	Eng. 2	Eng. 2	Coach/Conf	Coach/Conf
Ollman	ENGL							Eng. 2 H/T(6)	
@Seale	SCI	CONF	Chem H/T	Phy Sci	Coach(UC)	Chem	Phy Sci	CONF	Chem
Connolly	MATH	Geom	CONF	Geom	EXCEL	Alg 4B	Alg 2H	CONF	Alg 4B
Patterson	SOC. ST.	Coach/S.H.	Wor Hist	W. Hist H	CONF	Co/S.H.	Wor Hist	CONF	Wor Hist
TEAM 7									
Ollman	ENGL	CONF	Eng. 2	Eng. 2	Eng. 2	EXCEL	Eng. 2 H/T	x	CONF
Uplinger	SCI	CONF	Phy Sci	Phy Sci	Chem H/T	EXCEL	Phy Sci	CONF	Chem
@ Burke	MATH	CONF	Alg 4B	Geom	Geom	EXCEL	CONF	Alg 4B	Alg 2H
Hoover	SOC.ST.	CONF	W. Hist H	Wor Hist	I.S.S.	CONF	Wor Hist	Wor Hist	Coach/S.H.
TEAM 8									
@ Wasserman	ENGL	Eng. 2	Eng. 2	Eng. 2	EXCEL	Eng. 2 H/T	CONF	Eng. 2	Eng. 2
* New	SCI	Phy Sci	Chem	Phy Sci	EXCEL	Chem	Chem H/T	CONF	Phy Sci
Richards	MATH	Alg 2H	Inf Geom	Geom	EXCEL	CONF	Inf Geom	Geom	Geom
Ramos	SOC. ST.	Coach/S.H.	Wor Hist	CONF	EXCEL	Co/S.H.	Wor Hist	W. Hist H	CONF
Stokes	SOC. ST.	W. Hist (8)				W. Hist (8)			
Parker	SOC. ST.								

only if the contract does not work out. As a result, over the first three years of teaming at ORHS, ninth grade referrals to the office are down dramatically. Teachers point out proudly that they solve their own problems and that this improved behavior also carries over into the tenth grade.

During the first nine weeks of the school year, teams at ORHS meet to confer with every student, not just those who present special challenges, ensuring that team–student relationships get off to the best start. Teachers on teams group and regroup their students as the teachers choose, for behavioral or academic reasons; all that is required is that the team send notes to the counselors informing them of the moves. Some attempts at curriculum integration have begun. Team leaders serve without financial supplements.

From interviews it seems clear that the faculty is extremely positive about teaming. They offer as evidence of their success the extremely low rate of staff turnover at the school since the implementation of teaming. Team members describe in glowing terms the mutual support they say is present among the members of each team. They point to a substantial decline in the number of discipline referrals each team has had to make to the office; they feel more in control of their own classroom management. Nonetheless, the teachers on the teams suggest that academic teaming is in fact different at the high school level than it has been at the middle schools with which they are familiar. Teachers who are enthusiastic about teaming point out that they still have loyalty to their departments. Teams at ORHS are more academic, teachers say and much less social than teams at the middle school seem to be. Teachers at ORHS make it obvious that they did not want students to think they were still in middle school. Teachers want ninth grade to be more rigorous than middle school, with appropriately higher standards. At ORHS, teachers point out that from the beginning they must impress their students with the understanding that the student can no longer just "pass along," that they need credits, beginning in the ninth grade, to graduate three years later.

School leaders at ORHS say that teams have been an important catalyst for change in the school—sharing the same students, and sharing authority and responsibility with other teachers on the team, has given teachers professional ambition. Teaming has been the key to the overall change in the school insofar as teaching is concerned. Educators at ORHS investigated tenth grade teams but concluded that the mathematics choices were too limiting. Math choices would have determined which team a student would be on, leading to ability-grouped teams, a choice educators at ORHS were not willing to make. To team at the tenth grade level at ORHS, teachers might have had four different preparations, a situation perceived as so difficult that it outweighed the benefits of teaming.

Even though teaming has not yet been implemented at the tenth grade level, educators at ORHS have "de-departmentalized" the whole school at the same time academic teaming was implemented, by moving all the social studies, English, and mathematics teachers from department locations to classrooms dispersed around the school. Science, of course, remains housed in the laboratory area. It was hoped that these moves would put teachers in contact across the curriculum, enabling them to talk about students as well as curriculum. Consequently, teachers in grades ten through twelve are organized in loose interdisciplinary clusters of social studies,

English, and mathematics. The result, according to school leaders, has been increased sharing among teachers. The move to de-emphasize departments has lessened the opposition and turf protection that often accompanies hardened department positions, and it has promoted much more positive cross-department interaction.

Teams at ORHS do attempt to integrate the curriculum, especially when it can be based on English. Examples of three interdisciplinary units developed and taught by ninth grade teams are *My Antonia* with a Global Studies parallel; a Research Skills unit in which other teachers give the English teacher their vocabulary and topics to research; and *Jurassic Park,* which included vocabulary, genetics, and maps (in Global Studies). Efforts such as these could not have been easily accomplished in the absence of academic teaming.

At Troup High School (THS) in La Grange, Georgia, ninth grade academic teaming began in the fall of 1996 under the leadership of principal Darrell Dean and assistant principal Janet Johnson. In this case, teaming was implemented in anticipation of substantially greater racial desegregation of the schools in the district. According to Johnson (personal communication, October 14, 1996) "the 'Freshmen Academy' exists to provide each ninth grade student the skills needed to make a successful transition from the nurturing environment of the middle school to the more academically rigorous environment of the high school without sacrificing the traditionally high expectations of Troup High School." As is the case in many districts, it was formed when evaluations continued to indicate difficulties ninth grade students encountered year after year: high failure rates, poor examination performance, and large numbers of discipline referrals.

The goals of academic teaming at THS include:

- To empower teachers to develop, implement, and evaluate new strategies for enhancing student success
- To develop classroom management and discipline techniques that cultivate student maturity, responsibility, and sense of mutual respect
- To provide teachers with a better understanding of the developmental needs of ninth grade students
- To instruct and model organization, time management, and study skills
- To improve and promote teacher/parent communication
- To promote teacher/teacher contact
- To promote interdisciplinary instruction and employ cooperative learning strategies
- To help integrate freshmen into the collective student body
- To provide incentives for and recognition of student success

At THS, the ninth grade has three teams of teachers with approximately 125 students on each team. Members of a given team have the same four classes with the same four teachers, but do not necessarily travel together with the same class group to the same classes in order. Students are rotated out of the teams for their two electives. Each team has established its own discipline plan, including rules, procedures, and expectations.

The teams at THS have agreed to use some common tools:

- The same three-ring binder for the four core classes
- The same THS assignment book/planner; and students use the planner for recording permission to leave class, major assignments, as a discipline record, and for communication to parents. Teams of teachers have agreed that their students must have the planner or they will not be able to leave class for any reason other than an emergency.
- "Do Now" assignments to begin each class on each team
- Similar seating charts and grading software
- Similar note-taking systems
- The use of a special parent contact phone line for teachers
- The use of an assignment line for students to call and get assignments
- Regular and structured team planning
- Increased peer tutoring
- Increased use of cooperative learning as an instructional tool

To be a member of a ninth grade team at THS, teachers have to volunteer and then undergo training in teaching new applied courses. The result was 12 teachers (three teams of four each) and 360 students (120 students per team), balanced to represent the population of the school—one section of students with a primarily vocational program of study, two with tech-prep interests, and two college-prep sections are assigned to each team. Teams are heterogeneous at THS. Each team spends the first four days of the school year in a high school orientation program with its students. Students are taught note-taking procedures that are used in every class on the team, get their schedules and information about clubs and other activities, are introduced to the school planner and handbook, take tours of the building, and complete other necessary tasks. Wisely, teachers at THS had interviewed the previous freshmen class to identify problems that needed to be addressed by teams (e.g., lockers, buses, failures).

Teachers on teams at THS have common planning times but no common planning space, and teams do not have the visual identity of middle school teams. Each team meets once a week in the principal's conference room so that meetings can more easily involve the administration. Meeting time is most often used for parent conferences. Each team of teachers develops a greater knowledge of their students, leading to schedule changes for particular students, conferences, and related activities. Team leaders at THS are the English teachers on each team because they have fewer preparations. No stipend is attached to this role, but teachers appear to accept the responsibility eagerly.

Typically teaching assignments for teachers on each THS team include:

- Mathematics teacher: one vocational mathematics class, two applied mathematics 1 (tech-prep) classes, one Algebra 1 class, and one geometry class
- Science teacher: One vocational biology class, two applied biology classes, and two physical science classes
- Social Studies teacher: three college prep citizenship and economics classes and two regular citizenship and economics classes
- English Teacher: five regular and college prep English 1 classes

In addition, teams at THS use what they describe as a "Facilitator Model" of inclusion of gifted students. Each gifted student is on a contract, similar to an individualized education plan (IEP). The English and social studies teachers on each team work together with the teacher of gifted students.

As elsewhere, teachers on teams at THS focus on the development of "class pride" rather than team pride as in the middle school. Teachers bought "Class of 2000" T-shirts, arranged group photos, selected class officers from team representatives, and engaged in other activities to enhance the students' sense of themselves as a class/year group.

The first year's experience with teaming at THS has yielded the following results:

- Teachers on the ninth grade teams want some of their priorities (e.g., note-taking system) to be used in the tenth grade, and in the eighth grade at the feeder middle schools;
- The student planners are now in use in the tenth grade as well;
- Cross-discipline work has grown just from teachers talking together during planning time;
- Teachers on teams have had very little interpersonal conflict;
- Teams keep coming up with new ideas (e.g., peer tutoring, using *USA Today* for all students);
- Each Wednesday teams have advisory time or activity time. The ninth grade holds grade/year activities at least once a month during this time. The time is used for guest speakers, clubs, SADD, teaching cheers, learning the school alma mater, and so on. Teachers believe that these activities help "class" cohesiveness grow. In fact, the freshman class sponsor, who teaches health, has focused even more intensely on the development of class spirit now that teaming has made it more feasible.
- Principal Dean says that "Discipline problems are way down in the ninth grade; we have eliminated 80 percent of the problems at that grade level and we have more tardies in the tenth grade than in the ninth grade. In-school suspension rates for freshmen are down by 38 percent. I believe that it has come from the strong emphasis on teaching responsibility to ninth graders that has emerged from academic teaming."
- Educators in the district had anticipated a dramatically higher failure rate in the 1996 ninth grade as a consequence of demographic changes in the school but actually experienced a 60 percent drop in failures in the first 9 weeks. THS educators believe they can improve that, because, said Janet Johnson, "Most of our failures are in the 60s, percent-wise. Teachers are really energized to work to decrease the failure rate further. So at the end of the first 9 weeks teachers examined failure rates, identified students in real need, and set up more parent conferences for students who are failing more than two courses."

Illustrative teacher comments from a focus group of teachers, administrators, and media specialists include these:

"Teaming gives me moral support. I know that if I have a problem, it's probably not just me."

"Teaming provides tremendous support for parent conferences."

"We can separate students who aren't good for each other, in collaboration with parents."

"Students have adjusted their behavior, because they know that teachers talk together frequently (e.g., students can't skip class as easily)."

"Teaming saves me pencils and paper, since the students are more focused. Our team gives students a list of necessary materials and reinforces it in each class."

"Students confide in the teachers because they are more secure with team teachers."

"I can see the difference in the tenth grade students in the media center as a result of the Freshmen Academy. It has helped to pull the whole school together."

"Teaming cuts down on my isolation."

"I can talk with my teammates about common curriculum problems."

"I feel in control."

"It's worth three preps."

"We actually raised standards because students have more instructional time since we get much of the other stuff done as a team."

"Make sure teachers are team players."

SCHOOL-WITHIN-SCHOOL STRATEGIES

Career Academies

In the mid-1980s the federal government began to articulate what came to be known as "Tech/Prep." This was an attempt to resolve the centuries-long divisions within the comprehensive high school by organizing the high school so that college preparation and vocational studies were no longer two opposite and alienated ends of a curriculum continuum. Eventually the Southern Regional Education Board (SREB) and similar groups in other parts of the nation developed programs to encourage the design and implementation of new models of high school organization and curriculum that would unify the high school curriculum.

The program for SREB, "High Schools That Work," has emphasized academic and vocational teachers working together, getting students to complete an upgraded program of academic and vocational study, integrating high-level academic and vocational instruction, replacing the general track, having students complete a career or academic "major" equivalent to about 500 hours of instruction, and using assessment and other data to improve student achievement. The central goal of these efforts is to raise the academic achievement of students enrolled in general and vocational studies to the level and quality expected in college preparatory programs. Career academies have resulted from this attempt to more productively weave together college preparation and vocational studies (Bottoms, 1997). Programs offer three levels of preparation: preparation for immediate entry into the world of work; the option of vocational school, then work; and the choice of college, then work. In this chapter, however, we direct our attention to the organizational nature of the career academy, rather than to the content of the programs.

Taft High School (THS) in Cincinnati, Ohio, is an example of a school moving in the direction of the career academy approach. At THS all students enroll in one component of T-CAP, which stands for the Taft Career Academic Program, a program that is both career-focused and solidly academic. Teachers and students are organized into academic teams, each student has a "Youth Advocate" from the tenth grade onward, and students have the opportunity to enroll in newly designed internships beginning in their junior year. Four career clusters are available: Health and Human Services; Science, Engineering, and Manufacturing; Commercial and Professional Services; and Information, Communication, and the Arts.

Every student at THS takes a series of three special career exploration and preparation classes. In the ninth grade Freshman Focus introduces students to a broad range of careers and concludes with visits to local colleges. A Career Focus—10 course continues the career exploration, helping students focus their efforts where their interests lie. A similar course in the junior year prepares students for internships.

The school district of Orange County, Florida, is an example of major efforts being made to restructure high schools to incorporate career academies. According to Eugene Pickler, Senior Administrator for Secondary Education in Orange County (Personal communication, January 17, 1997), academies are "a marriage of vocational and academic studies. We are trying to make the high school vocational programs so that they are not just unfairly viewed as the 'rejects' anymore. A strenuous effort has gone into attracting the "middle level student" to the heterogeneously grouped career academy program. "We want to help students who are serious about career preparation. The student has to be committed. We are more eager to counsel students out of the academy when they aren't motivated."

Career academies in Orange County have four guiding principles, which make it clear how similar this organizational strategy is to academic teaming. First, they seek to establish a "sense of community" such that bonds are created among teachers, students, and parents. In these groupings, more individual attention would be paid to students, to provide guidance and allow students to "work on life as well as academic skills." As in academic teaming, members of career academies are expected to experience enhanced teacher professionalism as a result of the ability to use their expertise and judgment to modify the curriculum, alter class schedules, and modify the allocation of time for teaching and learning. Third, teachers and students are invited to integrate the curriculum, to explore and expand the use of thematic units, and to incorporate cooperative learning and other instructional strategies requiring teamwork. Students are expected to acquire a first-hand understanding of teamwork, to help prepare them for a "workplace where teamwork is the industry standard." Finally, the career academy is devoted to the facilitation of students' transition from high school to career involvement.

Academic teaming and career academies have so much in common that teachers in career academies frequently think and talk of themselves as members of teams. As the teachers at Dr. Phillips High School in Orlando planned for the implementation of the first of their career academies, a business academy, they worked to develop a "team vision" that captured what the faculty believed would be the best possible outcomes for students participating in an academy there. Career academy teachers established team goals that would help to bring the vision to reality, and an action plan that would implement the goals. Individual teachers were challenged to develop their courses in ways that would incorporate the goals and vision of the academy.

At Oak Ridge High School (ORHS) in Orlando, Florida, the career academy concept has evolved into a form that has many similarities to the academic team offered to ninth grades in that school and elsewhere. Teachers in an academy at ORHS have the same general group of students, usually occupy the same space in the school, operate on the same schedule, and assist each other and their common students with the same curriculum theme. At ORHS about 50 percent of the students were involved in career academies in 1997. Students sign a contract to follow a course of study that has a clear vocational focus. The career academy program at ORHS spans a 4-year time frame, beginning in the eleventh grade and extending (2 + 2) to community college.

At ORHS, students can opt for the Public Works Academy, a dual program with Mid-Florida Tech, a local community college. The entire curriculum of the academy is concerned and focused on various aspects of city management: traffic, power, sewage, waste management, surveys, and water treatment. Students may be aiming for a career in public administration, involving a minimum of a master's degree, or immediate full-time employment after graduation; both students are equal members of the Public Works Academy. Students take numerous field trips, pursue internships with municipal government, and focus their other studies on the field of public works. In a large and growing community like Orlando, the opportunities for careers in public works are expanding dramatically, offering students a vision of an attractive future on several levels.

Not surprisingly, a new career academy at ORHS, located near major nationally known tourist attractions, features a program focus in Hotel/Motel Management. A local hotel made a substantial contribution to the start-up of the program in the fall of 1996 by redecorating a portion of the high school to resemble a modern hotel lobby; other lodging property managers have contributed opportunities for field trips, internships, guest speakers, and curriculum materials. Students in this career academy can work toward college preparation in hotel administration at the local university, similar but less extended programs at community colleges, or immediate employment after graduation. Teachers in the academy share the same students, space, schedule, and commitment to the special curriculum focus.

Career academies such as these build on Tech Prep ideas and School-to-Work concepts by moving away from the traditional smorgasbord high school curriculum to a much narrower career focus inside the structure of several years together in the same "school inside the school." Success in these programs requires substantial staff development for new teachers, who need to adjust their curriculum to the focus of the academy. Based on teacher surveys, ORHS staff development offered more use of technology in teaching, alternative assessments more in line with the product/process style of the curriculum, and additional techniques for motivating students who had become discouraged. An extensive effort went into building the curriculum around student needs—moving away from the textbook to offer students alternative, academy-based materials.

Apopka High School in Apopka, Florida, has 2,200 students in grades ten through twelve; 800 additional students are housed in the adjoining Ninth Grade Center. According to Joyce Clark, assistant principal, the goal is to have every student in a career academy career pathway. A new Technology Academy (pre-engineering) had enrolled 150 students in grades ten through twelve, during the 1996–97 school year. An Arts and Communications Academy is in preparation for the beginning of the 1997 school year. In 1996 the Health Careers Academy, the first such effort in Orange County, enrolled 430 students with 22 teachers in grades nine through twelve. A ninth grade Health Careers Academy would be organized into an academic team within the career academy. A common core curriculum is planned for the four years in each academy. In the Health Careers Academy, for example, each student would have his or her English, social studies, science, and Health/Medical Careers in common with other academy students. Clark says that because teachers share so much they "come to know the students intimately over a four-year period." A sense of team exists throughout the four years of the career academy.

A number of components make the career academy a powerful force in shaping the school lives of high school students and teachers. Entrance into an academy, including those in Orange County, requires exemplary conduct in eight and ninth grades. Like all other career academies in Orange County, the Health Academy is heterogeneously grouped, including students aiming for careers as paramedics and those whose aim is medical school. Honors and regular sections are offered in many subjects within the academy, but many common courses contain students from every achievement level. Each academy has a "Council of Twelve"—eight students and four teachers who meet to solve problems within the academy on a quarterly basis. Students do a lot of "shadowing" of career professionals in tenth and eleventh grades, also in heterogeneous groups. Every student has an internship in his or her senior year. Educators report that students who participate in a career academy with these features have a very different feeling about their high school experience.

Joyce Clark and many other educators in Orange County have recognized a number of important benefits arising from the career academy related to the organizational structure of the program. Students have an entirely new sense of identity and much sharper focus for their studies. The common group of students and teachers, combined with a curriculum tailored to their career interests, provides students with a substantially greater motivation to attend and do well in high school. Grade point averages are rising among students who have opted for a career academy, the result of focus and motivation. At Apopka High School, educators report that students do not ask "Why do we need to know this?" when they have chosen an academy.

Like the academic team, the career academy is as important for teachers as it is for students. Teachers who share the same students over two to three years derive a great deal of mutual support from their common efforts; traditional high school teacher isolation is sharply reduced by participation in the career academy. Scheduling refinements as simple as a common lunch time for teachers in academies, plus 45 minutes of after-school planning time, make it possible for teachers to work together in a number of ways. Additionally, at Apopka and other high schools in Orange County, each academy staff meets once a month. Orange County high school teachers are willing to assume more course preparation duties in exchange for teaching all day in an academy; knowing their students, having them for up to 3 years, working collaboratively with other faculty on a regular basis, and having "students with a focus" makes teaching in a career academy rewarding.

THE HOUSE CONCEPT

Building on the concept of the Russian nesting doll strategy, the house concept goes a long way toward creating the feeling of smallness inside bigness. In a high school organized in this way, students and teachers opt for membership in a smaller organization similar to a career academy, but with one important difference. The house concept tends to center more on a group of teachers, students, and parents who concur on an educational philosophy about the most appropriate strategies for effective teaching and learning at the high school level.

At Salem High School in Conyers, Georgia, positive experiences with academic teaming led principal Robert Cresswell and his staff to consider several other options that they believed might contribute to "increased personalization" of their high school. Among the options considered (but eventually rejected) was a concept known as "looping," in which a group of teachers and students stay together as a team for more than one year, with the students eventually moving on and the teachers on the team moving back to an earlier grade to begin the process again with a new team of students. Increasingly common in elementary and middle schools, looping appears to offer a number of benefits to teachers, students, and parents (George & Lounsbury, in press; Rasmussen, 1998). At Salem, faculty decided that mandating such a new and complex process would have produced too much "anxiety and unnecessary stress for teachers who really wanted to stay at their current grade level. A plan was developed that permitted teachers and students to be together for two years, but gave teachers the option whether to loop or not." (Cresswell, 1996, p. 29).

Cresswell describes the plan:

> At Salem, the combination of a ninth and a tenth grade team is called a "house." The eight teachers (two English, two math, two science, and two social studies) have the same opportunities as a team does, i.e., planning for instruction and developing interdisciplinary units (including cross grade level interdisciplinary units.)
>
> The benefits for the student with regard to personalization are obvious. If students are in a house that loops the English teacher, for example, they do not have

to try to build a new relationship with a new teacher; they will continue the relationship they have already built and can focus on the task of learning. If students are in a house that does not loop, the students still know who the next English teacher will be, and have a general idea of the teacher's expectations.

Either way, there is a sense of stability for the students, an atmosphere conducive to building a relationship within which learning can take place. Teachers also have a stronger sense of accountability to both communicate expectations and pass on students capable of meeting those expectations (Cresswell, 1996, p. 29).

The addition of teaming to the eleventh and twelfth grades at Salem, combined with the house concept, led to houses called the Junior College (grades nine and ten), and the University (grades eleven and twelve). Both houses include teachers of English, social studies, mathematics, and science. The focus is on breaking down the isolation of teachers and increasing personalization of the teaching and learning process.

Winter Springs High School in Seminole County, Florida, opened its new building in the fall of 1997, with 2,500 students organized into a new and unusual school-within-school organization, with four pods including grades nine through twelve, and 600 students in each pod. Each house was planned so that all of the basic academic courses are available to students without the necessity of leaving the house and traveling around the school from department to department. AP courses, ROTC, and art are also offered in each pod. Each house or pod contains planning areas and offices for teachers; laboratories are also available in each pod instead of being placed together in a more traditional science wing. The authors expect and predict that the early years of the 21st century will see many more high schools organized in this manner.

Cambridge Rindge and Latin High School (CRLS) in Cambridge, Massachusetts, is one of the first, albeit still few, high schools to organize teachers and students in this way. CRLS, the only public high school in Cambridge, enrolls 2,200 students, a student body much more diverse than the national norm. In 1996, the faculty continued to utilize the house concept and to "explore ways of restructuring this large school into smaller, more manageable units to provide more personalized learning and closer monitoring" (Personal communication, Edward Sarasin, July 7, 1995).

CRLS has six houses, or schools-within-the-school. Students make the choice of the house they wish to join in the eighth grade, with 80 percent receiving their first of three choices. They then spend the ninth grade largely in one house. Later they may take more and more courses outside the house, depending upon their curriculum choices. Each house at CRLS has approximately 200 students and 35–40 teachers, and each house has its own school site council of parents, students, faculty, community representatives, "teacher-leaders," a house administrator, and an assistant administrator. As of the fall of 1996, CRLS offered the following choices of houses to its incoming students:

RSTA House   Rindge School of Technical Arts, established in 1988, offers courses that merge the mechanical arts with academies and fine arts. The goals of this program include: integration of vocational and academic knowledge and skills;

connecting classroom learning to community and worksite learning; preparing students for college and careers by teaching broad-based transferable skills. RSTA House is one of eleven programs nationally to receive a grant from the United States Department of Education to develop new ways to integrate academic and vocational learning. The school has created four new career paths for juniors and seniors: Health and Human Services; Arts and Communications; Business and Entrepreneurship; and Industrial Technology and Engineering. Career paths function like a concentration or major in college, offering clusters of related courses, internships, and community projects. Much like a career academy, career paths add focus and meaning to academic studies, connecting them to practical applications and work contexts.

The ninth grade core program in RSTA House, City Works, combines 10 credits in social studies, language arts, science, and mathematics, and students work on individual and team projects that focus on Cambridge's neighborhoods and industries. Students communicate what they find out by making maps, taking photographs, drawing blueprints, building models, and writing up interviews and oral histories. Ninth grade students are also introduced to the career paths of RSTA. The technical, academic, and critical thinking skills taught in City Works, say teachers in that house, prepare students for success in their future vocational and academic studies as well as in the workplace.

The tenth grade core curriculum, Pathways, also comprises ten credits, and leads students to explore a variety of careers within the four broad pathways of RSTA. The curriculum for the tenth grade program includes job-shadowing, work biographies, and student exhibitions. The goal is not to discover what a student wants to do for the rest of his or her life, but "to discover the value and meaning that work can have in life."

Pilot House   Pilot House was perhaps the country's first school-within-school alternative, the "oldest progressive public school program still in existence in the Untied States," say educators at CRLS. It was founded in 1969 and maintains its emphasis on cross-grade curriculum electives, a strong teacher-based advising program, and community-building activities. Students are drawn from all areas of the city and represent the city demographically with regard to sex, geographical area, race, and ethnic background. The students in Pilot House dress more casually, are invited to address their teachers by first names, and generally are involved in the sort of learning community that was typical of the 1960s. Over 80 percent of the school's graduates go to college, report educators at CRLS.

Unique features of Pilot House include heterogeneity of classes, untracked and including all grade levels; shared decision making; close student–teacher relationships, and student-centered guidance and counseling. All students belong to one of ten advising groups that meet daily as a homeroom and during an activity period whenever possible. Each teacher serves as an advisor to about 25 students in academic and personal areas both in and outside of school. Within these groups, students and teachers interact informally on ad-hoc committees and in special interest activities. The basic principles of Pilot House arise from an unusual philosophy for a high school program. In essence, Pilot House is a community of students, parents, and educators mutually accountable to each other for the goals, the programs, and the successful operation of the school. The operational principles of Pilot House are:

- Diversity and cross-cultural education. "Recognizing that the development of cross-cultural understanding and respect are essential to a genuinely pluralistic American society, Pilot House is committed to the development of these qualities within its own richly diverse student population. But this diversity represents more than a principle of selection—it is a basic foundation of the school from which other principles and much of the program arise. Classes within the school are heterogeneous with respect to grade level and ability; and curriculum offerings, course materials, and school activities represent a variety of cultural traditions" (CRLS Course Catalog, 1995–96).

- Human relationships. "In the Pilot School community, every effort is made to foster human relationships . . . characterized by informality, relative non-authoritarianism, mutual trust, and an absence of regimentation. The fact that students call their teachers by their first names is only a surface manifestation of this principle; more important is the fact that students often participate on an equal basis with teachers in class discussions, in conferences, and in other school activities. However, the Pilot School notion of human relationships not only emphasizes direct person-to-person relationships—it also implies a commitment to the group as well, to the successful maintenance of the school" (CRLS Course Catalog, 1995–96, p. 52).

- Governance. Decision-making within the Pilot School, report the educators involved, is based on the premise that people affected by decisions have the right to participate in those decisions. One of the essential principles upon which the PS was founded and has functioned for over 25 years, is a large degree of community control over school policies. Closely related to this is the Pilot School's commitment to shared responsibility for policy implementation. The important areas where students, parents, and staff have shared decision-making power include program and structure (curriculum planning, selection of courses, use of resources) and staffing.

- Individual needs and concerns. Pilot House is characterized by a focus on the needs of the individual. The conviction is not that individualism should flourish at the expense of the community, but that any successful educational community must attend to the needs of its individual members. The advising system is perhaps the most significant effort in this area, according to educators.

- Learning. The Pilot House faculty is committed to learning: to the acquisition of the intellectual skills necessary to survive and contribute in the world, to the development of self-awareness, and to the development of social awareness and responsibility among its participants.

Fundamental School   Located on the fourth floor of CRLS, Fundamental School, which houses 400 students, began in 1976; the house continues to emphasize a traditional curriculum in an atmosphere of discipline and respect. Fundamental School stresses academic challenge and student accountability, enlisting parental involvement and support in reinforcing the discipline code. Educators at CRLS say that this house emphasizes the "foundations of education in a setting that focuses on the discipline of learning and the development of high standards of achievement, manner, dress, and respect for self and others." Fundamental School boasts a strong sense of community in spite of the fact that it seems so strict. This house has developed a 4-year core curriculum that offers a solid foundation in grammar and literature, mathematics, history, science, foreign language, and study skills. The house offers its own academically oriented electives, and the courses are open to students from other houses at CRLS on a space-available basis.

House A   Instituted in 1977, House A is located on the third floor of CRLS and included (in 1996) 370 students. Characterized by a focus on the specific needs and concerns of each student, House A "strives to advance further the capabilities and maximize the potential of all students in the attainment of increased academic, social, and cultural development." It includes and intentionally capitalizes upon the rich diversity of the student body, using a core curriculum for ninth and tenth graders in English and social studies. All House A students receive instruction in study skills. "The primary purpose of our program," teachers say, "is to provide a setting for the maximum academic growth of every student in our charge. It is our intent to help every student to look upon their high school experience as a new beginning." In addition, House A has a Learning Center that aids students in developing speed reading, research report preparation, memory skills, and SAT preparation.

Academy House   Established in 1989, Academy House emphasizes collaborative learning through team-teaching, heterogeneous class groupings, and integrated studies. The Academy at CRLS is a "diverse but close-knit community of students and staff who work together in active partnership. Our ultimate goal is to prepare students for a lifetime of learning and personal development. To do so, we focus on the dynamics of how to learn—across the curriculum." Six core ideas form the basis of the Academy's philosophy (CRLS Course Catalog, 1995–96):

1. Cooperative learning. Cooperative learning is an exciting educational strategy that engages the student directly in the learning process. Students learn to work together in small, self-motivated groups that process the information and practice the skills their instructors are teaching. This hands-on method teaches the positive behaviors required for successful social interaction.

2. Team teaching. Experienced, outstanding teachers and counselors work together in teams with small groups of students to create a personalized learning environment. The teams meet weekly to discuss students' progress and to plan and evaluate curriculum. The result, say teachers in this house, is some of the most dynamic successful teaching to be found at CRLS.

3. A challenging curriculum. Faculty members assert that the highest standards are the basis for a rigorous, practical, and innovative curriculum. Academic subjects, once taught in isolation, are fused into an integrated whole that stresses the major themes of human knowledge and experience. Students explore the arts and modern technology as part of their course of studies. In all its programs the Academy stresses both individual excellence and group achievement."

4. Democratic decision making. The Academy is a democratic, culturally diverse community committed to the participation of students, teachers, and parents in

decision making. Elected councils represent the students, faculty, and parents. Regular community meetings provide students a strong voice in all aspects of the educational process. The Academy is unique in that its administration consists of a team of teacher-leaders, elected by the faculty for a rotating term.

5. Cross-cultural education. The student body reflects the ethnic and social diversity of the neighborhoods of the city of Cambridge. Students from more than 25 countries attend the Academy; this rich heritage promotes a true sense of cross-cultural awareness and understanding of the diversity of the world. It also affords students of varying language and culture the chance to take courses with native speakers of Portuguese, Spanish, Creole, Amharic, and Chinese.

6. A strong sense of community. Teachers believe that the democratic, flexible, and personalized learning program guarantees the participation of all in the life of a school small enough to offer a true sense of community. Group-building activities are a regular part of the curriculum. Students and staff come to know and respect each other well. A strong sense of community arises; people genuinely care about each other.

The Academy House offers core programs in ninth and tenth grades. In the ninth grade program most students take two interdisciplinary blocks, one in English and social studies, using cooperative learning and teaming with inclusion. The second is a mathematics and science block—geometry and a science course. Students also take PE and electives. The tenth grade is also part of a block of English, social studies, and PE, called "Project America." Most tenth grade students also take Algebra II along with chemistry or biology as a block.

Leadership School   Founded in 1990, Leadership School places an emphasis on the teaching and learning of leadership skills, a working knowledge of effective decision making, and collective mediation in conflict resolution. A course in community service, created and constantly being re-developed by the teaching staff, is greatly encouraged for all students in the program. A ninth grade core program offers students the opportunity to learn in small group settings experiencing truly collaborative efforts by the instructors. All students in this school are being prepared for college. Students in grades nine and ten take a heterogeneously grouped core curriculum from an interdisciplinary team within the school.

The teachers in these Leadership School teams spend a significant amount of time challenging and encouraging students, monitoring student progress, and reviewing and developing the curriculum. Students are encouraged to take at least one course a year in either the performing or visual arts, business, or home economics. Students have mentors who monitor and support their progress through graduation and help them to be productive members of the community by providing them with opportunities to develop a respect and responsibility for self and others. As members of the community, students, staff, and parents take part in making decisions about the operation of Leadership School.

In addition to these schools within the school, there is a Transitional Bilingual Program for about 280 students, offering English and a full component of courses in Chinese, Haitian-Creole, Portuguese, and Spanish. It is a priority at CRLS to have all students enrolled in programs they have chosen, programs that are a heterogeneous representation of the overall demographics of the school. All students are "citizens" of both the house and CRLS as a whole. All students have access to all the electives in the whole school, extracurricular activities, and to many special services. Students in all houses represent a range of performance levels on standardized tests and other evaluation measures. Students in each house pursue major college preparation subjects, as well as sequential courses in visual and performing arts, technical arts, business, media, and technology. Students in all schools have representatives on the school-wide Student Government. "The school-within-school model creates the advantages of a home base, the opportunity for close monitoring of student progress, and a stronger, more personal relationship between families and the school. At the same time, it provides student access to the widespread resources of a large, comprehensive high school." (CRLS Course Catalog, 1995–1996, p. 3).

HETEROGENEOUS GROUPING

A half century of research on instructional grouping consistently points to the wisdom of reducing the degree to which registration in a high school course is leveled on the basis of the supposed ability or prior achievement of the students (see, for example, Bellanca & Swartz, 1993; Lynn & Wheelock, 1997; Pool & Page, 1995; Oakes, 1985; Slavin, 1990, 1995). Generally, research on the effects of curriculum tracking indicates that the practice is related to highly differentiated and dramatically inequitable treatment of students in general (as opposed to honors) tracks (Rosenbaum, 1976; Damico, 1992). Students in high tracks experience a "culture of accomplishment," with many course options, high participation in extracurricular activities, and more privileges; in contrast, students in lower tracks experience a "culture of fatalism" in which their course choices are fewer, their participation in extracurricular activities is at a minimum, and their privileges sharply curtailed.

A great deal of controversy has accompanied the attempts of educators to act on these findings. Although relatively few high schools have made dedicated attempts to reduce curriculum tracking in their schools, the number of high school educators interested in detracking is increasing. Bert Linder, principal of Benjamin Cardozo High School in Bayside, New York, was spurred to action in his school when he discovered in the early 1980s that the "only real difference between the regular and honors physics courses in the school was that students in one track were required to read *Scientific American* and the others were not." After study and discussion, the faculty at Cardozo did away with the basic, non-Regents level classes in English and social studies; they found that the percentage of students in the school passing the Regents examination stayed the same, with dramatically higher numbers of students taking the exam. Now all students except those in exceptional education do a senior English thesis.

It appears that high schools moving to implement academic teaming, career academies, and houses, as described previously, are also likely to act to reduce tracking in their schools. In fact, virtually every school identified in this chapter has taken action to reduce tracking. Apparently, the commitment that makes faculty willing to de-departmentalize their school if it will benefit the students is strong enough to move them to soften the levels of tracking as well.

Nobel High School (NHS), a school of 950 students in rural southern Maine (Berwick), is typical of high schools that have made a commitment to the belief that all students can learn to a much higher standard. Addressing a culture of under-achievement and low expectations at Nobel has meant a rejection of rigid curriculum tracking for this member of the Coalition of Essential Schools. In 1996 members of the Class of 2000 were organized into one of three heterogeneous "learning communities," academic groups taught by a team of teachers. Students on these teams enrolled in a block of heterogeneously grouped courses in English, physical and earth science, algebra, and America and the World, as well as several electives. Tenth grade students were also part of one of three heterogeneous teams at that level, with a core curriculum in English, biology (AP biology is an option), history, geometry, and health and physical education. Juniors and seniors take a similar program, with the only tracking being the differentiation between a standard course and the AP parallel.

Because students come to Nobel from a traditionally tracked junior high school, it is important to point out that classes at NHS have shown substantial increases across all subjects in the percentage of students performing in the top quarter on the annual Maine Educational Assessment. At the same time, the percentage of students performing in the lowest quarter of the test has dropped dramatically, the gender gap in mathematics and science performance was virtually eliminated, and NHS students are "significantly outperforming comparison groups of students with similar rural, poor, blue-collar demographics." In 1995, for the first time, students at NHS scored above the state average in every category (Personal communication, Pam Fisher, December 12, 1996).

In 1984, teachers at Pioneer Valley Regional School in Northfield, Massachusetts, under the leadership of principal Evrett Masters, decided that they would eliminate the tracked curriculum in their school. After examining the research and examples of successful alternatives, the faculty, school administration, and school board agreed to implement heterogeneous grouping. But first the faculty and administration pursued a year's thorough preparation; their work included staff development and a college course in learning styles and instructional strategies. Changes in grouping were implemented in the 1985–86 school year.

Pioneer curriculum requirements ensured that a solid academic foundation was available to every student. Each student was scheduled individually in untracked programs of heterogeneously grouped classes. Ample choice was provided through topical electives beyond basic courses, and supplementary programs remained available in reading, writing, mathematics, and independent study. Services required under Chapter 766 and Public Law 94–142 were also provided in the regular classroom as well as a resource setting.

Thirteen years later, in 1997, the program of heterogeneous grouping was still in place and like some other faculty members, Roger Genest, chairperson of the English department and once one of the most vigorous opponents of heterogeneous grouping, had become its most fervent supporter. Genest says that the turning point for him came a decade earlier when he decided to try the new ideas he encountered in the staff development program with a pilot group of ninth graders who were still tracked in honors, college, general, and low tracts. His experiences convinced him of his need to move away from a direct instruction model of teaching to a more student-centered classroom style. According to principal Masters, "all courses at Pioneer are now college prep" (Personal communication, November 9, 1996).

The results, says Masters, have justified the detracking experiment. He credits the move to heterogeneous grouping with everything from improving individual students' self esteem to moving the school climate in markedly more positive directions and nearly doubling the percentage of students at Pioneer who go on to college. The number of seniors going on to further education increased from 37 to 80 percent. Students entering 4-year colleges increased from 17 to 45 percent. Students going directly to work dropped from 26 to 8 percent, and the percentage of students enlisting in the military immediately after high school has dropped from 17 percent to nearly zero (Wheelock, 1992, p. 270). Seventy-three percent of the Class of 1996 planned on further education following graduation. Masters reports that the move to heterogeneous grouping has been followed by a reduction in vandalism, fewer discipline referrals to the office, and the dramatic reduction of difficulties associated with school cliques. Student performance on college scholarship examinations ranks Pioneer in the 99th percentile compared with other schools in the area.

Donna Cadwell, a school counselor involved in the transition, believes that she can document changes in attitude among the students she sees, both about themselves and their chances of success in more challenging classes. She recalls one of her students saying to her "You know, I like school this year. I feel 'in.' Having everyone all mixed up in classes makes me feel part of the whole group, not just with my own friends. I can understand what we're reading just as well as the 'scholars.' I just read slower."

Amy Pelletier, a student who had been in the advanced sections when Pioneer had tracking, wrote about her experience with the transition to heterogeneous grouping in a letter published in the *Boston Globe* in December, 1990. We excerpt sections of her lengthy letter here:

> I am a first year student at Mount Holyoke College. I was in homogeneously grouped classes in seventh grade and changed to heterogeneously grouped classes in the eighth grade.
>
> When the transition was first made, I did not really understand what was happening, and therefore saw little change. Then I began to notice that there were different students in all my classes. I was no longer 'stuck' in the 'high-level' rotation where I saw all the same people all the time . . .
>
> There was also a change in the style of teaching. Much more work was done in groups, rather than lectures. As a result, teachers were able to work more one-on-one with students. With this, students learn to be responsible to each other, not just to the teachers. I remember one particular project which required that our group read a short story, come up with a script, and make a movie. While I had no problem writing the dialogue, I did not know where to start in making the video. Luckily, the others in my group (from the 'lower' levels) were very

creative and knowledgeable when it came to acting, recording, and film editing. It is in these groups that people learned to respect everyone's interest and talent.

Another example is from my senior physics class, where there were many different levels ranging from the top five percent of my class to the lowest quarter. Our teacher combined mathematical problems and book learning with many hands-on activities. . . . Ironically enough, the 'lower' levels were far more successful than the 'upper' level students in these assignments that applied our book knowledge to real life. I recall that in the debate over the change to heterogeneous grouping, many 'upper level' students were afraid of becoming bored in their classes. However, I did not experience this . . .

I feel there is a great deal of discrimination among students grouped homogeneously. Not only do the 'upper' level students look down on those in 'lower' levels, but the 'lower' students have many stereotypes of those in 'higher' levels. These stereotypes are unfair since the level where students are placed is often determined by a standardized test which does not truly measure their capabilities. Heterogeneous grouping, on the other hand, lessens this discrimination by allowing more students to interact with each other about these preconceived notions.

I believe that heterogeneous grouping is also more realistic. . . Life in the 'real world' involves dealing with people who are not at the same level as you. Therefore, I feel that heterogeneous grouping does not disadvantage any student academically, and that the social and psychological gains are tremendous (Steinberg & Wheelock, 1992, p. 3)

In spite of the dozen or so high schools engaged in detracking cited in this chapter, and the many others where similar efforts are underway, it is likely that changes in instructional grouping methods will lag behind changes in schedules, team organization, and other strategies. Many educators in senior high schools, particularly in districts where students have been tracked throughout elementary and middle school, perceive sizable achievement and motivation gaps between the highest and lowest achievers and believe that it is impossible to offer a single, high-quality curriculum that can accommodate this wide range, especially in hierarchically designed subjects like mathematics. Oakes (1992, p. 450) writes:

English and social studies teachers often seem less daunted, but even they find that their efforts to combine honors or gifted programs with regular classes—even regular college preparatory classes—generate enormous resistance from parents. In some districts, parents have used their political clout to halt any detracking efforts, and in others they have threatened to withdraw their children and enroll them in private schools. For both substantive and political reasons, many senior highs choose to leave their honors and gifted programs in place, particularly for 11th and 12th graders. Some, however, adopt a more 'open admissions' policy, recruiting students into honors and advanced placement classes, rather than enforcing strict entry criteria.

Even where educators are persuaded that rigid tracking must be discontinued, says Oakes, educators in senior high schools face tough challenges when they try to change their grading and reporting practices to accommodate more heterogeneous grouping. Traditional textbook-centered instruction also changes slowly, even in the best of circumstances; cooperative learning cannot be the only alternative. In regard to grouping for instruction, then, a few pioneers have blazed a trail that the great majority of high school educators have as yet declined to follow. The authors predict, however, that as public high school populations become ever more diverse, tracking will become a less and less viable strategy for organizing the curriculum and grouping students.

THE TALENT DEVELOPMENT HIGH SCHOOL

In the late 1990s educators at the Johns Hopkins University Center for Research on the Education of Students Placed At Risk (CRESPAR, 1996) attempted to articulate a model for the high school that incorporated many of the components described in this and other chapters, including academic teaming in the ninth grade, career academies, and heterogeneous grouping. Researchers at CRESPAR believed that a clear and concrete model was essential to successful restructuring—that ideas and principles were not sufficient. Patterson High School in Baltimore was identified as the first such "Talent Development High School," and the program was implemented there in 1995.

A "Ninth Grade Success Academy" pulls together all of the school's ninth graders into their own program. The Success Academy has its own entrance and classrooms, principal, and teaching staff. The ninth grade staff is divided into five academic teams with 150–180 students on each team, served by a common group of teachers with common planning time each day (CRESPAR, 1996). All ninth graders take Algebra 1.

At Patterson, four upper-level career academies of the sort described earlier in this chapter were organized for students in grades ten through twelve, each as a separate "school within the school" with is own wing of the school and separate entrance: Arts and Humanities; Business and Finance; Sports Studies and Health/Wellness; and Transportation and Engineering Technology. Each academy also has its own faculty and administrators. Toward the end of ninth grade, students apply for admission to one of the academies, each of which lays out specific career pathways students can follow toward employment after graduation or further education, or both.

Other components included in the CRESPAR Talent Development High School model include:

- Home room teacher-based advisement
- A four-period day in the career academies
- Progress-based grading
- Voluntary academic assistance before and after school
- Full-time health education staff
- Regular instruction and discussion of topics like teenage sexuality and substance abuse
- A "Twilight School" for students who have serious discipline problems

Evidence of the effects of the model at Patterson High School are preliminary but positive. It appears that school climate, student attendance, and promotion to the next grade have all improved. Educators believe that "one of the worst high schools in an urban district, designated for reconstitution by the state, is well on its way to becoming a very good high school in the very first year of its operation as a Talent Development High School" (Center for Research, 1996, p. 5) The authors of this text believe that in the years directly ahead, research and experience will continue to affirm the importance of reorganizing high school teachers and learners along the lines of the concepts and practices described in this chapter.

SUMMARY

A major step being taken by many high schools engaged in reform is that of creating smaller units of learning in which personal anonymity is diminished. This restructuring moves high schools rather dramatically away from traditional departmentalization and toward a more integrated and interdisciplinary approach to curriculum and instruction. To accomplish these and related goals, many high schools are adopting block schedules, organizing instructional teams, creating schools-within-schools, and moving to more flexible forms of instructional grouping. By using such strategies, educators hope to restore the balance between curriculum and community. They seek both a rich and rigorous curriculum and a strong sense of community where students feel known and cared about.

Academic teaming is a key component of restructuring high schools. Teams of teachers typically share the same students and combine their talents to offer most or all of the core subjects. Members of the team frequently have a common planning time and sometimes have classrooms located in a common part of the building. They work collaboratively to deliver quality teamed instruction, share information about the students they teach, hold team–parent conferences, integrate curricula, and build community. Teams can also become an important locus of control for decision-making, problem-solving, and the development of school guidelines.

High schools have utilized a number of strategies to move to the school-within-a-school organization. Some schools, for example, have established career academies that focus on weaving more closely together college preparation and vocational studies curricula. These academies typically offer three levels of preparation, including immediate entry into the workforce, vocational school, and/or college. These career academies typically seek to: (1) establish a sense of community where bonds are created among teachers, students, and parents; (2) enhance teacher professionalism; (3) integrate the curriculum while expanding the use of thematic units, cooperative learning, and other instructional strategies; and (4) facilitate students' transition from high school to career involvement.

An additional method for moving to a school-within-a-school organization is the "house plan." High schools using this plan tend to focus on a group of teachers, students, and family members who concur on an educational philosophy. Some of these schools also utilize "looping," which means that a group of students and teachers stay together as a team for more than 1 year.

Although research has shown for many decades that it is wise to reduce the degree to which high schools track classes based upon predicted ability and prior achievement, the practice remains ingrained in most high schools. Generally, research shows that tracking is related to differentiated and dramatically inequitable treatment of students in the "general" tracks. Students in the honors tracks experience a "culture of accomplishment," with many course options, high levels of participation in extracurricular activities, and many privileges. By contrast, students in the lower tracks more often experience a "culture of fatalism" where their course choices are limited, participation levels in extracurricular activities are minimal, and privileges are limited. In some high schools, however, including several discussed in the chapter, measures are being taken to reduce or eliminate traditional tracking practices, with positive results.

CONNECTIONS TO OTHER CHAPTERS

One purpose of making big schools feel smaller is to make them less intimidating and more inviting to students, their families, and to members of the community who might be productively involved in high school programs. The more personal the school feels to family and community members, the more likely these adults will become positively connected to the school.

ACTION STEPS

1. Identify a high school where teachers, perhaps at the ninth grade level, are involved in academic teaming. There are at least two possibilities for learning more about that strategy. This activity requires that you visit a high school, or at least have the opportunity to question a high school educator about his or her school. Try to select a high school where you can be assured that academic teaming is functioning as it was intended. Once you have identified such a school, you must secure permission to explore the existence of team life in *one* or *both* of these ways:

   a. Conduct your own "shadow study" of life on a team by spending a day with the team. Look for evidence of the extent to which team members are involved in the phases of team life you have read about. You can discover this evidence by observing the team area, students, and the teachers before, during, and after school. When you finish collecting data on your shadow study, pull it all together with a two-page essay on "Four Phases of Academic Teaming: A Matter of Degree." Here are nine important sets of evidence to collect as you "shadow" the team:

      i.   What evidence do you find that the teachers share the same students, part of the building, schedule, and interest in each other's subject areas?

    ii.   What evidence do you find that the teachers have tried to use the team as a professional support system by developing common team rules, procedures, parent conferences, or expectations for students?

    iii.   What evidence is there that the teachers have worked to build a sense of community in which students feel involved?

    iv.   Is there a special time and place teachers regularly use for team planning? What is the arrangement?

    v.   Is there any evidence that teachers have worked at interrelating their separate subject areas or at coordinating major assignments or units of study?

    vi.   What evidence is there that the teachers make decisions as a team on things like the use of time, money, or curriculum?

    vii.   Can you discover ways in which members of the school administration or the counseling staff work regularly with individual teams?

    viii.   Is there a school-wide decision-making group where teams are represented? How does it work?

    ix.   What do members of the team say about the success of the team and their satisfaction with their work together?

b. Interview a team of teachers during their planning time. If you are unable to arrange a shadow study, perhaps you can secure permission to interview a team about the extent to which they are involved in an interdisciplinary team organization. Here are a series of questions that should help you identify how the team process is functioning. After the "yes" or "no" response, be sure to probe for details. When you have completed the interviews, pull it together in the essay "Four Phases of Academic Teaming: A Matter of Degree."

    i.   To what extent do you [the teachers you are interviewing] work with others who share the same students? In what ways?

    ii.   Is your classroom near those of other teachers who (a) teach the same students but different subjects, or (b) the same subjects but different students? [Repeat for clarity]

    iii.   Do you have a common planning time with other teachers who teach the same students you do?

    iv.   Can you give an example of how you have recently become involved in planning, teaching, or evaluating curriculum beyond the subject for which you are responsible?

    v.   Do you typically work with other teachers in areas like managing student discipline, meeting with parents, or working with people like the school counselor? What are some examples?

    vi.   How often do you meet with other teachers to talk about students you have in common?

vii.   Would students be able to tell me what academic teaming was if I asked them? If so, how would they describe it? If you have the opportunity, ask several students about their team.

viii. Are there ever times when you and other teachers work together with a large group of students at once?

ix.   If you need to find funds for a field trip, a video rental, or a similar expense, to whom would you turn for assistance?

x.   Is there a schoolwide decision-making group that affects your life as a teacher? How is it structured?

DISCUSSION QUESTIONS

1. Which of the methods for creating "smallness inside bigness" described in this chapter do you believe to be most likely to become a permanent part of large numbers of high schools?

2. What aspects of contemporary high school programs might work against the widespread adoption of these programs?

3. What might be the negative consequences of widespread adoption of these practices?

REFERENCES

Beane, J. (1995). *Toward a coherent curriculum.* Alexandria, VA: Association for Supervision and Curriculum Development.

Bellanca, J., & Swartz, E., Eds. (1993). *The challenge of detracking: A collection.* Palatine, IL: IRI/Skylight Publishing.

Bottoms, G. (1997). Improving high schools by replacing the general track. *The High School Magazine, 4,* 12–17.

Breaking ranks: Changing an American institution, A report of the National Association of Secondary School Principals in partnership with the Carnegie Foundation for the Advancement of Teaching (1996). Reston, VA: National Association of Secondary School Principals.

Center for Research on the Education of Students Placed At Risk (October, 1996). *CRESPAR Research and Development Report.* Baltimore, MD: Johns Hopkins University and Howard University.

Cresswell, R., & Rasmussen, P. (1996). Developing a structure for personalization in the high school. *NASSP Bulletin, 80,* 27–30.

Damico, S. (1992, March). *When good intentions go bad.* Paper presented to the faculty, University of Florida, Gainesville, Florida.

Dyer, T. (1996). Personalization: If schools don't implement this one, there will be no reform. *NASSP Bulletin, 80,* 1–8.

George, P., & Lounsbury, J. (in press). *Long-term teacher-student relationships: A national study of an emerging middle school practice.* Columbus, OH: National Middle School Association.

Lynn, L, & Wheelock, A. (1995). Making detracking work. *The Harvard Education Newsletter, 13(1),* 1–5.

Oakes, J. (1992). Detracking schools: Early lessons from the field. *Phi Delta Kappan, 73,* 6, 448–454.

Oakes, J. (1985). *Keeping track: How American schools structure inequality.* New Haven: Yale University Press.

Peterson, K. S. (1996). New approaches help ninth-graders adjust. *USA Today,* Tuesday, September 2, 1–2D.

Plodzik, K., & George, P. (1989). Interdisciplinary team organization. *Middle School Journal, 20,* 15–19.

Pool, H., & Page, J. (1995). *Beyond tracking: Finding success in inclusive schools.* Bloomington, IN: Phi Delta Kappa.

Rasmussen, K. (1998, March). *Education Update, 40(2),* 1, 3–4.

Rosenbaum, J. E. (1976). *Making inequality: The hidden curriculum of high school tracking.* New York: Wiley.

Slavin, R. E. (1990). Achievement effects of ability grouping in secondary schools: A best-evidence synthesis. *Review of Educational Research, 60,* 3, 471–99.

Slavin, R. E. (1995). Detracking and its detractors: Flawed values. *Educational Leadership, 77(3),* 218–219.

Steinberg, A., & Wheelock, A. (September/October, 1992). After tracking—what? Middle schools find new answers. *The Harvard Education Letter, 8,* p. 3.

Wheelock, A. (1992). *Crossing the tracks: How "untracking" can save America's schools.* New York: The New Press.

CHAPTER 8

SCHOOL/FAMILY/COMMUNITY PARTNERSHIPS

WHAT YOU WILL LEARN IN THIS CHAPTER

Family, community and high school partnerships

National standards for parent/family involvement

Successful strategies for outreach activities and programs

Effective communication with families, community, and other stakeholders

Building strong partnerships

Meaningful partnership roles for family and community

The high school will engage students' families as partners in the students' education (Breaking Ranks, p. 89).

The school will accord meaningful roles in the decision-making process to students, parents, and members of the staff to promote an atmosphere of participation, responsibility, and ownership (Breaking Ranks, p. 32).

Each high school will establish a site council to work with the principal in reaching decisions to make the school an effective organization for student learning (Breaking Ranks, p. 75).

High schools, in conjunction with agencies in the community, will help coordinate the delivery of health and social services for youth (Breaking Ranks, p. 89).

The high school will foster productive business partnerships that support and supplement educational programs (Breaking Ranks, p. 89).

The high school will require each student to participate in a service program in the community or in the school itself that has educational value (Breaking Ranks, p. 89).

The leadership of students, parents, and others in the school community will enhance the work of the principal, who should recognize this potential for leadership by nurturing and supporting it (Breaking Ranks, p. 99).

The *Breaking Ranks* recommendations listed, as well as those found in other influential publications, reflect a growing recognition of the importance of engaging family and community members in school reform. High school educators have been slow to recognize the importance of this engagement and have often underutilized the rich resources that family and community members can provide for improving student learning. Unfortunately, family and community members in most communities are neither involved nor well informed about their schools (Brandt, 1998; Cavarretta, 1998; Cawelti, 1997; Lewis & Henderson, 1997).

A quiet revolution that signals a fundamental shift in the actions of citizens on behalf of children and their schools is now taking place. This change, usually called public engagement, arises from new conceptions about the notions and structures of power in education. The engagement of citizens in shaping the institutions that serve them is not a new idea. What is new, however, is the increasing use of engagement techniques for public education (Annenberg Institute on Public Engagement for Public Education, 1998).

The increased focus on the importance of authentic public engagement is embedded in a new vision of the goals and purposes of education. This vision acknowledges that if high schools are to be successful, profound changes in concepts of curriculum, instruction, and student learning are required. These and other changes in traditional programs and practices require authentic collaborative relationships between schools, families, and community members that are significantly different from those in most contemporary high schools.

This new vision, that higher standards are to be achieved by every student, is the most ambitious challenge public education in this nation has ever faced. "For the first time in our history, the nation has adopted policies that promise all students, rich or poor, no matter where they live or the language of their families or how long it takes them to learn, a quality education" (Lewis & Henderson, 1997, p. 1). For this vision to become reality, schools must no longer be allowed to focus almost exclusively on students who are viewed as potentially successful while the remaining students are largely disregarded. If high schools are going to make the curricular and instructional changes needed for this vision to become a reality, relationships between schools, communities, and families must also undergo a major metamorphosis.

The renewed recognition of the importance of family participation in the education of their children is a logical and positive development because for many years research has shown that parental participation in the education of their children is more important to student success, including scores on standardized achievement tests, than family income or education level. This is true whether the family is wealthy or poor, whether family members finished high school, or whether the child is in preschool or in the upper grades (Epstein, 1991; Stevenson & Baker, 1987; de Kanter, Ginsburg, & Milne, 1987; Henderson & Berla, 1994; Keith & Keith, 1993; Liontos, 1992). The confirmation of the importance of close collaborative working relationships with family members offered by this research and by "wisdom of practice" makes it crucial that high school educators take the steps necessary to fully utilize the valuable resources families have to offer. The importance of high schools working closely with community members is also very clear (*Breaking Ranks*, 1996; Danzberger, Bodinger–de Uriarte, & Clark, 1996; Rutherford, 1995; United States Department of Education, 1995).

This chapter reviews the knowledge base on family and community partnerships and presents examples of successful practice drawn from information provided by the exemplary high schools participating in this project. Emphasis is placed on working closely with parents and other family members and on developing strong partnerships with community members, including representatives from business and industry.

FAMILY, COMMUNITY, AND HIGH SCHOOL PARTNERSHIPS

Historically, the involvement of family members has decreased as their children have become older and have advanced to higher grades (Epstein, 1995, Epstein & Conners, 1992). For many years this decreasing involvement was taken for granted, and usually represented the status quo at the high school level. However, as increasing numbers of high schools restructure—make significant changes that contribute to increased productivity and effectiveness—they are taking steps to re-engage family and community members through new and exciting partnerships. These partnerships are designed to draw upon the rich resources that are available in all homes and communities.

Successful high schools are capitalizing upon the interest of family members, teachers, administrators, representatives from the business community, and other stakeholders, for developing stronger home–school collaborations (Chavkin & Williams, 1987; Epstein, 1995; Finney, 1993; Louis Harris & Associates, 1993; National Commission on Children, 1991; Perry, 1993; Rutherford, 1995). This new surge of interest is at least partially the result of a growing consensus that partnerships are desirable and necessary if high schools are to reach their full potentials and serve all their students effectively. This consensus has evolved from a number of factors which include concern about the quality of education at high schools, the success of schools that have strong partnerships, and the expanding research base which supports the importance of collaborative partnerships.

The most important goal of these partnerships is to help adolescents gain the knowledge, skills, and dispositions needed to be successful in high school and in later life. However, family members also benefit from involvement as they develop a greater appreciation of their role in their childrens' education, an improved sense of self-worth, stronger social networks, and the desire to continue their own education. They develop a more complete understanding of schools, teaching, and learning activities in general (Henderson & Berla, 1994; Liontos, 1994). Some additional reasons for establishing and maintaining strong partnerships between high schools, families, and community members include: (1) improving school programs and school climate; (2) providing family services and support; (3) increasing parents' skills and leadership; (4) connecting families with others in the school and in the community; and (5) helping teachers with their work (Epstein, 1995).

CHANGING PERSPECTIVES OF PARTNERSHIP ROLES

The era of equating family and community involvement with cookie baking and fundraising is rapidly ending in America's schools. Raising funds is still crucial to schools, but many family and community members now seek expanded roles that include a wide variety of activities, such as serving on governance and management teams that plan academic programs and school improvements.

Despite positive trends that point to improved efforts to create meaningful family and community partnerships, some educators continue to welcome this involvement only when it is needed in specific ways and when times are convenient. This model of total control of parental and family involvement by educators represents one extreme. Another extreme would be attempts by parents and other family members to run the school, control expenditures, and be involved in hiring and firing of staff. However, reality in most high schools is typically somewhere between these two extremes (Coulombe, 1995; Jesse, 1995).

Fortunately, the majority of families, community members, and educators want to provide high-quality teaching and learning experiences in their schools and are willing to put forth the effort to help ensure success in student learning. However, differences in opinion about how to reach the goals can impede progress. This situation points out the importance of having a framework for understanding the perspectives of all concerned so that children can receive the best schooling possible (Jesse, 1995).

PARENT AND FAMILY INVOLVEMENT IN A CHANGING SOCIETY

Because schools are a mirror of both society and the family, they must change as society and families change. As society, communities, and schools restructure themselves, the nature of parental/family involvement must also restructure itself (Davies,

1991). Schools have already changed, even when this change was independent of any conscious reform agenda. For example, dispositions, practices, expectations, and visions of the breadth and depth of the responsibility of schools have changed dramatically in recent years in response to changes in society and the family (Elkind, 1995). Welcome or not, these changes are a reality.

Along with this shifting paradigm regarding family involvement have come encouraging new beliefs regarding parents and other family members. Examples of these beliefs are:

- All families have strengths.
- Parents can learn new techniques.
- Parents have important perspectives about their children.
- Most families care about their children.
- Most teachers and administrators want to involve families.
- Most students, at all levels, want their families to be more knowledgeable partners about schooling.
- Cultural differences are both valid and valuable.
- Many family forms exist and are legitimate. (Epstein, 1995; Liontos, 1992)

As these new beliefs become more widespread, it is increasingly likely that the quantity and quality of school/family/community partnerships will increase, with high school students, their families, and their communities reaping the benefits of these efforts.

The transformations represented in the emerging definitions of effective family and community involvement are not always welcomed by educators and others in the community. However, these changes have led to reconsideration of the proper role of parents, families, community members, and others in collaborative partnerships with high schools. It should be remembered, however, that some people continue to long for the "good old days" as they become caught up in the nostalgia trap of remembering things the way they wish they had been rather than the way they really were (Coontz, 1992, 1995). Special efforts to involve these persons in the planning and implementation of successful school/community partnerships are crucial. Frequently, they become supporters and valuable participants in partnership activities as they learn more about the efforts of high schools to provide quality schooling for adolescents.

MEANINGFUL PARTNERSHIP ROLES FOR FAMILY AND COMMUNITY

Effective ways to strengthen family and community involvement have been widely identified in the literature (Comer, Haynes, Joyner, & Ben-Avie, 1996; Epstein & Conners, 1992; Fredericks & Rasinski, 1990; Jackson & Cooper, 1992; Schurr, 1992; Thousand, Villa, & Nevin, 1998). Family members have been discussed by Hester (1989) in terms of their roles as teachers, supporters of activities, learners, and advocates, and Epstein (1995) has developed a framework of six types of partnership involvement, which include parenting, communicating, volunteering, learning at home, decision making, and collaborating with community. These and other frameworks are valuable resources for those seeking a better understanding of successful collaborative partnerships involving families, community members, educators, students, and other stakeholders.

NATIONAL STANDARDS FOR PARENT/FAMILY INVOLVEMENT PROGRAMS

A valuable resource that provides guidance for those establishing new parent/family involvement programs or improving existing ones is provided by National Standards for Parent/Family Involvement Programs. These six standards, written by the National Parent Teachers Association (1997), are as follows:

- Communicating—Communication between home and school is regular, two-way, and meaningful.
- Parenting—Parenting skills are promoted and supported.
- Student learning—Parents play an integral role in assisting student learning.
- Volunteering—Parents are welcome in the school, and their support and assistance are sought.
- School decision making and advocacy—Parents are full partners in the decisions that affect children and families.
- Collaborating with community—Community resources are used to strengthen schools, families, and student learning.

These standards and their quality indicators are research-based and grounded in sound philosophy and practical experience. The purpose of these standards is to (1) promote meaningful parent and family participation; (2) raise awareness regarding the components of effective programs; and (3) provide guidelines for schools and other programs that serve children and families that wish to improve their programs. The standards are designed to be guidelines for leaders of institutions with programs serving parents and families. The research used in writing them is also included in the publication. The importance of these standards should not be overlooked by high schools as they work to improve the effectiveness and quality of parent/family involvement efforts.

BARRIERS TO SUCCESSFUL PARTNERSHIPS

Barriers likely to prevent partnerships from reaching their full potential must be identified so that strategies to remove them can be planned. These barriers can originate from beliefs, perceptions, and attitudes of teachers and other educators, and can include: (1) a lack of commitment to family involvement; (2) confusion about the proper role of educators; (3) concerns about territory and turf problems; (4) doubts about being able to work with at-risk parents; (5) low teacher expectations for at-risk children; (6) schools assuming passive roles and not making family members feel welcome; and (7) a focus on negative communications. Other barriers that are constructed by family members may include feelings of inadequacy, failure, and poor self-worth. The school may be viewed by some adults with suspicion or anger for a number of reasons, including their lack of success when they were students (Castro–Lewis, 1994; Jesse, 1995).

Barriers related to culture and language may also be present in high schools (Liontos, 1992). Minority family members may feel intimidated and awkward when interacting with educators, and may think that they have little to contribute to the education of their children. Special efforts must be made to invite minority families and community members to join partnership activities. This is especially important because research has shown that minority parents are less commonly invited to become involved in school activities (Chavkin, 1993). Effort to involve these hard-to-reach family members is time consuming and challenging. However, minority family members have as much to offer toward their children's educations as other families. Making the efforts necessary to involve them results in handsome payoffs when serious, long-term commitments are made (Castro-Lewis, 1994).

SUCCESSFUL STRATEGIES FOR OUTREACH ACTIVITIES AND PROGRAMS

At a time when schools have increasingly come under attack on many fronts, high school educators can ill afford to ignore the importance of meaningful partnerships with families and community members. Doing so places their schools, and public schooling itself, at risk. Educators at highly successful high schools do not assume that it is widely believed that schooling is so inherently valuable that it sells itself. If that were the case, all that would be needed is a means to deliver instruction and the proper place and time to do so (Haas, 1996). Educators at successful high schools avoid the naivete of this view and are aggressive in establishing authentic partnerships that build trust, support, and loyalty for their schools. They engage in long-term efforts to welcome partners outside their school not just as allies, but as full partners. Examples of outreach strategies follow.

Involving Partners in Decision-Making Roles

A major recommendation in *Breaking Ranks* (1996, p. 32) directly addresses the importance of meaningful roles in decision-making for parents and other family members. The information provided by the successful high schools featured in this book confirms the importance of this shared decision making. These schools ensure that participation in decision making is a reality. Programs and practices implemented at these high schools demonstrate an understanding that students, families, community members, and others more readily commit themselves to schools that offer them authentic opportunities for engagement.

Site-based councils serve as an example of ways to establish and maintain successful school/family/community partnerships. They allow principals to work closely with stakeholders toward making schools effective organizations for student learning. These councils can carry out important functions such as determining educational needs and priorities, setting goals, and making budget recommendations. Participation on these councils demonstrates to all concerned that their high school sincerely welcomes them to become full partners in the educational process. Membership typically includes students, family members, community members without children in school, public officials, and representatives from business and industry (*Breaking Ranks,* 1996).

Many opportunities are provided for participation on site-based councils, evaluation groups, and other policymaking bodies at successful high schools featured in this book. Care has also been taken at these high schools to include representation and participation from those who are most directly affected by the high school experience—students and teachers. Inclusion of teachers and other educational personnel on these policymaking groups provides them with opportunities to get to know and work with family and community members, and demonstrates a recognition that their participation leads to increased dedication and intensified efforts to improve the quality of teaching and learning. Students are also often included because they have a vested interest in the decisions made. They need to know that they have some control over their own destiny (*Breaking Ranks,* 1996).

Successful high schools use various governance structures to involve family and community members through service on site-based committees. For example, Copperas Cove High School in Copperas Cove, Texas, is governed through shared leadership, with the principal acting as a facilitator to determine administrative policies. The Copperas Cove Board of Directors consists of eight educators, two students, and two patrons (Figure 8.1). Issues addressed by this board vary in response to needs that emerge. Members of the board discuss and respond to important issues and concerns (e.g., tutorial policies, memorial program for deceased employees, elimination of lunch duty for teachers) brought to them by staff, administrators, community members, students, and other stakeholders. Administrative policies are developed, presented for adoption, implemented, and monitored either by cross-functional task forces or by traditional departments. The task forces are made up of educators, students, and patrons, and are led by a non-administrator or counselor. Each department has a patron advisory group.

The Copperas Cove shared-leadership method of school governance is built around the concept that the most damaging error that educational leaders historically have made is failing to use the innovative abilities of the educational staff, students, and patrons. Within this system of governance, the principal becomes a leader of other leaders and the head learner in a community of scholars. Quality education through systemic change is the ultimate goal, with problem solving through reflection, risk taking, and collaboration becoming the tenets of a culture of growth.

Other high schools contributing information for this book described similar governance plans, as well as councils that focus more specifically on special areas

FIGURE 8.1   Copperas Cove High School Leadership and Governance

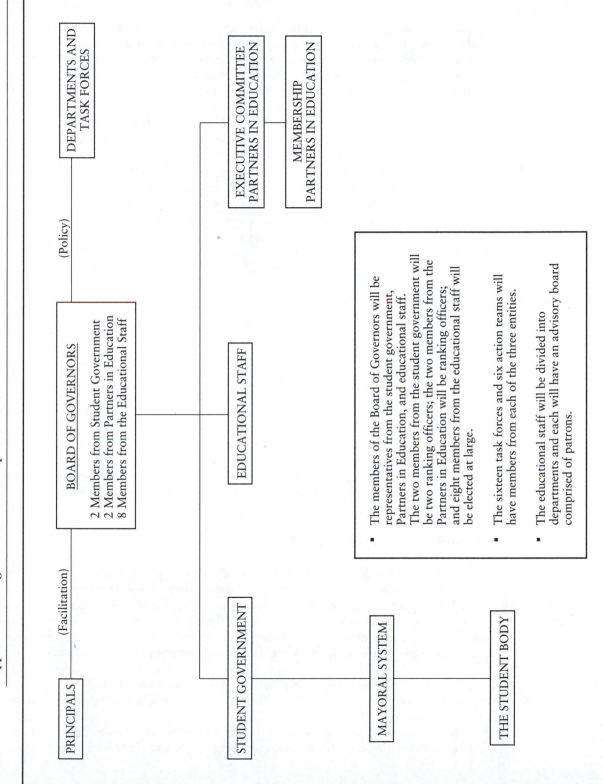

PRINCIPALS

(Facilitation)

(Policy)

DEPARTMENTS AND TASK FORCES

BOARD OF GOVERNORS

2 Members from Student Government
2 Members from Partners in Education
8 Members from the Educational Staff

EXECUTIVE COMMITTEE PARTNERS IN EDUCATION

MEMBERSHIP PARTNERS IN EDUCATION

EDUCATIONAL STAFF

STUDENT GOVERNMENT

MAYORAL SYSTEM

THE STUDENT BODY

- The members of the Board of Governors will be representatives from the student government, Partners in Education, and educational staff. The two members from the student government will be two ranking officers; the two members from the Partners in Education will be ranking officers; and eight members from the educational staff will be elected at large.

- The sixteen task forces and six action teams will have members from each of the three entities.

- The educational staff will be divided into departments and each will have an advisory board comprised of patrons.

(e.g., business councils and bilingual advisory councils). Fairdale High School in Fairdale, Kentucky, operates through a site-based council consisting of eight teachers, two non-parents, four students, one classified staff representative, one University of Louisville representative, one ex-officio Teenage Parent Program representative, and the principal. All policies and plans are approved, supported, and evaluated by this council.

Parents at Maritime and Science Technology School (MAST) Academy in the Dade County School District in Miami, Florida, are provided many opportunities to become involved in virtually all phases of the school's operation. They participate as voting members of the Board of Directors, sit on department committees, and serve on the School Advisory Council. The Parent Teacher Student Association is a large, active group that targets different areas of the school for action each year. Participation in governance and other decision-making activities has become a part of the culture at this innovative high school.

Duncan U. Fletcher High School in Jacksonville, Florida, has established a Business Advisory Council that meets periodically to provide input on key issues, including local language proficiency needs and perceived business trends. This council provides speakers, participates in career fairs, operates interview-skills workshops, and provides job shadowing experiences and other student internships. Through contacts facilitated by this advisory council, students learn about businesses and their need for employees proficient in a second language.

The decision-making board at Roosevelt High School in Fresno, California, consists of representatives from every major entity at the school, including four parent groups—Bilingual Advisory Council, Boosters Clubs, Volunteer Partnership Council, and the School Site Council. The Bilingual Advisory Council is made up of five groups of parents—African American, Hmong, Khmer, Lao, and Spanish. This council addresses issues that affect students and family members from homes where languages other than English are spoken. Special meetings are held at which parental involvement in school-related activities is strongly encouraged and facilitated. These and other special boards, councils, committees, and task forces are typical of those found in highly successful high schools.

Establishing Parent/Family Resource Centers

Many successful high schools have established parent resource centers to support the efforts of family and community members. These resource centers, often created in a spare classroom or a corner of the school library, provide family members a "place of their own" to serve as a base for activities. These centers not only show that family and community members are truly welcome at the school, but also serve many other valuable purposes. Some examples of these purposes include provision of:

- A meeting place for parent/family member groups and workshops
- An informal location for individual parent-teacher or parent-principal discussions
- Lounges and waiting rooms for family members in school on other business
- A welcoming environment for recruiting tutors and classroom volunteers

■ Opportunities to provide information and guidance about higher education opportunities, cultural and community services, and agencies to help families (*Reaching All Families: Creating Family-Friendly Schools,* 1996)

Establishment of a parent-visitation office is one of many efforts made at Lubbock High School in Lubbock, Texas, to encourage the involvement and support of family and community members. This office is a place where parents and other family members work on school projects, store materials, and hold conferences and meetings. This work space enhances the many other comprehensive efforts made at Lubbock High School to encourage meaningful parent involvement. Family members are regularly invited to participate in school activities and serve as resources for instruction (e.g., guest speakers, substitute teachers, clerical duties). Volunteers typically contribute over 10,000 hours of time per school year and make significant contributions to the many successes of this school.

Utilizing Home–School Coordinators

Some high schools have established the practice of utilizing home–school coordinators. These coordinators, sometimes called parent liaisons, can focus exclusively on developing family involvement programs without adding to the workload of teachers and other educators. Activities of these coordinators typically include establishing and coordinating parent clubs, helping to build parenting skills, and developing trust between families and schools. They establish personal contacts with family and community members, such as immigrants who are sometimes difficult to reach through traditional means (Goodson, Swartz, & Millsap, 1991; *Strong Families, Strong Schools,* 1994).

In some high schools, an important duty of the home school coordinator is the coordination of parent liaison programs. These liaisons are community members who work closely with teachers, administrators, and family members to promote high-quality involvement in partnerships that improve teaching and learning. Liasons often serve as primary contacts who respond to the needs and concerns of parents and families. They also typically perform other functions such as: (1) coordination of outreach efforts to traditionally nonparticipating families; (2) discussion of recommended home learning activities; (3) creating and publishing newsletters; and (4) conducting school tours and orientation sessions for new families (*Reaching All Families,* 1996).

Improving the Quality of Home Learning Activities

An important responsibility of schools is the provision of "information and ideas to families about how to help students at home with homework and other curriculum-related activities, decisions, and planning" (Epstein, 1995. p. 6). In other schools, traditional homework assignments are being converted into more interactive ones involving family members. Some high schools hold workshops for parents and their children that teach them about stimulating activities that can be used to learn at home. Resource people from the community (e.g., family members, school personnel, volunteers from community organizations) are sometimes used to conduct these workshops. Helping family members understand the importance of home-learning activities and teaching them how to participate in them successfully is a key to student success. Research has shown that the majority of parents who participate in these kinds of workshops engage in more learning activities at home with their children (Fruchter, Galleta, & White, 1992).

Parent home-learning networks can also be used to help organize parent networks that supervise afternoon and evening home-learning activities. These sessions are particularly useful for single or working parent and are typically organized so that volunteer parents agree to host a group of students on a rotating basis and to provide them with a supervised and quiet place to study and work on home-learning activities. These networks require careful coordination that might be provided by a parent liaison, volunteer, or teacher with released time from other instructional responsibilities (*Reaching All Families*, 1996). Additional examples of positive actions that can strengthen learning include providing: (1) information on skills required in specific subjects; (2) information on home learning policies; (3) calendars with activities for parents and students to use at home; (4) family mathematics, science, and other subject activity nights; and (5) summer learning packages (Epstein, 1995).

Many successful high schools are making special efforts to help parents better understand the purposes of home learning activities, and to provide parents with suggestions about ways to help their children with homework. This is being accomplished in a variety of ways (e.g., conferences, workshops, electronic avenues). For example, Cambridge Rindge and Latin School in Cambridge, Massachusetts, has produced a colorful brochure titled *Homework: The Parents' Role* that is widely distributed to family members. It answers questions such as: "Why is homework necessary?" and "What is the role of parents in relation to daily homework assignments?" Resources include information on obtaining help with specific study techniques, and names of specific teachers who can provide further assistance are also included. The use of brochures and other communication procedures are examples of efforts made by successful high schools to communicate more effectively with family members while assisting them in the complex task of parenting.

Conducting Home Visits

In an effort to demonstrate to the public the sincere desire to welcome all family members as partners in the education of their children, some high schools have initiated home visit programs. Home visits allow teachers to show sincere interest in their students' families and to better understand them by seeing them in their home environment. Teachers who have made home visits say they build stronger relationships with parents and their children and improve attendance and achievement.

Careful planning is essential to a home visit program. Administrators and teachers should agree to participate in the program and be involved in planning it. For example, teacher schedules will need to be adjusted to provide time for these visits. It is highly recommended that teachers visit homes of students in their classes. When this is not possible, homes that have requested visits are usually given priority. All families receive letters explaining the desire to make informal visits to students' homes. These letters are carefully worded so that parents understand the purpose of the visits, and include forms that allow parents to accept or decline the visit (*Reaching All Families,* 1996).

Home visits are made to parents who have children attending Garfield Alternative Education Center in Middletown City, Ohio. This charter school serves 200 at-risk students in grades nine through twelve. Because of the special needs of the students, the 16 faculty members and special personnel try to establish a supportive environment that allows students to experience personal growth. There is a deliberate plan at Garfield to engage parents/custodians on their own turf, with home visits being made at unusually high rates. Before students enter the school, they have been visited at home at least one time by a staff member. Additionally, entering students and their parents/custodians have an interview with the building principal and the school psychologist before attending Garfield. Although this interviewing process is important, staff members believe that the home visits throughout the school year truly support the positive image they wish to project. Staff members also go to the homes to pick up students for proficiency testing days and pick them up if they miss the bus. Vocational teachers, as a part of their state program requirements, visit homes regularly to talk about matters of concern with students and their parents/custodians. Home visit participants have found that moving out of the school building and not someone else's territory changes the power relationships and promotes cooperation and mutual respect.

Sponsoring and Coordinating Family and Community Education Programs

Family education programs can include activities, workshops, and materials that provide parents with skills and experiences to help them be successful. A popular topic at these workshops is understanding, supporting, and parenting adolescents. As is the case with other important efforts, careful planning and implementation is essential. Successful high schools typically assess parent needs in several ways (e.g., surveys, home visits, parent conferences) and take advantage of the great wealth of resources available in all communities to strengthen these outreach efforts. Continuing evaluation is also an important aspect of these programs (*Reaching All Families,* 1996).

Family and community education efforts are an important function of successful high schools. These outreach programs, however, require significant efforts to be successful. Some steps that should be included to help ensure the success of these programs include: (1) comprehensive efforts to assess the needs of the community are made; (2) resources are located; (3) participants are recruited; (4) support services are provided; and (5) provision for assessment and evaluation of the courses are included (*Reaching All Families,* 1996). When these steps are taken, success is much more likely.

Building Partnership Alliances

Establishing alliances that allow for and promote beneficial collaborative efforts is more than rhetoric at successful high schools. In a section of *Breaking Ranks* titled

"Relationships: Reaching Out to Form Alliances in Behalf of Students," (p. 89) it is recommended that a high school: (1) regard itself as a community in which members of the staff collaborate to develop and implement the school's learning goals; (2) engage students' families as partners in the students' education; (3) in conjunction with agencies in the community, help coordinate the delivery of health and social services for youth; (4) develop political and financial relationships in the community to foster ongoing support for educational programs and policies; (5) foster productive business partnerships that support and supplement educational programs; (6) form partnerships with agencies for youths that support and supplement the regular programs of the school; and (7) require each student to participate in a service program in the community or in the school itself that has educational value. The nature of programs and practices in the high schools participating in this project confirmed the importance of these recommendations.

Coordinating Health and Social Services

High schools cannot possibly provide sufficient staff and facilities to meet all the health and social needs of their students. However, they can coordinate these services. Otherwise many students and their families will never be aware of the assistance available, or will lack the knowledge to deal with the bureaucratic processes that are required to receive this assistance. High schools can and should provide the assistance needed to help families break down barriers to needed health and social services.

At many high schools providing information for this book, a broad range of services that help equip young people for learning, such as infant and child care, public housing information, and health care, are coordinated. The need for such health and social services is often inseparable from the support that students require for successful academic achievement. School-based health clinics that provide a wide range of health services, and national projects such as the Cities in Schools Program, surround students with teachers, mentors, social workers, health care providers, and employment counselors who provide them with help that will enable them to successfully complete high school and prepare them for life after they leave school (*Breaking Ranks*, 1996).

Facilitating and brokering roles for provision of health and social service is more difficult in districts where potential partners are not as readily available. Special efforts may be required, especially in economically deprived and rural locales. In the long run, the extra efforts required to make these services available also make economic sense. Every obstacle removed from the path of adolescents as they work toward success in school increases their chances of becoming contributing members of society.

Educators at Fairdale High School Magnet Career Academy in Louisville, Kentucky, working collaboratively with the Jefferson County Health Department, the University of Louisville Medical School Division of Family Practice and Community Health, and the Jefferson County Board of Education, have organized a comprehensive health care center. High-quality health care for students is available during school hours, which is of great convenience to students and their parents. The project is designed to help students: (1) get early detection and treatment of illness; (2) communicate with parents about health and personal concerns; (3) use health services sensibly; (4) choose health behaviors that are good for them; and (5) become worry-free learners. Among the services are health education/disease prevention, nutrition counseling, physical examinations, health screenings, and immunizations.

Students are treated at the center for physical as well as mental health concerns by highly qualified doctors, nurses, social workers, and health educators. The predominant reason for student visits to the health care center is treatment of acute health problems. However, students also attend the center to receive assistance with health maintenance, mental health counseling, nutrition advice, health education, and care for chronic conditions. Health services are provided free of charge to students and their families.

The mission of the Juneau Teen Health Center at Juneau Douglas High School in Juneau, Alaska, is to improve the health of their students and to promote health awareness. Arrangements have been made through the center for the services of local health professionals who are experienced and interested in adolescent health. A nurse practitioner and public health nurse provide physical examinations, diagnosis, and treatment of minor health concerns. A health promoter works in classrooms on and off-campus to deliver consistent, culturally relevant information about the importance of staying healthy. There is also a mental health clinician who assesses a variety of psychological problems. Short-term counseling is provided and referrals are made for long-term treatment. The medical director at the center oversees the quality of clinical services and ensures that procedures and protocols are effectively handled. There is no fee for the services of the center.

Professional Development for Teachers and Other Personnel

Although teachers typically agree on the importance of increased parental involvement, they often report that they do not know how to accomplish this important task. For example, two thirds of the teachers in one survey indicated that they needed professional development focusing on how to work with parents effectively (Conners & Epstein, n.d.). Evidence is scarce that prospective teachers receive specialized knowledge, skills, and dispositions needed to work closely with families and other community members. Furthermore, schools and school systems seldom offer formal preparation focusing on working successfully with family members or on "understanding the varieties of modern family life" (Shartrand, Weiss, Kreider, & Lopez, 1997; *Strong Families, Strong Schools,* 1994, p. 17).

Teacher roles that are important to successful partnerships include those that are family-centered. Nurturing, supporting, guiding, evaluating, and decision making are examples of teacher roles that focus on family involvement (Swick, 1992). Family members and teachers can make important contributions to the success of partnerships through collaboration, planning, communicating, and evaluating. However, as noted previously, teachers and other educators may need high-quality inservice professional development to fulfill their roles successfully. Professional development that focuses on working with parents and other family members is a good investment that pays many dividends.

Integrating Community Service Programs Into the Curriculum

The health of our democracy depends on students gaining a sense of their connection to the larger community. One of the best ways to create such ties is through service learning. These experiences enable high school students to contribute their efforts to activities that are useful to the community, and help them reflect on what they learn from their participation (*Breaking Ranks,* 1996).

Educators planning service programs at successful high schools have clearly defined goals that provide them with opportunities to consider systematically a range of possible priorities and the relationship of those priorities to curriculum. They are also aware that the choices they make, as with other curricular choices, have political dimensions. For example, it is not assumed that all educators share the same vision and values. Educators understand that is important to the ultimate success of these programs that the different visions that drive the creation and implementation of service learning are carefully explored, and that the program implemented be continually evaluated and improved (Kahne & Westheimer, 1996).

Despite the widespread support of service programs, some critics object to the requirement that students participate in activities that society often considers voluntary. However, supporters of these programs note that high school students take many kinds of courses to obtain diplomas—courses in English, social studies, mathematics, and science. These mandates stem from a belief that particular courses have some intrinsic value. Service learning, too, they point out, has merit not simply as an act of altruism, "but a duty of free men and women whose freedom is itself wholly dependent on the assumption of political responsibilities" (*Breaking Ranks,* 1996; Wirthlin Group, 1995, p. 246). Whatever the political implications of service learning projects, they clearly have earned the support of a wide spectrum of high schools, including those contributing materials to this book. The following are examples of these efforts.

At Alice High School in Alice, Texas, all juniors and seniors are provided opportunities to serve their school and community through a community service class. A variety of opportunities are provided, including participation in a weekly news program broadcast to the entire school district, working with the parent involvement program, volunteering at the Boys and Girls Clubs, and assisting with the work of the Alice Counseling Center.

The School Without Walls in Rochester, New York, includes an extensive community service component in the curriculum that requires all students to contribute to the community and learn from their experiences. Figure 8.2 shows the application form used by students to contract for their community service experiences; Figure 8.3 is a partial listing of cooperating community services. This highly successful community service program contributes measurably to the vision of the school, which includes graduating students who are community participants and leaders who: (1) work and live cooperatively with others; (2) contribute to the community; (3) explore career opportunities; (4) make informed choices in using and sustaining the natural environment; (5) know and use community resources; and (6) can express and apply their values and rights. This innovative school, established in 1971,

Sample Community Service Contract   FIGURE 8.2

CONTRACT FOR COMMUNITY SERVICE

DATE _____

NAME OF STUDENT _____

NAME OF COMMUNITY SERVICE SUPERVISOR _____

NAME OF AGENCY OR BUSINESS _____

ADDRESS OF AGENCY/BUSINESS _____

PHONE NUMBER _____

DAY(S) STUDENT IS EXPECTED TO WORK _____

HOURS STUDENT IS EXPECTED TO WORK _____

REPRESENTATIVE TASKS EXPECTED OF STUDENT _____

_____

_____._____

SKILLS THE STUDENT WILL ACQUIRE _____

_____

_____

SIGNATURES OF AGREEMENT

_____
COMMUNITY SERVICE SUPERVISOR

_____
STUDENT

_____
SCHOOL WITHOUT WALLS ADVISOR

FOR ANSWERS TO QUESTIONS OR PROBLEMS PLEASE CALL THE STUDENT'S

ADVISOR _____ AT _____ .

FIGURE 8.3   **School Without Walls: Partial Listing of Community Service Sites**

Government and Municipal Services

Monroe County Department of Planning
Center for Environmental Conservation
Rochester Department of Community Planning
Monroe County Water Authority
Monroe County Parks Division
NYS Assemblyman Gary Proud's Office
Center for Governmental Research

Media

WHEC-TV Channel 10
Greater Rochester Cablevision
Portable Channel
WHAM
WROC-TV CHANNEL 8
WDKX Radio Station
Rochester Radio Reading Service
WCMF Radio Station

Human Services

Call-A-Friend
The Center for Youth Services
Eastside Community Center
Genesee Settlement House
Jewish Community Center
Puerto Rican Youth Development and Resource Center
St. Joseph's House of Hospitality
Threshold

Legal

Greater Upstate Law Project
Judicial Process Commission
Monroe County District Attorney's Office

Day Care

Twelve Corners Day Care Center
Park Avenue Day Care Center
Genesee Valley Day Care Center
Edgerton Day Care Center
ABC Day Care Center

Business

Business Mate Corporation
Dorschel Buick-Toyota, Inc.

School Without Walls: Partial Listing of Community Service Sites—cont'd   FIGURE 8.3

John Fayko, Architect
Lester Green Company
Hollink Honda and Suzuki
Al Pardi, Architect

Education

School #14
School #23
School #58
School Without Walls
Rochester City School District Administrative Offices
Holy Family School
Rochester Association for the United Nations
Rochester Museum and Science Center
Rochester Youth Hockey
The Strong Museum
Center for Educational Development

Medical and Health

St. Mary's Hospital
Holiday Health and Fitness Center
Leukemia Society of America
Red Cross
Al Sigel Center
Pinnacle Nursing Home
Rochester Friendly Home
Rochester General Hospital
Strong Memorial Hospital

Animal Care

Seneca Park Zoo
Pittsford Animal Hospital
Animal Control Center
Monroe County Humane Society, Lollipop Farm

Political Agencies

Green Peace
Monroe County Democratic Campaign Headquarters
Republican Campaign Headquarters

Arts and Theater

GEVA
Blackfriars

has an outstanding record of success and offers much encouragement to those who believe all adolescents can learn and can do so in a variety of environments.

All community service activities do not have to be based off the campus, because students can provide meaningful service on school campuses in many ways. For example, a recycling project at Armuchee High School in Rome, Georgia, has been very successful. The recycling program at Armuchee encourages wide participation and makes a significant contribution to the environment. This plan, which began as the vision of one teacher, demonstrates that each person is capable of making a difference in the school, community, state, and nation.

Money from the project is used to help improve the environment for students, staff, and community members. An outdoor student commons area, basketball court, and walking path have been added to the school grounds and are maintained through funds generated by the program. The success of the program has been recognized with many awards and much recognition in the media. More importantly, however, many opportunities are provided for large numbers of students to learn about the importance of individual and group efforts in accomplishing worthy goals that serve the common good.

An additional way students have been involved in service roles is through the provision of service by groups of students rather than by individuals (e.g., whole class community service, grade-level projects, student civic clubs). For example, the Social Service School, one of the schools-within-a-school at Crater High School in Central Point, Oregon, "adopts" students from a Headstart program. These students are taken to a senior citizen's center to celebrate holidays and engage in other activities that promote cross generational awareness and understanding for all three age groups—children, adolescents, and seniors. Students in this school meet in classes 4 days per week and participate in community service actions 1 day per week. While students are participating in these community-based activities, their teachers are preparing curriculum that helps them explore the human life span while building upon their service learning experiences.

Single special events can also be important to the goals of community involvement and community service. At East Hartford High School in East Hartford, Connecticut, students sponsor a Senior Citizens Prom. Over 250 senior citizens are entertained in a brightly decorated cafeteria. Students serve as waiters and waitresses, kitchen help, and dance partners. The senior citizens are served dinner and dance to an oldies band. Events like this not only lead to new understanding by the adolescents and seniors involved, but carry important messages about making special efforts to learn about others and contribute unselfishly to their happiness and welfare.

Building Positive Political and Financial Relationships

It is essential that positive and productive political and financial relationships are established and maintained by high schools. If beneficial long-term alliances are to be formed, political events that affect high schools cannot be left to chance. Educators from the high schools that were part of this project offered many examples of ways in which they cultivate opportunities to be politically active while advocating in ways that serve the best interests of all their students and their families. They understand the value of building board bases of support at many levels. They recognize, for example, that the majority of households in school districts do not have school-age children, and they work to gain the approval and support of the total community.

The kind of support needed is built on continuing efforts by school personnel to keep the public informed rather than using short-lived media campaigns before elections to increase support for school district bond issues. Further, they understand that developing a reservoir of goodwill with government representatives, elected officials, and philanthropies is essential as they compete with many other worthy recipients for support and funding. Positive, accurate messages are kept in public view at all times so that the interests of the schools do not get obscured or forgotten (Carroll & Carroll, 1994).

Establishing Productive Business Partnerships

Gaining the support of the business community is of great importance because of its powerful influence. This support is especially crucial because many businesspersons have an image of high schools as "underachieving" institutions. To help change these beliefs, high schools can provide businesses with many legitimate reasons why they are worthy of confidence and trust. High schools can constantly keep track of what businesspeople expect of employees, so that students can be appropriately prepared. It is also important that businesses take collaborative partnerships with high schools seriously and regard the partnerships as much more than public relations showcases (*Breaking Ranks*, 1996; United States Department of Education, 1995).

True partnerships with businesses require long-term commitments and involvement that the schools can count on as educators work hard to respond to the constructive criticism of employers. The involvement of businesses, which often begins with the adoption of an individual school, now tends to focus more directly on system reform. More and more companies are becoming actively engaged in reforming the entire system of education (*Breaking Ranks*, 1996; Gorman, 1995).

Educators can also gain a deeper understanding of the application of knowledge by participating in summer internships in business and industry. People from business and industry can reciprocally serve as visiting lecturers and visiting faculty members. Furthermore, now that business regards pre-collegiate education as a legitimate recipient of its philanthropy, high schools can identify projects and programs that merit the support of business (*Breaking Ranks*, 1996).

Many examples were given by schools providing information for this book regarding ways high schools and businesses can work collaboratively. Adult education classes can provide courses to meet specific needs of neighborhood businesses and their employees. Also, businesses can provide opportunities for students to participate in valuable experiences such as job shadowing, apprenticeships, work–study, and summer employment (*Breaking Ranks*, 1996).

Primary business partners for Bellaire High School in Bellaire, Texas, are valuable resources. They provide financial assistance, mentoring, scholarships, use of facilities for staff development, grants to teachers for continued education, speakers for Career Day, and resource materials for teachers. For example, one partner solved a parking problem that was blocking progress on career day by volunteering vans and drivers to provide a guest shuttle service from a church parking lot more than a mile from school. Another business partner has donated a satellite dish to the school, employs students, maintains a school/community bulletin board in its community-based stores, and provides food for student and/or faculty activities. Business partners also support a German Exchange program, the Houston Hispanic Forum–Career/Job Fair, and the Junior Achievement Program. Business consultants work with teams of students competing in the applied economics program, and the Teachers of Russian provide support for the Russian Exchange program. Many other partners, such as the Italy and American Association, contribute to the overall excellence of Bellaire High School. A survey distributed to the business community each year obtains their perceptions of the strengths and weaknesses of the school, and the results are used to plan curriculum and programs.

Without question, high schools need to demonstrate their connection to the community and discover ways to familiarize businesses with the accomplishments of students and teachers, while seeking their support and direct involvement in efforts to create even more successful high schools. Ways to effectively build business and community partnerships for learning identified by the United States Department of Educational Resources project are shown in Figure 8.4 (U. S. Department of Education, 1995):

Encouraging Leadership from All Partners

Breaking Ranks (1996, p. 75) recommends that "Each high school will establish a site council to work with the principal in reaching decisions to make the school an effective organization for student learning." This statement recognizes the importance of nourishing leadership attributes among students, family members, and others in the school community. Principals, teachers, and other educators in successful high schools nurture this leadership potential, which helps them provide greatly enhanced opportunities for teaching and learning. The leadership of students, for example, enriches a high school and provides valuable experience for the young people who assume leadership roles. Student leadership also adds credibility to the goals of reform. Students who have the opportunity to lead in high school gain experience that will serve them well (*Breaking Ranks*, 1996).

The likelihood of high schools enlisting the support of the community in the cause of reform grows to the extent that schools truly embrace members of the community as partners in the effort. This means that parents, neighborhood residents, and others in the community should have the chance to assume some of the responsibility and leadership for improving schools. The synergy unleashed by this openness enables high schools to achieve more of their goals. Educators should not have to labor in isolation. They should be able to feel that the community supports the aims and objectives of schools, particularly at a time when reform puts fresh demands on education (*Breaking Ranks,* 1996).

Developing Partnerships With Youth-Serving Agencies

Although high schools work with the same adolescents as youth-serving groups, they rarely collaborate with these agencies (e.g., Boys and Girls Clubs, church youth

Ways to Effectively Build Business and Community Partnerships for Learning   FIGURE 8.4
United States Department of Educational Resources Project

Everywhere today, home-school-work partnerships are promoting family
involvement in the education of children. Among the options, businesses can:

Create and promote policies that make it possible for employees to be involved

Time off for participation in school and child care activities
Time off for first day of school
Beginning and end of day flextime
Lunchtime flex
Work-at-home arrangements
Compressed work week
Part-time work
Job sharing

Support employee parents through worksite programs

Lunchtime parenting seminars
Parent support groups
Education and parenting newsletters
Family resource libraries
Worksite-based PTA
Literacy training
National parent-school partnership programs
Parent hotlines

Work to improve child care and schools through internal and community programs

On-site or consortium child care, or on-site satellite schools
Child care resource and referral services
Child care subsidies such as vouchers and discounts
Training, development, and accreditation for community child care providers
In-kind donations or pro bono consulting to schools and child care
School-employee partnerships and volunteer programs
Advocacy

Work with schools to help them better meet the needs of employed parents

Parent volunteer programs
Employee-friendly scheduling of school events
Improved parent-teacher communication through newsletters or voice mail
Interpreters for non–English-speaking parents
Translation of parent materials
Family resource centers in the schools

groups). Successful high schools cultivate these organizations as potential partners, promoting them to students and linking the school to programs sponsored by the various groups and agencies. This collaboration serves many worthy purposes, including demonstration of the connections between high schools and the community. Effective partnerships with youth organizations, among other benefits, may help adolescents avoid gang membership by offering them a sense of belonging for which many have unfulfilled yearnings (*Breaking Ranks,* 1996).

Promoting Collaboration Among Students and Staff Members

A major prerequisite for working successfully with family and community members is the existence of an internal school community whose staff members collaborate to help attain the learning goals of the school. The commonality of faculty interests holds much promise when they work together in a collegial manner. Authentic collaboration among educators leads to productive change and helps reduce the sense of isolation experienced by many educators. Teachers who share ideas and engage in continuing professional dialogue have greater capacity to enhance student learning and provide models that help students understand the value of cooperation (Anderson, 1995; *Breaking Ranks,* 1996).

The majority of schools providing information for this book have moved beyond traditional kinds of student roles toward involving students in ways that recognize that they are capable of helping make sound decisions that move beyond self-interest. With good adult modeling and guidance, participation of these youth can not only improve the end results of policymaking and other activities, but also provide abundant opportunities for students to find satisfaction and fulfillment in the process (*Breaking Ranks,* 1996).

Providing Opportunities for Informal School-Family Gatherings

The use of more formalized opportunities, such as open houses and parent–teacher conferences can be supplemented and strengthened by more informal gatherings that may encourage larger numbers of parents and other family members to participate. These gatherings might include meeting with individual teachers or groups of teachers, meeting with the principal, and neighborhood coffees (*Reaching All Families,* 1996). For example, neighborhood meetings are held by educators at Dixie High School in St. George, Utah. Invitations are sent to parents and other community members. These meetings are attended by at least two staff members and about 10 to 15 other participants. Meeting in small groups in neighborhoods has increased communication and improved public relations significantly.

At Mountlake Terrace High School in Mountlake Terrace, Washington, a Dessert With the Principal program has been established to provide family and community members opportunities to communicate with the principal in less formal atmospheres. These dessert meetings are held at least once each month. Messages are sent to parents indicating that the principal would like to be invited to their homes for an evening to talk about school. Once volunteers are identified, the school sends out letters of invitation. Dessert is brought by the principal with the volunteer parents providing beverages. The potentials of efforts such as these may seem limited because of the relatively small number of persons involved in each meeting. However, schools using these kinds of outreach efforts report that they are well worth the time and effort needed to ensure that they will operate with a minimum of difficulty.

At McMain High School in New Orleans, Louisiana, parents are encouraged to communicate with teachers in many ways. One example of efforts that clearly has carried the message that teachers are genuinely interested in working closely with parents and are interested in their children is the provision of home telephone numbers of teachers. Also, teachers call parents personally when their children miss school.

Special events, whether held in the community or on the school campus, can also provide more informal settings that foster improved communication and understanding. These activities can make significant contributions to the development of positive attitudes in family members, educators, and other key individuals. The Roosevelt Pyramid Multilingual Family School Conference that is held at Roosevelt High School in Fresno, California, is an example of such an event. This conference, typically attended by about 800 people, offers home workshops in five languages. Community information booths, child care, and international food and entertainment are part of this special event. Numerous public and private agencies have booths and disseminate information. Speakers have included Jaime Escalante of *Stand and Deliver* fame and Dr. Yang Dao, the first Hmong to earn a Doctor of Philosophy in the U.S. Over 50 workshops are offered on topics such as drug presentation, gang awareness, computers and technology, and college entrance. Carefully planned events such as this one carry powerful positive messages to family and community members and strengthen efforts of the high school on many fronts.

EFFECTIVE COMMUNICATION WITH FAMILIES, COMMUNITY, AND OTHER STAKEHOLDERS

A warm and welcoming environment is vital to the success of partnerships with families and other community members. Educators at successful high schools work at learning about the needs of family and community members. They know that they must do much more than simply wait for family members and others outside the school to become active partners in activities that enhance student learning. The importance of this involvement is substantiated by research that shows that when parents sense an inviting school climate, they emphasize nurturing and supporting behaviors in their interactions with teachers and increase their levels of participation in school activities (Comer & Hayes, 1991).

There are numerous ways, many of which are discussed in this chapter, to let family and community members know that they are truly welcome at school and that their involvement and contributions are valued rather than trivialized. Some examples, followed by the name of the school submitting information about each item, follow:

- Coffeehouse Program—Provides weekend activities with a safe place for creative expression. This program is run totally by parents and other volunteers. (Champlain Valley Union High School, Hinesburg, Vermont)
- School Information Center—Designed to greet and direct school guests and visitors and to answer the telephone. The center, run by parent volunteers, makes the school more user-friendly and efficient, and releases secretaries from some duties so that they can concentrate on assisting students and teachers. (Bellaire High School, Bellaire, Texas)
- Honors Desserts—Demonstrates appreciation for agencies involved in serving students. (Crater High School, Central Point, Oregon)
- Close Up for New Americans—A year-round program for students who have recently immigrated to the United States. This program provides new Americans with a better understanding of government and the role individuals play in a democracy. Academic study, educational travel, and community service experiences are included in the program. (Del Valle High School, El Paso, Texas)
- Important Notices Mailed to Homes—Helps ensure that information needed by family members really reaches them. (Lubbock High School, Lubbock, Texas)
- Academic Symposium Program—Provides students opportunities to attend, facilitate, or conduct conference-style sessions on a wide array of topics. Some sessions are hosted by faculty and community experts who are knowledgeable on specific topics. (Marine and Science Technology High School, Miami, Florida)
- Congratulation Letters—Sent to parents congratulating them when their children earn awards or are inducted into the school hall of fame. Student accomplishments are also published in the district newsletter. (Metro High School, Cedar Rapids, Iowa)
- Home Language Parent Councils—Addresses the concerns and needs of second-language parents and students. Councils have been established: Hmong, Khmer, Lao, Spanish, and Vietnamese. (Roosevelt High School, Fresno, California)
- Parent and Student Switch (PASS)—Parents and students switch roles for a day or half a day. (Troy High School, Troy, Ohio)

Marketing the High School

It can no longer be assumed that high schools will automatically receive widespread support. Reasons for this phenomenon include: (1) there are now fewer adults with school-age children; (2) the image of public education has gotten worse while the cost has increased; and (3) the media has depicted American education as disappointing and inferior to the education systems of other industrialized nations (Carroll & Carroll, 1994; Postman, 1995). Although much of the negative image perpetuated in the media and elsewhere is unjustified, it should be remembered that perceptions are realities until they are changed. This situation has caused many high schools to realize that it is necessary to market their schools so that the public will have more accurate information upon which to base their beliefs.

Marketing images presented by successful high schools are accurate, positive, and compelling. The positive images of these schools are widely communicated and heavily advertised to educate the public and to correct misconceptions. Highly effective marketing efforts are a part of the normal activities of the school culture and are a function of every member of the school community. Of course, the ultimate success of these activities depends on the quality of communication practiced by all concerned. Many of the practices that lead to high levels of success in these marketing efforts include common sense knowledge such as wording communication in plain language that people outside the education profession readily understand, and developing positive, continuing relationships with representatives from the media (Haas, 1996). It should not be assumed, however, that all faculty and staff know how to present positive and accurate images of the school. Specific professional development activities should be conducted on a regular basis to help all concerned be successful in the image they present regarding the school (Carroll & Carroll, 1994).

High schools providing materials for this book have recognized the importance of "marketing—the creation of a positive school image that clearly and accurately conveys the school's purposes and product, and that stimulates a demand for school services" (Hass, 1996, p. 2). Examples provided throughout this chapter offer models for consideration. Many of these schools use colorful, well-designed brochures and other printed materials to provide information to parents, community members, and others who play important roles that help determine the quality of teaching and learning in high schools.

Successful high schools target potential students and their parents in their marketing efforts. Information sessions are held in the community, special mailings are sent, announcements are made on radio and televisions stations, and other means of communicating information about schools are used. These activities are typically more pronounced in districts where magnet schools, charter schools, and other schooling options are widely available. Technology (e.g., Internet, electronic mail, video tapes) also provides many opportunities to present information to the public. Mid Peninsula High School in Palo Alto, California, for example, has produced an outstanding video that describes their school.

Utilizing Technology to Strengthen Partnerships

The use of technology (e.g., Internet, electronic mail, faxes, automatic calling software) for communicating with families, community members, and other stakeholders offers major advantages. As the number of families with access to the Internet grows rapidly, excellent opportunities to make current information available emerge. Additionally, several aspects of the Internet now focus on families and can serve as a valuable resource to them while strengthening the efforts of the high school. Many families who do not have computers in their homes have access to the internet through locations such as their workplaces and public libraries. In districts where access is likely to be problematic for most, special projects at schools can include innovative ways to provide such access and to help family and community members learn how to use the available technology. These efforts benefit students and their families in ways that extend beyond the purpose of building school/community partnerships (e.g., National Parent Information Network).

Other, more accessible technologies should not be overlooked. For example, the use of audio and video tapes are alternatives to written messages at some high schools. This has many advantages, including provision for offering these resources in languages other than English. These tapes can improve communication and include those family and community members who are unlikely to participate in person at the school site.

Home pages are excellent ways for high schools to communicate information to their constituencies. Mountlake Terrace High School in Mountlake, Washington, uses a homepage that provides a wealth of useful information (e.g., daily bulletins, newsletters, newspapers, school calendars, letters, notices). With dramatic increases in access to and use of the Internet, it seems only logical that all high schools would develop home page sites and find new and innovative ways to strengthen the school program while increasing family and community involvement.

BUILDING STRONG PARTNERSHIPS

If high schools are to truly reinvent themselves to become more effective in serving students and their families, partnerships and public engagement must become more than buzz words. Crucial efforts to make family members and other stakeholders welcome and valued largely determine the levels of success of school-home-community partnerships. In highly successful partnerships, all sectors of the community are involved in careful and personal ways that permit and promote authentic engagement. The suggestions of these participants are taken seriously rather than being dismissed as uninformed and meddlesome. Carefully planned public dialogues are held at these high schools to engage the corporate community and people from neighborhoods, churches, and agencies serving youth so that common ground can be established. Mobilizing the public and sustaining support for high schools is viewed as an attainable goal and includes efforts to close the gap between what school experts and family members know (Cortes, 1995; Dilley, 1995).

It is also clear that educators are not solely responsible for creating highly successful school-home-community partnerships The American public needs to become engaged constructively in education. Successful high schools recognize this and invite participation on many levels from all citizens. They do not simply wait for volunteers to step forward. They work hard at making their schools inviting places where all people are valued and given opportunities to make meaningful contributions.

Representatives from these high schools, in collaboration with their partners, work to build trust and support for reform. They help all involved understand that reform is not a quick fix, but is instead a long-term process requiring sustained effort. Their high schools are organized and managed in ways that provide opportunities for people of different backgrounds to connect with one another, share information, debate, deliberate, and make recommendations. These opportunities allow participants to transcend their private lives and form public relationships that promote trust and consensus. In these partnerships, a "rule driven, hierarchical, command-and-control mentality has given way to a more collaborative atmosphere" (Cortes, 1995, p. 2).

CONCLUDING REMARKS

Successfully rearing and educating the youth of our nation requires cooperation from all stakeholders. However, the difficulty involved with this task does not justify being satisfied with high schools that do not serve all students, families, and communities well. As demonstrated at high schools contributing materials for this book, strong partnerships that include mutual respect, hard work, and long-term efforts pay off in many ways. The results of these collaborations are not always immediately evident, and at times may appear trivial compared with some of the other responsibilities involved in education. However, the long-term impact on the lives of those involved is circumscribed only by a limited vision of what is possible.

One need only consider the success of the students, educators, and community members of Rothsay School in Rothsay, Minnesota, to comprehend the potential of collaboration. The 260 students at that small rural school have taken over the operation of the town's last grocery store and lumberyard, which would otherwise have closed and left the citizens without their services. Projects such as these help us better understand the power that adolescents have, when assisted and encouraged by adults, to make significant contributions to their communities.

The time is long past, if indeed it ever existed, when high schools could operate effectively in isolation from, and with the blind trust of, the public. Carefully planned partnerships in which all participants become allies and full partners in education can help ensure that all young people attending high school will be provided with opportunities to gain the essential knowledge, skills, and dispositions needed to be productive citizens in this democratic nation.

SUMMARY

Recognition is growing regarding the importance of engaging family and community members in school reform. Although high schools have been slow to realize the importance of this engagement, highly successful high schools are making efforts to better utilize the rich resources the community can provide. They are increasingly capitalizing upon the interest of family members, teachers, administrators, representatives from the business community, and others for developing stronger home–school collaborations. These initiatives are emerging, at least in part, because of increased understanding that partnerships are desirable and necessary if high schools are to reach their full potential and serve all their students effectively.

There are many successful strategies for outreach activities and programs. Educators at successful high schools, including those featured in this book, understand that aggressive efforts must be made to establish authentic partnerships that build trust, support, and loyalty for their schools. They engage in long-term, comprehensive efforts to welcome people outside their schools as full partners. Some examples of outreach activities that are appropriate include: (1) involving partners in decision-making roles; (2) establishing parent/family resource centers; (3) utilizing home school coordinators; (4) improving the quality of home learning activities; (5) providing opportunities for informal school–family gatherings; (6) sponsoring and coordinating family and community education programs; (7) building partnership alliances; and (8) coordinating health and social services.

Building positive political and financial relationships is important to the development of productive business relationships and the establishment of opportunities to be politically active. Establishing effective communication with families, communities, and other stakeholders is also essential. Several examples of ways successful high schools can let family and community members know that they are welcome and that their contributions are valued were presented in this chapter.

CONNECTIONS TO OTHER CHAPTERS

The topics addressed in this chapter relate closely to the content found in other chapters because high levels of understanding and support among family and community members are essential to the success of all reform efforts.

ACTION STEPS

1. This chapter includes several examples of strategies used at successful high schools to encourage authentic involvement of family and community members in school affairs. Contact educators at a high school in your area and find out what strategies they use to involve family and community members in their schools. Prepare a brief written report about what you learn.

2. Interview members of two different families that have children enrolled in high school. Select families that are as representative as possible of the diversity in the schools. Prepare a set of questions to help you and your classmates better understand parents' perceptions of high schools. This same procedure can be used with community members who are not parents of high school students. Share what you learn in class.

3. Investigate the community service activities/programs at high schools in your community. Interview administrators, teachers, and students involved in the activities/programs to learn more about them. For example: What is the nature of these activities/programs (e.g., goals and objectives, participants, scheduling arrangements). Is participation voluntary? What kind of support has been received

from family and community members? Share what you learn with your classmates.

4. Explore the nature of business partnerships at a high school of your choice. Prepare a list of interview questions for selected educators at the school and for a representative of at least one of the school's business partners. Your questions should address factors such as the rationale for the partnership, related activities, and any other area that might help you and your classmates better understand these kinds of relationships.

DISCUSSION QUESTIONS

1. Why do you think the literature on high school reform places so much emphasis on the importance of engaging family and community members in schools? What barriers to this involvement will have to be overcome to make authentic engagement a reality?

2. The authors of this chapter include a discussion of "new beliefs" regarding parents and other family members. Using the list provided and other resources, discuss these new beliefs and their implications for working with family members.

3. What are some ways that the barriers to successful partnerships addressed in this chapter might be overcome?

4. Several examples of ways high school educators can communicate effectively with family and community members, as well as with other stakeholders, are included in this chapter. Using your own experience and knowledge, what are some additional ways to increase effective communication among these individuals and groups? What special roles do teachers play in this communication?

REFERENCES

Anderson, R. D. (1995). Curriculum reform: Dilemmas and promise. *Phi Delta Kappan, 77(1)*, 33–36.

Annenberg Institute on Public Engagement for Public Education (1998). *Reasons for hope: Voices for change.* Providence, RI: Author.

Brandt, R. (1998). Listen first. *Educational Leadership, 55(8)*, 25–30.

Breaking ranks: Changing an American institution, A report of the National Association of Secondary School Principals in partnership with the Carnegie Foundation for the Advancement of Teaching (1996). Reston, VA: National Association of Secondary School Principals.

Carroll, S. R., & Carroll D. (1994). *How smart schools get and keep community support.* Bloomington, IN: National Educational Service.

Castro-Lewis, M. (October 5, 1994). A better life for their children, *Education Week on the Web,* 1–2.

Cavarretta, J. (1998). Parents are a school's best friend. *Educational Leadership, 55 (8),* 12–15.

Cawelti, H. (1997). *Effects of high school restructuring: Ten schools at work.* Arlington, VA: Educational Research Service.

Chavkin, N. F. (1993). *Families and schools in a pluralistic society.* Albany, NY: State University of New York Press.

Chavkin, N. F., & Williams, D. L. (1987). Enhancing parent involvement: Guidelines for access to an important resource for school administrators. *Education and Urban Society, 19,* 164–184.

Conners, L., & Epstein, J. (n. D.). *Taking stock: Views of teachers, parents, and students on school, family, and community partnerships, Report 25.* Baltimore, Maryland: Center on Families, Communities, Schools, and Children's Learning, John Hopkins University.

Coontz, S. (1995). The American family and the nostalgia trap. *Phi Delta Kappan, 76 (7),* K1–K20.

Coontz, S. (1992). *The way we never were: American families and the nostalgia trap.* New York: Harper Collins.

Comer, J. P., & Hayes, M. (1991). Parent involvement in schools: An ecological approach. *Elementary School Journal, 91,* 271–278.

Comer, J. P., Haynes, N. M., Joyner, E. T., & Ben-Avie M. (1996). *Rallying the whole village: The Comer process for reforming education.* New York: Teachers College Press.

Cortes, E. (November 22, 1996). Making the public the leaders in education reform. *Education Week on the Web,* 1–3.

Coulombe, G. (1995). Parental involvement. A key to successful schools. *NASSP Bulletin, 79 (567),* 71–75.

Danzberger, J., Bodinger-deUriarte, C, & Clark, M. (1996). *A guide to promising practices in educational partnerships.* Washington, DC: United States Department of Education.

Davies, D. (1991). Schools reaching out: Family, school, and community partnerships for student success. *Phi Delta Kappan, 72 (376–382).*

de Kanter, A., Ginsburg, A. L., & Milne, A. M. (1987). *Parent involvement strategies: A new emphasis on traditional parent roles.* Washington, DC: U. S. Department of Education.

Dilley, B. (November 22, 1995). Building a broad constituency for change. *Education Week on the Web,* 1–3.

Elkind, D. (1995). School and family in the postmodern world. *Phi Delta Kappan, 77 (1),* 8–14.

Epstein, J. L. (1991). Effects on student achievement of teacher practices of parent involvement. In S. Silvern (Ed.), *Advances in reading/language research, Vol. 5, Literacy through family, community, and school interaction.* Greenwich, CT: JAI Press.

Epstein, J. L. (1995). School/family/community partnerships: Caring for children we share. *Phi Delta Kappan, 76 (9),* 701–712.

Epstein, J. L., & Conners, L. J. (1992). School and family partnerships. *NASSP Practitioner: or the On-line administrator,* National Association of Secondary School Principals.

Finney, P. (May, 17, 1993). The PTA/Newsweek national education survey. *Newsweek.*

Fredericks, A. D., & Rasinski, T. V. (1990). Working with parents: Involving the uninvolved—how to. *The Reading Teacher, 43 (6),* 424–425.

Fructher, N., Galletta, A., & White, J. L. (1992). *New directions in parent involvement.* New York: Academy for Educational Development.

Goodson, B. D., Swartz, J. P., & Millsap, M. A. (1991). *Working with families: Promising programs to help parents support young children's learning.* Cambridge, MA: Abt Associates.

Gorman, J. T. (June 21, 1995). Harsh reality at graduation season. *Education Week, 60.*

Hass, J. (1996). Countering bad facts attacks: Correcting public misperceptions of public schools. *NASSP Practitioner, 23 (2),* 1–6.

Henderson, A. T., & Berla, N. (1994). *A new generation of evidence: The family is critical to student achievement.* Washington, DC: National Committee for Citizens in Education.

Hester, H. (1989). Start at home to improve home-school relations. *NASSP Bulletin, 73 (513),* 23-27.

Jackson, B. L., & Cooper, B. S. (1992). Involving parents in improving urban schools. *NASSP Bulletin, 73 (513),* 30–38.

Jesse, D. (1995). Increasing parental involvement: A key to student achievement. In *What's noteworthy on learners, learning, schooling.* Aurora, CO: Mid-continent Regional Educational Laboratory, 19–26.

Kahne, J., & Westheimer, J. (1996). In the service of what? *Phi Delta Kappan, 77 (9),* 592-599.

Keith, T. Z., & Keith, P. B. (1993). Does parental involvement affect eighth-grade student achievement? Structural analysis of national data. *School Psychology Review, 22 (3),* 474–496.

Lewis, A. C., & Henderson, A. T. (1997). *Urgent message: Families crucial to school reform.* Washington, D.C.: Center for Law and Education.

Liontos, L. B. (1992). *At-risk families and schools becoming partners.* Eugene, OR: University of Oregon, ERIC Clearing House on Educational Management. *Metropolitan Life survey of the American teacher 1993: Violence in American public schools.*

Louis Harris & Associates (1993). New York: Author.

National Commission on Children (1991). *Speaking of kids: A national survey on children and parents.* Washington, DC: Author.

National Parent Teacher Association (1997). *National standards for parent/family involvement programs.* Chicago: Author.

Perry, N. (November 29, 1993). School reform: Big pain, no gain. *Fortune, 128,* 130–38.

Postman, N. (1996). *The end of education: Redefining the value of school.* New York: Alfred A. Knopf.

Reaching all families: Crating family-friendly schools (August, 1996). United States Department of Education.

Rutherford, B. (1995). Creating partnerships: The context of parent and community involvement programs. In B. Rutherford (Ed.) *Creating family/school partnerships.* Columbus, OH: National Middle School Association.

Schurr, S. L. (1992). Fine tuning your parent power: Increasing student achievement. *Schools in the Middle, 2 (2),* 3–9.

Shartrand, A. M., Weiss, H. B., Kreider, H. M., & Lopez, M. E. (1997). *New skills for new schools: Preparing teacher's in family involvement.* Cambridge, MA: Harvard Graduate School of Education.

Stevenson, D. L., & Baker, D. P. (1987). The family-school relation and the child's performance. *Child Development, 58,* 1348–1357.

Strong families, strong schools: Building community partnerships for learning (1994). Washington, DC: U. S. Department of Education.

Swick, K. J. (1992). Teacher-parent partnerships, *ERIC Digest,* Urbana, IL: Clearing House on Elementary and Early Childhood Education. EDO-PS-92-12.

Thousand, I., Villa, R., & Nevin, A. (1998). Meeting across the divide: Effective parent-professional collaboration. *The High School Magazine, 5(3),* 22–25.

United States Department of Education (1995). *Employers, families, and education: Promoting family involvement in learning.* Washington, DC: Author.

Wirthlin Group (August, 1995). *The prudential spirit of community initiative.* Washington, DC: Author, 14–15.

CHAPTER 9

THE HIGH SCHOOL TEACHER

WHAT YOU WILL LEARN IN THIS CHAPTER

Teacher roles in reformed high schools

Effects of an expanding knowledge base on high school teaching

Teaching a new high school curriculum

Professional development for the new high school

Teacher preparation for the new high school

Teachers will design work for students that is of high quality to engage them, cause them to persist, and, when successfully completed, result in their satisfaction and their acquisition of learnings, skills, and abilities valued by society (Breaking Ranks, p. vi).

Each student will have a personal plan of progress to ensure that the high school takes individual needs into consideration and to allow students, within reasonable parameters, to design their own methods for learning in an effort to meet high standards (Breaking Ranks, p. 11).

Teachers should have the ability to develop activities for students that— while embodying the learning objectives—are clearly linked to intellectual products that the students value (Breaking Ranks, p. 15).

Teachers should regard curriculum as more than some inert substance lying on the pages of textbooks, waiting to be absorbed by students (Breaking Ranks, p. 14).

*Each high school teacher will have a broad base of academic knowledge with depth in at least one subject area (*Breaking Ranks, *p. 21).*

*Teachers will know and be able to use a variety of strategies and settings that identify and accommodate individual learning styles and engage students (*Breaking Ranks, *p. 21).*

*Each educator will develop a Personal Learning Plan that addresses his or her need to grow, stressing knowledge and skills related to improved student learning (*Breaking Ranks, *p. 63).*

*Educators cannot improve high schools without the proper preparation to take on new roles and responsibilities. Their education in teacher colleges should equip them for changing demands in teaching and learning, and continuing inservice education must have a valued place in their day-to-day professional lives once they are on the job. Each educator in the school, including the principal, should have a Personal Learning Plan (*Breaking Ranks, *p. 5).*

THE CHANGING ROLES OF TEACHERS IN THE NEW HIGH SCHOOL

The changing roles of high school teachers are significant in both number and implications. The growing belief that all students can learn and have the right to do so under the direction of capable, caring teachers, is influencing the expectations being placed on high school teachers. Many other important factors (e.g., real and perceived failures of the traditional high school, increasing diversity of high school students, growing professionalism among high school educators) help determine what teachers should know and be able to do. The increasing knowledge base regarding best practice at high schools also informs the redefinition of successful high school teaching. For example, the complex challenges and opportunities of teaching all high school students effectively have led to greatly expanded expectations for teacher performance from both the public and the education profession itself. Simply knowing the subject matter and focusing on successfully teaching those students perceived to be the most capable is no longer sufficient.

Some teacher roles that serve as examples of new directions being taken at successful high schools are briefly described in this section, followed by an examination of related trends and issues in staff development and teacher preparation. The purposes of this chapter are to help prospective and practicing teachers better conceptualize the important roles they are likely to assume in high schools, and to explore some of the implications of these new roles for staff development and teacher preparation.

Emerging Roles for High School Teachers

A statement by Darling-Hammond (1996) captures the essence of the new expectations being placed on America's teachers:

A more complex, knowledge-based, and multi-cultural society creates new expectations for teaching. To help diverse learners master more challenging content, teachers must go far beyond dispensing information, giving a test, and giving a grade. They must themselves know their subject areas deeply, and they must understand how students think, if they are to create experiences that actually work to produce learning (p. 194).

All teachers today are responsible not only for teaching their students basic knowledge and skills, but for helping them "master new information technologies in order to enter a world of work where there are fewer and fewer routine jobs, where a career will span a number of different jobs of varying complexity, and where flexibility and teamwork are necessary to make the grade throughout life" (National Foundation for the Improvement of Education, 1996, p. 7).

Teachers are now expected to take on more responsibilities for student academic growth, to tailor curriculum and assessment to student and community needs, and even to help manage their schools. Examples of the expectations placed on high school teachers include: (1) teaching students from a variety of diverse backgrounds; (2) being aware of and sensitive to social demands and expectations; (3) successfully meeting the individual learning and developmental needs of students; (4) utilizing information technologies in their instruction; (5) making decisions about which knowledge to teach in a time when new knowledge is growing at unprecedented rates; and (6) working with family and community members more closely than ever before. Many high school teachers are taking on these and other challenges as the public makes clear its expectations for immediate school improvement. However, teachers need time and opportunities to master the new knowledge and to work with others to improve their practice (National Foundation for the Improvement of Education, 1996).

It is widely accepted that reforming the American high school must include major shifts in the ways adolescents are taught. Achieving the quality of instruction sought will require new and expanded roles for high school teachers that extend beyond past norms. Some examples of these roles, as described in *Breaking Ranks* (1996), are provided here. These examples do not constitute an exhaustive list of the roles important for successful high school teaching; they are intended simply to stimulate thought and discussion. Many of these roles have long been associated with the teaching profession, but others would not have appeared on a list like this one even a few years ago:

- Using instructional strategies that engage students while making them part of the learning process
- Teaching students in ways that help them think critically and reason well in specific academic disciplines
- Providing a climate that is supportive of teaching and learning, where academics are honored and distractions are not tolerated
- Providing learning experiences that help students meet district, state, and national standards
- Teaching students to apply what they learn
- Making learning stimulating and challenging for all students

- Teaching abstract principles and basic concepts as a necessary prelude to the application of knowledge
- Providing students with individual personal plans for progress and allowing them to be involved in designing their methods for learning
- Conveying a genuine sense of caring to all students
- Understanding and accommodating individual student learning styles
- Helping all students acquire a broad base of academic knowledge
- Acting as coaches and facilitators of learning to promote active involvement of students in their own learning
- Using technology in instruction in ways that improve student learning
- Integrating assessment into instruction so that it becomes an important part of the learning process
- Serving as personal advocates for a selected group of students
- Teaching in ways that help students approach knowledge from a multidisciplinary perspective
- Working collaboratively with educators from teacher preparation programs to help prepare future teachers and to improve teaching and learning in high schools

Clearly, these roles move beyond the didactic ones so commonly associated with high school teaching. Teachers who assume these roles are no longer defined by the subjects they teach, and are focusing on both content and student affect. Although they arc knowledgeable in their subject areas and demonstrate the importance of a deep understanding of content to their students, they no longer allow the subjects they teach to determine who they are professionally, how they teach, where and with whom they work, and how they are perceived by others.

EFFECTS OF THE EXPANDING KNOWLEDGE BASE ON TEACHER ROLES

Changing teacher roles and accompanying high expectations for performance are evolving not only because of changing attitudes among the public and those in the profession, but also because of the expanding base of knowledge concerning teaching, learning, and schooling. As advances are made in such areas as effective programs and practices, authentic assessment, brain-compatible learning, multiple intelligences, and learning styles, it becomes more difficult for high school teachers and other educators to continue in more traditional roles (e.g., dispensing knowledge primarily through lecturing; reserving the most effective instructional experiences for selected students who are viewed as "capable") that have defined successful practice in past generations.

An example of the influence of the expanded knowledge base is the impact of two major theories: that of *learning styles* (the different ways people think and feel as they solve problems, create products, and interact) and that of *multiple intelligences* (the effort to understand how cultures and disciplines shape human potential) (Gardner, 1991; Silver, Strong, & Perini, 1997). These theories are not discussed here; however, they do represent an expanding knowledge base that offers many possibilities for improving teaching and student learning. Teachers taking these major theories into consideration as they plan instruction depart from traditional instructional models that follow the pattern: give a lecture, have students take notes and memorize facts, give a test, and assign a grade.

An additional example of the forces that are changing the roles of high school teachers is associated with "authentic pedagogy." This term has evolved, at least in part, from the concern of some reformers that too much teaching does not reflect best practice. The following statement is typical of that concern (Newmann, Marks, & Gamoran, 1995).

> Educators and reformers often worry that today's students spend too much of their time simply absorbing—then reproducing—information transmitted to them. They fear that students aren't learning how to make sense of what they are told. Also, reformers often see little connection between activities in the classroom and the world beyond school. Students can earn credits, good grades, and high test scores, they say, demonstrating a kind of mastery that frequently seems trivial, contrived, or meaningless outside the school. The reformers call instead for authentic achievement, representing accomplishments that are significant, worthwhile, and meaningful (p. 1).

Authentic pedagogy, as defined by Newmann, Marks, and Gamoran, accepts the importance of active learning, problem solving, and construction of meaning that is grounded in real-world experience. However, they propose a concept of instruction and assessment that also recognizes that all active learning is not effective simply because it is active and being enjoyed by students. Classroom instruction under this model focuses on the standards of: (1) higher-order thinking; (2) substantive conversations; (3) deep knowledge; (4) connections beyond the classroom; (5) problem solving connected to the real world; and (6) an audience beyond the school. Neither these standards nor the authentic assessment tasks and academic performances that accompany them are described in any detail here. However, their focus on viewing instruction in ways that differ from common practice serves as another example of an expanding knowledge base that is reshaping the roles of high school teachers.

TEACHING THE NEW CURRICULUM

As discussed in Chapter 2, the new high school curriculum differs in many ways from more traditional concepts of curriculum, and changes in attitudes concerning the nature of student learning have many profound implications for teaching in high school. For example, reforms called for in *Second to None: A Vision of the New California High School* include a concept-driven curriculum instead of one based solely on learning facts and skills. This report recommends that the scope, content, and sequence of core disciplines be redesigned so that every student can succeed in the full academic curriculum. It also stresses the importance of teachers working with clusters of students and teams of teachers while strengthening the subject areas they teach and integrating curriculum (California State Department of Education, 1992). These recommendations are representative of major shifts occurring in the nature of teaching and learning, and schooling, and are typical of changes being recommended in the reform literature. Allocation of significant resources will be necessary if these new professional roles are to become reality in the nation's schools. The good news is that the major changes recommended are neither unrealistic nor simply theoretical. Many exemplary high schools have already moved to new and successful models that hold great promise for the youth of our nation and the teachers who serve them.

THE NATIONAL BOARD FOR PROFESSIONAL TEACHING STANDARDS

Another event that helped reshape the roles of high school teachers was the establishment of the National Board for Professional Teaching Standards (NBPTS). The mission of this independent, nonprofit, nonpartisan organization is: (1) to establish high standards for what highly accomplished teachers should know and be able to do; (2) develop and operate a national, voluntary system to assess and certify teachers who meet these standards; and (3) to advance related reforms that improve student learning. The efforts of NBPTS have advanced the professionalization of teaching on many fronts, including defining the knowledge, skills, and accomplishments that result in teaching excellence. Standards are being established in more than 30 certificate fields, including those for high school teachers (National Board for Professional Teaching Standards, 1990).

The core propositions upon which NBPTS are based offer insights into the standards themselves. These propositions are:

- Teachers are committed to students and their learning.
- Teachers know the subjects they teach and how to teach those subjects to students.
- Teachers are responsible for managing and monitoring student learning.
- Teachers think systematically about their practice and learn from experience.
- Teachers are members of learning communities (NBPTS, 1990, pp. 13–14).

These core propositions are used in developing the standards for each national certification. Examples of standards drawn from the *Adolescence and Young Adult Standards,* which include high school science teachers, are given below (National Board for Professional Teaching Standards, 1996):

> Accomplished science teachers must know how students learn, actively come to know their students as individuals, and determine students' understandings of science as well as their individual learning backgrounds (p. 15).

Accomplished science teachers have a broad and current knowledge of science and science education, along with in-depth knowledge of one of the subfields of science, which they use to set important learning goals (p. 19).

Accomplished science teachers take steps to ensure that all students, including those from groups which have historically not been encouraged to enter the world of science, participate in the study of science (p. 29).

The implications of the work of NBPTS are numerous and far-reaching. The fact that the majority of all members of boards charged with writing standards are practicing classroom teachers has provided much legitimacy to the process. These new standards offer much to both high school teachers and teacher educators. The standards are helping redefine the roles of all teachers, whether or not they elect to go through the process of becoming board-certified. The historic effort of defining highly accomplished teaching provides guidance for effective teaching that has never before been available.

PROFESSIONAL DEVELOPMENT FOR THE NEW HIGH SCHOOL

Teaching and learning are unlikely to improve significantly unless substantial improvement occurs in professional development activities. Major reports issued by government bodies, business associations, and other groups all emphasize the central role professional development must play if all students are to succeed. Those responsible for staff development at the local, state, and national levels recognize that high-quality staff development is essential if lasting, positive changes are to be accomplished (Sparks & Hirsh, 1997).

Quality staff development, along with other key factors (e.g., team building, shared decision making, collaboration, comprehensive long range planning), is essential to the restructuring of high schools. Teacher learning, provided at least in part through staff development activities, is prerequisite to meaningful and lasting high school reform. This teacher knowledge is essential to accomplishing the cultural and structural changes that are crucial components of successful high school reform (Kaplan, 1997).

Dynamic professional development efforts that surpass the meager offerings of many traditional staff development plans must become a reality if high school teachers and other educators are to successfully meet the challenge of teaching all students well. Staff development that is confined to a few specific days in the school calendar simply cannot provide teachers with the ongoing, job-embedded development of new knowledge, skills, and dispositions essential to successful teaching. The kinds of staff development opportunities required allow and encourage high school teachers to continually refine their skills, inquire into practice, and construct craft knowledge (National Staff Development Council and National Association for Secondary School Principals, 1995).

STANDARDS FOR STAFF DEVELOPMENT AT THE HIGH SCHOOL

Publication of national standards for staff development sponsored by the National Staff Development Council and the National Association of Secondary School Principals has changed perceptions of effective professional development. The staff development standards for high schools are organized into the following three categories (Hirsh, 1997; National Staff Development Council and National Association for Secondary School Principals, 1995):

- *Context:* the organizational, system or culture in which new learning will be implemented (e.g., effective high school staff development provides adequate time during the work day for staff members to learn and work together to accomplish the school's mission and goals) (National Staff Development Council, p. 12)
- *Process:* the means for ensuring that adults acquire the knowledge, skills, and dispositions necessary to ensure high levels of learning for all students (e.g., effective high school staff development uses content that has proven value in increasing student learning and development) (p. 23)
- *Content:* skills and knowledge educators require to ensure student learning (e.g., effective high school staff development increases administrators' and teachers' understanding of how to provide school environments and instruction that are responsive to the developmental needs of adolescents) (p. 38)

Context, process, and content standards are all necessary for effective staff development. Those responsible for staff development activities and programs, whether at the building or district level, should give these standards careful consideration while planning, implementing, and assessing their efforts.

NEW PARADIGMS FOR STAFF DEVELOPMENT

Research and experience have demonstrated that a new kind of staff development, considerably different from previous practices, is needed. Influential educational leaders advocate a radical departure from a traditional "sit and listen" style of staff development that is currently so prevalent. (Darling-Hammond & McLaughlin, 1995; Liberman, 1995; Sparks & Hirsh, 1997). A continuum of practices that incorporates new and expanded concept of staff development and encourages professional growth is recommended. As noted by Liberman (1995), teachers need opportunities to "discuss, think about, try out, and hone new practices" by taking new roles (e.g., teacher as researcher), creating new structures (e.g., problem-solving groups), working on new tasks (e.g., creating new standards), and creating a culture of inquiry.

There is a strong and growing consensus that staff development must be intensive, continuous, and focused on producing measurable advances in student learning. However, this high-quality staff development cannot occur unless it is part of fundamental reform in the culture of the school and the ethos of the profession of education. Staff development should be directly linked to reform efforts and supported by a learner-centered view of teaching and a career-long conception of teachers' learning (Darling-Hammond & McLaughlin, 1995; Joyce & Showers, 1995).

Trends in Staff Development

Sparks and Hirsh provide some examples of major shifts in staff development that offer hope that the reform efforts of high schools will endure, and will benefit students and their teachers for many years. These shifts are:

- From individual development to individual development *and* organizational development
- From fragmented, piecemeal improvement efforts to staff development driven by a clear, coherent, strategic plan for the school district, each school, and the departments that serve schools
- From district-focused to school-focused approaches to staff development
- From a focus on adult needs and satisfaction to a focus on student needs and learning outcomes, and changes in on-the-job behaviors
- From training conducted away from the job as the primary delivery system for staff development to multiple forms of job-embedded learning
- From an orientation toward the transmission of knowledge and skills to teachers by "experts" to study by teachers of the teaching and learning processes
- From a focus on generic instructional skills to a combination of generic and content-specific skills
- From staff developers who function primarily as trainers to those who provide consultation, planning, and facilitation of services as well as training
- From staff development provided by a central office to staff development as a critical function and major responsibility performed by all administrators and teacher leaders
- From staff development directed toward teachers as the primary recipients to continuous improvement in performance for everyone who affects student learning
- From staff development as a "frill" that can be cut during difficult financial times to staff development as an indispensable process without which schools cannot hope to prepare young people for citizenship and productive employment (Sparks & Hirsh, pp. 12–16)

These and other shifts in staff development practices are significant, powerful, and essential to the creation of learning communities in which students, teachers, principals, and support staffs are both learners and teachers. These shifts can "unleash the most powerful source of success for all students—the daily presence of adults who are passionately committed to their own lifelong learning within organizations that are continually renewing themselves" (Sparks & Hirsh, p. 16).

The Central Role of School-Based Staff Development

The importance of the school-based staff development efforts is now more widely recognized as a crucial component of staff development than in past years. "Both district and school initiatives depend on concerted study and action at the faculty level. Individuals are greatly enhanced if the quality of the school is good, and they are impeded if it is not healthy" (Joyce & Showers, 1995, p. xv). A major key to student growth is educator growth, as the two are mutually beneficial. Designing schools in ways that provide teachers opportunities to work together to improve their practice (e.g., continuous data collection, analysis, and interpretation) helps to transfer the content of staff development into practice whether the content focuses on teaching and curriculum or on processes for collegial efforts.

This new model of staff development is conceived as a large-scale research project and improved continually as the community of people operating it studies its effects. It moves beyond the concept of staff development as something for only those who are interested, and makes it a vital matter involving all responsible for the education and welfare of high school students (Joyce & Showers, 1995).

Effective Staff Development Models

Teachers in highly successful high schools engage in a variety of staff development activities that support their ongoing professional development, such as "study groups, action research groups, observation and assessment, peer coaching, training and follow up, participation on school improvement and/or curriculum writing teams, and problem solving sessions throughout the school year" (National Staff Development Council, 1995, p. 7). These kinds of activities are important because teachers who develop sustained and challenging learning opportunities for their students are typically those who address problems and find solutions together (McLaughlin & Talbert, 1993).

Research on effective staff development has identified characteristics of effective programs, including: (1) connectedness to school settings and schoolwide efforts; (2) involvement of teachers and planners; (3) provision of choice and differentiated learning; (4) use of demonstration, supervised practice, and feedback as part of training; and (5) ongoing assistance and support (National Council for Staff Development, 1995).

The kind of staff development needed by high school educators is much more comprehensive and effective than the traditional model of relatively passive participants sitting and listening to experts. Although it is sometimes appropriate to have knowledgeable persons make large-group presentations (e.g., reports on promising practices, new research results, innovative models of schooling), educators at innovative high schools are active participants in a great variety of effective staff development activities. Staff development "not only must affect the knowledge, attitudes, and practices of individual teachers, administrators, and other school employees, but it must also alter the cultures and structures of the organizations in which individuals work" (Sparks & Hirsh, 1997, p. 2).

STAFF DEVELOPMENT PRACTICES IN THE NEW HIGH SCHOOLS

If staff development is to move beyond the traditional "presentation by one or more outside experts" mode, a variety of opportunities must be provided at both the district and individual school levels. Jefferson County Public Schools District in Louisville, Kentucky, is a good example of a district that provides a plethora of professional development options. Their design and delivery models for professional development reflect a recognition that educators are at different levels in their professional development needs and interests. These levels are:

- *Orientation:* Practitioners develop knowledge and understanding of key concepts, processes, and organizational structures of the program.
- *Application:* Practitioners develop the skills and processes to begin implementation.
- *Implementaiton:* Practitioners learn to master the required tasks for implementation of the program in their workplace.
- *Refinement:* Practitioners vary the use of practice to achieve maximum impact on student achievement.

Several opportunities of progressing through these levels can be selected, including those found in Figure 9.1. A wide variety of available professional development activities helps ensure that professionals in the Jefferson County Public Schools can become more effective educators, with their students ultimately being the greatest beneficiaries.

Educators in successful high schools use a variety of staff development delivery models that includes but is not limited to those that are part of the Jefferson County Public Schools plan. For example, second and fourth Wednesdays at La Grande High School in La Grande, Oregon, are devoted to Faculty Forum, which deals primarily with staff development. Classes start on these days at 10:04 A.M., which provides 4 hours per month for professional development. Educators at La Grande report tremendous gains in professional development because of this reassigned time. They have divided themselves into five subgroups and make decisions about staff development and other important matters based on an 80 percent consensus model. This scheduling arrangement, which recognizes the importance of making time available during the school day, provides numerous opportunities for staff members to work together to enhance their knowledge and skills.

Central Park East Secondary School in New York City also provides time for teachers to work collaboratively toward a number of important goals, including staff development. Staff members meet every Monday from 3:00 until 4:30 P.M. and from 1:30 until 3:00 P.M. on Fridays (classes meet from 8:00 A.M. until 1:00 P.M.).

Delivery Models for Staff Development: Jefferson County Public Schools   **FIGURE 9.1**

Summer Institutes: Sessions revolving around integrated themes, with expert consultant presentations and opportunities for collegial discussion and planning

Seminars: Events with a central theme, utilizing expert consultants and group participation

Retreats: District-wide or site-specific, 1 or more days, for work-group expansion of knowledge and for implementation planning for a particular theme

Professional Conferences: Local, state, and national experiences selected to broaden knowledge and to assess adaptability of outside programs

Support Groups: Network experiences selected to broaden knowledge and to assess adaptability of outside programing to share information and to develop strategies

Workshops: Introductory 3–6-hour sessions to build awareness, provide basic information, and allow participants to determine future areas of concentration

Strands: 12–18 hours of concentrated study in selected areas

Peer Coaching: A strand of concentrated study plus a collegial support component

Training of Trainers: A strand of concentrated study with a commitment to provide professional development training for the district in the area of concentration; includes training in preparation and presentation of professional development sessions

Video Study: Independent or group study through the use of commercial or locally produced videotapes

Cadre Team Development: The training of a group of individuals in a core concept with the responsibility to assist implementation of the concept at the local school level

Partners in Professional Growth: Establishment of cross-role study groups, including parents, to effect change

Teleconferences: Nationally organized transmissions that allow for local participation

University Partnerships: Continued development of action research projects with institutions of higher education

Action Labs: Practical, hands-on sessions featuring a high degree of participant involvement

Study Groups: A small number of colleagues meeting to study specific educational topics at the district or school level

Additionally, teams of teachers have 3 hours each week to plan while students are involved in community service placements. Staff development occurs at Central Park during the formal and informal gatherings. "They are where the newest teacher learns his or her trade, and senior staff reexamine and revisit old issues" (Meier & Schwarz, 1995, p. 38).

Some high schools provide a series of "mini-courses" that can be selected by faculty members based on their individual needs and interests. However, the topics of these mini-courses are carefully matched with the goals of the school. Cambridge Rindge and Latin School in Cambridge, Massachusetts, provides a series of mini-courses for faculty members that directly address the goals of the school. Some selected titles are:

- Toward Creating Student Performances of Deep Understanding: Toward Cultivating the Life of the Mind
- Authentic Assessment as a Tool to Improve Instruction
- Portfolios in the Classroom
- Introduction to Cooperative Learning
- Peer Coaching
- Using Drama in the Classroom
- Teachers on Line: A Classroom Teacher's Journal and Idea Bank

Effective high schools use many additional staff development models according to their needs. Some examples are:

- *Intensive Summer Institutes:* These institutes focus on themes such as "Writing in Schools" (Eastern High School in Lon, Kentucky) and "Interdisciplinary Learning" (Satellite Academy and University Heights High Schools in New York, New York).
- *Professional Development School Partnerships:* Information on these is presented later in this chapter (Independence High School in Columbus, Ohio, and Fairdale High School Magnet Career Center in Fairdale, Kentucky).
- *Comprehensive Annual Inservice Plan:* These plans include a variety of opportunities, focusing on identified needs and interests of staff and on school goals (Parkway South High School in Manchester, Missouri, and Providence High School in Charlotte, North Carolina).
- *Staff Development Professional Days:* These professional days have themes such as "Teaching for Deeper Meaning" (Cambridge Rindge and Latin School in Cambridge, Massachusetts).
- *Vertical Teaming Staff Development Days:* Elementary, middle, and high school teachers attend staff development activities together to discuss curriculum, instructional strategies, student transition, and other issues of mutual interest that benefit students at all school levels (McNeil High School in Austin, Texas).
- *First Year Teacher Program:* A comprehensive plan to make sure new teachers receive the information and support they need to be successful (Vestavia Hills High School in Vestavia, Alabama).

TEACHER PREPARATION FOR THE NEW HIGH SCHOOL

An influential report, *What Matters Most: Teaching for America's Future,* (National Commission on Teaching and America's Future, 1996) pointed out what would seem to be obvious: that the single most important strategy for achieving America's educational goals is "a blueprint for recruiting, preparing, supporting, and rewarding excellent educators in all America's schools" (p. vi). The Commission's work was based on three premises: (1) what teachers know and can do is the most important influence on what students learn; (2) recruiting, preparing, and retaining good teachers is the central strategy for improving our schools; and (3) school reform cannot succeed unless it focuses on creating the conditions in which teachers can teach, and teach well.

The goal of the commission's plan is ensuring that all schools have teachers with the knowledge and skills needed to enable all children to learn. "If a caring, qualified teacher for every child is the most important ingredient in education reform, then it should no longer be the factor most frequently overlooked" (Darling-Hammond 1996, p. 194). Unfortunately, at many institutions the professional preparation of high school teachers remains largely unchanged after decades of dramatic changes in the nature of teaching and learning. One of these challenges is to create schools that "help the vast majority of young people reach levels of skill and competence that were once thought to be within the reach of only a few" (Darling-Hammond, 1996, p. 194).

The Problems of Teacher Preparation

Numerous state and national reports and other literature addressing teacher preparation have found it inadequate. The problems in teacher preparation have been well documented (Goodlad, 1990; Cruickshank and Associates, 1996; The Holmes Group, 1996; Sarason, 1993; Tyson, 1994; *What Matters Most,* 1996; Zeichner, 1993) and include:

- *Inadequate time:* This often results in elementary teachers with too little content knowledge and high school teachers with inadequate knowledge about teaching, learning, and their students.
- *Fragmentation:* Many of the key elements of teacher preparation are disconnected from each other (e.g., professional skills are segmented into separate courses, arts and sciences professors are insulated from teacher education coursework).
- *Uninspired Teaching Methods:* Too much lecture and recitation continues to dominate in higher education, including teacher preparation programs.
- *Superficial Curriculum:* Many traditional preparation programs lack a focus on how to understand and handle real problems of practice.
- *Traditional View of Schooling:* Pressures to prepare prospective teachers for schools as they are traditionally viewed, rather than in innovative, more effective ways often leads to prospective teachers learning to work in isolation

using chalkboards, rather than in teams using technology (*What Matters Most*, p. 32).

The lack of success cannot be attributed to lack of concern or effort. Rather, failures occur primarily because most schools and teachers do not know how to produce the kind of learning demanded by new reforms and today's youth. Many teachers, including teacher educators, simply do not know how to teach all students well (Darling-Hammond, 1996; *What Matters Most,* 1996). Additionally, the systems they work in do not adequately support their efforts. It is a situation of not knowing rather than not caring—of teaching and teacher preparation programs that were designed for a society that no longer exists. For these and many other important reasons, teacher preparation and staff development must be redesigned if high schools are to successfully meet the complex challenge of serving all students well.

PROFESSIONAL DEVELOPMENT HIGH SCHOOLS AND OTHER COLLABORATIVE PARTNERSHIPS

Teachers, who are often critical of teacher preparation programs, acknowledge that significant changes are taking place in some education programs. However, they advocate improvements such as: (1) making sure that all teachers know their content areas well, (2) teaching pedagogy in the context of academic content; and (3) giving prospective teachers varied school experiences. Many teachers recommend that teacher preparation programs focus more on practice and less on theory while emphasizing school-based experiences (Rigden, 1996). One means of carrying out these recommendations is through collaborative relationships such as professional development schools. These kinds of arrangements permit and encourage teachers and other educators to work closely with teacher preparation personnel to prepare tomorrow's teachers.

Increasing numbers of educators at teacher preparation institutions and in P–12 schools are forming new partnerships that promise to improve both teacher preparation and student learning at the precollegiate level. These partnerships take many forms, among which is the establishment of professional development schools. These schools, sometimes called clinical schools or professional-practice schools, are both a product of the movement toward educational reform and a means for achieving some of its goals (Abdal-Haqq, 1989; Dodd, 1996).

Professional development schools are not envisioned simply as laboratory schools for research, demonstration schools, or clinical sites for field experiences. Rather, they are intended to encompass all these and additional functions. They are schools "for the development of novice professionals, for continued development of experienced professionals, and for research and development of the teaching profession" (Holmes, 1995, p. 1). As noted by Darling-Hammond (1994):

> A major aspect of the restructuring movement in education is the current effort to invent and establish professional development schools (PDSs). PDSs aim to

provide new models of teacher education and development by serving as exemplars of practice, builders of knowledge, and vehicles for communicating professional understandings among teacher educators, novices, and veteran teachers. . . . PDSs are a special case of school restructuring; as they simultaneously restructure schools and teacher education programs (p. 1).

The purposes of professional development schools are to: (1) provide an exemplary education for some segment of P–12 students, (2) provide high-quality clinical settings, and (3) promote and conduct inquiry that advances knowledge of schooling (Clark, 1997 p, 5). Osguthorpe, Harris, Black, Culter, and Harris (1995) identify four basic goals of professional development (partnership) schools that are all aimed at increasing student learning: They include:

- *Educator Preparation:* Collaboration between partners to assure that those entering the education profession are prepared to serve students effectively
- *Professional Development:* Collaboration between partners to provide opportunities for teachers to strengthen their ability to contribute to the students they serve
- *Curriculum Development:* Collaboration between partners to improve the education and school experience of all students
- *Research and Inquiry:* Collaboration between partners to raise questions and conduct research that will promote educational renewal at both the school and the university (p. 5)

Clearly, these are worthy goals that will improve the success of teacher preparation programs and high schools. Professional development schools and other initiatives that focus on collaborative efforts offer new opportunities that benefit students and their teachers at both the high school and collegiate levels.

Independence High School in Columbus, Ohio, is an urban professional development high school with a 78 percent minority student population. Educators at Independence work closely with faculty members from the College of Education at Ohio State University to redesign preservice and inservice teacher education and to improve student learning at both institutions. Areas of focus include; (1) meeting the needs and interests of a very diverse student population, (2) implementing an innovative block scheduling plan, (3) assessing the staff's professional development needs and planning professional development opportunities, and (4) providing on-site research opportunities for participants. Educators involved in the professional development school program report that they have developed an increased awareness of the real needs at each institution and of what can be done to better meet those needs. One high school educator stated that:

> We have developed an understanding of each other's culture, context, concerns, and frustrations. We began to realize that we are all working toward the same end—providing an educational experience in which all learners can be successful. Involvement in this program has enabled us to recognize that we are as much learners as the students we teach—whether the learners are university students aspiring to be teachers or high school students in Independence High School classrooms. . . . All involved have come to realize and appreciate how hard we

all are working and how dedicated the professional development school participants are to making a difference in the lives of learners" (Personal communication, B. Carnate, 1997).

Participants at Independence High School and Ohio State University believe that the professional development high school partnership has much to offer all participants. A rich environment that provides prospective teachers with valuable, direct experiences with innovative schooling models and professional practice greatly increases the chance that effective teachers will be available for high school students and that students at Independence will benefit significantly from the collaborative efforts of faculties from both institutions.

Fairdale High School Magnet Career Academy in Fairdale, Kentucky, is a professional development school in partnership with the University of Louisville in Louisville, Kentucky. Faculty members from Fairdale report that the collaborative relationship established has been an enormous help to them in numerous ways, including assistance with school restructuring efforts. Interns typically complete observation-oriented activities during the fall semester and student teach in the spring semester. Approximately 50 graduate-level interns per year participate in the program.

One way these prospective teachers become involved in school restructuring at Fairdale is through a requirement that they successfully complete a project that advances restructuring in some manner. University of Louisville professors and Fairdale High School teachers meet during the summer preceding the year interns will become participants to determine what those projects will be (Figure 9.2). Through these projects prospective teachers receive valuable direct experience in high school classrooms and learn first-hand about assessing and improving schools and professional practice. Participants from both institutions support these collaborative efforts and believe that all involved become more effective professionals while improving the quality of their practice. One indication of the success of this professional development school partnership is that several teachers currently employed at Fairdale are products of this collaborative venture.

Other high schools work closely with teacher preparation institutions without entering a formal professional development school partnership. For example, when the faculty at Cabot High School in Cabot, Vermont, was faced with the question of what teachers and other educators needed to fulfill the new the mission of their school, they responded with a list of 30 concepts that were consolidated into eight major strands and ranked by importance. Faculty members from St. Michael's College helped develop an inservice curriculum that addressed the identified needs. Inservice activities then focused on those specific topics and teachers earned graduate credit for the work they completed during inservice days.

The Cabot faculty also endorsed a professional development plan that included an opportunity for the entire faculty to enroll in a course from the University of Vermont titled "Linking Assessment to Instruction." This course taught high school educators about current best practices of assessment and instruction in mathematics, social studies, writing, and science. Persons in this class interacted, experimented, reflected, and planned with colleagues while receiving support from the instructor.

FIGURE 9.2

Restructuring Project Assignments at Independence High School

- *Interviewing parents of students who reside in the Fairdale attendance district.* Parents who have and have chosen to have their children attend Fairdale will be included. This group will work with Mrs. Alma and other staff members to organize a process for interviewing parents. The group will conduct interviews under the supervision of Fairdale staff members and prepare a report summarizing the results.

- *Publishing an "Ideas that Work" summary for the Critical Friends Group.* This group will work with Fairdale's Critical Friends Group of teachers to gather and compile successful lesson plans, curriculum materials, assessments, and other resources that have proven successful with students. Additionally, the group will identify resources (e.g., articles, internet sites, professional organizations) that have been the most influential in shaping the thinking and practice of members of the Critical Friends Group. A summary of the results will be published or otherwise disseminated to Fairdale faculty members and prospective teachers.

- *Profiling Fairdale's successful seniors and graduates.* This group will interview Fairdale's most successful seniors and recent graduates. A set of attributes of successful students will be developed, curriculum experiences that these seniors and graduates cite as contributing to their success will be summarized, and feedback will be provided to be used in proposals aimed at enhancing current courses/experiences and developing new ones. The group will also research information about programs at other Coalition Schools.

The course also focused on aligning the Vermont Core Framework with New Standards and Cabot Standards with lessons and activities.

Partnerships such as the ones just described offer renewed hope that educators at high schools and teacher preparation institutions can work collaboratively to better accomplish their goals. Staff members from each type of institution have much to gain by learning from the other while combining their professional knowledge to better educate our nation's adolescents and their teachers.

The Significance of Effective Teacher Preparation Programs

Despite the problems faced by teacher preparation programs and the legitimate call for significant redesign, their crucial importance is evident. For many years, numerous research studies have shown clearly that the most successful teachers know their subjects deeply, understand how students learn, and have mastered a wide variety of teaching strategies (*What Matters Most,* 1996; Olsen, 1985; Wise, 1997). These research results help debunk the myths that anyone can teach and that teaching skills cannot or need not be taught.

Research results refute the belief of many policymakers and education critics that teacher education is ineffective. Teachers who earn more hours in professional education obtain higher ratings from supervisors and have students who score higher on tests than do students of colleagues who have less extensive teacher preparation. Graduates of teacher education programs are rated as more effective by supervisors than are graduates from the liberal arts or other non-education majors. Additionally, teachers with regular state licensure receive higher supervisor ratings and have higher student achievement than teachers who do not meet certification standards (Ashton, 1996; Ashton & Cocker, 1996).

Research studies show that teachers who are admitted to the teaching profession through quick-entry routes have difficulties in the areas of curriculum development, pedagogical content knowledge, addressing the learning styles and levels of students, classroom management, and student motivation (Darling-Hammond, Wise & Klein, 1995; Lenk, 1989; Feiman-Nemser & Parker, 1990; Grossman, 1990; Mitchell, 1987). Novice teachers who have not completed professional preparation programs show more ignorance about student needs and differences and about the basics of teaching than do those with formal professional preparation. Many studies have also revealed that teachers without the benefit of professional preparation programs are less sensitive to students, less able to plan and redirect instruction to meet student needs, and less skilled in instruction (Bents & Bents, 1990; Rottenberg & Berliner, 1990). As noted by Darling-Hammond, Wise and Klein, 1995:

> An unprepared teacher is likely to teach in the way he or she was taught. When a powerful teacher education process does not intervene, new knowledge does not have an opportunity to transform teaching across generations. Yet prospective teachers cannot profit from these insights if they have no opportunity to encounter them (p. 21).

Of course, the proven benefits of formal teacher preparation programs do not mean that they are all of high quality or that continuous improvements are not needed. Problems, including those discussed in this chapter, are real, and they demand serious reforms. Programs that prepare high school teachers are especially in need of attention and substantial reform.

Directions for Change in High School Teacher Preparation

Those responsible for the professional preparation of high school teachers must make major changes in order to provide new teachers with the knowledge, skills, and disposition needed to succeed. Old models designed for different eras of history will simply no longer suffice. The following recommendations, adapted from those commonly associated with innovative middle level teacher preparation programs, are provided for consideration by those planning new high school teacher preparation programs or revising existing ones.

It might not be surprising that the specialized preparation for middle and high school teachers includes some common components and areas of emphasis. After all, many of the results sought in the two levels of schooling are similar (e.g., teacher advisory programs, use of a variety of instructional strategies, content area knowledge, integration of instruction). This is not to suggest, however, that the professional preparation programs for both levels should be identical. The kind of teaching needed by young adolescents in grades five through eight differs sufficiently from that needed by older adolescents in grades nine through twelve to justify separate professional preparation programs.

The following recommended components for high school teacher preparation programs are based on those identified by McEwin and Dickinson (1995, 1996) as essential for middle level teachers. The list is limited to elements that are unique to high school teacher preparation and does not include elements essential for all quality preparation programs (e.g., diversity, technology). The list is intended to stimulate thought and discussion rather than to represent a complete description of a comprehensive high school teacher preparation program. High school teacher education programs should include:

- Collaborative teacher preparation partnerships between high school-based educators and university-based teacher preparation faculty members
- A thorough study of adolescence and the needs of adolescents
- A comprehensive study of high school philosophy and organization for the reformed American high school
- A thorough study of high school curriculum
- An intensive focus on planning, teaching, and assessment using developmentally and culturally responsive practices
- Preparation for teacher-based guidance (advisory) roles
- Early and continuing field experiences in a variety of good high school settings
- Study and practice in the collaborative role of high school teachers in working with colleagues, families, and community members
- Comprehensive academic content preparation in at least one subject area

If high school teachers successfully completed professional preparation programs that included these components, reforming America's schools would not be such an arduous task. Teachers would enter their professional careers with the specialized knowledge, skills, and dispositions necessary to help high schools become the kinds of institutions needed by adolescents and the nation. Establishing and maintaining significant and long-lasting reforms in the nation's high schools will be difficult, if not impossible, if teacher preparation programs do not also make major changes. The new high school teacher preparation programs can be created only if high school and higher education professionals collaborate and consider teacher preparation and high school improvement joint responsibilities.

HIGH SCHOOL TEACHERS MEETING THE CHALLENGES OF NEW HIGH SCHOOLS

Many factors will determine the degree of authentic change that will occur in the American high school. Perhaps the most important factor is the willingness of high school teachers and other key educators to not only accept the fact that reform is needed, but also become staunch advocates of efforts to accomplish the goals identified. These educators and their teacher preparation colleagues clearly will have to become involved in intense professional development efforts to get the job done. However, much of the end result will depend as much on attitude as on newly acquired professional knowledge and skills. As noted by Lounsbury (1996):

> What must occur among secondary schools is a comparable commitment that will lead to a reconceptualization, a re-visioning of the high school, one that takes hold of a new and greater vision, one that enlarges its definition and grips the emotions (p. 19).

Lounsbury warns that the changes needed will not come easily because change always brings with it resistance. He points out that the American high school has a "long legacy of significant service, deeply ingrained traditions, and millions of successful graduates who believe the education they received was completely satisfactory—and for them it probably was" (p. 24). It will be up to high school teachers and other stakeholders to help the nation understand that times, society, and youth have changed significantly, and that bold changes in high schools are not only appropriate, but absolutely necessary.

The new mission of education requires "substantially more knowledge and radically different skills for teachers" (Darling-Hammond, Wise, & Klein, 1995, p. 2). The kind of teaching necessary to meet the demands of new high schools "cannot be produced through teacher-proof materials or regulated curricula" (p. 2). To create links between challenging high school curriculum and adolescents' needs and experiences, teachers must: (1) understand cognition and the many different avenues to learning, (2) have a working knowledge of human growth and development, (3) have a deep understanding of pedagogy and its applications, and (4) understand a variety of alternatives for assessment (Shulman, 1987; Darling-Hammond, 1990; Darling-Hammond, Wise, & Klein, 1995).

Merely adding new regulations and tinkering with innovation will not transform America's high schools. Teachers must work with administrators, family members, and other stakeholders to accomplish lasting, positive reforms that profoundly affect the nature and quality of teaching and learning in the nation's high schools. Diez (1996) states that "formal preparation of a teacher is the joint responsibility of college and university teachers of liberal arts and sciences, college- and university-based teacher educators, teacher educators in local schools, and communities that support local schools" (p. 31).

One of the most important ways to accomplish the goals of the new high school is through "rebuilding the human infrastructure of the educational system through strategic investment in the recruitment, induction, and ongoing learning of teachers" (Darling-Hammond, 1995, p. 23). As stated by Sizer:

> We know now that the status quo of shopping-mall high schools and lecture-drill-and-test systems demonstrably do not work for too many pupils, and that the skimpy tests that are often administered distort and mask the depth and shape of our problems and seriously mislead the public. Maintaining this system while waiting for some foolproof model is utterly irresponsible. We should act now on what we know. It is clear that tackling change is less risky than stubbornly sticking to old and discredited habits (pp. 79–80).

Perhaps more than ever before, a highly prepared teaching force is needed to meet the new challenges of teaching all students rather than a select few, and teaching in ways that lead to universal understanding rather than "subject coverage." This teaching force will not become a reality unless staff development is greatly improved, teacher preparation programs are changed in meaningful ways, and perhaps most important, high school teachers themselves make the personal commitment to take advantage of every opportunity to improve their practice as they carry out their important work.

SUMMARY

The growing acceptance of the belief that all students can learn and have the right to do so under the direction of a capable, caring teacher is a major influence on the new expectations placed on high school teachers. Examples of forces redefining teacher roles include: (1) the increasing knowledge base regarding best practice; (2) increased teacher responsibility for student learning growth; (3) expectations that curriculum be tailored to better meet the needs of all learners; and (4) increased responsibility for assessment that better meets student and community needs. Furthermore, high school teachers are expected to: (1) teach students from a wide variety of diverse backgrounds; (2) be aware of and sensitive to social demands and expectations; (3) successfully meet the individual learning needs and developmental needs of students; (4) utilize information technologies in instruction; (5) make decisions about what to teach at a time when new knowledge is growing at record rates; and (6) work more closely than ever before with family and community members.

It is widely acknowledged that high school reform must include major shifts in the way high school students are taught. Achieving the necessary quality of instruction requires new and expanded instructional roles, as well as strategies that extend far beyond past and current norms. Examples of these new roles (e.g., utilizing instructional strategies that engage students while making them part of the learning process; providing a climate that is supportive of teaching and learning where academics are honored and distractions are not tolerated) were provided in the chapter.

Several other developments have contributed to the changing concept of effective high school teachers. These include the creation of the National Board for Professional Teaching Standards, which has established high standards for what accomplished teachers should know and be able to do, and the establishment of national standards for high school staff development. These and related events have more clearly spelled out the roles and responsibilities of today's high school teachers. Changes in staff development include moving away from fragmented, piecemeal improvement efforts to staff development driven by clear, coherent, strategic planning. Examples of effective staff development models, including those implemented at high schools featured in this book, were provided in this chapter.

Teacher preparation must also be improved if prospective high school teachers are to enter the profession with the knowledge, skills, and dispositions needed to succeed. The single most important strategy for reforming high schools is that of significantly improving professional preparation programs at the undergraduate and graduate levels. Much work remains to be done in this area because at many institutions, the professional preparation of high school teachers has undergone few changes for decades. An encouraging trend emerging at growing numbers of teacher preparation institutions, however, is the professional development school model, which focuses on high school teachers and other school-based educators.

CONNECTIONS TO OTHER CHAPTERS

The crucial roles high school teachers play in determining the degree of success high schools reach in achieving in their primary goal of increasing student learning connect this chapter to all the others in this book. The topics included are closely associated with the chapters that address instruction, the affective needs of adolescents, the organization of teachers and learners, and working with family and community members.

ACTION STEPS

1. Interview two or more teachers who have excellent reputations for successful high school teaching. Ask questions that will help you learn more about their perspectives on the changing roles of teachers, and share what you learn with your classmates.

2. It is suggested in this chapter that learning styles and multiple intelligences are examples of an expanding knowledge base that is helping reshape high school

teaching. Learn more about one of these theories and write a succinct paper that provides examples of ways the theory you select influences your concept of high school instruction.

3. Using the National Board for Professional Teaching Standards website and other resources, examine the national certification standards for a teaching field in which you are interested. How do you believe these standards influence the nature of high school teaching? Share what you learn with your classmates.

4. Arrange to interview someone (central office supervisor, high school principal, teacher leader) who is responsible for designing staff development for practicing high school teachers. Ask them questions that will help you better understand what they believe are the most effective ways to provide successful staff development opportunities. Share what you learn with you classmates.

Discussion Questions

1. After reading about some of the emerging roles of high school teachers in this chapter, discuss the ways, if any, that these roles have changed since you attended high school.

2. One of the *Breaking Ranks* recommendations at the beginning of this chapter is that all high school students should have individual learning plans. What do you think this recommendation means? How can this recommendation be carried out in large high schools?

3. In what ways do you believe teacher preparation needs to change to reflect the new kinds of expectations placed on high school teachers today?

4. Prepare a brief list of characteristics you believe successful high school teachers should have. Include the three categories of knowledge, skills, and dispositions. Discuss the characteristics you included as compared with those listed by your classmates.

References

Abdal-Haqq, I. (1989). The nature of professional development schools. *ERIC Digest,* Washington, DC: ERIC Clearinghouse on Teacher Education. ED316548 89.

Ashton, P. T. (1996). Improving the preparation of teachers. *Educational Researcher, 25,* 21–22, 35.

Ashton, P. T., & Crocker, L. (1996). *Does teacher education make a difference?* Gainesville, FL: University of Florida.

Bents, M., & Bents, R. (1990). *Perceptions of good teaching among novice, advanced beginner and expert teachers.* Paper presented at the annual meeting of the American Research Association, Boston, Massachusetts.

Breaking ranks: Changing an American institution: A report of the National Association of Secondary School principals on the high school for the 21st Century (1996). Reston, VA: National Association of Secondary School Principals.

California State Department of Education (1992). *Second to none: A vision of the California high school.* Sacramento, CA: California High School Task Force.

Carnate, B. (May 25, 1997). Personal communication.

Clark, R. W. (1997). *Professional development schools: Policy and financing—A guide for policymakers.* Washington, DC: American Association of Colleges for Teacher Education.

Cruickshank, D. R. & Associates (1996). *Preparing America's teachers.* Bloomington, IN: Phi Delta Kappa Foundation.

Darling-Hammond, L. (1994). Developing professional development schools: Early lessons, challenge, and promise. In Darling-Hammond L. (Ed.) *Professional development schools: Schools for developing a profession.* New York: Teachers College Press.

Darling-Hammond, L. (1996). What matters most: A competent teacher for every child. *Phi Delta Kappan, 78(3),* 193–200.

Darling-Hammond, L. (1990). Teacher professionalism: Why and how. In Liberman, A. (Ed.). *Schools as collaborative cultures: Creating the future now.* Philadelphia: Falmer Press, pp. 25–50.

Darling-Hammond, L., & McLaughlin, M. (1995). Policies that support professional development in an era of reform. *Phi Delta Kappan 76(8),* 597–604.

Darling-Hammond, L., Wise, A. E., & Klein, S. P. (1995). *A license to teach: Building a profession for 21st-century schools.* San Francisco: Westview Press.

Dodd, A. W. (1996). A very different kind of teacher education program: Professional development schools. *NASSP Bulletin, 80(580),* 30-37.

Feiman-Nemser, S., & Parker, M. B. (1990). *Making subject matter part of the conversation of helping beginning teachers learn to teach.* East Lansing: National Center for Research on Teacher Education.

Gardner, H. (1991). *The unschooled mind. How children think and how schools should teach.* New York: Harper Collins Publishers.

Goodlad, J. (1990). *Teachers for tomorrow's schools.* San Francisco, CA: Jossey-Bass.

Grossman, P. L. (1990). *The making of a teacher: Teacher knowledge and teacher education.* New York: Teachers College Press.

Hirsh, S. (1997). Breaking ranks recommendations require standards-based staff development. *The High School Magazine, 4(4),* 4–13.

Holmes Group. *Tomorrow's schools of education* (1995). East Lansing, MI: Author.

Joyce, B., & Showers, B. (1995). *Student achievement through staff development: Fundamentals of school renewal.* White Plains, NY: Longman Publishers.

Kaplan, L. S. (1997). Professional development for restructuring: Teacher leadership for classroom change. *The High School Magazine, 4(4),* 14–21.

Lenk, H. A. (1989). *A case study of two alternative route social studies teachers.* Dissertation: Teachers College, Columbia University.

Liberman, A. (1995). Practices that support teacher development. *Phi Delta Kappan 76(8),* 591–596.

Lounsbury, J. H. (1996). Personalizing the high school: Lessons learned in the middle. *NASSP Bulletin, 80(584),* 17–24.

McEwin, C. K., & Dickinson, T. S. (1996). *Forgotten youth, forgotten teachers: Transformation of the professional preparation of teachers of young adolescents.* Background paper prepared for the Middle Grade School State Policy Initiative. New York: Carnegie Corporation of New York.

McEwin, C. K., & Dickinson, T. S. (1995). *The professional preparation of middle level teachers: Profiles of successful programs.* Columbus, OH: National Middle School Association.

McLaughlin, M., & Talbert, J. (1993). *Contexts that matter for teaching and learning.* Stanford, CA: Center for Research on the Context of Secondary School Teaching, Stanford University.

Meier, D., & Schwarz, P. (1995). Central Park East Secondary School: The hard part is making it happen. In Apple, M. W., & Beane, J. A. (Eds.). *Democratic schools*. Alexandria, VA: Association for Supervision and Curriculum Development.

Mitchell, N. (1987). *Interim evaluation report of the alternative certification program*. REA87-027-2. Dallas, TX: Dallas Independent School District, Department of Planning, Evaluation and Testing.

National Board for Professional Teaching Standards (1996). *Adolescence and young adulthood/Science standards for national board certification*. Southfield, MI: Author.

National Board for Professional Teaching Standards (1990). *Toward high and rigorous standards for the teaching profession*. Washington, DC: Author.

National Foundation for the Improvement of Education (1996). *Teachers take charge of their learning: Transforming professional development for student success*. Executive summary. West Haven, CT: Author.

National Staff Development Council and National Association of Secondary School Principals (1995). *Standards for staff development: High school edition*. Oxford, OH: Author.

Newmann, F. M., Marks, H. M., & Gamoran, A. (1997). *Issues in Restructuring Schools*, Report Number 8, University of Wisconsin, Madison, Center on Organization and Restructuring of Schools.

Olsen, D. G. (1985). The quality of prospective teachers: Education vs. Non-education graduates. *Journal of Teacher Education, 37*, 56–59.

Osguthorpe, R. T., Harris, R. C., Black, S., Cutler, B. R., & Harris, M. F. (1995). Introduction: Understanding school-university partnerships. In Osguthorpe, R. T., Harris, R. C., Harris, M. F., Black, S. (Eds.) *Partner schools: Centers for educational renewal*. San Francisco: Jossey-Bass Publishers.

Ridgen, D. W. (December 11, 1996). How teachers would change teacher education. *Education Week on the Web*.

Rottenberg, C. J. & Berliner, D. C. (1990). *Expert and novice teachers conceptions of common classroom activities*. Paper presented at the annual meeting of American Educational Research Association, Boston, MA.

Sarason, S. B. (1993). *The case for change: Rethinking the preparation of educators*. San Francisco, CA: Jossey-Bass Publishers.

Shulman, L. S. (1987). Knowledge and teaching: Foundations of the new reform. *Harvard Educational Review, 57 (1)*, 1–22.

Silver, H., Strong, R., & Perini, M. (1997). Integrating learning styles and multiple intelligences. *Educational Leadership, 55 (1)*, 22–27.

Sizer, T. R. (1996). *Horace's hope: What works for the American high school*. Boston: Houghton Mifflin Company.

Sparks, D., & Hirsh, S. (1997). *A new vision for staff development*. Alexandria, VA: Association for Supervision and Curriculum Development and Oxford, OH: National Staff Development Council.

Tyson, H. (1994). *Who will teach the children? Progress and resistance in teacher education*. San Francisco, CA: Jossey-Bass Publishers.

What matters most: Teaching for America's future: Report of the National Commission on Teaching and America's Future (1996). New York: Author.

Wise, A. E. (1997). New teachers say they are well prepared: Study in Kentucky reveals Progress—NCATE a factor. *Quality Teaching, 6 (2)*, 1–2, Washington, DC: National Council for Accreditation of Teacher Education.

Zeichner, K. M. (1993). Traditions of practice in U. S. preservice teacher education programs. *Teacher and Teacher Education, 9*, 1–13.

CHAPTER 10

LEADING HIGH SCHOOLS IN THE NEW CENTURY

WHAT YOU WILL LEARN IN THIS CHAPTER

The nature of instructional leadership

New directions in leadership training and certification

A comprehensive approach to assessing a school's learning environment

The value of school-based decision making in developing school improvement plans

Designing action research projects to improve teaching and learning

New projects to reform high schools— Coalition of Essential Schools, Outcome-based education and total quality management

The principal will provide leadership in the high school community by building and maintaining a vision, direction, and focus for student learning.

Selection of high school principals will be based on qualities of leadership rooted in established knowledge and skills that result in dedication to good instructional practice and learning.

Current principals will build and refine the skills and knowledge required to lead and manage change.

The principal will foster an atmosphere that encourages teachers to take risks to meet the needs of students.

Teachers will provide the leadership essential to the success of reform, collaborating with others in the educational community to redefine the role of the teacher and to identify sources of support for that redefined role.

—*Breaking Ranks*, p. 99

The late science educator Paul Brandwein liked to chide audiences of principals by saying, "Leaders go too far in order for others to go far enough." These words, spoken in the 1960s, appear timely for high school principals in the 1990s and beyond. Meeting the needs of youth and society today requires knowledge, understanding, and faith in one's convictions. Two key concepts important to leadership at the high school level appear embedded in Brandwein's assertion: (1) leaders are risk takers and (2) leaders stretch the behavior of those they lead.

Although the importance of the high school principal cannot be overestimated, the concept of leadership applies to teachers as well. The quality of their work with students and the quality of their contributions to school reform are key variables in high school reform. William Glasser, a psychiatrist who has written widely about schools, sees leadership as the ability to manage all workers in a way that gets them to do high quality work (Glasser, 1994). He contends that managing workers to produce quality requires different behavior than was true of the traditional boss manager who told people what to do. Lead managers are people who help others see that it is in their best interests to do quality work.

Glasser (1990) lists four essential elements of lead management: (1) leaders engage the workers in an ongoing discussion of the quality of work to be done and the time needed to do it so that they have a chance to add their input, (2) leaders model the task so that the workers know what is expected of them, (3) leaders ask the workers to inspect or evaluate their own work for quality, (4) leaders show the workers that they have done everything possible to provide them with the best tools and the best workplace as well as a noncoercive atmosphere in which to do the job (pp. 31–32). Interestingly, he believes that the definition of good teaching is embodied in the four elements of lead management.

Historically, as the complexity of schools increased, it was deemed necessary to appoint someone to superintend the enterprise. This person, usually selected by the teachers, was called the *principal-teacher*. In theory, and often in practice, the principal-teacher was considered the best teacher in the school. He or she continued to teach but also served as the nominal leader of the school. The use of the term *principal-teacher* was considered an Americanized version of the British headmaster and remained a valid description of the position until consolidation created larger schools and ostensibly less time to teach students. As a result, principal-teachers became principals with no teaching responsibilities.

The original intention of the principalship gradually evolved to a point at which instructional dimensions were de-emphasized. Accepting Glasser's premise, however, seems to restore the mission of the principal as a teacher of teachers. In working with the teachers, he or she models the behavior that they are expected to demonstrate to students. If the purpose of the high school is to get all students to produce quality work, then instructional leadership advances to center stage.

THE NATURE OF INSTRUCTIONAL LEADERSHIP

Keefe and Jenkins (1984, 1991) define instructional leadership as "the principal's role in providing direction, resources, and support to teachers and students for the improvement of teaching and learning in the school" (p. vii). They conceptualize the role in four broad domains: formative, planning, implementation, and evaluation.

Formative: The instructional leader operates from a secure knowledge base. An effective instructional leader does not have to be omniscient, but knows the trends in school curriculum, understands ways to organize schools differently and the ramifications of each, knows how to build a schedule to fit a variety of instructional needs, and knows how to integrate instructional resources and strategies to match the learning needs of individual students.

Planning: Understanding educational trends gives the principal an appropriate knowledge base for the planning dimension of instructional leadership. It means helping teachers organize for instruction by:

- Assessing current student and program needs
- Establishing goals for the school
- Helping teachers see the relationship of goals to the instructional program
- Developing goals for instructional areas
- Translating instructional goals into operational objectives
- Formulating plans for school improvement
- Securing the necessary resources to support the program.

Instructional planning means working with teachers and other stakeholders to formulate a direction for the high school that incorporates national exigencies, state mandates, and local circumstances. It means aligning the written, taught, and tested curriculum as closely as possible (English, 1994).

Implementation: The planning process leads naturally to activities for enhancing the quality of teaching and learning. The instructional leader understands that students learn in different ways; what works for some students may not work for others. Research on school effectiveness shows that academic emphasis and the quality of student–teacher interactions affect student outcomes (Edmonds, 1982). A high school's climate for learning is the product of the collaborative efforts of the principal, the teachers, the parents, and the students. Successful leaders know how to orchestrate the special talents and abilities of these groups and individuals within them for the benefit of students. Classrooms are replaced with learning environments and teaching teams that respond to the learning needs of individual students so that the likelihood of success for all is increased.

Evaluation: A high school's increased effectiveness is evident from a number of vital signs:

- Average daily attendance
- Library and media center usage
- Participation in cocurricular activities
- Number of referrals for disciplinary reasons
- Percentage of students making adequate progress
- Number of students enrolled and succeeding in high-level academic courses

Student performance on standardized tests is compared with local, state, and national norms. Teachers monitor student achievement using criterion-referenced tests. Surveys of parents and other community members provide feedback on the impact of school programs. Evidence collected systematically by school leaders can serve as the basis for school improvement and community support (Keefe & Jenkins, 1991).

Instructional leadership, though a key dimension of the effective principal, can be extended to include teachers as well. The four domains are just as relevant for teachers as they are for principals. At the successful high school, instructional leadership is every professional's responsibility. At the Middle High College High School in Long Island City, New York, for example, all faculty members serve on one of three assessment committees. Each committee is responsible for translating schoolwide outcomes into broadly defined student projects that include a system for collecting student work, a procedure for assessing it, and a means for determining standards for graduation.

THE PERFORMANCE-BASED PRINCIPALSHIP

In 1990 the National Policy Board for Educational Administration in Fairfax, Virginia, identified "21 performance domains of the principalship, organized in four areas that blend traditional content with leadership and process skills" (NASSP University Consortium, 1992, p. v). The intent was to provide universities specific direction for the preparation of principals. Eleven of the domains are skill-oriented, and ten are content-oriented. In reality, however, most of the domains combine skill and content. The domains are described in terms of performance standards that can be used for preparation programs and certification, and as benchmarks for practicing principals to engage in self-evaluation and to map courses for self-improvement. The nature of the domains and performance standards are such that entry and advanced levels of performance are accommodated within a single domain (Thomson, 1993).

A typical domain from each of the four areas (functional, programmatic, interpersonal, and contextual) is described here with selected performance standards or behaviors as example.

Leadership: "Providing purpose and direction for individuals and groups; shaping school culture and values; facilitating the development of a shared strategic vision for the school; formulating goals and planning change efforts with staff, and setting priorities for one's school in the context of community and district priorities and student and staff needs" (Thomson, 1993, pp. 1–3). To be competent in the leadership domain, principals should be able to:

1. Articulate a personal vision for their school and a well-developed educational philosophy, and set high standards for themselves and others

2. Gain insights into the school's culture and school members' personal hopes and dreams

3. Foster innovation within their schools

4. Facilitate the development of school improvement efforts

5. Utilize the leadership skills of staff and students to plan and implement the change process (Thomson, pp. 1–12)

Curriculum Design: "Understanding major curriculum design models, interpreting school district curricula; initiating a needs analysis; planning and implementing with staff a framework for instruction; aligning curriculum and anticipated outcomes; monitoring social and technological development as they affect curriculum; adjusting content as needs and conditions change" (Thomson, 1993, p. 9). To be competent in curriculum design, principals should be able to:

1. Connect curriculum design to instructional objectives

2. Describe procedures for improving quality control in implementing curricula

3. Identify and define the relationships among the written curriculum, the taught curriculum, and the tested curriculum

4. Describe how schools can use data disaggregation to improve pupil performance

5. Conduct the basic steps in needs assessment (Thomson, pp. 9–20).

Motivating Others: "Creating conditions that enhance the staff's desire and willingness to focus energy on achieving educational excellence; planning and encouraging participation; facilitating teamwork and collegiality; treating staff as professionals; providing intellectual stimulation; supporting innovation; recognizing and rewarding effective performance; providing feedback, coaching, and guidance; providing needed resources; serving as a role model" (Thomson, 1993, p. 14). To be competent at motivating others, principals should be able to:

1. Encourage teamwork and collegiality among teachers

2. Practice participative decision making

3. Provide face-to-face and written performance feedback

4. Enhance individual productivity

5. Articulate performance expectations (Thomson, pp. 13–14).

Policy and Political Influences: "Understanding schools as political systems; policy issues; examining and affecting policies individually and through professional and public groups; relating policy initiatives to the welfare of students; addressing ethical issues" (Thomson, 1993, pp. 20–23). To be competent in this domain, principals should be able to:

1. Describe how an existing or proposed policy interacts with other policies and how it complements or challenges the norms and routines of the school

2. Develop if/then scenarios outlining alternative political strategies that could be employed to mobilize support for or resistance to particular policy proposals

3. Profile the power relationships in the local school setting and indicate how these power relationships affect the likelihood that particular proposals can be enacted and implemented

4. Assess policy options and political strategies in light of their moral and ethical implications

5. Assess the political interests and ideals of relevant constituent groups inside and outside the school setting (Thomson, pp. 20–22)

Some critics of the National Policy Board standards believe they are much too ambitious for the majority of principals to achieve. They believe that mastering the performance standards in all 21 domains would require a lifetime of study (Sacken, 1994), but then one could argue that the principal should also be a life-long learner. The significance of the standards, however, resides in the scope of the content and skills judged important for successful leadership, the acknowledgment that the quest for higher standards is appropriate for educational leaders as well as students, and the realization that the standards can be considered in terms of tiers of learning. With regard to the latter, reaching the ultimate tier might result in a national certification similar that used in the profession of architecture. A volume on each of the 21 domains is being published by Eye on Education.

REFORMING HIGH SCHOOLS

Reform seems a better word than restructure for describing what is required to improve the education of all high school students. *Webster's New Collegiate Dictionary* defines *reform* as putting an end to a fault or an abuse by introducing a better course of action. Restructuring implies the changing of the makeup, organization, or pattern of something. Reform appears to include restructuring and is a stronger concept. Restructuring may allow for tinkering with change without a corresponding change in the substance. For example, the adoption of an external innovation may bring notoriety to a school without addressing a major problem in the school.

The change process is often described as a series of steps that good leaders implement in improving schools. The term *process,* however, implies a dynamic that may frustrate attempts to think of change in a mechanistic fashion. Yet high school leaders are continually reminded of the need to understand the change process and how it takes place. Successful change in any institution requires a critical mass of people who have internalized certain principles about change.

Education is a complex business. Its reform requires hard work, skill, commitment, and depth of understanding. In a speech at the annual convention of the National Association of Secondary School Principals in February, 1994, Charles Letteri, University of Vermont, Burlington, reminded his audience that learning and teaching are extremely difficult undertakings. He lamented that the present high school milieu has yet to internalize the notion that teaching is as arduous a task as learning.

Reforming high schools, like teaching and learning, is hard work. It requires skill, commitment, and a willingness to *do* something, rather than just talk about it. Changing schools rarely goes easily. Teachers, parents, community members, and even students often resist attempts to make needed changes in schools. It is the principal's responsibility to teach others why changes are appropriate and to provide opportunities to learn the new behaviors necessary to implement the changes. As a teacher of teachers, the principal goes the extra mile during the transition stage of change to offer support, encouragement, and pertinent staff development.

Fullan and Miles (1992) derive seven basic themes from current knowledge of successful change that reflect the current state of the art:

- Change is learning—loaded with uncertainty.
- Change is a journey, not a blueprint.
- Problems are our friends.
- Change is resource-hungry.
- Change requires the power to manage it.
- Change is systemic
- All large-scale change is implemented locally.

They write, "We can say flatly that reform will not be achieved until these seven orientations have been incorporated into the thinking and reflected in the actions of those involved in change efforts" (p. 749).

Embedded within these seven themes is a belief that change is a systematic and unified process which occurs in a context influenced by international, national, state, and local variables. Its success relies heavily on the knowledge, skills, and personalities of local participants.

Strategic planning is a key element in any attempt to reform a school. The term *strategic* means that it is based on data systematically collected and interpreted. One excellent tool for collecting data about a specific high school is the Comprehensive Assessment of the School Environment (CASE), produced by the National Association of Secondary School Principals. The CASE model provides a systematic framework for school improvement. The data collected through the CASE process provides answers about student achievement and its distribution among various subgroups within a high school student population and whether a school operates efficiently (Keefe, 1994).

CASE is a new conceptual model of the school environment which incorporates 34 variables in a computerized information management system (IMS) for schools to profile productivity and efficiency. Thus the system is referred to as CASE-IMS. The model includes a range of inputs and outputs important to school improvement. It is devised to suggest that climate, satisfaction, and productivity are determined by many different factors interacting with each other. In this sense, the model captures the spirit of Margaret Wheatley's premise that a system can only be fully understood as a whole system and that the relationships among discrete variables are given primary value. When systems are viewed from a holistic perspective, there is a landscape of connections with each component important to the other (Wheatley, 1992).

Figure 10.1 depicts the contextual, input, mediating, and outcome variables of school environments as formulated in CASE.

FIGURE 10.1   An Interactive Model of the School Environment

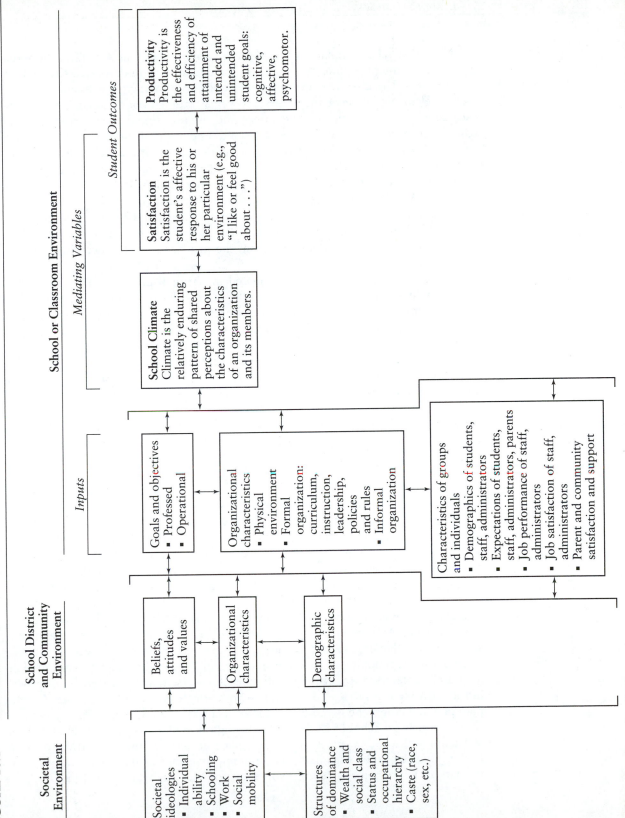

Note that school climate is a mediating variable and that societal, school district, and community contexts are part of the overall system that affects school improvement. "The model is an interactive one. . . . Implicit are hypotheses that societal elements influence the values and organizational characteristics of the district which, in turn, influence the values and organizational characteristics of the school which, in turn influence the values and operation of the school, teacher, student, and parent perceptions of the school climate and ultimately student satisfaction and productivity" (Keefe, 1994, p. 58). A basic assumption of the model is that school climate does not define effectiveness; it only predicts it.

The CASE battery consists of four survey instruments: the NASSP School Climate Survey, designed to be used with students, teachers, and parents, and three separate NASSP Satisfaction Surveys, one for each of the aforementioned groups. Three report forms gather additional data from the principal, the teachers, and the students, respectively.

The survey instruments were validated in national and normative surveys of 1,500 teachers, 14,600 students, and 4,400 parents. Each survey has between eight and ten subscales addressing important aspects of the school environment. Computer scoring programs provide a separate climate and satisfaction profile for a high school (National Association of Secondary School Principals Task Force, 1987).

The NASSP School Climate Survey collects information about student, teacher and parent perceptions of: (1) teacher–student relationships, (2) security and maintenance, (3) administration, (4) student academic orientation, (5) student behavioral values, (6) guidance, (7) student–peer relationships, (8) parent and community relationships, (9) instructional management, and (10) student activities. This data becomes part of a comprehensive database that helps identify a school's strengths and weaknesses. The CASE-IMS program also assists in planning school improvement projects in two different ways.

An "Interventions Command" offers possible actions to identify school strengths and to improve identified weaknesses. A "What If" analysis predicts the effect of specific inputs on particular school outcomes. The interventions command accesses more than 600 suggestions stored by CASE. The "What If" analysis estimates the degree of impact on a specific outcome if a school leadership team made certain changes in a moderator or input variable. The result of the CASE-IMS analysis gives a leadership team greater insight into a school's status relative to key variables, suggests experientially validated steps to improve a situation, and provides estimates of the relative effects of a planned change before its implementation.

The CASE-IMS process is one component of a larger strategy for diagnosing school needs, planning desired changes, and further evaluating the effects of planned interventions. School improvement is a long-term process that requires careful planning and implementation at the building level. Its essential characteristic is growth in the outcome measures used to define school effectiveness and excellence. Careful planning and comprehensive assessment are necessary conditions (Keefe, 1994).

Capital High School in Olympia Washington, and Mills Godwin High School in Richmond, Virginia, participated in a pilot project for the CASE-IMS process. Both schools began by organizing a school improvement management team (SIMT) to plan an initial priority-setting workshop for the faculty, students, parents, and community, and to support the task forces that emerged from the workshop. At the workshop, representative small groups focused on several of the environmental areas. The groups were asked to identify the current status of each area and to describe how they thought it should be.

At Capital High School, three major concerns were identified and resulted in the formation of three task forces: Academic Preparation, Student Discipline, and Curriculum. Within 6 months the three task forces expanded to 27, leading the principal to observe that the task force concept was "an ongoing, never-ending process." The task forces, using data collected from CASE, suggested interventions to reduce the gap between the status quo and the school's vision in various areas related to the three major concerns. At Mills Godwin High School, each task force had a leader, usually a teacher, who was responsible to the SIMT. Interventions were recommended to the SIMT and action plans were implemented. One intervention resulted in 54 percent reduction in the number of students referred to the administration for minor disciplinary offenses, and a 46 percent reduction in the number of referrals for major offenses. Interventions at Capital High School resulted in improved communication between the high school and its middle-level feeder schools, the establishment of a technology lab in business education, and a communications link between the social studies department and a school in Beijing (Howard & Keefe, 1991).

School-based Decision Making

Optimally, school improvement planning includes representatives from several key stakeholder groups, but at the very least should involve the administration and faculty. These representatives form the leadership team responsible for making decisions about school improvement. The team may be called a school site council, as it is at Minot High School in Minot, North Dakota, a school improvement management team, as recommended by the CASE-IMS process of NASSP, a leadership team, or any number of creative titles. The point is that the group is empowered to make decisions. It is not merely advisory. Some type of school improvement team exists in most high schools today. In many instances, site-based management for school improvement is mandated by state statute.

At Minot High School, the site council includes representatives from the administration, teachers, classified personnel, parents, and students. Parents, teachers, and classified personnel are elected for 1- to 3-year terms by the vote of their constituent groups. The principal and the assistant principals automatically serve on the council. The council makes decisions in five specific areas: goal setting, personnel selection, staff development, curriculum modifications, and faculty improvement. It submits an annual plan for school improvement and a year-end evaluation of the plan to the district.

In the area of personnel, the Minot High School site council prioritizes the needs of the school program and assigns staff to meet the needs in accordance with the specifications of the negotiated contract. When staff vacancies exist, the council works with the appropriate department chair to develop a position analysis and appropriate interview questions. The district office and the principal then screen applicants against the position analysis. The best applicants are interviewed by a site selection team that includes the department chair and other members of the specific department.

With regard to curriculum modification, the site council makes recommendations to the district curriculum committee when the school wishes to deviate from the approved district curriculum. They develop a modification proposal that includes the rationale for the change, an outline of the revised content, a listing of the district outcomes that will be affected, an explanation of how they will be addressed, a sample of the instructional strategies to be used, and an evaluation design. Obviously, this process is complex and involves staff members beyond the site council.

The function of the school-based leadership teams is to plan, coordinate, and manage the change process. In so doing it may interface with other groups whose primary role is advisory. For example, in Florida, School Advisory Councils (SACs) exist in all public schools. The primary responsibility of the SAC is to give advice and to approve school improvement plans before they are submitted to the district school board. The school-based leadership teams steer the activities that result in school improvement planning and involve as many members of the school community as possible. They may establish permanent task forces, as is done at the Mann High School in Greenville, South Carolina. There the school management team asks teachers to volunteer annually for one of three standing task forces: budget, policy and procedures, and staff development. Other task forces are appointed on an ad hoc basis.

The leadership teams arrange for staff development activities that raise the awareness levels of faculty, staff, students, and parents. Initially the awareness activities help faculty and staff master the skills necessary for conducting school improvement. If, for example, the CASE-IMS system is to be used, people need to understand the processes of data collection, interpretation and analysis. The faculty and staff must also understand the components of a school improvement plan. Usually these components include a mission statement, a set of assumptions or beliefs, and as list of goals. These elements are crucial to the ultimate success of an improvement plan. Later, as a school improvement plan evolves, staff development related to instruction, scheduling, advisement, teaming, and other innovations may be needed.

School-based management means changing school governance. It is a way for the total school community to buy into making schools better places for students and teachers. As Sarason (1971) reminded educators over two decades ago, schools are cultures, and cultural change requires more than simply plugging in the latest innovations in sporadic attempts to keep pace with one's colleagues. Cultural change means that the school community will identify and question the assumptions that undergird the school's operation in light of new data reflecting changes in a school's population and in society. At Rancho Verde High School in Moreno, California, the school site council approves the school improvement plan, approves the school budget, and reviews policies and programs.

School Improvement Plans

School improvement plans may differ from school to school or state to state. Typically they involve the development of a mission statement and a set of goals consistent with the statement. The goals are developed annually and establish targets for school improvement. In many cases school improvement plans embrace larger goals established by the state. For example, many states have adopted the eight goals listed by the *Goals 2000: Educate America* Act passed by Congress in March, 1994, or they have used the six goals identified in *America 2000,* a product of the Bush administration. The goals, such as "all children in America will start school ready to learn," or "U.S. students will be first in the world in mathematics and science" by the year 2000, become the targets for each school district and each school in the district. The school improvement plan then focuses on ways that a particular school can enable the district and the state to achieve each goal. Unfortunately, this process has resulted in an overabundance of activity to create plans to meet local and state deadlines, but little substantive change at the school level. In 1982, Larry Cuban at Stanford University found that high schools have changed very little since 1900. The implication of his study is that until classroom structures change, not much else will (Keefe, 1994).

The school design statement developed by the National Association of Secondary School Principals seems a better option (Keefe & Howard, 1997). It is a set of specifications for a school of the future. Unlike the school improvement plan, all components are interdependent and consistent with one another. The design statement addresses the total school as a system. For example, the school schedule is an outgrowth of the school's mission statement, its key assumptions, and its stated outcomes for students. Schools do not adopt a schedule because it appears to be more flexible; they adopt a schedule because it fits the overall configuration that the faculty and staff deem appropriate.

The design statement consists of twelve steps. The first three set the tone for the other nine. They are basic and must be defined before decisions are made about aspects of the school. The first step is the *mission and vision statements,* which state why the school exists as a school and the characteristics of the desired school of the future. The second is a *compilation of assumptions* about the nature of leaders, learning, motivation, the purposes of high schools, school organization, and budgeting that are basic to the high school's design. For example, "Students have different learning styles which affect their response to different forms of instruction," "Learning tasks chosen by students tap intrinsic motivation and facilitate understanding," or "Teaching teams composed of teachers with complementary talents are superior to the self-contained assignment of teachers." The third basic component is *a list of four to six competencies deemed essential for effective living in the 21st century.* These exit outcomes define the performance expectations that the school holds for its students. For example, "Students will be global citizens who interact positively with people of varied cultures, identify the environmental impact of decisions, promote the health of the world's environment, and promote the welfare of all people in the world." "Students will be socially responsible contributors who participate in the political process; live in accordance with the just laws of society; process, assimilate, and synthesize information to determine actions; and participate in lifelong learning" (Keefe & Howard, 1997, p. 67).

The nine system components that follow are derived naturally from the three basic components. The first system component is the *curriculum.* Here the leadership team or their designees write short descriptive statements about the nature of curriculum content and the opportunities offered students. These specifications must be consistent with the assumptions and the student outcomes statement. *Instructional techniques* to be used are defined next, based on research and practice that indicate their success in achieving student outcomes. The instructional use of technology is included in this component. The third component describes the *school structure and organization.* This section includes descriptors of the school schedule and the relations of staff to each other and to students. The fourth addresses *school culture and climate.* Key characteristics of the school's culture are defined in this section. The customs, traditions, and ceremonies of the school are described, especially as they directly affect the identified student outcomes. If CASE is used, the results of the climate surveys point out school strengths and areas in need of attention.

The *school leadership, management, and budgeting* section explains how the school's site-based management is expected to function. The use of technology as a management tool is included in this area. The next component is *school staffing and staff development.* Questions such as "what are the primary staffing roles?" "Who will participate in the hiring and induction of new personnel?" and "What staff development activities are needed to support the mission, assumptions, and outcomes?" frame the discourse in this area.

Communication and political structures are included in the seventh system component. Specification for the school's internal and external communication linkages are described. Vertical and horizontal flowcharts show connections within the school, such as voice mail, e-mail, and networking capabilities; articulation with feeder schools; and relationships with the school district and the community. The next section outlines the short- and long-term *school resources, physical plant, and equipment* needed to actualize the curricular and instructional design. The final piece is the development of an *evaluation plan* to determine the extent to which the desired outcomes are being accomplished. The plan should include several means of reporting the results to interested stakeholders (Howard & Keefe, 1991).

Obviously, a school design statement for a high school cannot be short-circuited without seriously damaging its effectiveness. It requires considerable time, lots of reflective thinking, and a faculty and staff willing to collaborate to make a school a better place for the students and themselves. Once in place, the process breeds a professional atmosphere for enhancing the knowledge and skills of all concerned and a sense of ownership for school reform not usually found in piecemeal efforts. The design approach looks at the school as a system and as part of a system. As a result it is both comprehensive and systemic in its scope.

A PROTOTYPE DESIGN STATEMENT

The Thomas Haney Secondary School in Maple Ridge, British Columbia, opened for students in 1993. As part of an overall plan for improvement in the district, the school developed its own school design statement consistent with the mission of the total system. The following is a summary version of that statement.

1. Mission statement: All students will seek challenge and experience success.

2. Philosophical, psychological and organizational Assumptions:

   a. Whether one learns is more important than when.

   b. Learning requires the active participation of the learner.

   c. People learn in a variety of ways and at different rates.

   d. Learning is both an individual and a social process.

   e. Learning takes places in safe, healthy, orderly environments.

   f. All learners can be successful learners.

   g. Learning is a life-long process

3. Student outcomes statement: Students will be:

   a. High-quality producers who create products and services that consistently reflect high standards, take responsibility for results, and use time management skills effectively.

   b. Collaborative workers who express ideas and needs, accept and value the ideas and needs of others, work closely with others in a changing environment, find creative options and look for consensus, act with integrity, and work cooperatively in both non-competitive and competitive environments.

   c. Global citizens who interact positively with people of varied cultures, identify the environmental impact of decisions, promote the health of the world's environment, and promote the welfare of all people in the world.

   d. Socially responsible contributors who participate in the political process; live in accordance with the just laws of society; process, assimilate, and synthesize information to determine actions; and participate in life-long learning.

   e. Self-actualized individuals who value themselves as positive, worthwhile people; set and achieve personal and social goals; assess information to solve problems; and take responsibility for their own emotional and physical well-being.

   f. Communicative persons who can interact using a variety of communication processes and information sources.

   g. Creative contributors who develop creative solutions and implement new ideas, experiment and take risks, and participate in and influence change.

4. Curriculum and instructional programs:

   a. Students are required to meet the minimal requirements of the Ministry of Education, which include English, social studies, mathematics, science, business education, and at least one of physics, chemistry, or science and technology.

   b. The curriculum has been reorganized into learning guides to permit self-pacing and independent learning. Each course is divided into units and learning guides. Five learning guides are written for each unit.

5. Instructional techniques:

   a. Teachers act as subject matter coaches. Teachers supervise students in independent study, provide tutorial help, offer preview seminars, and follow up cooperative learning groups.

   b. A variety of learning activities are offered for each learning guide objective to accommodate individual student learning styles and capabilities.

   c. Testing is conducted when students are ready.

   d. In physical education and choral and instrumental music, students meet in groups two or three times per week.

6. School structure and organization:

   a. Every professional participates in the teacher adviser program. Teachers and administrators work with multi-age groups of 18 advisees.

   b. Advisees meet with their adviser 60 minutes on Mondays and Thursdays and 30 minutes on other mornings to plan their daily schedules.

   c. There is no master schedule except for the advisory group meetings.

   d. Advisers monitor student progress in each of four subjects the students pursue each semester.

   e. Each student develops a personalized educational plan (PEP) with the help of the teacher adviser.

   f. Each student is administered the Learning Style Profile from the National Association of Secondary School Principals to help in selecting activities in the learning guides and in choosing appropriate environments for learning.

7. School Culture and Climate:

   a. The school is developing a tradition of excellence for all students in an environment where all individuals are valued.

   b. Initial climate and satisfaction data will be collected using the NASSP CASE-IMS process.

8. School leadership, management and budgeting:

   a. The administrative organization is founded on the belief that all staff be provided the opportunity to be meaningfully involved in the decision-making process. The role of the principal is to help define, support and implement the creative decisions sought by staff, students, and parents.

   b. Role definitions exist for the principal, vice-principal, and department heads.

   c. The department heads committee focuses attention on matters related to budget, resources, curriculum, and instruction.

   d. The staff committee includes seven elected teachers and the principal. The committee makes recommendations about issues fundamental to fulfillment of the school's mission and to the essence of the search for effective methods to individualize instruction and learning.

e. Other important groups include student government, parents' advisory, and professional development.

f. The school-based team is composed of the vice principal, the student services department head, special programs teachers, and teachers whose students may be affected by the decisions of the team. The team assesses the needs of any student experiencing unusual difficulties in school.

9. School staffing and staff development:

a. Teachers serve as subject matter coaches and student advisers.

b. All teachers have common planning areas and access to private offices for student and parent conferences.

c. Teachers are selected for their commitment to personalized education, student advisement, and continuous progress learning.

d. Staff members devote considerable time to learning about "Outcomes Based Education," learning style and advisement.

10. School Resources, Physical Plant, and Equipment:

a. The building design provides individual and small group areas, a centrally located library/information center, a building-wide computer network for data access from all terminals, a computer-equipped staff planning area, natural lighting in all instructional areas, carpet tile and "flat wire" in many resource areas to allow for flexible configurations of electrical and computer outlets, air conditioning to provide a comfortable environment year-round and a full range of student support facilities.

b. Traditional classroom spaces have been replaced by spaces designed to implement an innovative educational program. Independent study occurs in a spacious area called "The Great Hall" where students obtain study guides and work on their own, with another student, or in small groups. Here students work on mathematics, English, social studies, and French. Other spaces have been constructed to facilitate individualized science, technology, art, music, drama, physical education, and business education.

11. Evaluation Plan:

a. The formative evaluation will focus on the school's mission statement and its exit outcomes.

b. The process will also examine the "three pillars" of Thomas Haney: advisement, curriculum organization, and information management.

c. An external audit team will be formed annually to examine the curriculum, student and administrative services, the teacher adviser system, human and social development, community relations, and information management.

d. Test results will be analyzed and compared with results from other high schools in the province.

e. Individual data about student academic progress will be filed daily in the information control center.

f. Traditional report cards will be replaced by a report of student progress whenever it is requested (School Design Statement, 1994).

ACTION RESEARCH

Action research appears as a final piece in the reform puzzle. Introduced to educators by Stephen M. Corey in 1953 as an effort to narrow the chasm between educational practice and theory, action research directly involves teachers in efforts to improve their instructional decision making. The idea that teachers can engage in hands-on research was an adaptation of the work of Kurt Lewin, who used action research as an intervention strategy for solving social problems (Corey, 1953). Applied to education, action research asks teachers to develop a systematic approach to answering questions they have about teaching and learning. When implemented properly, it is the essence of school-based decision making (Jenkins, 1994).

Today's climate for school improvement seems ideal for a resurgence of the notion that teachers individually and collectively can raise the level of education in their schools and in the nation. Traditionally educators have been content to take direction from external sources such as research, textbooks, publishers, or tradition. Questions were rarely raised as to the efficacy of a given approach for certain students or for achieving specific school goals, and if they were raised it was by professors at a university whose involvement with a high school was minimal. The current emphasis on local decision making and university–school collaboration, however, encourages research in the real-world setting of the school.

In order for teachers to do action research, they need the appropriate knowledge and skills. Working with university professors and school colleagues, teachers can learn to do research. Teachers who are directly involved in the process tend to pay attention to the results. As the novice teacher-researcher gradually acquires mastery of the research process, he or she gains control of the teaching-learning process, becoming more of a generator of knowledge than a consumer. Additionally, the discipline that accompanies the research process affects his or her planning and teaching (Jenkins, 1994).

The questions that guide the action research may originate from an individual teacher, a team of teachers, or from the school's plan for improvement. They lead to a review of salient literature, the development of a plan of action, data gathering, interpretation and analysis of the data, a report of the findings, and conclusions drawn from the findings. The results of the research project then inform the teacher-researcher and can be disseminated to other interested teachers in the school. When action research projects are conducted in several district schools, a structure for disseminating the results across schools is appropriate.

Including action research in the process of school improvement yields numerous benefits. Staff development is integrated into a teacher's regular school day and is conducted on site. Universities and schools expand their collaborative efforts toward school improvement. Teachers become more systematic in their overall conduct. Interest in other research is generated. The overall quality of practical problem solving is enhanced. In the emergent high school, teachers accept more responsibility for school change.

EFFORTS TO REFORM HIGH SCHOOLS

Major projects to change high schools date back to the Eight Year Study conducted from 1932–1940. This study, under the auspices of the Commission on the Relation of School and College, involved 30 public and private high schools. They were invited to redesign their course offerings in order to achieve: (1) greater mastery in learning, (2) more continuity in learning, (3) the release of students' creative energies, (4) a clearer understanding of the problems of contemporary civilization, (5) better individual guidance for students, and (6) better teaching materials and more effective teaching (Aiken, 1942). Three hundred colleges agreed to waive their formal admissions requirements for graduates of the experimental high schools. The results showed that graduates of the experimental schools outperformed their conventional school cohorts on a number of significant dimensions (see Chapter 1). Unfortunately, the effects of the study were diminished by our involvement in World War II.

The 1970s brought a major project in secondary education jointly sponsored by the Danforth Foundation and the National Association of Secondary School Principals. The Model Schools Project, as it was called, involved 34 junior and senior high schools. They were charged with implementing several innovative practices simultaneously. Among the practices were differentiated staffing, continuous progress education, independent study, advisement, a flexible master and daily schedule, and new approaches to evaluating student progress. Although only a few of the schools managed to implement all of the innovative practices, the results, as reported by the principals and staffs of individual schools, were impressive (Model Schools Project Report, 1977). Although the failure to conduct a comprehensive evaluation of the effects of all-at-once change diminished the impact of the project, many of the practices were adopted by nonparticipating secondary schools.

Currently the best known national reform initiatives are the Coalition of Essential Schools and Outcome-Based Education. Both involve many high schools. The Coalition of Essential Schools currently enrolls many high schools. Each school is encouraged to implement nine basic principles judged essential for creating good schools (see Chapter 1). According to the Coalition's principles, good schools focus on helping adolescents use their minds well, keep goals simple, apply their goals to all students, personalize teaching and learning, adopt the concept of the student-as-worker, award the diploma upon the successful final demonstration of mastery, stress values of patient expectation, perceive the principal and teachers as generalists first, maintain class loads of 80 students per teacher, and allow for substantial planning time. Each school is expected to actualize the nine principles in ways respectful of the local community and consistent with the strengths of the faculty. Consequently, no two schools are the same (Sizer, 1992).

Although the Coalition is high in conceptual strength, it is modest in suggesting practical steps for local implementation. It relies on the member schools to suggest ways in which the nine principles can be implemented. Several practices have emerged from this approach. For example, exhibitions have replaced the traditional credit accumulation at Central Park East High School and the Urban Academy in New York City. Noble High School in Berwick, Maine, has instituted the "senior celebration." The celebration consists of three parts: an exhibition, a portfolio, and the completion of citizenship and service activities. The exhibition is a celebration of the students' lives thus far, their special talents, their dreams of the future, their accomplishments, and their opinions. It is presented before a panel of three, one of whom must be a teacher.

The portfolio includes a current resume, three letters of recommendation, a copy of a completed application for college or for military service, a personal statement of introduction written by the student, special writings, a one-page statement of how the student plans to apply his or her knowledge of health to take care of himself or herself as an adult, and documentation of the citizenship and services activities. Citizenship embraces several activities: volunteering in a school for up to 5 hours, completing a tax form, participating in cocurricular activities, registering to vote (if 18), participating in local government, completing an approved job shadow experience, or designing one's own citizenship project. The citizenship project is in addition to 20 hours of community service that the student must complete during his or her four years in high school. Graduation by exhibition and portfolio is also found at Fenway Middle College High School in Boston, Massachusetts.

Many of the Coalition schools have given up the traditional subject matter departments in favor of interdisciplinary ones. The Thayer Junior-Senior High School in Winchester, New Hampshire, is organized in three-person teams responsible for four academic areas. The ninth grade team is responsible for math, science, social studies, and computers. A special education teacher or aide is added to the team so that all special educations can be mainstreamed. The Social History Project at University Heights High School, located at the Bronx Community College in New York City, combines English, social studies, and art. The Social History Project traces American history through four themes: slavery, immigration, industrialization, and unions. In many of the Coalition schools, the role of the teacher has been expanded to include the academic advisement of individual students (Lear, 1992).

The Coalition conducts research on the effects of the nine principles on school change. A publication entitled *Horace* is produced five times each year and offers examples from the member schools in implementing different aspects of the principles. For example, the November 1991 edition contained information on how to initiate conversation about school redesign. The teacher-as-coach metaphor was discussed by several athletic coaches at Fairdale High School in Jefferson County, Kentucky.

Outcome-Based Education (OBE) is built on the notion that schooling must start with an analysis of what students should be able to do when they graduate. Rather than think simply of accumulated credits and grades, course requirements and graduation requirements are redefined in terms of specific behaviors. For example, at Crestline High School in Crestline, Ohio, emphasis is placed upon the application of acquired knowledge. Culminating activities in each course require students to demonstrate real-life applications.

Proponents of OBE attempt to apply four basic principles to the design, delivery, documentation, and decision-making work of schooling: (1) Culminating demonstrations become the focal point of curriculum design and instruction, (2) curriculum and instruction proceed backward from the culminating demonstrations (outcomes) ensuring all components of a successful culminating demonstration are in place, (3) the outcomes should represent a high level of achievement and apply to all students, and (4) time should be flexible rather than a predefined absolute (Spady, 1992).

Implementation of the principles occurs in three broad categories: traditional OBE, transitional OBE, and transformational OBE. Traditional OBE applies the principles to the existing curriculum content. Transitional OBE defines outcomes in broader terms that cut across specific subject matter content. Transformational OBE means that curriculum content is no longer the defining element of outcomes; student learning is judged on the ability to perform in contexts that simulate life situations and challenges (Spady, 1992).

Littleton High School in Littleton, Colorado, has rewritten graduation requirements in terms of student outcomes which embrace both single disciplines and multidisciplines. Students must complete 19 outcomes to graduate rather than the traditional number of credits. Under their system, all students must demonstrate what they know and can do, in written and verbal communication in English and a foreign language, in mathematical problem solving and computation, history and geography, personal health, and ethics and technology. Thirty-six demonstrations, such as writing letters to public figures, writing a theater review, and designing science experiments enable students to demonstrate proficiency in the 19 requirements for graduation (Westerberg, Thomas, & Stein, 1994).

Like the Coalition of Essential Schools, OBE seems long on vision but lacking in specific implementation strategies. The substance of OBE, in some respects, resembles previous efforts at continuous progress education. In continuous progress education students completed learning packages, or UNIPAKS, which began with behavioral objectives accompanied by activities to achieve the objectives and an assessment to determine successful completion. Students were pretested to check entering behavior and placed in the material at a point commensurate with their knowledge and skills. They were then able to proceed through the packet at their own rate of speed.

Recent manifestations of OBE have been criticized by several groups representing an ideological spectrum. The biggest problem has arisen from a tendency to write outcomes in vague terms that are often associated with the affective domain. For example, to graduate from one Ohio high school, students should be able to "function as a responsible family member and maintain physical, emotional, and social well-being." Additionally, some analysts cite the fact that there is little or no hard evidence that OBE works, especially tranformational OBE. Others argue that transformational OBE will "dumb down" the curriculum by teaching to the least common denominator (Manno, 1995). Fundamentalist Christians often object to any outcome that hints at critical thinking on the grounds that "critical thinking means teaching children to empty themselves of their own values (transmitted from parents, church, and culture) and accept a set of suggested values" (Simonds,

1993–94). Problems with OBE seem to have occurred when traditional OBE was augmented by transitional and transformational OBE.

TOTAL QUALITY MANAGEMENT (TQM)

Total quality management is another approach that is making inroads into school practice. Based on the work of business consultant W. Edwards Deming, TQM favors empowering teachers and students (Holt, 1993). One important contribution is the notion that failure is often the result of the system rather than individuals within the system. The school system is often configured in such a way as to preclude the creation of quality products from all but a few students.

Deming defines the aim of leadership as helping people do a better job. He believes that it is the overall climate of an organization that influences a person's contribution more than the individual him/herself. As a result he avoids traditional systems of evaluation, claiming, "You cannot measure the performance of people. Measured performance is a function of the system" (Deming, 1993). The effectiveness of the system is the degree to which each component part works in harmony with the others. According to Deming, competition among people and departments within an organization is the enemy of quality.

He lists 14 points that managers must understand if they wish to attain quality and raise productivity. These 14 points include: (1) helping workers to evaluate the quality of their own work, (2) eliminating deficits, (3) driving out the fear of failure, (4) breaking down the barriers that divide members of a staff, (5) eliminating slogans and other external reward devices, (6) removing the barriers to pride in workmanship, (7) providing continuous programs of education and improvement, and (8) eliminating numerical quotas.

With regard to the last point, he saw the current trend toward formulating higher standards and enforcing them with performance assessments as wrongheaded. He felt that goals in and of themselves are meaningless. It is method alone that counts (Holt, 1993). Although Deming did not work in schools nor did he develop his approaches with schools in mind, a definite connection between TQM and better high schools can be drawn.

Applying several of Deming's 14 points to the improvement of high schools, one might conclude that the notion of zero deficits means that failure of any kind is detrimental to the system. When one student fails, the system fails. He often chided American industry for placing quality control at the end of the assembly line. What is needed is constant and continuous evaluation of the total process. When students fail, they go to summer school or repeat a grade or course. These remedies are costly and often come too late. They do neither the system nor the individual much good. When evaluation of student progress is continuous, nonproductive practices can be modified. Deming believed strongly in the power of the individual to resolve organizational and personal problems.

William Glasser (1990, 1992) has taken many of the ideas of TQM and applied them to schools. In his book *The Quality School: Managing Students Without*

Coercion, he defines a quality school as one where: (1) staff and students are friends; (2) teachers are required to explain how what they teach can be used in the students' lives now or later; (3) the skills of speaking, writing, calculating, and problem solving are emphasized; (4) subjects such as social studies, health, science, and foreign language are taught the way the teachers of these subjects think best; (5) all students are asked to evaluate their work for quality; (6) all tests are open book; (7) grades can be raised if the students want to redo their work; (8) a corps of students are trained to serve as tutors for students needing one-on-one help; (9) there is no busy-work or compulsory homework; and (10) all students and teachers will be taught control theory (Glasser, 1990, 1992).

LEADERSHIP AND SCHOOL ACCOUNTABILITY

The final system component of the school design statement is the development of an evaluation plan. Evaluation is critical to all efforts for school improvement. It is the fuel with which design statements are modified and new directions are undertaken. B. Frank Brown, principal of the first nongraded high school in the United States, liked to remind the faculty of Melbourne High School in Melbourne, Florida, that, "As soon as an innovative program is in place, we must work to make it obsolete." His challenge seems to capture the essence of evaluation practices in the emergent high school. The quest for continuous improvement in teaching and learning for all students is the driving force for high schools in the 21st century.

The present is admittedly ambiguous in the messages sent to high school leaders about evaluation. On one hand is a national movement toward searching for new ways to assess student learning; on the other, legislators and policy makers are looking to the results of norm-referenced tests as an assessment of school effectiveness. Statistics indicating student performance on standardized instruments are often included in school report cards to the community. Several states have enacted legislation that categorizes high schools based on test results. When a school is judged unsatisfactory, it is given a specified time period in which to improve or risk takeover by the state department of education.

Although results will continue to be important measures of school success, the development of alternative forms of assessing student achievement offer expanded data. Portfolios of student work, exhibitions presented to panels of adults, applications in the settings in which they are appropriate, writing samples and problem-solving activities yield more valid and reliable information than decontextualized multiple choice questions. Aligned with the curriculum and the intended school outcomes, they assess the curriculum, the instruction, and the individual student. On the wall of a high school in Cleveland, Mississippi, the following admonition was found: "If students don't learn the way we teach them, then teach them the way they learn." It places the responsibility for student learning on the system rather than the student.

Regional accrediting associations are offering outcomes accreditation as an option to accreditation for member high schools. Outcomes accreditation focuses on student success and allows high schools to combine accreditation with efforts toward school improvement. The North Central Association of Colleges and Schools suggests CASE-IMS as one of the options available for schools. The Southern Association of Colleges and Schools employs a school renewal process and the School Improvement Process developed by the National Study of School Evaluation (NSSE) as alternatives to traditional evaluation procedures. In the school renewal approach high school faculties address five areas: school climate, planning, staff development, curriculum and instruction, and communication over the course of a 5-year period. In the NSSE approach the faculty addresses four areas: student and community characteristics, beliefs and mission, desired results, and instructional and organizational effectiveness. The gathering of data in these four areas leads to the development of an action plan to improve student performance. Both approaches acknowledge the value of continuous school improvement.

School leaders should also be aware of the need to assess the process of school-based decision making. Even though this aspect of evaluation is not of general interest to the public, it is important to improving the means by which stakeholders are involved. Measures should be adopted or designed that ask teachers, students, parents, and community members to comment on the degree of their involvement in school improvement. Measures should be designed or adopted that ask teachers to comment on their understanding of the school improvement plan and what can be done to make it better. Leaders at the school level must balance assessment and evaluation between student competence and stakeholder participation. Both means and ends are important to establishing and continuing a school culture that values continuous growth.

According to the knowledge and skill base of the National Policy Board for Educational Administration, the key behaviors that define the assessment role of the effective principal include: (1) describing curriculum goals valued at the building level and explaining each goal's importance; (2) linking valued achievement targets to proper assessment formats; (3) understanding and knowing how to control for sources of extraneous interference that can cause the incorrect measurement of student achievement; (4) understanding and applying sampling methods that ensure fair, complete, and efficient assessment of student achievement, and (5) training others to apply these attributes to their assessments (Thomson, 1993.)

Understanding the nature and use of assessment to measure school effectiveness seems crucial for building a bridge to the high schools we need. Leadership is more than merely applying skills and strategies. It is knowing what questions to ask and when to ask them. It is raising the level of consciousness of the total school community.

SUMMARY

The quality of leadership from principals and other administrators in efforts to reform high schools has a powerful influence on the levels of success achieved. Principals who are effective leaders provide direction, resources, and support to teachers and students in their efforts to improve teaching and learning. However, the concept of leadership in successful high schools includes teachers and other stakeholders as well as administrators. The quality of teachers' work with students and their contributions to school reform are key variables in helping high schools become institutions that serve all students well. This is especially important because change of any magnitude requires that a critical mass of people within an institution have internalized certain principles about change.

Strategies that have proven helpful to successful high schools as they engage in reform efforts were discussed in this chapter (strategic planning, school-based leadership teams). Examples of ways teachers can exert leadership were also presented (participation in leadership teams for staff development and school-site councils). The role of teacher involvement in action research projects and the potential of these projects to help close the gap between theory and practices was also discussed.

ACTION STEPS

1. Arrange a brainstorming session by dividing the class into several groups of five to ten students. Select a leader for each group who will also serve as the recorder. Place chart paper on the wall in front of each group. Each group takes 3 to 5 minutes to call out synonyms for leader. The recorder writes all responses on the chart paper. After the time period elapses, each group should discuss each of the synonyms and select the best three in rank order, seeking consensus. Share the group responses with the whole class. Write group responses on chart paper, the chalkboard, or an acetate. The total group is then asked to select the best three to five synonyms and place them in rank order. The synonyms then are used as a template for judging a person's leadership behavior or leadership potential.

2. Using the answers derived from the brainstorming session, have each student read a biography, a biographical sketch, or some portrait of a leader, living or dead, and apply the class synonyms. How does this person measure up to the class standards? Report the findings to the class. Students may also wish to consult *Theory in Educational Administration,* chapter five, "Ancient traces and heroic portraits: Prescientific views of leadership" and chapter six, "Schemers, popes, and princes: Protoscientific portraits of leadership" (English, 1994).

3. Investigate the National Association of Secondary School Principals Assessment Center. How do the dimensions of leadership assessed by this procedure compare with the class standards? What similarities can be found? What differences?

4. Select a high school in your area. Review data from the school on each of the vital dimensions listed under the evaluation domain cited from Keefe and Jenkins, *Instructional Leadership Handbook.* What preliminary observations can be made? What recommendations can be made for school improvement?

DISCUSSION QUESTIONS

1. How does the school design statement described in the chapter compare with what you know about the school improvement process as practiced in most high schools? What similarities exist? What differences exist?

2. Do you agree with Glasser's premise that the concept of leadership applies to both high school administration and high school teaching? Why or why not?

3. How do you expect colleges and universities to react to the use of portfolios and exhibitions as graduation requirements from high schools? Will students from high schools using this approach be penalized? What objections to the use of portfolios and exhibitions might be raised? What are the strengths of this approach as compared with the traditional Carnegie Unit?

4. Differentiate between instructional leadership and educational leadership. Is instructional leadership the responsibility of every professional on a high school staff? Why or why not?

5. Investigate each of the 21 domains described in *Principals for Our Changing Schools: Knowledge and Skill Base*. Investigate one of the domains in depth and report your findings to the class.

6. Design an action research project focused on improving teaching and learning in some aspect of a high school. Include the following ingredients: (1) need for the study, (2) focus question, (3) review of the salient literature, (4) a description of the school setting with the students to be included, (5) at least four techniques for collecting data, and (6) how the data will be processed.

REFERENCES

Aiken, W. M. (1942). *The story of the eight year study.* New York: McGraw-Hill.

Breaking ranks: Changing an American institution (1996). Reston, VA: National Association of Secondary School Principals.

Corey, S. M. (1953). *Action research to improve school practices.* New York: Teachers College, Columbia University.

Deming, W. E. (1993). *The new economics for industry, government, education.* Cambridge, MA: Massachusetts Institute of Technology, Center for Advanced Engineering Study.

Edmonds, R. (1982). Programs for school improvement: An overview. *Educational Leadership, 40,* 4–11.

English, F. W. (1994). *Theory in educational administration.* New York: Harper Collins College Publishers.

Fullan, M. G. & Miles, M. B. (1992). Getting reform right: What works and what doesn't. *Phi Delta Kappan, 73(10),* 745–752.

Glasser, W. (1994). *The control theory manager.* New York: Harper Collins.

Glasser, W. (1990, 1992). *The quality school: Managing students without coercion.* New York: Harper Collins.

Holt, M. (1993). Deming on education. *Phi Delta Kappan, 75(4),* 329–330.

Howard, E. R. & Keefe, J. W. (1993). *Suggested components for a school design statement.* Reston: VA: National Association of Secondary School Principals.

Jenkins, J. M. (1994). Action research: School improvement at the grass roots. *International Journal of Educational Reform, 3(4),* 470–473.

Keefe, J. W. (1994). School evaluation using the CASE-IMS model and improvement process. *Studies in Education, 20,* 56–67.

Keefe, J. W. & Howard, E. R. (1997). *Redesigning schools for the new century: A systems approach.* Reston, VA: National Association of Secondary School Principals.

Keefe, J. W. & Jenkins, J. M. (Eds). (1984, 1991). *Instructional leadership handbook.* Reston, VA: National Association of Secondary School Principals.

Lear, R. (1992). Integrated teaching and learning in essential schools. In Jenkins, J. M. & Tanner, D. Restructuring for an interdisciplinary curriculum. Reston, VA: National Association of Secondary School Principals.

Manno, B. V. (1995). The new school wars: Battles over outcome-based education. *Phi Delta Kappan, 76(9),* 720–726.

Model schools project report (1977). *NASSP Bulletin, 61,* 412.

National Association of Secondary School Principals Consortium for the Performance-Based Preparation of Principals. (1992) *Developing school leaders.* Reston, VA: National Association of Secondary School Principals.

NASSP Task Force. (1987). *Comprehensive assessment of school environments: Examiner's manual.* Reston, VA: National Association of Secondary School Principals.

Sacken, D. (1994). No more principals. *Phi Delta Kappan, 75(9),* 664–670.

Sarason, S. (1971). The culture of the school and the problem of change. Boston: Allyn and Bacon.

School Design Statement. (1994). Thomas Haney Secondary School. School District No. 42. Maple Ridge, British Columbia.

Simonds, R. (1993–94). A plea for children. *Educaitonal Leadership,* December/January, 15.

Sizer, T. R. (1992). *Horace's school: redesigning the American high school.* Boston: Houghton Mifflin.

Spady, W. G. (1992). Outcome-based education. In NASSP Commission on Restructuring. *A leader's guide to school restructuring.* Reston, VA: National Association of Secondary School Principals.

Thomson, S. (Ed). (1993). *Principals for our changing schools: The knowledge and skill base.* Fairfax, VA: The National Policy Board for Educational Administration.

Westerberg, T., Thomas, R., & Stein, T. (1994). Direction 2000—rethinking the American high school. In Jenkins, J. M., Louis, K. S., Walberg, H. J., & Keefe, J. W. *World class schools: An evolving concept.* Reston, VA: National Association of Secondary School Principals.

Wheatley, M. J. (1992, 1994). *Leadership and the new science: Learning about organization from an orderly universe.* San Francisco: Berrett-Koehler.

Roster of High Schools

Alabama
American Studies Center
2803 6th Street
Tuscaloosa City Schools
Tuscaloosa, AL 35401

Shelby County High School
101 Washington Street
Columbiana, AL 35051

Vestavia Hills High School
2235 Lime Rock Road
Vestavia Hills, AL 35216

Alaska
Juneau Douglas High School
10014 Crazy Horse Drive
Juneau, AK 99801

Arizona
Catalina Foothills High School
4300 E. Sunrise Drive
Tucson, AZ 85718

Arkansas
Ridgecrest Secondary Complex
1701 West Court Street
Paragould, AR 72450

California
Escondido High School
1535 North Broadway
Escondido, CA 92026

Florin High School
7956 Cottonwood Lane
Sacramento, CA 95828

Los Angeles Educational
Partnership
315 West Ninth Street
Suite 1110
Los Angeles, CA 90015

Mid-Peninsula High School
870 N. California Avenue
Palo Alto, CA 94303

Rancho Verde High School
17750 Lasselle Street
Moreno, CA 92551

San Clemente High School
700 Avenida Pico
San Clemente, CA 92673

Theodore Roosevelt High School
4250 East Tulare Street
Fresno, CA 93702

West Covina High School
1609 Cameron Avenue
West Covina, CA 91791

Woodlake Union High School
400 West Whitney
Woodlake, CA 93286

Colorado
Colorado's Finest Alternative High
  School
2323 West Baker
Englewood, CO 80110

Eaglecrest High School
5100 South Picadilly Street
Aurora, CO 80015

Pueblo County High School
1050 Lane 35
Pueblo, CO 81006

Wasson High School
2115 Afton Way
Colorado Springs, CO 80909

Connecticut
East Hartford High School
869 Forbes Street
East Hartford, CT 06118

Delaware
Paul M. Hodgson Vocational-
  Technical High School
2575 Summit Bridge Road
Newark, DE 19702

Florida
Apopka High School
55 West Martin Street
Apopka, FL 32712

Atlantic High School
1250 Reed Canal Road
Port Orange, FL 32119

Community Education in Florida
Stewart Mott Davis Center for
  Community Education
University of Florida
Gainesville, FL 32611

Duncan U. Fletcher High School
700 Seagate Avenue
Neptune Beach, FL 32266

Flagler Palm Coast High School
PO Box 488
Bunnell, FL 32110

Haines City High School
2800 Hornet Drive
Haines City, FL 33844

Lake Brantley High School
991 Sand Lake Road
Altamonte, FL 32714

Lake Region High School
1995 Thunder Road
Lake, FL 33839

Lyman High School
865 South County Road
Longwood, FL 32750

MAST Academy (Maritime and
  Science Technology High School)
3979 Rickenbaker Causeway
Miami, FL 33149

Melbourne High School
74 Bulldog Avenue
Melbourne, FL 32901

Newberry High School
400 Southwest 7th Street
Newberry, FL 32669

Oak Ridge High School
6000 S. Winegard Road
Orlando, FL 32809

Okeechobee High School
2800 Highway 441 North
Okeechobee, FL 34972

Palm Beach Gardens
4245 Holly Drive
Palm Beach, FL 33410

Rutherford High School
1000 School Avenue
Panama City, FL 32401

Rutherford High School
1000 School Avenue
Springfield, FL 32401

Saint Augustine High School
3205 Varella Avenue
Saint Augustine, FL 32095

Suncoast Community High School
600 West 28th Street
Riveria Beach, FL 33404

University High School
11550 Lokanotosa Trail
Orlando, FL 32817

Winter Park High School
2100 Summerfield Road
Winter Park, FL 32792

Georgia
Armuchee High School
4203 Martha Berry Highway
Rome, GA 30165

Salem High School
3551 Underwood Road
Conyers, GA 30208

Troup High School
1920 Hamilton Road
La Grange, GA 30240

Illinois
Barrington High School
616 West Main Street
Barrington, IL 60010-1799

Center for Applied Technology
Township High School District
Wheeling High School
900 S. Elmhurst Road
Wheeling, IL 60090

Champaign Central High School
610 W. University Avenue
Champaign, IL 61820

Elmwood High School
301 West Butternut
Elmwood, IL 61529

Flower Vocational High School
3545 West Fulton Boulevard
Chicago, IL 60624

Malta High School
5068 Rt. 38
Malta, IL 60150

Mundelein High School
1350 W. Hawley Street
Mundelein, IL 60060

Waukegan High School
2325 Brookside
Waukegan, IL 60085

Wheaton-Warrenville South High
  School
1993 Tiger Trail
Wheaton, IL 60187

Wheeling High School
900 South Elmhurst Road
Wheeling, IL 60090

Indiana
Lebanon Senior High School
Essex Drive
Lebanon, IN 46052

Penn High School
56100 Bittersweet Road
Mishawaka, IN 46545

Iowa
Metro High School
1212 7th Street
Cedar Rapids, IA 52401

Kansas
Blue Valley North High School
12200 Lamar
Overland Park, KS 66209

Kentucky
DuPont Manual Magnet High
  School
120 West Lee Street
Louisville, KY 40208-1999

Eastern High School
12400 Old Shelbyville Road
Middletown, KY 40243

Fairdale High School
1001 Fairdale Road
Fairdale, KY 40118

Seneca High School: Magnet
Career Academy
3510 Goldsmith Lane
Louisville, KY 40220

Valley High School Magnet Career
Academy
10200 Dixie Highway
Louisville, KY 40272

Louisiana
McMain Magnet Secondary School
5712 S. Claiborne Avenue
New Orleans, LA 70125

Maine
Nobel High School
PO Box 1180
Berwick, ME 03901

Presque Isle High School
16 Ft. Street
Presque Isle, ME 04769

Maryland
Patterson High School
100 Kane Street
Baltimore, MD 21224

Wilde Lake High School
5460 Trumpeter Road
Columbia, MD 21044

Massachusetts
Brookline High School
115 Greenough Street
Brookline, MA 02146

Cambridge Rindge and Latin
School
459 Broadway
Cambridge, MA 02138

Fenway Middle College High
School
250 Rutherford Avenue
Boston, MA 02129

Mt. Everett Regional High School
Berkshire School Road
Sheffield, MA 01257

Pioneer Valley Regional School
97 F Summer Turner Road
Northfield, MA 01360

Rindge School of Technical Arts at
Cambridge Rindge and Latin
High School
Cambridge Public Schools
459 Broadway
Cambridge, MA 02138

Michigan
Coloma High School
PO Box 550
Coloma, MI 49038

Jackson High School
544 Wildwood Avenue
Jackson, MI 49201

SeaHolm High School
2436 West Lincoln
Birmingham, MI 48009

Sturgis High School
216 Vinewood
Sturgis, MI 49091

Minnesota
Rothsay School
Box 307
Rothsay, MN 56579

Missouri
Hillcrest High School
3319 North Grant
Springfield, MO 65803

Parkway South High School
801 Hanna Road
Manchester, MO 63021

Nebraska
Columbus High School
2200 26th Street
Columbus, NE 68601

New Hampshire
John Stark Regional High School
618 North Stark Highway
Weare, NH 03281

Souhegan High School
PO Box 1152
Amherst, NH 03031

Thayer Junior-Senior High School
85 Parker Street
Winchester, NH 03470

New Jersey
Wood Ridge Junior Senior High
   School
258 Hakensack Street
Wood Ridge, NJ 07075

New Mexico
Mayfield High School
1955 North Valley Drive
Las Cruces, NM 88005

New Futures School
5400 Cutler Avenue, NE
Albuquerque, NM 87110

Twin Buttes High School
PO Drawer 680
Zuni, NM 87327

New York
Central Park East Secondary
   School
1573 Madison Avenue
New York, NY 10029

City as School—National Defusion
   Network Project
16 Clarkson Street
New York, NY 10014

Croton-Harmon High School
Old Post Road, South
Croton-on Hudson, NY 10520

Fiorello H. LaGuardia Community
   College
31-10 Thomson Avenue
Long Island, NY 11101

John F. Kennedy High School
3000 Bellmore Avenue
Bellmore, NY 11710

Middle College High School
31-10 Thomson Avenue
Long Island City, NY 11101

Satellite Academy High School
51 Chambers Street
New York, NY 10007

School Without Walls
480 Broadway
Rochester, NY 14607

Urban Academy — An Inquiry
   High School
317 East 67th Street
New York, NY 10021

Westinghouse High School
21 Rockaway Place
Massapequa, NY 11758

North Carolina
Cape Lookout High School
1108 Bridges Street
Morehead City, NC 28557

Midwood High School
1817 Central Avenue
Charlotte, NC 28205

Northwest Guilford High School
5240 Northwest School Road
Greensboro, NC 27409

Providence Senior High School
1800 Pineville-Matthews Road
Charlotte, NC 28270

Thomasville High School
410 Unity Street
Thomasville, NC 27360

North Dakota
Minot High School
1100 11th Avenue
Minot, ND 58701

Ohio
Butler County Joint Vocational
   School District
3606 Hamilton-Middletown Road
Hamilton, OH 45011

Columbus Alternative High School
2632 McGuffey Road
Columbus, OH 43211

Crestline High School
7854 Oldfield Road
Crestline, OH 44827

Dublin Coffman High School
7030 Coffman Road
Dublin, OH 43017-1008

Fort Hayes Metropolitan Education
   Center
546 Jack Gibbs Boulevard
Columbus, OH 43215

Franklin Heights High School
1001 Demorest Road
Columbus, OH 43204

Garfield Alternative Education
   Center
1830 Yankee Road
Middletown, OH 45044

Independence High School
5175 E. Refugee Road
Columbus, OH 43232

Lorain County Joint Vocational
   School
15181 State Route 58
Oberlin, OH 44074

Mayfield High School
6116 Wilson Mills Road
Mayfield, OH 44143

New Albany High School/Middle
   School
6425 New Albany-Condit Road
New Albany, OH 43054

Reynoldsburg City Schools
6549 E. Livingston Avenue
Reynoldsburg, OH 43068-3585

Robert Taft High School
420 Ezzard Charles Drive
Cincinnati, OH 45214

Troy High School
151 W. Staunton Road
Troy, OH 45373

West High School
179 S. Powell Avenue
Columbus, OH 43204

Westland High School
146 Galloway Road
Galloway, OH 43119

Oklahoma
Tulsa Area Voc-Tech School
3420 South Memorial Drive
Tulsa, OK 74145

Oregon
Asheland High School
201 South Mountain Drive
Asheland, OR 97520-2194

Crater High School
4410 Rogue Valley Highway
Central Point, OR 97502

Grant High School
2245 N.E. Avenue
Portland, OR 97212

La Grande High School
708 K Avenue
La Grande, OR 97850

Reynolds High School
1698 SW Cherry Park Road
Troutdale, OR 97060

Pennsylvania
North Hills Senior High School
53 Rochester Road
Pittsburgh, PA 15229-1189

Philadelphia High School
Academies Inc.
230 South Broad Street, 18th Floor
Philadelphia, PA 19102

South Carolina
Irmo High School
6671 St. Andrews Road
Columbia, SC 29212

J. L. Mann High School
61 Isbell Lane
Greenville, SC 29607-3799

Riverside High School
1300 South Suber Road
Greer, SC 29650-9599

Tennessee
Farragut High School
11237 Kingston Pike
Knoxville, TN 37922

Twenty-First (21st) Century
   Preparatory School
4201 Cherryton Drive
Chattanooga, TN 37411

Texas
Alice High School
#1 Coyote Trail
Alice, TX 78332

Bellaire High School
5100 Maple
Bellaire, TX 77401

Canutillo Independent School
   District
PO Box 100
Canutillo, TX 79835

Copperas Cove High School
400 South 25th
PO Box 580
Copperas Cove, TX 76522

Del Valle High School
950 Bordeaux Drive
El Paso, TX 79907

Greenville High School
3515 Lion's Lair Road
Greenville, TX 75402

Hico Independent School District
PO Box 218
Hico, TX 65457

James Bowie High School
4103 W. Slaughter Lane
Austin, TX 78749-6914

Lubbock High School
2004 Nineteenth Street
Lubbock, TX 79401

McNeil High School
5720 McNeil Drive
Austin, TX 78729

Midland High School
906 West Illinois
Midland, TX 79701

Robert E. Lee High School
1400 Jackson-Keller
San Antonio, TX 78213

Utah
Dixie High School
350 East 700 South
St. George, UT 84770

Granger High School
3690 South 3600 West
West Valley, UT 84119

Vermont
Cabot School
25 Common Road, PO Box 98
Cabot, VT 05647

Champlain Valley Union High
  School
RR2 Box 160
Hinesburg, VT 05461

Virginia
Mills Godwin High School
2101 Pump Road
Richmond, VA 23233

Parry McCluer High School
2329 Chestnut Avenue
Buena Vista, VA 24416

Thomas Jefferson High School for
  Science & Technology
6560 Braddock Road
Alexandria, VA 22312

York High School
9300 George Washington Highway
Yorktown, VA 23692

Washington
Capital High School
2707 Conger Street
Olympia, WA 98501

Mountlake Terrace High School
21801 44th Avenue West
Mountlake, WA 98043-3598

Wheeling Park High School
1976 Park View Road
Wheeling, WV 26003

Wisconsin
Walden III Middle and Senior High
  School
1012 Center Street
Racine, WI 53403

Canada
L. V. Rogers Secondary School
1004 Cottonwood Street
Nelson, B.C. Canada, V1L 3W2

AUTHOR INDEX

Abdal–Haqq, I., 310, 319
Adler, E., 162, 165
Adler, M., 30, 39, 40, 50, 64
Ahlgren, A., 46, 65
Aiken, W.M., 15, 16, 17, 39, 40, 338, 346
Aikenhead, G., 54, 64
Ancess, J., 49, 65
Anderson, R.D., 293
Archibald, D.A., 49, 64
Argys, M., 75, 111
Armstrong, D.G., 79, 111
Armstrong, L., 126, 130
Ashton, P.T., 314, 319
Atchley, D., 55, 64

Baker, D.P., 265, 295
Beane, J., 224, 261
Bell, T.P., 122, 130
Bellanca, J., 253, 261
Ben–Avie, M., 267, 294
Bennett, W.J., 50, 64
Bents, M., 314, 319
Bents, R., 314, 319
Berla, N., 266, 295
Berliner, D.C., 314, 321
Bestor, A., 19, 40
Bishop, H., 207
Black, S., 311, 321
Boix–Mancilla, V., 53, 65
Block, 94, 111
Bodinger–deUriarte, C., 265, 294
Bottoms, G., 58, 59, 64, 261
Bowles, S., 26, 37, 40
Boyd, S.M., 50, 66
Boyer, E.L., 31, 40, 165
Brandt, R., 114, 130, 264, 293
Brewer, D.J., 75, 111
Bronkhorst, B., 55, 65
Brooks, J.G., 74, 111
Brooks, M.G., 74, 111
Brophy, J., 69, 111
Brown, B.F., 26, 40
Bruder, I., 122, 130
Bruner, J., 20, 40, 122
Bunte, K., 50
Burns, R.B., 94, 122
Buschbaum, H.M., 122, 130
Bushnell, D., 144, 165
Button, H.W., 4, 15, 20, 22, 40
Butts, F., 3, 6, 8, 14, 40

Canady, R.L., 76, 77, 111, 169, 170, 178, 186, 187, 203
Carnate, B., 312, 320
Carroll, D., 169, 170, 178, 282, 288, 289, 293
Carroll, S.R., 169, 170, 178, 282, 288, 289, 293
Carter, K., 115, 117, 130
Castro–Lewis, M., 269, 293
Cavarretta, J., 264, 294
Cawelti, H., 183, 264, 294
Chavkin, N.F., 265, 269, 294
Clark, M., 265, 294
Clark, R.W., 311, 320
Clerk, F.E., 138, 165
Cohen, D., 31, 32, 41
Cole, C.G., 142, 147, 157, 165
Comer, J.P., 267, 284, 294
Conant, J., 21–23, 37, 40
Conners, L.J., 265, 267, 277, 294
Coontz, S., 267, 294
Cooper, B.S., 267, 295
Corey, S.M., 338, 346
Cortes, E., 290, 291, 294
Cortese, A., 114, 130
Coulumbe, G., 265, 294
Cox, N.D., 42, 165
Cresswell, R., 74, 230, 231, 247, 248, 261
Crocker, L., 314, 319
Cruikshank, D.R., 309, 320
Cusick, P., 27, 34, 40
Cutler, B.R., 311, 321

Damico, S., 253, 261
Danzberger, J., 265, 294
Davies, D., 265, 294
Darling–Hammond, L.,49, 65, 297, 310, 314, 317, 320
de Kanter, A., 265, 294
Deming, W.E., 342, 346
Dennison, G., 25, 40
Dickenson, T.S., 315, 320
Diegmueller, K., 46, 65
Dilley, B., 291, 294
Dodd, A.W., 310, 320
Doyle, D.P., 114, 129, 130
Dyer, T., 212, 261

Eads, L.J., 121, 130
Early, M., 51, 65
Edmonds, R., 342, 346
Ephrim, H.E., , 94, 111
Eggen, P., 78, 111
Eineder, D., 207

Elkind, D., 267, 294, 324
English, F.W., 324, 325, 346
Epstein, J.L., 266, 267, 268, 294
Erekson, T.L., 122, 130

Fang, F., 122, 130
Farivar, S., 80, 112
Farrer, E., 31, 32, 41
Feiman–Nemser, S., 314, 320
Finney, P., 265, 294
Fiore, Q., 114, 130
Fredericks, A.D., 294
Freidenberg, E., 25, 40
Frick, T.W., 130
Fructher, N., 274, 294
Fullan, M.G., 328, 346

Galassi, J.P., 142, 165
Galletta, A., 274, 294
Gamoran, A., 300, 321
Gardner, H., 53, 65, 300, 320
George, P.S., 30, 146, 165, 226, 247, 262
Ginsburg, A.L., 265, 294
Glasser, W., 323, 342, 343, 346
Goldberg, M.F., 147, 165
Gomez, L.M., 119, 130
Goodlad, J., 31, 32, 40, 309, 320
Goodman, P., 25, 40
Goodson, B.D., 273, 294
Gorman, J.T., 283, 294
Graham, D., 142, 165
Gregory, T., 34, 35, 40
Grossman, P.L., 314, 320
Gulledge, S.A., 142, 165
Guskey, T., 95, 111
Gutek, G., 3, 4, 7, 10, 24, 28, 40

Haller, E., 40
Hamburg, D.A., 132, 165
Hamdy, M., 207
Hampel, R., 18, 19, 24, 26, 31, 32
Harris, M.F., 311, 321
Harris, R.C., 311, 321
Hass, J., 269, 289, 294
Hawkins, M., 142, 165
Hayes, M., 287, 294
Haynes, N.M., 267, 294
Henderson, A.T., 266, 267, 295
Hester, H., 295
Highland, W., 138, 165
Highland, M., 138, 165

Hill, M., 122, 130
Hirsh, S., 302, 303, 305, 306, 320, 321
Holden, J., 50, 65
Holt, M., 342, 346
Holt, J., 25, 37, 40
Holubec, E., 79, 111
Howard, E.R., 331, 333, 334, 347
Hufty, H., 119, 120, 130

Illich, I., 25, 40
Irmsher, K., 207

Jackson, B.L., 267, 295
Jackson, D., 79, 111
Jenkins, J.M., 48, 65, 121, 130, 137, 138, 147, 165, 324, 324, 325, 338, 345, 347
Jesse, D., 266, 269, 295
Johnson, R., 111
Johnson, D., 79, 82, 111
Jones, A., 111
Jones, D., 126, 130
Joyce, B., 87, 111, 304, 305, 320
Joyner, E.T., 267, 294

Kagan, S., 80, 111
Kahne, J., 16, 40, 278, 295
Kaplan, L.S., 302, 320
Kauchak, D., 78, 111
Keefe, J.W., 56, 57, 65, 324, 325, 330, 331, 334, 335, 345, 347
Keith, P.B, 295
Keith, T.Z., 295
Kendall, J.S., 63, 65
Killin, T.E., 132, 165
King, B., 208
Kline, S.P., 314, 316, 320
Kozol, J., 23, 41
Kramer, S., 208
Kreider, H.M., 277, 295
Krug, E., 3, 4, 5, 7, 12, 13, 15, 18, 40

Labaree, D., 2, 3, 41
Lear, R., 340, 347
Lenk, H.A., 314, 320
Leonard, G., 127, 128, 130
Lewis, A.C., 264, 295
Liberman, A., 303, 320
Liontos, L.B., 266, 267, 269, 295
Lopez, M.E., 277, 295
Lounsbury, J.H., 163, 165, 320

Lynch, W., 130
Lynd, A., 19, 41
Lynn, L., 253, 262

Manno, B.V., 341
Marks, H.M., 300, 321
Marzano, R.J., 63, 65
McEwin, C.K., 141, 147, 165, 315, 320
McKenzie, J., 118, 130
McLaughlin, M., 303, 304, 305, 320
McLuhan, M., 114, 129, 130
Meier, D., 35, 41, 308, 321
Metzger, M., 61, 65
Miles, M.B., 328, 346
Millsap, M.A., 273, 294
Milne, A.M., 294
Mitchell, N., 314, 321
Monahan, B., 119, 130
Myrick, L.S., 137, 138, 144, 147, 157, 165
Myrick, R.D., 137, 138, 139, 144, 147, 157, 165

Neill, A.S., 25, 41
Nevin, A., 267, 295
Newmann, F.M., 49, 64, 321

O' Neil, J., 120, 130
O' Neil, M., 141, 165
O' Neill, D.K., 119, 120, 130
Oakes, J., 75, 111, 253, 256, 262
Olsen, D.G., 314, 321
Orfield, G., 23, 41
Orlando, L., 122, 130
Osguthorpe, R.T., 311, 321

Page, J., 253, 262
Parker, M.B., 314, 320
Perini, M., 300, 321
Perry, N., 265, 295
Peshkin, A., 51, 65
Peterson, K.S., 221, 222, 223, 262
Plodzik, K., 226, 262
Podl, J.B., 61, 65
Pool, H., 253, 262
Postman, N., 288, 295
Powell, A.G., 31, 32, 41
Preskill, S., 11, 12, 41
Provenzo, Jr., E., 4, 15, 20, 22, 40
Pulliam, J., 5, 6, 8, 41

Rasinski, T.V., 294
Rasmussen, K., 247, 262
Rasmussen, P., 247, 261
Rees, D.I., 75, 111
Reese, W., 4, 5, 7, 8, 9, 11, 41
Reich, R., 44, 65
Reneke, F., 121, 130
Rettig, M.D., 76, 77, 111, 169, 170, 178, 186, 187, 203, 204
Rickover, H., 20, 41
Ridgen, D.W., 321
Rogers, C., 25, 41
Rosenbaum, J.E., 253, 262
Rosenshine, B., 68, 112
Rottenberg, C.J., 321
Rutherford, B., 265, 295
Rutherford, E.J., 46, 65

Sacken, D., 327, 347
Sarason, S.B., 309, 321, 347
Savage, T.V., 79, 83, 111
Schroth, G., 208
Schurr, S.L., 78, 83, 88, 112, 267, 295
Schwarz, P., 113, 308, 321
Sharan, Y., 81, 112
Sharan, S., 81, 112
Shartrand, A.M., 277, 295
Shewey, K., 247, 262
Showers, B., 304, 305, 320
Shulman, L.S. 317, 321
Silberman, C., 25, 37, 41
Silver, H., 300, 321
Simonds, R., 341, 347
Sizer, T.R., 41, 112, 137, 165, 168, 317, 321, 339, 347
Slavin, R.E., 79, 81, 84, 112, 253, 262
Smagorinsky, P., 47, 66
Smith, G., 34, 35, 40
Spady, W.G., 325, 326, 327, 341, 347
Sparks, D., 302, 303, 305, 306, 321
Stein, T., 49, 66, 347
Steinberg, A., 256, 262
Stevenson, D.L., 295
Stewart, W.J., 112
Strong, R., 300, 321
Swartz, E., 253, 261
Swartz, J.P., 273, 294
Swick, K.J., 277, 295

Takanishi, R., 132, 165
Talbert, J., 305, 320
Thomas, R., 49, 66, 326, 344, 347
Thomason, J., 78, 83, 88, 112

Thompson, M., 78, 83, 88, 112
Thomson, S., 325, 326, 327, 347
Thornburg, D.D., 114, 130
Thousand, I., 267, 295
Tomko, S., 119, 130
Tomlinson, C., 91, 92, 112
Trump, J.L., 24, 41
Tyson, H., 309, 321

Van Patten, J., 5, 6, 8, 41
Vars, G.F., 142, 165
Vessels, G.G., 51, 66
Viadero, D., 59, 66
Villa, R., 267, 295

Wagner, R., 119, 130
Wasserman, S., 83, 84, 112

Webb, N., 80, 112
Weil, Marsha, 87, 111
Weiss, H.B., 277, 295
Westerberg, T., 49, 66, 341, 347
Westheimer, J., 278, 295
Wheatley, M.J., 328, 347
Wheelock, A., 253, 255, 256, 262
White, J.L., 274, 294
Williams, D.L., 264, 294
Williams, R.L., 132, 165
Winebrenner, S., 89, 92, 94, 112
Wise, A.E., 314, 316, 320, 321
Wollman, R., 138, 165
Wynne, E., 51, 66

Zeichner, K.M., 309, 321

INDEX OF HIGH SCHOOLS

Alice High School, 143, 278, 355
American Studies Center, 349
Apopka High School, 246, 350
Armuchee High School, 351
Asheland High School, 143, 355
Atlantic High School, 176, 350

Barrington High School, 53, 56, 351
Bellaire High School, 283, 288, 355
Blair High School, 121
Blue Valley High School, 351
Brookline High School, 352
Butler County Joint Vocational School District, 354

Cabot School, 49, 61, 312, 356
Cambridge Rindge and Latin School, 52, 59, 136, 248, 274, 308, 352
Canutillo Independent School District, 355
Cape Lookout High School, 354
Capital High School, 331, 356
Catalina Foothills High School, 140, 349
Center for Applied Technology, 351
Central Park East Secondary School, 49, 52, 61, 133, 143, 306, 340, 353
Champagne Central High School, 351
Champlain Valley Union High School, 148, 179, 288, 356
City as School—National Defusion Network Project, 353
Coloma High School, 60, 118, 181, 182, 352
Colorado's Finest Alternative High School, 349
Columbus Alternative High School, 354
Columbus High School, 353
Copperas High School, 179, 355
Crater High School, 270, 282, 288, 355
Crestline High School, 354
Croton–Harmon High School, 353

Del Valle High School, 133, 288, 355
Dixie High School, 356
Dr. Phillips High School, 245
Dublin Coffman High School, 354
Duncan U. Fletcher High School, 272, 350
DuPont Manual Magnet High School, 351

Eaglecrest High School, 52, 61, 349
East Hartford High School, 350
Eastern High School, 50, 352
Elmwood High School, 351
Escondido High School, 349

Fairdale High School, 271, 276, 308, 312, 352
Farragut High School, 133, 355
Fenway Middle College High School, 59, 143, 157, 340, 352
Fiorello H. LaGuardia Community College, 353
Flagler Palm Coast High School, 192, 350
Florin High School, 349
Flower Vocational High School, 351
Fort Hayes Metropolitan Education Center, 354
Franklin Heights High School, 354

Garfield Alternative Education Center, 275, 354
Governors School, 123
Granger High School, 356
Grant High School, 54, 355
Greenville High School, 356

Haines City High School, 121, 350
Hico Independent School District, 49, 356
Hillcrest High School, 181, 353

Independence High School, 308, 311, 354
Irmo High School, 355

J.L. Mann High School, 355
Jackson High School, 352
James Bowie High School, 356
John Stark Regional High School, 353
John F. Kennedy High School, 353
Juneau Douglas High School, 202, 277, 349

L.V. Rogers Secondary School, 356
La Grande High School, 202, 306, 355
Lake Region High School, 57, 350
Lake Brantley High School, 201, 350
Lebanon Senior High School, 351
Littleton High School, 49, 55, 341
Lorain County Joint Vocational School, 354
Los Angeles Educational Partnership, 349
Lubbock High School, 203, 272, 288, 356
Lyman High School, 185, 350

Malta High School, 351
MAST Academy (Maritime and Science Technology High School), 60, 211, 272, 288, 350
Mayfield High School, 191, 353, 354

McMain Magnet Secondary School, 287, 352
McNeil High School, 214, 218, 226, 228, 356
Melbourne High School, 343, 350
Mid–Peninsula High School, 349
Middle College High School, 49, 325, 353
Midland High School, 356
Midwood High School, 354
Minnetonka High School, 50
Mills Godwin High School, 356
Minot High School, 56, 331, 354
Mountlake Terrace High School, 286, 356
Mt. Everett Regional High School, 352
Mundelein High School, 351

New Albany High School/Middle School, 354
New Futures School, 353
New Trier High School, 119, 138
Newberry High School, 187, 190, 223, 350
Nobel High School, 254, 340, 352
North Hills Senior High School, 355
Northweat Guilford High School, 354

Oak Ridge High School, 184, 213, 226, 237, 239, 240, 255, 350
Okeechobee High School, 350

Palm Beach Gardens, 184, 350
Parkway High School, 224, 308, 353
Parry McCluer High School, 171–173, 356
Patterson High School, 352
Paul M. Hodgeson High School, 140–143, 158, 350
Penn High School, 150–157, 228, 229, 351
Philadelphia High School, 355
Pioneer Valley High School, 352
Presque Isle High School, 352
Providence Senior High School, 308, 354
Pueblo County High School, 349

Rancho Verde High School, 332, 349
Reynolds High School, 355
Reynoldsburg City Schools, 354
Ridgecrest Secondary Complex, 349
Rindge School of Technical Arts at Cambridge Rindge and Latin School, 352
Riverside High School, 120, 355
Robert Taft High School, 244, 354
Robert E. Lee High School, 230, 356
Roosevelt High School, 272, 288
Rothway High School, 291, 352
Rutherford High School, 183, 186, 350

Saint Augustine High School, 230, 231, 350
Salem High School, 230, 351
San Clemente High School, 349
Satellite Academy High School, 308, 353
School Without Walls, 278, 353
SeaHolm High School, 352
Seneca High School: Magnet Career Academy, 352
Shelby County High School, 349
Souhegan High School, 42, 149, 353
Steward Mott Davis Center for Community Education High School, 350
Sturgis High School, 135, 352
South Gate High School, 54
South Miami Senior High School, 59
Suncoast Community High School, 350

Thayer Junior–Senior High School, 353
Theodore Roosevelt High School, 349
Thomas Jefferson High School for Science & Technology, 59, 356
Thomasville High School, 191, 354
Troup High School, 240–243, 351
Troy High School, 288, 354
Tulsa Area Voc–Tech School, 355
Twenty–First (21st) Century Preparatory School, 355
Twin Buttes High School, 353

University High School, 194, 351
Urban Academy—An Inquiry High School, 140, 340, 353

Valley High School Career Magnet Academy, 352
Vestavia Hills High School, 308, 349

Walden III Middle and Senior High School, 356
Wasson High School, 193, 349
Waukegan High School, 56, 139, 143, 145, 157, 351
West High School, 355
West Covina High School, 349
Westinghouse High School, 353
Westland High School, 355
Wheaton–Warrenville South High School, 351
Wheeling High School, 118, 122, 351
Wheeling Park High School, 356
Wilde Lake High School, 138, 221, 352
Winter Park High School, 118, 351
Wood Ridge Junior Senior High School, 353
Woodlake Union High School, 349

York High School, 356

SUBJECT INDEX

Academic Teaming, 213, 258
  not team teaching, 213
  four areas, 214
    organization, 214
    community building, 221
    ninth grade, 221
    teamed instruction, 223
    governance, 226
  team planning, strategies, 227
  goal/objectives statements, 232
Academies, 3–4
Accountability, 343
Accreditation, 333, 374
Action Research, 338
  teacher research, 338
Adolescence and Young Adults Standards, 301
Advisory Programs, 133
  advisors, 133
  teacher advisory programs, 137
  as integral components of governance, 138
  nature of, 139
  goals and objectives, 140
  characteristics of successful programs, 141
  scheduling, 143
  roles of advisors, 144
  characteristics of effective advising, 146
  roles of principals, 146
  common themes, 150
  evaluation, 157
  Alternative day schedules, 179
Annenberg Institute of Public Engagement for Public Education, 293
America 2000, 45, 333
American High School Today, 21, 37
Apprenticeships (*See also* youth apprenticeships), 58
Assessment, 344
Apprenticeships, 58
Authentic Pedagogy, 300
Area Vocational–Technical School, 60

Block scheduling (*See also* scheduling), 68
  planning for, 77
  units, 78
Block Scheduling: A Catalyst For Change in High Schools, 187
Bobbitt, Franklin, 12
Boston Latin School, 5
Brown vs. Topeka, 18
Breaking Ranks: Changing an American Institution, 25, 33, 38, 42–43, 51, 131, 137, 144, 147, 168, 263, 269, 275, 278, 283, 284, 296, 298

BSCS Biology, 54
Business Partnerships, 283

CAD (Computer aided design), 123
California State Department of Education, 320
Career academies, 243, 257, 258
Career Choices, A Guide For Teens and Young Adults, 58
Carnegie Unit, 10, 34, 118, 168
Cardinal Principles of Secondary Education, 12–13, 36
Case studies and simulations, 82–88
CD–ROMs, 118–121, 123, 126
Center for Research on the Education of Students Placed At Risk (CRESPAR), 261
Change, successful (seven elements), 328
Charters, W.W., 12
Chemical Bond, 54
Chemical Study, 54, 64
Character education, 51
Chicken Soup for the Soul, 50
Computer laboratories, 120
Coalition of Essential Schools, 32, 33, 61, 168, 224, 254, 333, 339, 340
Cognitive Skills Center, 56
Collaboration partnerships, 265
College Entrance Examination Board (CEEB), 10
Commission on Achieving Necessary Skills, 58, 122
Commission on Accredited Schools, 10
Commission on Reorganization of Secondary Education, 12
Commission on Relations of School and College 15
Committee of Ten on Secondary School Studies, 9, 11, 118
Committee on Economy of Time in Education, 11
Community Service, 278
  contract, 279
  in curriculum, 278
Comprehensive Assessment of School Improvement (CASE), 328
CASE–IMS, 330–334
Comprehensive High School Concept, origin, 6
Comprehensive High School, The, 23
Cooley, Chief Justice, 7
Cooperative learning, 16, 79–82
Cooperative learning exercises, 81, 109
  Jigsaw, 81
  group investigation, 81
  student teams achievement programs, 82
  teams–games–tournaments, 82
  pro–con cooperation, 82
Copernican style scheduling, 170–172
Councils, site–based, 270
Counseling (*See also* Guidance and Counseling), 17, 132, 147

Craftsmanship 2000, 58
Crisis in the Classroom, 25
Curriculum
    academies, 4
    reformulation in the nineteenth century, 8
    evolution of, 8
    vocational education, 11
    tracking, 11, 19
    Commission on Reorganization of Secondary
        Education, 12
    Committee of Ten, 19
    1920's and 1930's, 14
    core curriculum, 8, 16, 45
    National Defense Education Act (NDEA), 20
    1960's and 1970's, 26–27
    Nation at Risk recommendations, 29
    definition, 42
    assessment, 44
    foreign language programs, 43
    interdisciplinary coursework, 43
    and assessment, 44
    portfolios, 44, 49
    national core curriculum, 45
    standards, 45–47
        localizing standards, 48–49
    Commission on High School Reform, 51
    values education, 51
    interdisciplinary curriculum, 52
    Writing Across the Curriculum, 55
    curriculum compacting, 70, 109
    team teaching, 224
    curriculum matrix, 224
    concept–driven, 300
*Curriculum and Evaluation Standards for School
    Mathematics,* 45

Decision–making, school based, 330
Deschooling Society, 25
Dewey, John, 15, 16
DIALOG, 121
Discipline management program, 217]

"Edutainment" programs, 126
"Education for All American Youth", 18
*Educational Wastelands: The Retreat From Learning In
    Our Public Schools,* 19
Eight Year Study, 15–17, 36, 339
Education and Ecstasy, 126
Eliot, Charles, 11
English for Speakers of Other Languages (ESOL), 121
Endangered Species: Children of Promise, 114
Evaluation plan, 343
Exhibitions, 60–61

Experimental schools, 18

Florida View Interest Survey, 58
Foreign languages, 43, 128
Franklin, Benjamin, 3
Freedom to Learn, 25
Families, 214
(*See also* Parents)
    involvement in a changing society, 266
    partnership roles, 266
    standards for parent/family involvement programs,
        268
    decision–making roles, 270
    parent–family resource centers, 272
    encouraging new beliefs about, 267

Gates, Bill, 114
Geography for Life: National Standards, 46
Gifted students, 22,29
Goal/objective statement for academic teaming, 232
Goals of education, 21
Goals 2000: Educate America Act, 333
Governance, shared leadership method, 270
Grading contracts, 91
Graded classroom, 7
Grouping, heterogeneous, 253
Greeley, Horace, 11
Guidance and Counseling, 132
    peer counseling, 134
    peer mediation, 136
    teacher advisement programs, 137
        as integral component of guidance,
        nature of, 139
    goals and objectives, 140
    characteristics of successful programs,
    scheduling advisement programs, 143
    advisor roles, 144
    and curriculum, 147
    scheduling, 201–202

Health clinics, 276
High Schools
    history, 1–41
    curriculum, 42–66
    instruction, 67–112
    technology, 113–130
    guidance and counseling, 131–166
    scheduling, 167–210
    academic teaming, 211–262
    school/family/community partnerships, 263–297
    teachers, 298–321
    leadership, 322–346

High Schools, history
    goals, 2, 3, 8, 9
    earliest American secondary education, 2
    first high school, 5
    comprehensive high school concept, 6
    Committee of Ten, 9
    vocational education and "socialization", 10
    Committee on Reorganization of Secondary
        Education, 12
    Progressive education, 14
    Eight Year Study, 15
    high school in 1940's and 1950's, 18,
    Sputnik and American education, 10
    Conant reports, 21
    comprehensive high school in 1960s and 1970s, 23
    A Nation at Risk, 28
Higher order thinking, 56
History Standards Project, 46
Holmes Group, 307
House concept, 247
    RSTA house, 248
    Pilot House, 249
    Fundamental School, 250
    House A, 251
    Academy House, 251
    Leadership School, 252
*Horace's Compromise: The Dilemma of the American High
    School,* 32, 66, 168
Horace's Hope: What Works For American High Schools,
    32, 66
Horace's School: What Works for American High Schools,
    32, 66

Image of high school, 281
Independent study, 91–94
Interactive Math Project, 53
Instruction
    long block schedule, 68–69
    differentiating instruction, 71–72
    teacher directed, limitations, 74
    alternative instructional strategies, 77
        unit planning and teaching, 78–79
        cooperative learning, 79–82
        case studies and simulations, 82–88
        learning contracts, 89–91
        independent study, 91–94
        grading contracts, 91
        mastery learning, 94–97
        learning centers and learning guides, 97
        reading writing workshops, 103–108
        learning guides, 101–103
Instruction, large group strategies, 109
    preassessment, 71
    flexible classroom strategies, 71

    compacting, 71
    alternative responses and assessments, 71
    support tactics for slower students, 72
    reviews, 72
In–school support groups Instructional leadership, 324
    formative, 324
    planning, 324
    implementation, 324
    evaluation, 324
Instructional Leadership Handbook, 345
Interact: Learning Through Involvement, 88
Interactive Mathematics Program, 65
Internet, 120
Jefferson, Thomas, 4
Kalamazoo decision, 7
Laser disc technology, 128
Latin Grammar School, 2–3
Learning activities packet (LAP), 101–103
Learning centers, 97
Learning contracts, 16–19, 89–91
Learning guides, 101–103
Learning styles, 117, 120
Life Adjustment Education, 18, 19
Lives of Children, The, 25
Limited English Proficient students (LEP), 122
Logical Reasoning in Science and Technology, 54
Long block schedule, 68

Magnet schools, 59
Marketing high schools, 285
Mastery learning, 94–97
Mid–continent Regional Educational Laboratory, 48
Mini–lessons, 124
Model Schools Project, 24, 50, 151
Multiple intelligences, 299

Nation at Risk, 28–29, 37, 195
National Association For Secondary School Principals, 327,
    333, 339
    School Climate Survey, 330
    School Design Statement, 333
National Association For Secondary School Principals Task
    Force, 347
National Board for Professional Teaching Standards
    (NBPTS), 301, 318
National Assessment of Education Program, 65
National Association for Special and Physical Education, 65
National Commission on Children, 295
National Committee on Excellence in Education, 28, 29,
    30, 41
National Commission on Industrial and Technical Educa-
    tion, 11
National Committee of Teachers of Mathematics, 62

National Committee on Science Education Standards and
    Assessment, 45, 65
National Council for Teachers of Mathematics, 65
National Council on Education, Standards, and Testing
    National Defense Education Act, 20
National Education Association, 18
National Foundation for Improvement of Education, 298
National Parents Information Network, 270
National Parents–Teachers Association (NTPA), 268
National Policy Board for Educational Administration,
    standards, 325–327
National Standards for Civics and Government, 47
National Standards for Parent/Family Involvement
    Programs, 268
National Staff Development Council, 303, 305
National Science Teachers Association, 65
New Directions in Distance Learning (NDDL), 119
New High Schools
    curriculum, 306
    staff development practices, 306
New Standards Project, 50
Non–graded high schools, 26
Non–English speaking students, 121
    and computer technology, 121–122
North Central Association of Schools and Colleges, 10

Ohio State University, 313
One Student At A Time: Report of Task Force on High
    School Education, 137, 165
Open Learning Agency, 120
Oracle Channel, 121
Outcome–based Education, 339–342
Outcomes For Physical Education Quality Education
    Programs, 47

Paideia Proposal, 30, 38, 50
Parents, 266
    involved in changing society, 266
    standards for parent/family involvement programs, 268
    outreach programs, 269
    decision–making roles, 270
    parent/family resource centers, 272
    home school coordinators, 273
    home visits, 274
Partnership roles, changing perspectives, 266
Partnerships with family and community, 265
    reasons for, 266
    barriers, 268–269
    successful outreach activities, 269
    site–based councils, 270
    family–parent resource centers, 272
    parent home learning network, 274
    home visits, 274

building alliances, 275
community education programs, 275
health and social services, 276
professional development, 277
Peer assistant teams, 135
Peer counseling programs, 134
Peer mediation program, 136
Peer helper program, 135
Performance Assessment Handbook, 63
A Place Called School, 31, 38
Portfolios, 340, 343
Principals, 323
    advisory roles, 146–147
    lead management, four elements, 323
    history, 323
    domains (National Policy Board) 325
        leadership, 325
        curriculum design, 326
        motivating others, 326
        policy and political influences, 326
    reforming high schools, 327
    change, themes, 328
Principals For Our Changing Schools, 346
Process of Education, 20
Professional Development, 310
Professional preparation (teachers) 315–318
Progressive education, 14, 19, 20
Progressive Education Association, 14–17
Project 2061, 46, 55
PSSC Physics, 54
Public Engagement, 264
Pueblo County High School Handbook, 165

Quackery in the Public Schools, 19
Quality School: Managing Students Without Coercion, 342

Reading–writing workshops, 103–108
Reaching All Families: Creating Family–Friendly Schools,
    272, 280
Reforming high schools, 327

"Shadowing" in career academies, 124
Scheduling, 68
    long block scheduling, 68
    traditional high school, 168
    Copernican style, 172
    alternative day (A/B) schedule, 178
    4 × 4 semester plan, 187
    combination schedules, 198
    issues, 203
    research, 207
    future of, 208

Scholastic Aptitude Test, 28, 29, 54
School Advisory Councils (Florida), 333
School design statement, 333–338
School–to–work, 57
School improvement plans, 332
School–within–a–school strategy, 243
   career academies, 243
   teaching in, 247
Schooling in Capitalist America, 26
Science curriculum, 53–55
Science for All Americans, 46
Scope, Sequence, and Coordination Initiative, 54
*Second to None: A Vision of the New California High
   School,* 300
*Selective Character of American Secondary
   Education,* 14
*Shopping Mall High School: Winners and Losers in the
   Educational Marketplace,* 31
*Simulation and Gaming: An International Journal of
   Theory, Design, and Research,* 88
Simulation, 85–88, 183
Slums and Suburbs, 23
Southern Regional Examination Board, 243
Special Education, 229
Sputnik, 19
Staff development
   trends, 304
   school–based, 305
   effective models, 305
   practices, new high schools, 306
   delivery models, 306,307
   professional development high schools, 310
   professional development goals, 311
   professional development with universities, 311, 312
Standards, 9,10
   simulations, 183
   foreign languages, 47
   geography, 46
   history, 46
   local, 48
   portfolios, 49
   science, 45
   new vision of higher standards for all students, 264
   for family/parent involvement programs, 269
Strategic planning, 328
Strong Families, Strong Schools, 277
STS (Science, Technology, and Society), 53
*Summerhill School: A Radical Approach to
   Childrearing,* 25
*Systematic Identification of of Content, Standards, and
   Benchmarks,* 48

Talent development high school, 257
Teacher Advisory Programs, 137

Teacher researchers, 338
Teachers, 298
   expectations, 298
   roles, 298–299, 317
   expanded knowledge base, 300
   authentic pedagogy, 300
   standards (NBPTS), 301
   professional development, 302
   staff development, 304
   preparation, 309–312
      problems, 309
      effectiveness, 314
      directions for change, 315
      new high schools, challenges, 316
Team planning for interdisciplinary units, 227
"Tech prep", 243
Technological education, 122
Technology
   impact, 114
   planning for, 115
      systems theory approach, 115
      commitment, 116
      implementation, 116
      assessment, 116
      coordinating use, 117
   instructional uses, 117, 128
   personalized learning, 118
      self–paced learning, 118
   computer assisted learning, 118
   distance learning, 119
   partnerships, 122
   as course, 122
   traditional academic programs, 123
   administrative uses, 124
   and future, 125
Technology Plus Program, 59
Theory in Educational Administration, 345
Thinking, continuum of, 56–57
Total Quality Management, 342
   application to high school by W. Glasser, 342–343
Tracking, 11, 13, 19, 26, 253–257
Trump, J. Lloyd, 24–25
Tyler, Ralph, 16

Unipacs, 101
Untracking, effect on test scores, 253–256
U.S. Department of Education, 295
University of Louisville, 313
University of Vermont, 31

The Vanishing Adolescent, 25
Values, 50–51
Vocational education, 11, 57, 58, 243

Wait time, 172
What Matters Most: Teaching for America's Future, 309
Web, 119
Word processing, 123, 128
Worthlin Group, 295
Writing Across the Curriculum, 55

Youth apprenticeships, 58
   Craftmanship 2000, 58
   National Youth Apprenticeship Act, 58
   Technology Plus Program (Alabama), 59
   California Partnership Academies, 60